חֲמִשָּׁה חֻמְשֵׁי תּוֹרָה

THE FIVE BOOKS OF MOSES

an

EASY-TO-READ

TORAH

Translation

חֲמִשָּׁה חֻמְשֵׁי תּוֹרָה

THE FIVE BOOKS OF MOSES

an

EASY-TO-READ

TORAH

Translation

by
SOL SCHARFSTEIN

KTAV PUBLISHING HOUSE INC.

Library of Congress Cataloging-in-Publication Data

Bible. O.T. Pentateuch. English. Scharfstein. 2005
    The five books of Moses: an easy-to-read Torah / translation by Sol Scharfstein.
        p. cm.
    Includes index.
    ISBN 0-88125-853-9
    1. Bible. O.T. Pentateuch—Liturgical use. 2. Bible. O.T. Pentateuch—History.
    3. Bible. O.T. Pentateuch—Criticism, interpretation, etc., Jewish.
    I. Scharfstein, Sol, 1921. II. Title.
BS1223.S43 2005
222'.105209—dc22

                        2004016987

Published by
KTAV Publishing House, Inc.
930 Newark Avenue
Jersey City, NJ 07306
Email: bernie@ktav.com
www.ktav.com
(201) 963-9524
Fax (201) 963-0102

TABLE OF CONTENTS

TO MY WIFE EDYTHE
Whose patience and support never wavered.
For enduring
"Just give me another ten minutes till I finish this paragraph"—
which often stretched into hours.

In Memoriam

In 1921 my parents, Asher and Feiga, came to America, where they established a Jewish bookstore in the Lower East Side ghetto of New York City. At first we lived in one room in back of the store, with a toilet in the hall. Every Friday we went to the public baths, where we purchased towels and soap for a penny. Sometimes we brought our own towels and soap to save the pennies.

Asher and Feiga were young, intelligent, and not content to just sell books and sundry religious items. So they began to create lead draydels, make Simchat Torah flags, and publish wedding certificates. From this small beginning they began to branch out and publish other books such as siddurim, machzorim, and chumashim. In 1947 my father had a brainstorm and assembled the first-of-its-kind Torah-reading text, entitled *Tikkun Torah*. This was an immediate success. This *Tikkun,* 60 years later, has gone through innumerable editions and has helped train tens of thousands of Torah readers. It is still in print and is selling well to this day.

In 1947, after World War II, my father received the devastating news that his brothers and their families in the little town of Dinivetz in Russia were murdered by the Nazis.

In 1950, with tears in his eyes and a quivering hand, he wrote this Hebrew memorial for a new version of the *Tikkun* entitled *Tikkun Encyclopedia.*

Asher's memorial reads:

In memory of my brother Yosef, son of Dov, and his lovely wife Sara, and their son Yisrael and his wife and their two children, who never even tasted life. They, with all the Jews in the village of Dinivetz, were thrown alive into a mine in the forest by the Nazis and the Polish villagers on the 8th day of the month of Mar Heshvan. May the memory of their murderers be wiped off the face of the earth.

To my nephew Aaron, son of Yosef, the engineer, who was killed in the Russian army during the battle for the city of Voronezh.

To my brother Shmuel and his wife Chava and their two children, who in 1942 were burnt alive during a pogrom near the city of Warsaw.

I will never forget them.
Asher son of Dov Scharfstein

There are times during a restless night, when I see their shadows and hear their cries echo through my dreams. I know that they are reminding me never to forget.

This book is dedicated to my nephews, cousins, aunts, and uncles whose joys I will never share and whose laughter I will never hear.

P.S. I was born in the murderous town of Dinivetz in 1921.

ABOUT THE TRANSLATION

The Torah is the eternal book of the Jewish people and must be made intelligible to both young and old, both the learned and those who have not yet enjoyed the opportunity to heed the rabbinical injunction to "go and study."

Much effort and time have been expended to make the translation of the Torah—The Five Books of Moses—as simple and comprehensible and as user friendly as possible.

Here are some of the modifications:

1. Besides a simplified translation, the major change is in the usage of the names of God. The original written Torah, which is read in the synagogue, uses three primary names of the Deity: Elohim, El, and most frequently, Adonai.

Elohim and El are found in the Book of Bereshit. The other four books use mostly the name Adonai. But strangely, the word Adonai does not appear in the Torah. Instead the text uses the tetragrammaton YHVH, which in the Torah appears as the Hebrew letters *yud, hay, vav, hay*. In Jewish tradition, the mysterious Holy Name is forbidden to be pronounced by ordinary laymen or even priests. It was pronounced only by the High Priest on Yom Kippur when he entered the Holy of Holies. Jews have always honored that tradition and read the Holy Name as Adonai.

Why does the Book of Bereshit have a different sytle than the four other books? Some Bible scholars believe that the scrolls were written by different people at different times. They called the Book of Bereshit the E scroll, referring to the use of Elohim there. The other four books or scrolls are named the J, D, and P scrolls. Non-Jewish scholars use the name Jehovah for Adonai.

The early talmudists were aware of the problem of multiple names and they suggested that the books had been written or edited by Moses during the forty-year trek through the wilderness. They posited that the different styles reflected the different pressures and situations during the wandering.

2. All weights, measures, and monetary units are converted into modern equivalents.

3. The Torah is a male-oriented text. Where possible, without disturbing the meaning of the sentence, the text is modernized by use of the word "person" instead of "man." Sometimes the sentence structure is modified to eliminate the masculine orientation.

4. The text is divided into the traditional sidrot (sections), with both Hebrew and English names.

5. All the *aliyot* are indicated in their proper places. In addition, titles have been added to the *aliyot.*

6. Most Hebrew place-names appear with Englisht translation since many of the names record an event or describe the area. The translation will make the text more meaningful.

7. The translation rigidly follows the Masoretic text, but it is not a word-for-word translation, since some phrases have been moved around to simplify the sentence structure and thereby clarify the meaning.

8. The text often joins sentences where continuity is required.

INTRODUCTION

The classic book *Sayings of the Fathers* is a tractate of the Mishnah, the Oral Torah of Judaism. It starts with the statement:

> Moses received the Torah at Sinai and handed it on to Joshua. Joshua handed it to the Elders, the Elders to the Prophets, and the Prophets handed it down to the Men of the Great Assembly.

Each of the leaders transmitted the teachings of the Torah not only to the leaders, rabbis, and teachers, but to all Israel. All Israel refers to all generations, directly to you.

The Torah was given on the top of Mount Sinai in a stark, silent wilderness, devoid of life. The cruel, harsh scene epitomizes the state of the world at that time. Nations were ruled by despots, kings, and warlords. Wars, disregard for human life, and the sacrifice of humans to man-made idols were prevalent. There was a complete lack of social justice, loving-kindness, and respect for human life.

In this wilderness, Adonai planted the seed of Torah, which, despite great odds, germinated and grew, spread and became the book of divinity for two other major religions, Christianity and Islam.

Why Torah?

Since the revelation at Mount Sinai, Jews have viewed the Torah as the spiritual adventure of a people seeking and learning how to serve Adonai through moral perfection. Possessing its rules and laws, a Jew can learn to live a disciplined and dedicated life.

With Torah in hand, study and the attainment of knowledge can become a religious pursuit.

The Mishnah Teaches:

> There are things of which a man enjoys the dividends in this world while the principal remains for him for the world to come. They are honoring father and mother; deeds of loving-kindness; regular attendance at the house of study and prayer—morning and

evening; hospitality to wayfarers; visiting the sick; dowering the bride; attending the dead to the grave; devotion in prayer; and making peace between man and his fellow; but the study of Torah is equal to them all, for it leads to them all.

About My Teachers

Unfortunately, I cannot remember all the Hebrew teachers and Rabbis that taught me Torah.

Almost every Saturday, my father Asher, after a grueling week of work, summoned the time and energy to review with me portions of the weekly sidrah and, in season, *Pirke Avot.*

Besides my studies at the five-day-a-week intensive Downtown Talmud Torah, my parents engaged a special tutor named Rabbi Chaim Brecher. Although he was educated in the shtetl, I especially appreciate him now because of his skill in Hebrew, Aramaic, Yiddish, French, Greek, Latin, Russian, mathematics, and science. My father discovered this hidden East Side intellectual pearl, and he soon became a consultant to the Hebrew scholarly elite.

I am eternally grateful to principal Zaslofsky of the Zitomer Talmud Torah located on 8th Street at Avenue B on the Lower East Side of New York. He tamed my youthful exuberance and introduced me to some lifelong friends, notably Rabbi Max Raiskin, who passed away before his time. Mr. Zaslofsky graduated ten of us, who then became students at the Herzlia Hebrew Teachers College.

Max revived the Talmud Torah into a vibrant day school of some three hundred students. Unfortunately, demographics, health, and monetary problems intervened, and the school combined with the Rabbi Arthur Schneir Park East Day School on the Upper East Side of New York City and lives on.

I had some marvelous teachers at Herzlia Hebrew Teachers College. I especially appreciate Mr. Epstein. He was a thin, white-haired, unassuming individual. But in front of a class he assumed the role of the prophet and delivered beautiful introductions to Isaiah, Jeremiah, and Ezekiel in clear concise Hebrew.

Unfortunately, World War II intervened and brought the end of my formal Hebrew studies. During my three and a half years of military service, I was too busy and there was no opportunity for Torah study.

After the war, my education continued with my scholarly editors at KTAV, Mr. Eliahu Persky and Mr. Isaiah Berger. KTAV has published hundreds of books, and every volume has been a learning experience.

Now, fortunately for me, every day is a continuing Torah learning experience.

ALL ABOUT THE TORAH

Contents

TORAH HISTORY

The Patriarchs and the Matriarchs

The patriarchs and matriarchs of the Jewish people lived in the Fertile Crescent, the region in the Middle East surrounded by the Tigris, Euphrates, and Nile Rivers. Ur, the chief city of this region, was a thriving market center visited by merchants from near and far. The people who lived there worshipped many different gods, but Abraham and his wife, Sarah, the parents of the Jewish people, believed in only one God—Adonai. Adonai promised the land of Canaan (Israel) as a homeland for them and for all their descendants.

Abraham and his descendants Isaac and Jacob established themselves in the land of Canaan. The Torah tells us that Jacob wrestled with an angel, a messenger of Adonai, who gave Jacob the name Israel, which means "he struggled with Elohim." Since that time, Jacob's descendants have been called the Children of Israel. They are also sometimes referred to as Hebrews.

There was a famine in the land of Canaan, so Jacob sent his sons to Egypt to purchase food. There they encountered their brother Joseph, whom they had sold as a slave. Joseph had risen to a position of great power, second in command

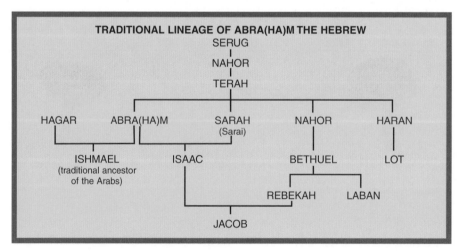

only to Pharaoh. At Joseph's invitation, Jacob, his family, and the Children of Israel moved to Egypt.

Moses and Pharaoh

After the Hebrews peacefully lived in Egypt for about two hundred years, a new Pharaoh came to power who did not remember Joseph's deeds. He enslaved the Children of Israel and issued a decree that all male children born to the Israelites must be killed. Soon after the decree, a male child was born to Jocheved, an Israelite woman, and her husband Amram, from the tribe of Levi. Jocheved placed the baby in a waterproof basket and floated it down the Nile River.

An Egyptian princess found the baby and named him Moses, which means "I took him from the water." Moses grew up in the palace of Pharaoh as an Egyptian prince. One day, Moses was enraged to see an Egyptian overseer beating an Israelite slave. Moses killed the Egyptian and fled to the land of Midian.

One day, as Moses was caring for his flock, Adonai called to him from the midst of a burning bush. Adonai told Moses to return to Egypt and to free the Hebrew slaves and lead them to freedom. Moses reluctantly agreed and returned to Egypt.

Moses and his brother Aaron again and again confronted Pharaoh and pleaded for the Israelites to be released. After ten miraculous and disastrous plagues against the Egyptians, Pharaoh relented and set the Hebrews free.

This scene of an overseer beating a slave was found in an Egyptian tomb.

The Israelites Leave Egypt

The march out of Egypt began in the middle of the night. The twelve Israelite tribes marched to the Sea of Reeds, where Adonai drove back the waters and miraculously created a dry path to the opposite shore. The Israelites quickly crossed to the other side, and Pharaoh's army followed them into the sea. Moses saw the pursuing Egyptians enter the Sea of Reeds. Adonai told him to raise his miraculous staff, and the walls of water

Rameses II was most likely the Pharaoh who enslaved the Hebrews.

collapsed, engulfing the chariots and drowning the Egyptian soldiers. The Israelites watched the miracle. They knew that ahead of them lay many dangers, but for the moment they danced joyously and sang for their newly found freedom.

This picture of Pharaoh Tutankhamen in his chariot was found in his tomb. The chariot reins are tied around the Pharaoh's waist, freeing his arms and enabling him to shoot his arrows. The Bible describes the pursuit of the Israelites by the "chariot of the king of Egypt."

The Holiday of Passover

The Israelites left Egypt so hurriedly that they had no time to bake their bread. They spread the raw unleavened dough in their kneading bowls and tied them onto their shoulders. The hot desert sun baked the dough into matzot. This was the origin of the custom of eating unleavened bread (matzot) on Passover, the festival that commemorates the victory won for freedom so many centuries ago.

The opening words of Psalm 114, which is the Hallel prayer. It begins, "When Israel left Egypt. . . ." This illustrated psalm shows the Children of Israel leaving Egypt. They are led by Moses and are passing through the gate of a medieval town from which the Egyptians are looking down.

Moses and the Torah

After the Israelites left Egypt, they camped around Mount Sinai. Moses ascended the mountain and remained there for forty days and nights. God presented the Ten Commandments to Moses during the forty days. Moses then presented them to the people.

Torah is the Hebrew name for the first five books of the Bible. In Hebrew it means "teaching" and "law." The rabbis of the Talmud explained that Moses wrote the Torah under the supervision of Adonai, scroll by scroll. During the forty years of desert trials, Moses recorded the history of Israel as well as his instructions and conversations with Adonai.

During his lifetime of 120 years, Moses had a long and difficult journey. He molded a group of slaves that he had freed from Egypt into a powerful holy nation that was to take center stage in the Middle East and later in world history.

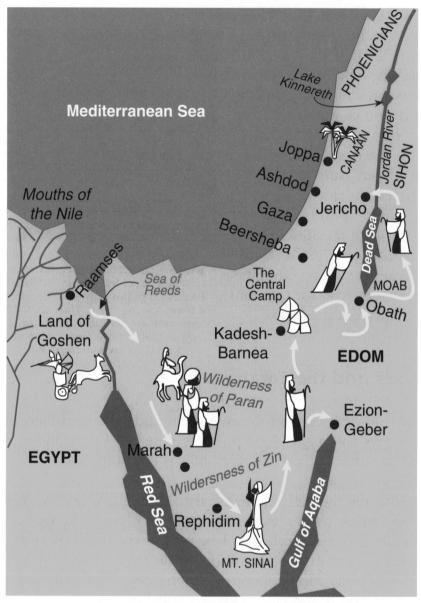

According to the Bible, the Israelites left Egypt and traveled along
the northern coast of the Sinai peninsula. During the forty years of
wandering, they passed through many kingdoms and endured great
hardships. The Israelites spent much time at the oasis of Kadesh-Barnea.
Moses sent twelve spies into Canaan from this oasis. At Marah,
the Israelites found bitter water. According to the Bible, God showed
Moses a plant that made the water drinkable. Before the Israelites
reached Mount Sinai, they battled the Amalekites at Rephidim.

**Moses bringing down
the Ten Commandments.
From the Sarajevo Haggadah.**

Moses, who was the prophetic leader to his last dying breath, addressed the Israelites and recorded the last section of the fifth scroll of the Torah before he died. His oration starts, "This is the blessing with which Adonai's prophet Moses blessed the Children of Israel before his death" (Deuteronomy 33:1).

After he finished his oration, Moses handed the completed fifth and last scroll of the Torah to the priests and then climbed Mount Nebo and disappeared.

The Torah in Israel and Babylon

After the First Temple was destroyed in the fifth century B.C.E., the Israelites lived under Babylonian captivity. Some went to Babylonia and some remained in Israel. During the Babylonian Exile, Ezra the Scribe and the Men of the Great Assembly ruled that a specific sidrah, or portion, from the Torah was to be assigned to each Sabbath, so that all five scrolls (the Five Books of Moses) could be completed in one full year. They divided the Torah into fifty-four sidrot according to the number of weeks in a leap year.

The rabbis in ancient Israel disagreed with their colleagues in Babylon. They divided the Torah into 155 smaller portions so that it would take three years to read the whole Torah. This system is called the triennial cycle, and it is now followed in Reform, Reconstructionist, and many Conservative congregations.

Ezra also instituted the reading of short sections of the Torah on Mondays and Thursdays as well as Saturday afternoons. Monday and Thursday were market days, when farmers came to the city to sell their produce and purchase supplies. Ezra recognized that these days were opportunities to assemble a group and teach Torah.

According to the Mishnah, by the end of the second century C.E., there were regular Torah readings on Mondays, Thursdays, Sabbaths, and the festivals, including Chanukah, Purim, and fast days. Today, Orthodox and Conservative synagogues continue the practice and read short sections of the Torah on Mondays, Thursdays, and Saturday afternoons.

Fragment of an ancient Torah scroll. It belongs to a Jewish family in the Israeli village of Peki'in in the Galilee. Peki'in has a record of Jewish settlement from the first century C.E. The inhabitants of this tiny agricultural village escaped Roman exile.

The systematic reading of the Torah has had an extraordinary educational and spiritual impact on the life of Jews throughout their history. The Torah is not just read, it is studied and explained and its ethical lessons are applied to the daily life of Jews no matter where they reside. The Torah is the cornerstone of the Jewish religion and has had a profound effect on Jewish survival.

The Five Books of Moses

The Torah is often called the Five Books of Moses. The Torah is the Hebrew book that was revealed to Moses on Mount Sinai in about 1280 B.C.E. It records the beginning history of the Jewish people as well as the basic laws that established the Jewish religion. Hundreds of years later, other religions, notably Christianity and Islam, adapted and interpreted the Torah as their own religious possession.

The Torah has been published in thousands of editions and hundreds of languages. It is by far the best-selling book of all time.

The Five Books of Moses with Greek and Hebrew names.

TORAH SCHOLARSHIP

The Targum

Throughout the Near East, and especially in Babylonia and Syria, Aramaic was the dominant language. After the Israelites returned from the Babylonian Exile, it also became the everyday spoken language of Judea. Since the Torah was written in Hebrew, it was necessary to provide a translation for the many people who were no longer able to understand it.

Ezra solved the problem by providing a translator who stood right next to the Torah reader during services and translated the Hebrew into Aramaic for the congregants. Eventually the oral translations provided in this manner were set down in writing. The Aramaic translation of the Torah is called the Targum. Note the close similarly between the name *Targum* and the word *meturgeman* (translator).

The Talmud mentions that in some synagogues the Torah was read twice: once in Hebrew and once in Aramaic.

Page from a Hebrew Bible with commentaries. The narrow column at the upper left is the Aramaic translation by Onkelos and is the most widely used Targum. It is still printed side by side with the original Hebrew text in modern editions of the Torah. Some Jews recite it with the regular weekly portion. Onkelos was a convert to Judaism.

There are three major Aramaic translations of the Torah: Targum Onkelos, Targum Jonathan, and the Palestinian Targum (Targum Yerushalmi).

The Septuagint – ca 285–246 B.C.E.

Under Ptolemy II Philadelphus, an Egyptian king of the second century B.C.E., the Bible was translated into Greek. This came about, we are told, because the library at Alexandria had a copy of every book in the world except the Bible. Wanting its collection to be complete, Ptolemy sent to Jerusalem for a Bible and asked the high priest for permission to have it translated. He invited seventy sages to Alexandria and set each of them to work by himself. The seventy sages had no contact with one another, but when they finished, all seventy translations were identical. We do not know whether this story is fact or legend, but whatever may be the case, the first Greek translation of the Bible came to be known as the Septuagint, meaning the translation "by the seventy."

A page from the Septuagint, Exodus 19.

The Septuagint created a great stir. At that time Greek was the most widely used language in the ancient world.

Many Jews in Egypt and other countries no longer knew Hebrew. Their knowledge of Judaism had suffered as a result, but now they were able to read the Holy Scriptures and study the laws of the Torah in Greek.

The Septuagint translation also enabled non-Jews to read the Bible. Before long the entire ancient world became acquainted with the history and ideas of the people of the little land of Judea. Many non-Jews, known as "God-fearers," began attending synagogues or adopting Jewish customs.

The Masoretes

In ancient times every copy of the Bible had to be written by hand. A group of scholars known as Masoretes, in the city of Tiberias in ancient Israel, were aware that over the centuries many errors had been made by the scribes who copied Torah scrolls. They decided to standardize the Torah text so that it could be handed down correctly to future generations. The term *Masorete* means "handed down."

Page from the Rules of Accents by Jacob ben Asher in the tenth century. This momentous work established the rules of punctuation and spelling in the Bible.

The scribes who copied the text made errors of various kinds. Then other scribes sometimes unknowingly copied an erroneous text and thus passed the error on to later generations. It was important to have an accurate text. The scholars who performed this task of establishing the correct text are called Masoretes. To this day, *soferim* (scribes) follow the Masoretic text when they copy scrolls of the Torah.

In order to preserve the true text and meaning of the Scriptures, the Masoretes carefully compared different versions of each biblical book and decided which corresponded to the pure, original form. They laid down the text word for word, letter for letter, and worked out a system of punctuation. They devised a system of vowel signs to ensure that every word was pronounced properly. In addition, they provided a system of accentuation and punctuation that also serves as musical notation (*trope*) for the chanting of the Torah and other parts of the Bible in the synagogue.

The Masoretes were active from the seventh through the tenth century. Their most outstanding scholars were Ben Asher and Ben Naphtali.

Torah Commentators

Commentators help you to understand things that at first seem complicated or unfamiliar.

The Torah also has commentators. This is so because the Torah is concise and sometimes its meaning needs a clarifying explanation. With the help of the commentators, we are better able to understand the early history of the Jewish people. They also explain the details of the laws, ordinances, and mitzvot in the Torah. In clarifying some of the Torah passages, the commentators made use of their immense knowledge of science, mathematics, history, medicine, language, Midrash, and Talmud.

Here are only four of the many thousands of Jewish commentators who wrote explanations of the Torah.

Page from the first edition of Abraham ibn Ezra's commentary to the Torah, Naples, 1488.

Abraham ibn Ezra (1092-1167) was a born wanderer who traveled through North Africa, France, Italy, and England, absorbing knowledge while preaching and writing. Ibn Ezra is famous for his Torah commentary.

Obadiah ben Jacob Sforno (1475-1550) was born in Italy and studied mathematics, philosophy, and medicine. In his commentaries he tries to discover the plain meaning of the text and to develop its ethical teachings.

Name	Hebrew	Rashi		Name	Hebrew	Rashi
Mem Sofit	ם	ם		Alef	א	ნ
Nun	נ	נ		Beit	ב	כ
Nun Sofit	ן	ן		Gimel	ג	ג
Samech	ס	ס		Daled	ד	ר
Ayin	ע	ט		Hay	ה	כ
Fay	פ	פ		Vav	ו	ן
Fay Sofit	ף	ק		Zayin	ז	ר
Tzadi	צ	ჰ		Chet	ח	ს
Tzadi Sofit	ץ	ך		Tet	ט	ט
Quf	ק	ק		Yud	י	ა
Resh	ר	ר		Khaf	כ	Ა
Sin	שׁ	ს		Khaf Sofit	ך	ך
Tav	ת	ր		Lamed	ל	ל

LEFT: Rashi was a prolific scholar and was constantly writing new commentaries. It was difficult and very time-consuming to write using the regular Hebrew alefbet. So Rashi used a cursive script that was much easier and faster to write. Most of the early commentaries on the Torah and the Talmud were printed in Rashi script.

RIGHT: The Rashi chapel in the city of Worms, Germany, in the synagogue where the great commentator worshipped and taught.

Rashi (1040-1105), whose full name was Rabbi Shlomo Yitzhaki, was the greatest of the Torah commentators. His brilliant mind developed so many new ideas that he had difficulty writing them down fast enough. So Rashi invented a shorthand Hebrew script that helped him to write faster. He wrote commentaries on the Torah and the Talmud.

Nachmanides (1194-1270) was born in Spain and lived there most of his life. His full name was Rabbi Mosheh ben Nachman. His commentaries are related to Halachah (law), moral values, and mysticism. He died in Israel.

He is also known as the Ramban.

Seal of Nachmanides, found near Akko, Israel.

TWO TORAH HOLIDAYS

The Torah is the centerpiece of all synagogue services. It is read and studied every Shabbat and on all Jewish holidays. There are also two holidays, Simchat Torah and Shavuot, that are dedicated to the honor of the Torah.

Simchat Torah

Simchat Torah, the Rejoicing in the Law, is a holiday dedicated to a book—the greatest book of all—the Torah. On this day we come to the end of the reading of the Five Books of Moses in the synagogue and begin again with the wonderful story of creation. The last chapter of Devarim is chanted, and then the first chapter of Bereshit. The cycle of Torah reading continues and the circle of the Torah is eternal, without beginning or end.

In the synagogue, Simchat Torah is celebrated with great merriment. Everybody comes—young and old, men and women.

Torah Procession

On this festive occasion, all the Torah scrolls are taken out of the Ark and carried lovingly around the synagogue in processions known as *hakafot*. Children follow the grown-ups, gaily waving colorful flags. Seven times the procession makes its rounds.

The *hakafot* are introduced by the reading of a collection of biblical verses called *Attah Horeyta*. As each line is read by the cantor or a member of the congregation, it is repeated by the participants. All the members of the congregation are given the opportunity of carrying a Torah scroll during the *hakafot*.

In many synagogues a beautiful ceremony called Consecration is held. The children who will be starting religious school that year are called to the *bimah* (pulpit) and each is presented with a miniature Torah. The rabbi blesses the group and wishes all the children a happy and meaningful Jewish experience in the years of study in the religious school.

Shavuot

Shavuot means "Weeks," and the holiday falls exactly seven weeks after the second day of Passover, on the sixth and seventh days of the month of Sivan. (Reform Jews observe only the first of the two days.) The Greek name for Shavuot is Pentecost, which in Greek means "fiftieth," because it takes place on the fiftieth day after the beginning of Passover.

Shavuot is a triple holiday—a threefold celebration which commemorates the giving of the Torah on Mount Sinai, the harvesting of wheat in Israel, and the ripening of the first fruits in the Holy Land.

The rabbis declared Shavuot to be the most pleasant of all Jewish holidays. In a way, it is the conclusion of the great festival of Passover. For on Passover, the Jews were freed from slavery, and on Shavuot, the freed slaves were made into free people by the Ten Commandments.

Many kibbutzim in Israel celebrate the wheat and the fruit harvest. The children wear wreaths and carry baskets of fruit and vegetables; the young men and women dance in the fields and the adults cut sheaves of grain. The entire kibbutz gathers and there is a display of the produce of the soil—the fruit of the kibbutz harvest from its orchards, vegetable garden, and field crops.

A Torah Festival

As a Torah festival, Shavuot is also known as *Zeman Matan Torateinu,* which means "The Time of the Giving of Our Law." It was on Shavuot that Adonai spoke to Moses atop Mount Sinai and gave the Israelites the Ten Commandments.

Mount Sinai

When the Israelites reached Mount Sinai, sometime around 1280 B.C.E., Moses ordered them to pitch their tents. Here there would occur the most important moment in Jewish history. Moses was going to receive the Ten Commandments from Adonai and pass them on to the people.

Israeli Shavuot stamp.

The Ten Commandments

Chapters 19 and 20 of the Book of Shemot vividly tell the story of how Adonai bestowed the Torah on the Jewish people.

In the third month after the Children of Israel left Egypt, they came to the wilderness of Sinai. There they camped in front of the mountain. While they waited, Moses went up to Adonai, and the Eternal called to him from the mountain, "Say to the Children of Israel: 'You saw what I did to the Egyptians, and how I saved you and brought you to Me. Now, if you will listen to My voice and obey My laws, you will be My treasure from among all peoples.'"

Moses told the people what Adonai had said, and the people answered, "All that the Eternal has said, we will do."

The people sanctified themselves and waited for the Ten Commandments. And there was thunder and lightning, and a thick cloud surrounded the mountain. Then the sound of a shofar blowing very loudly was heard and the people trembled. Soon the mountain was completely surrounded by smoke and flames; the shofar became louder and louder, and the whole mountain shook.

Then God spoke these words, saying:

1. I am the Almighty your God.
2. You shall have no other gods before Me.
3. You shall not take the name of the Almighty in vain.
4. Remember the Sabbath to keep it holy.
5. Honor your father and your mother.
6. You shall not kill.
7. You shall not be unfaithful to wife or husband.
8. You shall not steal.
9. You shall not bear false witness.
10. You shall not desire what is your neighbor's.

The Ten Commandments sealed a covenant between the young nation of Israel and the one God. No other nation had a code of laws so just and humane. The Israelites now truly abandoned the ways of Egypt and dedicated themselves to live by this lofty code.

Archaeologists unearthed this stone relief of the Holy Ark in the ancient synagogue in Capernaum. The original Holy Ark was built by Moses and was carried from place to place before being permanently enshrined in the First Temple. The Holy Ark safeguarded the Ten Commandments and the Torah during the forty-year journey through the wilderness.

TORAH ORNAMENTS AND SETTING

Because the Torah scroll is the most sacred object in Jewish tradition, Jews always try to ensure that it be "clothed" in the most aesthetically pleasing fashion possible. In every generation, among both Ashkenazim (from north and eastern Europe) and Sephardim (from Spain and the Mediterranean), distinctive sets of protective and decorative "garments" have been designed for the Torah, and these can be seen today in any synagogue in the world when the scrolls are removed from the Ark for the public reading of the Torah.

Mantle of the Law

The mantle (*me'il*) of the Law covers the holy scroll when it is not in use. It is usually made of embroidered silk or satin.

Choshen

When the Torah is taken out of the Ark, we see its beautiful breastplate, or *choshen,* suspended by a chain from the top of the rollers. In the center of the breastplate there is frequently a representation of a tiny Ark whose doors are in the form of the two tablets of the Law. The lower part of the breastplate has an area where small plates may be inserted. Each of these plates is engraved with the name of one of the Jewish festivals, to be displayed on the holiday or Shabbat on which the scroll is used.

A *choshen.*

Atzei Chayyim

The wooden rollers (*atzei chayyim* or "trees of life") on which the Torah scroll is wound are made of hard wood. They have flat round tops and bottoms to support the edges of the rolled-up scroll. The Torah itself is called *Etz Chayyim,* the "tree of life."

Keter Torah

Over the upper ends of the *atzei chayyim* is placed the *keter Torah,* the "crown of the Torah." It is usually made of silver and adorned with little bells, and it is one of the scroll's chief ornaments.

A keter Torah.

Yad

The pointer of silver or olive wood which is used to guide the reading of the Torah is called the *yad,* or "hand." It is shaped like a staff, and its end is narrow and in the form of a closed fist with the forefinger outstretched. When the Torah scroll is rolled, the yad is hung by a chain over the *atzei chayyim* and rests on the silver breastplate.

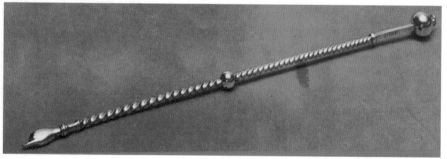

Yad.

Rimonim

The *rimonim* are the silver decorations with tinkling bells that are placed on top of the two *atzei chayyim* of the Torah. scroll. The word *rimon* means "pomegranate." In ancient Israel the robes of the priest were decorated with artistically knotted pomegranates.

Rimonim.

This beautiful *Aron Ha-Kodesh* is in the synagogue of the Italian city of Florence. This synagogue was built in 1882.

Aron Ha-Kodesh

The scrolls of the Torah are safely guarded in the *Aron Ha-Kodesh,* or Holy Ark. This chest is named after the *Aron Ha-Brit,* the Ark of the Covenant, which held the tablets of the Ten Commandments when our ancestors crossed the desert. The *Aron Ha-Kodesh* is usually placed against the synagogue wall facing east or toward Jerusalem.

Parochet

The Children of Israel, while wandering in the desert, hung a curtain before the Ark of the Covenant, and we follow their ancient example in many of our synagogues today. The *parochet,* or curtain, is made of fine material and hangs in front of the *Aron Ha-Kodesh.* It is often embroidered, usually with a rendering of the Ten Commandments.

A *parochet.*

Bimah

The *bimah* is the raised platform on which the desk stands for the reading of the weekly portion from the Torah and the prophets. The *bimah* is sometimes placed in the center of the synagogue, where it represents the altar that once stood in the middle compartment of the Temple, and sometimes it is at the front of the synagogue.

TORAH CEREMONIES AND HONORS

The Ba'al Koreh

In ancient times each person who was called to the Torah would read a portion aloud to the congregation. Today, the Torah reading is performed by a master reader called a *ba'al koreh*.

Aliyot

Even Jews who cannot read the Torah want to participate in the reading. This is made possible by calling people to the pulpit to recite special blessings before and after each of the Torah readings. These people are said to have had an *aliyah* (going up), (plural *aliyot*).

Gabbaim

It is customary for two people called *gabbaim* (*gabbai*) to stand near the *ba'al koreh* as an honor guard and assist the Torah reader. The *gabbaim* are in charge of calling honorees for their Torah *aliyot*. In addition the *gabbaim* follow the reading in a *Humash* (Bible) to assist and correct reading errors of the *ba'al koreh*.

The Trope

The Torah text has been handwritten on the parchment scroll with a feather pen and a special ink. As in the ancient Torah that Moses presented to the Israelites, there is no punctuation and there are no vowel symbols. In the synagogue the Torah is chanted with special musical notes called the *trope*.

The honor of lifting the Torah and showing it to the congregation is called *hagbah*.

The Honors

Aliyot and several other honors are distributed during the Torah service. The honor of opening the Ark and taking out the Torah scroll is called the *petichah*, meaning "opening." The honor of lifting the Torah scroll and showing it to the congregation is called *hagbah*. Another honor is called *gelilah;* the honoree ties and dresses the Torah scroll before it is returned to the *Aron Ha-Kodesh*.

The Order of the Aliyot

In Orthodox and most Conservative synagogues, the first *aliyah* goes to a *kohen,* a person who is descended from the priestly family of Aaron, the brother of Moses. The second *aliyah* is assigned to a *levi,* a descendant of the priestly tribe of Levi. The next five *aliyot* are reserved for Israelites, who are the majority of the Jews.

Many synagogues do not assign the first two *aliyot* to a *kohen* and a *levi,* because they feel that these divisions are outdated and that today all Jews are equal and should be treated equally.

After the reading ceremony, the Torah scroll is opened and raised aloft. This ceremony is called *hagbah*. The Torah scroll is raised in such a way that enables the congregation to see three written columns.

Then the honoree takes the scroll and sits down with it. Another honoree binds the Torah with a sash and dresses it with its mantle and ornaments. This honor is called *gelilah,* which in Hebrew means "rolling together."

The Ba'al Maftir

In addition to the seven Torah *aliyot,* there is the honor of reading the Haftarah. The person who reads the Haftarah is called the *ba'al maftir.* The reading of the Haftarah is preceded by and ends with a special blessing.

The Haftarah

The Haftarah is a portion from the Prophets that is also read on each Sabbath. The Haftarah always has a thematic relationship to the weekly sidrah. The custom of reading the Haftarah was instituted during the occupation of ancient

Israel by the Greek conquerors. The Greeks forbade the reading of the Torah, so the rabbis cleverly substituted the reading of a selection from the Prophets. Today, both the Torah sidrah and the Haftarah are read on Sabbaths and holidays.

The Sephardic System

Among Sephardim and in the Jewish communities of the East, the preservation and decoration of the Torah scrolls are different from the styles followed by Ashkenazim. The scroll is wound upon two wooden *atzei chayyim,* but these are enclosed within a wooden box, formed by two arch-shaped sections joined to the center by a hinge. The case is flat at the bottom to enable it to stand securely on a table, and when the Torah is read, the box is opened like a book to reveal a column of text, which is read without removing the scroll. The scroll is rolled to the appropriate place by manipulating the *atzei chayyim,* whose ends protrude through the top of the case.

A Sephardic Torah reader.

The *atzei chayyim* are usually capped with permanent carved handles, and the box itself is covered in leather or metal engraved with traditional symbols. Inside, colorful and decorative kerchiefs called *mitpahot* are used to protect the part of the parchment that is exposed when the case is opened.

Bar Mitzvah

At the age of thirteen, Jewish boys celebrate their Bar Mitzvah, "Son of the Commandments." In Reform temples and most Conservative synagogues, girls celebrate their Bat Mitzvah, "Daughter of the Commandments."

On the Sabbath following their thirteenth birthday according to the Jewish calendar, the youngsters are called to the

Torah and given *aliyot*. They read a section of the weekly Torah portion and also the Haftarah. Family members are honored by being given *aliyot* and special honors, such as opening and closing the Ark and dressing the Torah.

Zachary Scharfstein reading his Torah portion at his Bar Mitzvah.

According to traditional Jewish law, the thirteen-years-olds can now be counted as part of a prayer *minyan* (quorum) of ten people.

INSIDE THE TORAH

The Tanak

The complete Hebrew Bible is called TaNaK. It is divided into three divisions: Torah (the Five Books of Moses), Nevi'im (Prophets), and Ketuvim (Writings).

The name *Tanak* comes from the first letters of each of the three divisions. *T* is for Torah, *N* is for Nevi'im, and *K* is for Ketuvim.

There are a total of thirty-nine separate books in the Tanak. The Torah consists of five books, the Prophets of twenty-one books, and the Writings of thirteen books.

The chapter divisions and the numbering of the verses were introduced into the Tanak to make quoting from it easier.

The language of the Tanak is Hebrew except for portions of the books of Daniel and Ezra, which are in Aramaic.

GENESIS
EXODUS
LEVITICUS
NUMBERS
DEUTERONOMY

PROPHETS

JOSHUA
JUDGES
1 SAMUEL
2 SAMUEL
1 KINGS
2 KINGS
ISAIAH
JEREMIAH
EZEKIEL
HOSEA
JOEL
AMOS
OBADIAH
JONAH
MICAH
NAHUM
HABAKKUK
ZEPHANIAH
HAGGAI
ZECHARIAH
MALACHI

12 minor prophets

WRITINGS

PSALMS
PROVERBS
JOB
SONG OF SOLOMON
RUTH
LAMENTATIONS
ECCLESIASTES
ESTHER
DANIEL
EZRA
NEHEMIAH
1 CHRONICLES
2 CHRONICLES

The three divisions and thirty-nine books of the Tanak.

Writing a Torah Scroll

A Torah scroll must be written in a very special way, by someone who is specially trained. He is called a *sofer* (scribe). The Torah is written by hand in a special script. It is not written on paper but on parchment made from the skins of kosher animals. A special instrument is used to write the Torah. It is a feather pen or quill. The pieces of the scroll are sewn together with thread made from the sinews of kosher animals.

Writing a Torah scroll is long, hard, tedious work. There are very few people today who have the special skill and knowledge that is needed. A properly written scroll is rare. Not only are the words in it very precious, but the scroll itself is precious.

A *sofer*, or scribe, writing a Torah in the traditional way with a feather pen and special ink.

Here are some of the main steps followed by a *sofer* in writing a Torah scroll, or *Sefer Torah:*

For parchment, the *sofer* may use only the hide of a clean animal (one that, according to the Torah, is kosher to eat). With a sharp point, he draws lines on the parchment, dividing each piece into eight sections, with 42 to 72 lines for each section.

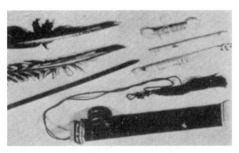

These tools are used in writing a Torah scroll. Here you see the inkwell, the reeds and their case, quills, and sinews (of kosher animals) for sewing parchment sheets together.

A *Sefer Torah* must be written in special black ink only. The pen is a feather of a clean (kosher) fowl, with the tip sliced off at an angle and the point slit. This writing tool can shape thick or thin strokes, as required.

The *sofer* uses a special script. He may not write even one word from memory, and he must pronounce each word out loud before writing it.

Only seven letters of the alefbet may have the decorative little crowns called *tagim.*

Some sections are written in a special form. For example, the Song of the Red Sea (Exodus 15) is arranged like bricks in

את הים ברוח קדים עזה כל הלילה ויׁשם את
הים לחרבה ויבקעו המים ויבאו בני ישׁראל
בתוך הים ביבׁשה והמים להם חומה מימינם
ומׁשמאלם וירדפו מצרים ויבאו אחריהם כל
סוס פרעׁה רכבו ופרׁשיו אל תוך הים ויהי

The *sofer* uses special script. The decorative little crowns on the top of some letters are called *tagim.* These crowns are used on seven letters. The *sofer* may not write from memory and must pronounce each word before writing it.

a wall, a reminder of how Adonai split the waters so that our ancestors might cross unharmed. The last few lines of the *Sefer Torah* are left unfinished. They will be filled in at a synagogue ceremony called the "Completion of the *Sefer Torah*," or *Siyyum Ha-Sefer*.

The sheets are sewn together with the sinews of kosher animals which are woven into long threads. The sewing must not be visible on the face of the *Sefer Torah*.

The scroll is attached to two wooden rollers, each called the a "Tree of Life," or *etz chayyim.*

The 613 Mitzvot

The Torah comprises the first five books of the Bible, the Five Books of Moses. But the word *Torah* is also a general term for the Jewish way of life. When a Jew lives according to the laws and customs of Judaism, it is said that he or she is living in the way of Torah. To live according to Torah, it is necessary to know what Torah is. Jews have always been encouraged to study Torah—the Jewish way of life.

According to Maimonides, there are 613 mitzvot in the Torah. They are known as the *taryag mitzvot* because the Hebrew letters that spell out the words *taryag mitzvot* have a numeric value of 613. There are 248 yes-do mitzvot. These are the mitzvot that Adonai wants each of us to do, such as praying and honoring our parents. These are called *mitzvot aseh*. There are 365 mitzvot that are of the don't-do kind. These are called *mitzvot lo ta'aseh*. Do not steal and do not kill are just two examples. The mitzvot are associated with every part of life: how a person behaves in school and how a person plays sport; how a person treats friends and family. Mitzvot tell a person how to be a good citizen and how to treat those less fortunate. Mitzvot are an essential part of the cycle of Jewish life: birth, Bar/Bat Mitzvah, marriage, and death. There are mitzvot about the food a person eats and how a person will act as a grown-up in business or in a profession.

The Names for Adonai

The Torah contains seven names for Adonai. The name that appears most frequently is the tetragrammaton, the four-letter holy name YHWH, which is pronounced *Adonai*. Next in frequency is *Elohim,* followed by *El.* Some scholars believe that the tetragrammaton is derived from the Hebrew root *hayah,* meaning "to be," thus signifying that Adonai is the one who is and will be forever.

The ancient rabbis taught that the tetragrammaton was the true name of Adonai. During the Second Temple period, the name *Adonai* was forbidden to be pronounced out loud except by the High Priest on Yom Kippur.

According to tradition, the Hebrew letters that comprise the tetragrammaton, YHWH, were not to be pronounced. Instead it is customary to substitute the word *Adonai* wherever the tetragrammaton appears in the Tanak, prayerbook, or any other holy text. In the sixth century, when vowels were introduced, Christian scholars placed vowels from *Elohim* under the consonants YHWH of the tetragrammaton and read Adonai's name as "Jehovah." The name "Jehovah" is used in many Christian Bibles, prayerbooks, and religious texts. Today, some non-Jewish scholars also read the tetragrammaton as "Yahweh," again using the vowels from under the Hebrew word for *Adonai.*

The Torah Is Alive and Well

Wherever Jews have settled, even in small numbers, they have always brought the Torah with them. The first Jews who came to America from Recife, Brazil, in 1654 brought a Torah scroll with them.

From the very beginnings of Jewish history, conquerors and tyrants have tried to destroy Jewish life physically and religiously by burning the Torah scrolls and forbidding the study of Torah. Despite the censorship and death threats, Jews continued to study and learn from it.

In ancient times, it was the Babylonians, the Greeks, and the Romans who tried to destroy Judaism and its holy Torah. In medieval and modern times the French, the Spaniards, the Russians, and the Nazis all tried to destroy Judaism by destroying the sacred scrolls and to prohibit Torah study by burning them. In spite of all of the book burnings, the pogroms, and the holocausts, the Jewish people live on and the study of Torah continues.

I hope that this will be just the beginning of your Torah studies.

The Touro synagogue in Newport, Rhode Island. It was designed by architect Peter Harrison and completed in 1763.

סֵפֶר בְּרֵאשִׁית

THE BOOK OF BERESHIT

Masoretic Torah Notes

Here is a list of some of the Masoretic notes for the Book of Bereshit.

1. The Book of Bereshit contains 1,534 verses.
2. The Book of Bereshit contains 50 chapters.
3. The Book of Bereshit contains 12 sidrot.

These are the sidrot in the Book of Bereshit.

סֵפֶר בְּרֵאשִׁית	50	*Book of Bereshit*
בְּרֵאשִׁית	53	**Bereshit**
נֹחַ	63	**Noah**
לֶךְ לְךָ	73	**Lech Lecha**
וַיֵּרָא	83	**Vayera**
חַיֵּי שָׂרָה	94	**Chayay Sarah**
תּוֹלְדוֹת	102	**Toldot**
וַיֵּצֵא	110	**Vayetze**
וַיִּשְׁלַח	121	**Vayishlach**
וַיֵּשֶׁב	132	**Vayeshev**
מִקֵּץ	141	**Miketz**
וַיִּגַּשׁ	152	**Vayigash**
וַיְחִי	160	**Vayechi**

סֵפֶר בְּרֵאשִׁית

THE BOOK OF BERESHIT

*The Hebrew name for the first book of the Torah is Bereshit.
The Hebrew word* bereshit, *which means "in the beginning,"
is the first word in the Torah. The Greek name of the book is
Genesis, which also means "beginning."*

*The first section of Bereshit (chapters 1–11) starts with the six
days during which the world and humanity are created. This
event is followed by the story of the first two humans, Adam
and Eve, and their expulsion from the Garden of Eden
because they disobey Adonai and eat from the Tree of
Knowledge. In time the human race becomes so evil that
Adonai sends a huge rain and floods the earth, killing every
living thing. Only Noah and his family and the animals in
the ark are spared. At the end of forty days the rain stops and
the ark comes to rest on Mount Ararat. From there a new
generation spreads out and repopulates the earth.*

*The second part of the book of Bereshit (chapters 12–24) tells
the stories of the Patriarchs and Matriarchs. According to the
Torah, Abraham and his wife, Sarah, were the first Jews and
the parents of a new nation. Adonai appears several times to
Abraham, concludes a covenant with him, and promises that
his descendants will someday be a great nation and inherit
the land of Canaan.*

*Abraham's son Isaac marries Rebekah, who has grown up
outside of Canaan. Like Abraham and Sarah, Rebekah
uproots herself from her home and its idol-based religion.
Adonai also renews the promise of the land of Canaan to
Isaac's son Jacob. Jacob leaves Canaan after a bitter quarrel
with his twin brother, Esau. Jacob marries his cousins Leah
and Rachel, who together with their handmaids bear him
twelve sons.*

Chapters 25–50 conclude the book of Bereshit. After twenty-five years Jacob returns to his homeland and reconciles with his brother, Esau. On his return to Canaan, after serving his uncle Laban, Jacob meets a man near the River Jabbok. After wrestling with Jacob, the man reveals that he is an angel, a messenger of Adonai. He gives Jacob the name Israel, which means "he who struggles with Adonai." From then on Jacob's descendants were called the Children of Israel.

Jacob is now a rich man with a large family and twelve stalwart sons. His favorite is Joseph.

The brothers resent Joseph and sell him as a slave. A famine in Canaan forces the brothers to go to Egypt to purchase food for the family. Their brother Joseph is now second to the Pharaoh of Egypt. He brings the Children of Israel to live with him in the land of Egypt. Joseph dies at the age of 110, and on his deathbed he says, "I am dying, but I know that Adonai will lead you to the Promised Land. Swear to me that you will take my body with you" (50:25).

The families of these brothers became the Twelve Tribes of Israel. The Jewish homeland of Canaan, which Adonai promised to the Patriarchs and Matriarchs and their descendants, is now known as the land of Israel.

Bereshit בְּרֵאשִׁית
AT THE BEGINNING

1 At the beginning Elohim created the cosmos, which included planet Earth.

2 The earth was shapeless and empty, with darkness on the face of the waters, and life-giving winds from Elohim whooshed over the surface of the water. **3** Elohim said, "Let there be light," and there was light.

4 Elohim saw that the light was good, and Elohim separated the light from the darkness. **5** Elohim called the light "Day," and the darkness He called "Night." And there was evening and there was morning, that very first day.

6 Elohim said, "Let there be a sky in the middle of the water, to separate the waters above from the waters below." **7** Elohim made the sky, and it separated the water below the sky from the water above the sky. And so it was. **8** Elohim named the sky "Heaven." And there was evening and there was morning, on the second day.

9 Elohim said, "Let the waters under the sky be gathered to one place, and let the dry land appear." And so it was. **10** Elohim named the dry land "Earth," and the great pools of water He named "Oceans." And Elohim saw that it was good.

11 Then Elohim said, "Let the earth be filled with vegetation, and plants with seeds and trees that grow all kinds of fruits." And so it happened. **12** The earth was carpeted with vegetation, with plants that produced their own kinds of seeds, and with fruit trees that produced their own kinds of seeds, and Elohim saw that it was good.

13 Then there was evening and it was morning, on the third day.

14 Elohim said, "Let there be bright lights in the sky to separate the day from the night and to mark the time of the holidays, the days, and the years.

15 They shall be lights in the sky, to illuminate the earth."

And so it happened. **16** Elohim made two large lights, the stronger light to shine during the day, and the weaker light to shine during the night. He also made the stars. **17** Elohim then positioned them in the sky to illuminate the earth, **18** and to shine by day and by night, and to divide the light and the darkness. And Elohim saw that it was good. **19** And there was evening and there was morning, on the fourth day.

20 Elohim said, "Now let the water be filled with schools of swimming fish. And let birds fly over the land and through the air." **21** Elohim also created huge sea monsters, creeping creatures and all kinds of flying birds. And Elohim saw that it was good.

22 Elohim blessed them all, saying, "Be fruitful and multiply, and fill the waters of the oceans and let the birds fill the air." **23** And there was evening and there was morning, on the fifth day.

24 Elohim said, "Now let the earth give birth to all kinds of tame and wild animals." And so it happened. **25** Elohim made all kinds of wild beasts and tame animals. And Elohim saw that it was good.

26 Then Elohim said, "Let us make a human being in our image like ourselves. Let the human beings be the masters of the fish of the sea, the birds in the sky, the tame animals, and every creature that lives on the earth."

27 Elohim now created a human being to be like himself. In the image of Elohim He created them, male and female.

28 Elohim blessed them. Elohim said to them,

> "Be fertile and multiply.
> Settle the land and preserve it.
> Care for the fish in the sea,
> the birds of the sky,
> and every creature
> that lives on the earth."

29 Elohim said, "I have given you all kinds of seed-producing plants, and trees that produce seed-bearing fruit, for food.

30 And also as food for every beast of the field, every bird of the air, and everything that walks the land and has a living soul." And so it was. **31** Elohim saw that everything that He had created was very good. And there was evening and there was morning, on the sixth day.

2 Heaven and earth, and everything in them were successfully completed. **2** On the seventh day Elohim completed all His work, and on the seventh day He rested from all His work. **3** Elohim blessed the seventh day, and He declared it to be holy, because on this day Adonai rested from the work of creation.

The Creation of a Human   *2nd Aliyah*

4 This is the account of the creation of the heavens and the earth.

5 All the plants as yet had not emerged out of the ground, and the grasses had not yet sprouted. This was so because Adonai had not yet sent rain to water the soil, and there were no people to farm the land. **6** Then water flowed up from the earth, and it watered the entire surface of the ground. **7** Now Elohim formed a man from the dust of the earth and breathed into his nostrils the breath of life. This is how man became a living person. **8** Now Elohim planted a garden in Eden in the east. There He placed the man that He had created. **9** Elohim planted trees that were beautiful to look at and with fruit that was good to eat, including the Tree of Life in the middle of the garden, and the Tree of Knowledge of Good and Evil.

10 A river flowed out of Eden and watered the garden. From there it divided and became four branch rivers.

11 The name of the first branch river is Pishon. It circles the entire land of Havilah, where gold is found. **12** The gold of that land is very pure. Pearls and precious stones were also found there. **13** The name of the second branch river is Gihon. It circles the land of Cush. **14** The name of the third branch river is the Tigris, which flows to the east of Assyria. The fourth branch river is the Euphrates.

15 Elohim placed the man in the Garden of Eden to farm and care for it. **16** Adonai gave the man a warning, saying, "You may eat from every tree of the garden. **17** But you must not eat from the Tree of Knowledge of Good and Evil, for on the day you eat from it, you will surely die."

18 Elohim said, "It is not good for man to be alone. I will make a companion for him." **19** Elohim had created every wild beast and every bird in the air. Now He brought the animals to the man to see what he would name each one. Whatever the man called each living thing would forever remain its name.

The Tree of Knowledge   *3ʳᵈ Aliyah*

20 The man named every tame animal and every bird in the air, as well as all the wild beasts. However, the man still did not have a suitable companion for himself.

21 Elohim then made the man fall into a deep sleep, and while he slept, He took one of his ribs and closed the place from which it was taken. **22** Elohim made the rib that he took from the man into a woman, and He brought her to the man. **23** The man exclaimed,

> "She is bone from my bones
> and flesh from my flesh:
> She shall be called WoMan
> because she was taken from Man."

24 This is why a man leaves his father and mother and marries. So he and his wife can become united as one family. **25** The man and his wife were both naked, but they were not ashamed by each other.

3 The snake was the trickiest of all the wild animals that Elohim had created. The snake asked the woman, "Did Elohim really say that you may not eat from any of the trees of the garden?"

2 The woman answered the snake, "We may eat from the fruit of all the other trees of the garden. **3** But Adonai warned us 'Do not eat, or even touch, the fruit of the tree that is in the middle of the garden, or else you will die.'"

4 The snake hissed to the woman, "No! You will certainly not die!

5 Elohim knows that on the day you eat from it, your mind will be opened, and you will be like the angels, and you will know good and evil."

6 The woman was convinced that the fruit of the tree was good to eat and that the tree was a way to gain wisdom. She took some of its fruit and ate it. She also gave some to her husband, and he ate it.

7 The minds of both of them were opened, and they became ashamed because they were naked. So they sewed together fig leaves and made loincloths for themselves.

8 Suddenly, toward evening, they heard Elohim moving about in the garden. The man and his wife hid themselves from Elohim among the trees of the garden.

9 Elohim called to the man, and said, "Why are you trying to hide?"

10 The man answered, "I hid because I heard Your voice in the garden, and I was afraid because I was naked."

11 Then Elohim asked, "Who told you that you are naked? Did you eat from the tree from which I warned you not to eat?" **12** The man answered, "The woman that you gave me, she brought me the fruit from the tree and I ate it."

13 Then Adonai said to the woman, "Why did you disobey me?"

The woman replied, "The snake tricked me and I ate it."

14 So Elohim said to the snake,

> "Because you did this,
> you will be cursed
> more than any other animal,
> of all the wild beasts
> You will crawl on your belly,
> and you will eat dust all the
> days of your life.

15 From now on, you and the woman will be enemies and your children and her children will also be enemies.

He will strike you in the head, and you will bite him in the heel."

16 To the woman He said, "You will give birth in great pain. You will love your husband, but he will be your master." **17** To Adam He said, "Because you listened to your wife, and ate from the tree about which I warned you, saying, 'Do not eat from it,' I have cursed the ground and your life will be a struggle to grow food from the soil. **18** It will grow thorns and weeds for you, and you will be forced to eat wild grass from the field.

> **19** By the sweat of your brow
> you will eat bread.
> And in the end
> you will return to the earth dead;
> From the earth
> you were created.
> You are dust,
> and to dust you shall return."

20 The man named his wife Eve (*Chavah*), because she was the mother of all life. **21** Elohim clothed Adam and his wife with leather garments that He made for them.

Expulsion from the Garden   *4th Aliyah*

22 Elohim said, "Man has now become like one of us in knowing good and evil. What if he decides to eat from the Tree of Life and live forever?" **23** So Elohim drove man from the Garden of Eden, to farm the earth from which he was created. **24** He drove the man away and stationed cherubim (angels) with the revolving sword at the east of Eden, to guard the path to the Tree of Life.

4 Eve became pregnant and gave birth to Cain. She said, "With Adonai's help I have given birth to a child." **2** Once again, she gave birth, this time to his brother Abel. Abel became a shepherd, while Cain became a farmer.

3 One time, Cain brought some of his crops as an offering to Adonai. **4** But Abel brought some of the finest lambs in his flock. Elohim was pleased with Abel's offering, **5** but He was not pleased with Cain's offering. Cain became very angry and sad.

6 Adonai said to Cain,

> "Why are you so angry and sad?
> **7** If you do good,
> your future will be special.
> But if you do not do right,
> Then only sin will be at your door,
> but you can overcome it."

8 One day when they were in the field, Cain said something to his brother Abel. Cain became angry at his brother Abel, and murdered him.

9 Adonai asked Cain,

> "Where is Abel your brother?"
> "I do not know," replied Cain.
> "Am I my brother's keeper?"

10 Adonai said, "What have you done? Your brother's blood is crying to me from out of the earth. **11** From now on you shall be cursed by the earth that opened up to receive your brother's blood spilled by your hand. **12** When you farm the earth, it will no longer give you new crops. And from now on you will be a fugitive and wander the world."

13 Cain wept and said, "I cannot survive your punishment. **14** Today you have driven me from my land. And also from your presence. Now whoever finds me will kill me." **15** Adonai said to him, "Very well! Then whoever kills Cain will be punished seven times as much." Adonai placed a mark on Cain to prevent anyone from killing him. **16** Cain left Adonai's presence and settled in the land of Nod, to the east of Eden.

17 Cain's wife became pregnant and gave birth to Enoch. Cain founded a city, and he named the city Enoch, after his son.

18 Enoch fathered a son named Irad.
Irad fathered a son named Mechuyael.
Mechuyael fathered a son named Methushael.
Methushael fathered a son named Lemech.

The Family of Lemech   *5ᵗʰ Aliyah*

19 Lemech married two women. The first one's name was
Adah, and the second one's name was Zillah. **20** Adah gave
birth to Yaval. He was the ancestor of all those who live in
tents and raise cattle. **21** His brother's name was Yuval. He
was the first to play the harp and flute. **22** Zillah also had a son
called Tuval Cain; he was a maker of copper and iron tools.
Tuval Cain's sister was called Naamah.

23 Lemech said to his wives, Adah and Zillah, "Listen to me;
listen to my confession. I have killed a man by attacking him,
and a child by beating him.

24 If Cain shall be punished seven times, then the revenge
against me is that I will be punished seventy-seven times."

25 Adam's wife became pregnant again, and she gave birth to
a son. She named him Seth, "Because Adonai has granted me
another child in place of Abel, whom Cain killed."

26 A son was also born to Seth, and Seth named him Enosh. It
was then that people started to pray to Adonai.

Descendants of Adam   *6ᵗʰ Aliyah*

5 This is the book of the history of mankind.
When Elohim created man, He made him in the likeness
of Elohim. **2** He created them male and female. On the
day that they were created, He blessed them and named
them humans.

3 Adam lived 130 years, and he had a son just like himself. He named him Seth. **4** Adam lived 800 years after he
fathered Seth, and then he had more sons and daughters.

5 In all, Adam lived 930 years, and he died.

6 Seth lived 105 years, and he fathered a son called Enosh.

7 Seth lived 807 years after he had Enosh, and he had

more sons and daughters. **8** Seth lived 912 years, and then he died.

9 When Enosh was 90, he fathered a son called Kenan. **10** Enosh lived 815 years after he had Kenan, and he fathered more sons and daughters. **11** Enosh was 905 years old when he died.

12 When Kenan was 70 years old, he fathered a son called Mahalalel.

13 Kenan lived 840 years after he fathered Mahalalel, and he had more sons and daughters. **14** Kenan was 910 years old when he died. **15** When Mahalalel was 65 years old, he fathered a son called Yered. **16** Mahalalel lived 830 years after he fathered Yered, and he had more sons and daughters. **17** Mahalalel was 895 years old when he died.

18 When Yered was 162 years old, he fathered a son called Enoch. **19** Yered lived 800 years after he fathered Enoch, and he had more sons and daughters. **20** Yered was 962 years old when he died.

21 When Enoch was 65 years old, he fathered a son called Methuselah. **22** Enoch walked with Elohim for 300 years after he fathered Methuselah, and he had more sons and daughters. **23** Enoch died when he was 365 years old. **24** Elohim was pleased with Enoch's way of life. And Enoch disappeared because Elohim had taken him.

The Birth of Noah   *7ᵗʰ Aliyah*

25 When Methuselah was 187 years old, he fathered a son called Lemech. **26** Methuselah lived 782 years after he fathered Lemech, and he had more sons and daughters.

27 Methuselah was 969 years old when he died. **28** When Lemech was 182 years old, he fathered a son. **29** He named him Noah, saying, "This one will relieve us from the drudgery and labor of farming the soil that Adonai has cursed." **30** Lemech lived 595 years after he fathered Noah, and he had more sons and daughters.

31 Lemech was 777 years old when he died.

32 When Noah was 500 years old, he had fathered three sons: Shem, Ham, and Yefeth.

6 Humanity began to increase on the face of the earth, and children were born to them. **2** The Nefilim (giants) appeared and saw that the daughters of the humans were beautiful, so they married them. **3** Adonai said, "From now on, I will not tolerate man forever, since he is nothing but flesh. From now on his life span will be 120 years."

4 In those days the giants were on the earth. Afterwards the giants married the daughters of man and they had children. The giants were the strongest ones who ever existed and men of great bravery.

The Wicked People   *Maftir*

5 Adonai saw that the people on earth were becoming more wicked. All day long they thought only of evil.

6 Adonai was angry and regretted that He had created man, and He was very sad. **7** Adonai said, "I will erase from the face of the earth the humans, animals, beasts, and birds of the sky that I have created. I am sorry that I ever created them."

8 However, Noah was a special person in the eyes of Adonai.

Noah נֹחַ
NOAH

9 This is the story of Noah's life:
Noah was the only righteous man in his generation and lived according to the rules of Elohim. **10** Noah fathered three sons: Shem, Ham, and Yefeth.

11 But the people were evil, and the land was filled with violence. **12** Elohim saw all the evil that was in the world. **13** Elohim said to Noah, "I have decided to destroy all the living creatures that have filled the world with violence. I will therefore wipe them off the face of the earth.

14 Hurry! Make an ark of cypress wood. Divide the ark into compartments. Waterproof the inside and outside with tar. **15** This is how you shall construct it: Make the ark 450 feet long and 75 feet wide, and 45 feet high.

16 Make a skylight for the ark. Make it slanted, so that it is 18 inches wide on top. Construct a door on the side of the ark and build three decks on the inside of the ark.

17 I am about to send a flood, and water will cover the earth and destroy every living creature. Everything that is alive on land will die. **18** But with you I will keep My pledge and keep you safe. Together you and your sons, your wife, and your sons' wives will be safe on the ark.

19 Bring into the ark two of each kind of living creature. They shall be male and female. **20** From each kind of bird, from each kind of cattle, and from each kind of animal, bring two of each kind so they will stay alive. **21** Make sure to take enough food to eat. Enough food for you and the animals."

22 Noah did exactly all that Adonai had commanded him.

The Flood   *2ⁿᵈ Aliyah*

7 Adonai said to Noah, "Now you and your family must come into the ark. I have seen that you are the only righteous person in this generation. **2** Take seven pairs of every clean animal, each consisting of a male and its mate. Of every animal that is not clean, take two, a male

and its mate. **3** Of the birds of the heaven, also take seven pairs, each consisting of a male and its mate. They will remain alive on the face of the earth. **4** For in another seven days I will bring rain on the earth for forty days and forty nights. I will obliterate every living creature that I have made from the face of the earth."

5 Noah did all that Adonai had commanded. **6** Noah was 600 years old when the flood started and water covered the earth. **7** Noah, and his sons, his wife, and his sons' wives, came into the ark ahead of the waters of the flood. **8** The clean animals, the animals that were not clean, the birds, and all that walked the earth **9** came two by two to Noah, into the ark. They were male and female, just as Adonai had commanded Noah.

10 Seven days passed, and the flood waters were on the earth. **11** It was in the 600th year of Noah's life, in the second month, on the seventeenth of the month. On that day all the wellsprings of the great deep burst forth and the floodgates of the heavens were opened. **12** It continued to rain on the earth for forty days and forty nights.

13 On that very day, Noah boarded the ark along with his sons, Shem, Ham, and Yefeth. Noah's wife and the three wives of his sons were with them.

14 They came along with every kind of beast, every kind of livestock, every kind of land animal, and every separate kind of flying creature—every bird and every winged animal. **15** All creatures that had a breath of life came to Noah, two by two into the ark; **16** those that came were male and female living creatures, just as Elohim had commanded Noah. Adonai then sealed them inside.

It Rained for Forty Days and Nights   *3rd Aliyah*

17 There was a flood on the earth for forty days. The waters increased and lifted the ark, and it rose from the ground. **18** The waters surged and increased very much, and the ark began to drift on the surface of the water.

19 The waters on the earth flooded upward, and all the high mountains under the heavens were covered. **20** The waters surged upwards to a height of twenty-three feet, and all the mountains were covered.

21 All the creatures that lived on the earth perished: birds, livestock, wild beasts, and everything that lived on the land, as well as every human being. **22** Everything on dry land whose life was sustained by breathing died. **23** The flood wiped out every creature that had been on the face of the earth: humans, livestock, beasts, and birds of the sky. They were all wiped out from the earth. Only Noah and those with him in the ark survived.

24 The waters flooded the earth for 150 days.

8 Elohim kept watch over Noah, and over all the beasts and livestock with him in the ark. Adonai made a wind blow over the earth, and the waters began to go down.

2 The wellsprings of the deep and the floodgates of heaven were sealed. The downpour from the heavens stopped.

3 The waters receded from the earth. They continued to lessen, and at the end of 150 days the water had decreased.

4 In the seventh month, on the seventeenth day of the month, the ark came to rest on the Ararat Mountains. **5** The waters continued to decrease until the tenth month. On the tenth month, on the first of the month, the mountain peaks became visible.

6 After forty days, Noah opened the window he had made in the ark. **7** He sent out the raven, and it departed. It flew back and forth until the water had dried up from the land's surface.

8 He then sent out a dove to see whether the water had disappeared from the land's surface. **9** The dove could not find any place to rest its feet, and so it returned to the ark. There was still water over all the earth's surface. Noah stretched out his hand and brought the dove back into the ark.

10 Noah waited another seven days, and he once again sent the dove out from the ark. **11** The dove returned to him toward evening, and there was a freshly picked olive leaf in its beak. Now Noah knew that the water had subsided from the earth. **12** He waited another seven days and again sent out the dove. This time the dove did not return to him.

13 In the 601st year of Noah's life, in the first month, on the first of the month, the land was drying, so Noah removed the roof of the ark. He saw that the earth's surface was beginning to dry. **14** By the second month, on the twenty-seventh day of the month, the land was completely dry.

Leave the Ark   *4ᵗʰ Aliyah*

15 Elohim spoke to Noah, saying, **16** "Leave the ark—you, your wife, your sons, and your son's wives. **17** Take with you all the living creatures, birds, livestock, and all the creeping things. Let them populate the land. Let them breed and multiply on the earth."

18 Noah left the ark along with his sons, his wife, and his sons' wives. **19** Every beast, every animal, and every bird—all left the ark by families.

20 Now Noah built an altar to Adonai. He took a few of the clean animals and clean birds, and he sacrificed them as offerings on the altar. **21** Adonai was pleased with the sacrifice, and Adonai said to Himself, "I will never again curse the soil because of man's evil. I will never again strike down all life as I have just done. **22** As long as the earth remains,

> seedtime and harvest,
> cold and heat,
> summer and winter, and
> day and night,
> shall never again cease to exist."

9 Elohim blessed Noah and his children. He said to them, "Be fruitful and multiply, and fill the earth. **2** All the wild beasts of the earth, and all the birds of the sky, all creatures on earth and all the fish in the sea, I have placed them in your hands.

3 Every living creature as well as the grain and vegetables are yours to eat as food. I have now given you everything. **4** But you must not eat the flesh of a creature that is still alive.

5 Murder is forbidden. Animals that kill humans must die. Any human who kills another must be punished. **6** Any human who spills the blood of another human shall have his own blood spilled, because Adonai made humans in His own image.

7 Now be fruitful and multiply, populate the earth."

The Rainbow   *5th Aliyah*

8 Elohim said to Noah and his sons, **9** "I am now making a covenant with you and with your descendants. **10** And with every living creature, the birds, the livestock, all the beasts of the earth who were with you in the ark.

11 I will make My covenant with you, and with all life. I will never again send a flood to destroy the earth."

12 Elohim said, "This is My sign of the covenant between Me, you, and every living creature that is with you, for all generations: **13** I have placed My rainbow in the clouds, and it shall be a sign of the covenant between Me and the earth. **14** When I send clouds over the earth, the rainbow will be seen among the clouds. **15** I will then remember the covenant that exists between Me, you, and every living creature. Never again will I send a flood to destroy all life. **16** The rainbow will be in the clouds, and I will see it to remember the eternal covenant between Elohim and every living creature on the earth."

17 Elohim said to Noah, "This is the sign of the covenant that I have made between Me and all living creatures on the earth."

The Descendants of Noah   *6th Aliyah*

18 The sons of Noah who emerged from the ark were Shem, Ham, and Yefeth. Ham was the father of Canaan.

19 These three were Noah's sons, and from them came all the nations of the whole world.

20 Noah began as a farmer, and he planted a vineyard.

21 He drank some of his own wine and became drunk and was naked in his tent. **22** Ham, the father of Canaan, saw his father naked, and he told it to his two brothers.

23 Shem and Yefeth took a garment and placed it over their shoulders, and walking backwards, they covered their father's naked body. They looked the other way and did not see their naked father.

24 When Noah awoke from his drunken sleep and understood what his youngest son had done to him,

25 he angrily said,

> "Cursed be Canaan!
> He shall be a servant
> to his brothers!"

26 He then said,

> "Blessed be Elohim,
> the Savior of Shem!
> Let Canaan be his slave!
> **27** May Elohim bless Yefeth,
> He shall dwell in the tents of Shem
> and let Canaan be their servant!"

28 After the flood Noah lived for 350 years. **29** Noah was 950 years old when he died.

10

This is the history of Noah's sons, Shem, Ham, and Yefeth. Many children were born to them after the flood.

2 The sons of Yefeth were Gomer, Magog, Madai, Yavan, Tuval, Meshech, and Tiras. **3** The descendants of Gomer were Ashkenaz, Riphath, and Togarmah.

4 The sons of Yavan were Elishah, Tarshish, Kittim, and Dodanim.

5 Their descendants became seafarers. Each one founded a nation and developed its own separate language.

6 The sons of Ham were Cush, Mitzraim, Put, and Canaan:

7 The sons of Cush were Sava, Havilah, Sabtah, Raamah, and Savteca. The sons of Raamah were Sheba and Dedan.

8 Cush was the father of Nimrod, who was a mighty ruler.

9 He was a mighty hunter before Adonai. There is a saying, "Like Nimrod, a mighty hunter blessed by Adonai!"

10 The foundation of his kingdom was in Babylon, as well as the cities of Erekh, Akkad, and Calneh, in the land of Shinar. **11** Asshur left Babylon and built the cities of Nineveh, Rechovoth-ir, and Calach, **12** as well as Resen, which is between Nineveh and Calach. Nineveh is a great city.

13 Mitzraim was the ancestor of Ludim, the Anamim, the Lehabim, the Naftuchim, **14** the Pathrusim, and the Casluchim from whom the Philistines descended and the Caphtorim. **15** Canaan fathered Sidon (his first-born) and Heth, **16** as well as the Jebusites, the Amorites, the Girgashites, **17** the Hivites, the Arkites, the Sinites,

18 the Arvadites, the Tzemarites, and the Chamathites: Later on the families of the Canaanites became scattered.

19 The Canaanite borders extended from Sidon as far as Gerar until Gaza, and as far as Sodom, Gomorrah, Admah, and Tzevoyim, until Lasha.

20 The descendants of Ham spread into many lands and nations with many languages.

21 Children were also born to Shem. He was the ancestor of all the descendants of Ever and was the older brother of Yefeth. **22** The sons of Shem were Elam, Asshur, Arpachshad, Lud, and Aram. **23** The sons of Aram were Utz, Chul, Gether, and Mash.

24 Arpachshad fathered a son Shelach. Shelach fathered a son Eber.

25 Eber fathered two sons. The name of the first was

Peleg, because during his lifetime the world spread out. His brother's name was Yoktan.

26 Yoktan was the father of Almodad, Shelef, Chatzarmaveth, Yerach,

27 Hadoram, Uzal, Diklah,

28 Obal, Abimael, Sheba. **29** Ophir, Havilah, and Yovav. These were all the sons of Yoktan. **30** Their settlements extended from Meshah toward the eastern mountain of Sepher.

31 These are the descendants of Shem, arranged according to their families and languages and by their territories and nations.

32 These were the families of Noah's sons, listed according to their descendants and their nations. After the flood, these nations spread over the earth.

The Tower of Babel   *7th Aliyah*

11
During this time the entire world spoke one language. **2** As the population spread eastward, they discovered a valley in the land of Shinar, and they settled there. **3** They said to one another, "Come, let us make strong bricks by firing them." So they made bricks as hard as stone and tar for cement. **4** They said, "Now we can build a city with a tower that reaches the sky. This will keep us together so we will not be scattered all over the face of the earth."

5 Adonai descended to see the city and the tower that the sons of man had built. **6** Adonai said, "They are a single people, all having one language, and this is the first thing they do! Now nothing they plan to do will be unattainable for them! **7** Come, let us descend and confuse their speech, so that one person will not understand another's speech."

8 From that place, Adonai scattered them all over the face of the earth, and they stopped building the city. **9** He named it Babel, because this was the place where Adonai confused the world's language. It was from there that Adonai dispersed [humanity] over all the face of earth.

10 These are the chronicles of Shem:

Shem was 100 years old when he fathered his son Arpachshad, two years after the flood.

11 Shem lived 500 years after he fathered Arpachshad, and he had more sons and daughters.

12 Arpachshad was 35 years old when he had a son Shelach. **13** Arpachshad lived 403 years after he had Shelach, and he had more sons and daughters.

14 Shelach was 30 years old when he fathered his son Eber.

15 Shelach lived 403 years after he had Eber, and he had more sons and daughters.

16 Eber was 34 years old when he fathered his son Peleg. **17** Eber lived 430 years after he fathered Peleg, and he had more sons and daughters.

18 Peleg was 30 years old when he fathered his son Reu. **19** Peleg lived 209 years after he fathered Reu, and he had more sons and daughters. **20** Reu was 32 years old when he fathered his son Serug. **21** Reu lived 207 years after he fathered Serug, and he had more sons and daughters.

22 Serug was 30 years old when he fathered his son Nachor. **23** Serug lived 200 years after he fathered Nachor, and he had more sons and daughters.

24 Nachor was 29 years old when he fathered his son Terach.

25 Nachor lived 119 years after he fathered Terach, and he had more sons and daughters.

26 Terach was 70 years old when he fathered Abram, Nachor, and Haran.

27 This is the history of Terach: Terach fathered Abram, Nachor, and Haran. Haran had a son, Lot. **28** Haran died in the land of his birth, Ur Kasdim, while his father, Terach, was still alive.

The Descendants of Terach   *Maftir*

29 Abram and Nachor married. The name of Abram's wife was Sarai. The name of Nachor's wife was Milcah, the daughter of Haran. **30** Meantime Sarai had no children.

31 Terach took his son Abram, his grandson Lot, and his daughter-in-law Sarai, and he left Ur Kasdim, and he traveled toward the land of Canaan. They came as far as Haran and settled there. **32** Terach was 205 years old when he died in Haran.

Lech Lecha לֶךְ לְךָ
LEAVE YOUR LAND

12 Adonai said to Abram,

"Leave your land, your birthplace,
and your father's house,
[and go] to the land that I will show you.
2 I promise to make your descendants
into a great nation.
I will bless them
and make them great.
You shall become a blessing.
3 I will bless those who bless you,
and curse those who curse you.
All the nations of the world
will be blessed because of you."

4 Abram went as Adonai had directed him, and Lot went with him. Abram was 75 years old when he left Haran.

5 Abram took his wife Sarai, his nephew Lot, and all their belongings, as well as the people they had gathered, and they left, heading toward Canaan. When they finally came to Canaan, **6** Abram traveled through the land as far as the area of Shechem, coming to the Plain of Moreh. At that time the Canaanites were in the land.

7 Adonai appeared to Abram and said, "I will surely give this land to you and your descendants." So Abram built an altar to Adonai, who had appeared to him there.

8 From there Abram traveled southward toward the mountains east of Bethel. There he pitched his tent between Bethel to the west and Ai to the east. He built an altar there and prayed to Adonai. **9** Abram then continued his journey, moving steadily toward the south.

10 There was a terrible famine in the land. So Abram traveled south to Egypt to stay there for a while, because the famine in the land had grown very strong. **11** As they approached Egypt, he said to his wife Sarai, "I am aware that you are a beautiful woman. **12** When the Egyptians see you, they will realize that you are my wife and will kill me, while allowing you to live. **13** If you would, say that you are my sister. They will, for your sake, treat me well, and because of you my life will be saved."

Abram in Egypt   *2nd Aliyah*

14 When Abram came to Egypt, the Egyptians saw that his wife Sarai was very beautiful. **15** Pharaoh's officials saw her and described her to Pharaoh. So Sarai was taken to Pharaoh's palace. **16** Pharaoh treated Abram well because of Sarai. Pharaoh gave Abram many gifts: sheep, cattle, donkeys, male and female slaves, she-donkeys, and camels.

17 But Adonai punished Pharaoh and his palace with plagues because of what he had done to Abram's wife Sarai.

18 Now Pharaoh sent for Abram and angrily said, "How could you do this to me? Why didn't you tell me that she was your wife? **19** Why did you say that she was your sister so that I should take her to myself as a wife? Now here is your wife! Take her and leave my land!"

20 Pharaoh sent Abram and his wife Sarai and all their belongings out of the country.

13 Abram, with his wife and all his belongings, and Lot, headed northward to the Negev.

2 Abram was very rich in livestock, silver, and gold. **3** He continued on his travels from the Negev toward Bethel, until he came to the place where he had originally camped, between Bethel and Ai, **4** the exact place where he had first built an altar. There Abram worshipped Adonai.

Abram and Lot Separate
3rd Aliyah

5 Lot, who accompanied Abram, also had many sheep, cattle, and tents. **6** However, there was not enough grass for both their flocks. **7** There were many quarrels between the shepherds of Abram's flocks and those of Lot. At that time the Canaanites and Perizzites were also living in the land.

8 Abram said to Lot, "We must stop the quarrels between your shepherds and my shepherds. After all, we're from the same family. **9** Look around, all the land is before you. Why not separate from me? If you choose to go to the left, I will go to the right; if you choose to go to the right, I will go to the left."

10 Lot looked around and saw that the entire Jordan Plain was fertile all the way to Tzoar. There was plenty of water. This was before Adonai destroyed Sodom and Gomorrah. It was like Adonai's beautiful garden, like the land of Egypt.

11 Lot chose for his flocks the entire Jordan Valley. And the two separated. **12** Abram remained in the land of Canaan, while Lot settled among the cities of the Plain, near Sodom. **13** But the people of Sodom were very wicked, and they sinned against Adonai.

14 After Lot left, Adonai said to Abram, "Open your eyes, and from where you are now standing, look as far as you can toward the north, toward the south, toward the east, and toward the west. **15** All the land that you see, I will give to you and to your descendants forever. **16** I will make your descendants as many as the dust of the earth. **17** Arise, walk the land and explore the length and breadth of all the land, and you will see what I am giving you."

18 Then Abram moved his tents. And he settled in the Plains of Mamre, at Hebron, and there he built an altar to Adonai.

Abram Rescues Lot
4th Aliyah

14 It was about this time that Amraphel king of Shinar, Arioch king of Ellasar, Chedorlaomer king of Elam, and Tidal king of Goyim **2** fought a war against Bera

king of Sodom, Birsha king of Gomorrah, Shinav king of Admah, Shemever king of Tzevoyim, and the king of Bela, which is now Tzoar.

3 All of these rulers banded together in Siddim Valley, now the Dead Sea. **4** They had for twelve years served Chedorlaomer, but now, in the thirteenth year, they rebelled. **5** In the fourteenth year, Chedorlaomer and his allied kings arrived. They defeated the Rephaim in Ashteroth Karnaim, the Zuzim in Ham, the Emim in Shaveh Kiryathaim, **6** and the Horites in the hill country of Seir, as far as Eyl Paran, at the edge of the desert. **7** Then they swung around and attacked Eyn Mishpat, now Kadesh, and they defeated the armies of the Amalekites and the Amorites, who lived in Charzatzon Tamar.

8 The armies of Sodom, Gomorrah, Admah, Tzevoyim, and Bela Tzoar prepared for battle. They set up fortified positions in Siddim Valley, **9** against Chedorlaomer king of Elam, Tidal king of Goyim, Amraphel king of Shinar, and Arioch king of Ellasar. There were four kings against the five.

10 The Siddim Valley was filled with tar pits, and when the kings of Sodom and Gomorrah tried to flee, they fell into them. The others escaped to the mountains. **11** The victorious invaders seized all the goods and all the food of Sodom and Gomorrah, and they returned home.

12 When they left, they also captured Abram's nephew Lot and his possessions, since he had been living in Sodom. **13** A fugitive who escaped came and brought the news to Abram the Hebrew, who was living quietly near the oak grove belonging to Mamre the Amorite, brother of Eshkol and Aner. They were Abram's allies.

14 When Abram heard that his relatives had been kidnapped, he mobilized all his 318 fighting men who had been born in his house. He pursued the kidnappers, catching up to them in Dan. **15** Abram divided his forces, and he and his servants attacked at night. He attacked, and pursued the kidnappers as far as Hovah, which is to the left of Damascus.

16 Abram recovered all the property. He also brought back his relative Lot and all his goods, the women, and all the other people. **17** After he returned from his victory over Chedorlaomer and his allies, the king of Sodom came out to greet him in Shavah Valley, now called King's Valley.

18 Melchi-tzedek king of Salem served bread and wine. He was a priest to Adonai the Most High. **19** He blessed Abram, and said,

> "Blessed be Abram by El,
>   the most high
> Creator of heaven and earth.
>   **20** And blessed be El,
>   the most high
> who helped you conquer your enemies."

Abram then gave king Melchi-tzedek a tenth of everything.

I Will Not Take Anything
That Is Yours
5th Aliyah

21 The king of Sodom said to Abram, "Give me back my people who were captured, and you can keep the goods that you recovered."

22 Abram replied to the king of Sodom, "I have sworn in an oath to Adonai Most High, Creator of heaven and earth! **23** I will not take anything that is yours! Not even a thread nor a shoelace! In this way you will not be able to say, 'It was I who made Abram rich.' **24** All I will accept is what my young men have eaten, and a share in the spoils for the young men, Aner, Eshkol, and Mamre, who went with me."

15 After these events, Adonai spoke to Abram in a vision, saying, "Abram do not be afraid, I am your shield. Your reward will be very great."

2 Abram said, "Adonai, what good are Your blessings that You will give me if I remain without a son? Will the heir to my household be my servant, Eliezer of Damascus?"

3 Abram continued, "You have given me no children. A member of my household will inherit what is mine."

4 Then Adonai said to him, "No one else will be your heir! A son born from your own body will inherit what is yours." **5** He then brought Abram outside and said, "Look at the sky and count the stars. See if you can count them." Adonai then said to him, "That is how numerous your descendants will be."

6 Abram believed in Adonai, and Adonai considered Abram righteous because he believed the promise.

Adonai Promises Abram   *6ᵗʰ Aliyah*

7 Adonai said to him, "I am Adonai, who took you out of Ur Kasdim to give you this land as a possession forever."

8 Abram asked, "Adonai, how can I really be sure that this land will be mine?"

9 Adonai replied, "Bring Me a heifer, a goat, a ram, a dove, and a young pigeon."

10 Abram brought all of them. He split them in half, and placed one half opposite the other. He did not split the birds.

11 Vultures then came down to feed on the bodies, but Abram chased them away.

12 As the sun was setting, Abram fell into a deep sleep, and he saw a terrifying vision.

13 Then Adonai said to Abram, "You can know for sure that your descendants will be strangers for 400 years in a land that is not theirs, and they will be enslaved and oppressed. **14** But I will punish the nation that enslaves them, and in the end they will leave with great wealth. **15** You will die in peace, and you will be buried at a ripe old age. **16** The fourth generation will return to this land, when the Amorites who are here now will be gone." **17** The sun had set, and it became very dark.

A smoking fire pot and a blazing torch passed between the halves of the sacrifice.

18 That day, Adonai made a covenant with Abram, saying, "I have given this land to your descendants, from the border of Egypt as far as the great river, the Euphrates; **19** the lands of the Kenites, the Kenizites, the Kadmonites, **20** the Hittites, the Perizzites, the Rephaim, **21** the Amorites, the Canaanites, the Girgashites, and the Jebusites."

16

Abram's wife Sarai still had not given birth to any children. Sarai had a slave-girl by the name of Hagar. **2** Sarai said to Abram, "Adonai has kept me from having children. Marry my slave, and hopefully she will have sons and they will be like my own children." Abram listened to Sarai.

3 After Abram had lived in Canaan for ten years, his wife Sarai took Hagar the Egyptian, her slave, and gave her to her husband Abram as a wife. **4** Hagar became pregnant. When she realized that she was pregnant, she treated her mistress with contempt.

5 Sarai said to Abram, "I gave you my slave. Now that she is pregnant, she despises me. Adonai will make you pay for doing this to me!"

6 Abram replied to Sarai, "She is your slave. Deal with her as you see fit." Sarai was cruel to her, and Hagar ran away from her.

7 An angel of Adonai found Hagar near a spring of water in the desert, along the road to Shur. **8** The angel said, "Hagar, maid of Sarai! Where are you coming from, and where are you going?"
She replied, "I am running away from my mistress, Sarai."

9 The angel of Adonai said to her, "Return to your mistress, and do what she says."

10 Then the angel of Adonai continued to speak: "I will grant you many descendants. They will be more than anyone can count."

11 Then the angel of Adonai said to her, "You are pregnant and will give birth to a son. You must name him Ishmael, for Adonai has heard about your complaint. **12** He will be like a rebel. His hand will be against everyone, and everyone will fight against him. He will live near all his brothers."

13 Hagar gratefully said to Adonai, who had spoken to her, "You are a God who sees me [El-Ro'i]," for she said, "I saw the One who appeared to me." **14** So she named the oasis, "Oasis to life [and] my vision of the God who sees me [Be'er LaChai Ro'i]." It is located between Kadesh and Bered.

15 Hagar gave birth to Abram's son. Abram named his son, who had been born to Hagar, Ishmael. **16** Abram was eighty-six years old when Hagar gave birth to his son Ishmael.

17 When Abram was ninety-nine years old, Adonai appeared to him and said, "I am Adonai Almighty [El Shaddai]. Obey Me and have faith in Me. **2** I will make a covenant between us, and I will make your descendants into a great nation."

3 Abram fell on his face. Elohim spoke to him again, saying, **4** "This is My covenant with you: You shall be the father of many nations. **5** From now on you shall no longer be called Abram. Your name shall be Abraham, for your descendants will become many nations. **6** You will be the father of many nations—kings will be among your descendants.

Adonai's Covenant with Abraham   *7ᵗʰ Aliyah*

7 "I will continue the covenant between us and your descendants. This is an eternal covenant; I, Adonai will be with you and your descendants after you. **8** Yes, to you and your descendants I will give the land of Canaan, where you are now living as a stranger. The whole land of Canaan shall be your eternal heritage, and I, Adonai, will be with your descendants."

9 Then Elohim said to Abraham, "You and your descendants must keep My covenant forever. **10** You must keep My covenant between Me and between you and your descendants. You must circumcise every male.

11 You shall circumcise the flesh of your foreskin. This shall be the sign of the covenant between Me and you.

12 Throughout all generations, every male child must be circumcised when he is eight days old. This shall include those born in your household as well as those servants who are purchased—everyone must be circumcised.

13 This shall be My eternal mark on your body.

14 Any male whose foreskin has not been circumcised shall be cut off from the community, for he has broken My covenant."

15 Then Elohim said to Abraham, "Sarai your wife shall no longer be called by the name Sarai. From now on she shall be called Sarah. **16** I will bless her, and she will give birth to a son. I will bless her, and she will be the mother of nations—kings will be among her descendants." **17** Abraham fell on his face and laughed. He said to himself, "Can a hundred-year-old man have children? Can Sarah, who is ninety years old, give birth?" **18** To Elohim, Abraham said, "May Ishmael receive a special blessing from you!"

19 Elohim then said, "Soon your wife Sarah will give birth to a son. You must name him Isaac. I will keep My covenant with him and his descendants as an everlasting treaty. **20** I have also heard your request with regard to Ishmael. I will bless him and make him fruitful, greatly increasing his numbers. He will father twelve princes, and I will make him into a great nation. **21** But I will keep my covenant with Isaac, to whom Sarah will give birth at this time next year."

22 When He finished speaking to him, Elohim left, leaving Abraham.

23 Then Abraham, on the very same day that Elohim had spoken to him, circumcised his son Ishmael, and everyone born in his house, and every servant and every male in his household.

Abram and Ishmael Are Circumcised   *Maftir*

24 Abraham was ninety-nine years old when he was circumcised.

25 His son Ishmael was thirteen years old when he was circumcised.

26 On the very day that Abraham and his son Ishmael were circumcised, **27** all the men of the household, both those born in Abraham's household and those who were bought, were circumcised with him.

Vayera וַיֵּרָא
AND ADONAI APPEARED

18 Adonai appeared to Abraham in the Plains of Mamre while he was sitting at the entrance of his tent in the hottest part of the day. **2** Abraham looked up, and he saw three strangers standing a short distance from him. When he saw them from the entrance of his tent, he ran to welcome them, bowing down to the ground.

3 He said, "My lords, please do not go any farther without stopping here with me. **4** My servants will bring some water to bathe your feet while you rest in the shade of the tree. **5** I will serve some food so you can refresh yourselves. Then you can continue on your journey. After all, you are passing by my house."

"All right," they replied. "We will do as you have said."

6 Abraham then rushed into Sarah's tent and said, "Quick! Get twenty-two quarts of the finest flour! And bake some bread."

7 Then Abraham ran to the herd and selected a tender, choice calf. He gave it to a young man who rushed to prepare it.

8 Abraham also brought some cheese and milk, and the meat that the servant had prepared, and served his three guests. Abraham served them as they ate under the tree.

9 They asked him, "Where is your wife Sarah?"

"She is here in the tent," he replied.

10 One of the men said, "Next year at this time I will return, and your wife Sarah will have a son."

Sarah was listening to the conversation from behind the entrance of the tent. **11** Abraham and Sarah were already old, and Sarah knew that she no longer could have children. **12** Sarah laughed to herself, saying, "I and my husband are very old. How can we possibly have a baby?"

13 Adonai said to Abraham, "Why did Sarah laugh and say, 'Can I really have a child when I am so old?'

14 Is there anything too difficult for Adonai? At this time next year, I will return, and Sarah will have a son."

Adonai Plans to Destroy Sodom   *2ⁿᵈ Aliyah*

15 Sarah was afraid, so she denied it. "I did not laugh," she said. Adonai said, "You really did laugh."

16 The three strangers got up from their places and continued their journey toward Sodom. Abraham accompanied them part of the way.

17 Adonai said, "Should I hide from Abraham what I plan to do? **18** Abraham's descendants shall become a great and mighty nation, and because of him all the nations of the world will be blessed. **19** I have chosen him so that he will teach his children and his descendants to keep Adonai's laws of doing charity and justice. Adonai will then do for Abraham everything He promised."

20 Adonai continued, "The reputation of Sodom is full of evil, and they are very wicked. **21** I myself must go down to see if the reports are true. Only then can I be sure." **22** The strangers continued toward Sodom. But Abraham was still standing before Adonai.

23 Abraham approached Adonai and said, "Would You really destroy the innocent together with the guilty?

24 Just suppose there are fifty innocent people in the city. Would You still destroy it, and not save the city for the sake of the fifty good people inside it? **25** I am sure that you will not kill the innocent with the guilty, so that the innocent are punished, and the righteous and the wicked fare alike. It would be sacrilege! Shall the whole world's judge not act justly?"

26 Adonai said, "If I find fifty innocent people in Sodom, I will save the entire area for the sake of them."

27 Abraham continued and said, "I have already said too much before my Lord! I am just dust and ashes! **28** But suppose that there are five missing from the fifty innocent? Would you destroy the entire city because of the missing five?"

"I will not destroy Sodom if I find forty-five innocents there," replied Adonai. **29** Abraham pleaded and said, "But suppose there are only forty there?" "I will not destroy for the sake of the forty innocent."

30 Abraham continued, "Adonai, do not be angry with me, but I must speak up. What if there are thirty innocent there?" "I will not destroy if I find thirty innocent there."

31 "I have already said too much now before my Lord! But what if twenty innocents are found there?" "I will not destroy for the sake of the twenty innocent."

32 Abraham persisted and said, "Adonai, do not be angry with me, but I must speak up just one more time. Suppose ten innocent are found there?" "I will not destroy for the sake of the ten innocent."

33 Adonai left when He finished speaking with Abraham. Abraham then returned home.

The Evil City of Sodom   *3rd Aliyah*

19 The two strangers came to Sodom in the evening, while Lot was sitting at the entrance of the city. Lot saw them and got up to greet them, bowing to the ground. **2** Lot said, "My lords, please come to my house. Be my guests, bathe your feet, and then in the morning continue on your journey."

"No," they insisted, "we will spend the night in the city square."

3 Lot kept insisting until they finally agreed and came to his house. He made a feast for them and baked matzah, and they ate.

4 Just as they were going to bed, the townspeople, the men of Sodom, surrounded the house. **5** They shouted to Lot and said, "Where are the strangers who came to you tonight? Bring them out to us so that we can molest them!"

6 Lot went out to the mob in front of the entrance, shutting the door behind him. **7** He said, "My brothers, please do not do such an evil thing! **8** I have two daughters who are virgins, and I will bring them out to you. You can do as you please with them. But do not harm these men. After all, they have come into my house, and I am responsible for their safety!"

9 The mob shouted, "Get out of our way!"

They said to Lot, "You came here as an immigrant, and now, all of a sudden, you tell us how to behave. We'll treat you worse than them!"

They pushed Lot, and tried to break down the door.
10 The two strangers inside the house reached out, pulled Lot into the house, and locked the door.

11 They blinded the Sodomites who were standing at the entrance and trying to find the door.

12 The strangers said to Lot, "Who else do you have in the house? Sons-in-law? Your own sons? Your daughters? If you have any relatives in the city, get them out of Sodom. **13** We are about to destroy the city, for the evil reputation of Sodom is very great. Adonai has sent us to destroy Sodom."

14 Lot hurried and spoke to his sons-in-law, who were married to his daughters. He said, "Quick! Get out of this area! Adonai is about to destroy the city!" But to his sons-in-law, it was a big joke.

15 The next morning, the two angels urged Lot. "Hurry, get moving!" they said. "Take your wife and two daughters who are here! You do not want to be caught in the coming destruction because of Sodom's sins!"

16 Lot still hesitated, so the strangers grabbed him, his wife, and his two daughters by the hand, and rushed them out to the outskirts of Sodom. Adonai had shown pity for Lot and his family. **17** The angel who had led them out said, "Escape for your life! Do not look back! Do not stop anywhere in the valley! Run to the hills, so that you will not die!"

18 Lot said to the strangers, "Please! **19** I know that you have been kind to me and have saved my life! But I cannot reach the hills to escape. The destruction will overtake me and I will die! **20** Please, there is a small village nearby, close enough for refuge! I will escape there and will be safe."

Sodom and Gomorrah   *4ᵗʰ Aliyah*

21 The angel replied to Lot, "I will accept your suggestion. I will not destroy the city you mentioned. **22** Hurry! Run to the village! I can do nothing until you get there."
The village was then called Zoar (Insignificant).
23 The sun was rising as Lot arrived in Zoar. **24** Now Adonai rained down sulphur and fire from the sky on Sodom and Gomorrah. **25** He destroyed the cities and everything in the entire plain. He destroyed everyone in the cities and everything that was growing from the ground.
26 But Lot's wife looked back, and she was turned into a pillar of salt.
27 In the morning Abraham woke up early and hurried back to the place where he had stood before Adonai.
28 He looked toward Sodom and Gomorrah, and all he saw was heavy smoke rising from the earth, like the smoke of a furnace.
29 When Elohim destroyed the cities of the Plain, Adonai remembered Abraham. When He destroyed the cities in which Lot lived, He kept Lot safe from the disaster. **30** Lot and his two daughters left Zoar and settled in the hills, because he was afraid to remain in Zoar. He and his two daughters lived alone in a cave.
31 The older girl said to the younger, "Our father is growing old, and there is no other suitable man that our father will allow us to marry. **32** Come, let's get our father drunk with wine and sleep with him. In this way our family will continue through our father."
33 That night, they got their father drunk with wine, and the older girl went and slept with her father. He was not aware that she had slept with him.
34 The next day, the older girl said to the younger, "Last night

it was I who slept with my father. Tonight, let's get him drunk again. Now it is your turn to sleep with him; in this way our family will survive through children from our father."

35 That night, they again made their father drunk. The younger girl got up and slept with him. Again he was not aware that she had slept with him.

36 Lot's two daughters became pregnant from their father.
37 The older girl gave birth to a son, and she named him Moab. He became the ancestor of the nation Moab that exists today.
38 The younger girl also had a son, and she named him Ben-Ami (Son of My People). He became the ancestor of the people of Ammon who exist today.

20

Abraham journeyed southward to the land of the Negev, and he settled between Kadesh and Shur. He would often visit Gerar.

2 There he announced that his wife Sarah was his sister, so Abimelech, king of Gerar, sent messengers for her and brought Sarah to his palace.

3 Adonai appeared to Abimelech in a dream that night. He said, "You will die because of the woman you took. She is already married."

4 Abimelech had not even touched her. He said, "Adonai, would you kill an innocent person? **5** Her husband told me that she was his sister. She too claimed that he was her brother. I did not harm her in any way."

6 Adonai said to him in the dream, "I realize that you have done this innocently. That is why I prevented you from sinning by not giving you the opportunity to touch her. **7** Now return the man's wife, for he is a prophet. He will pray for you, and you will live. But if you do not return her, then you and your kingdom are doomed."

8 Abimelech got up early in the morning and assembled all his servants. He told them everything that had happened, and everyone was very frightened.

9 Abimelech summoned Abraham and said to him, "What have you done to us?" **10** Abimelech asked Abraham, "Whatever made you think to do such a thing?"

11 Abraham replied, "I realized that the people here do not fear Elohim, and that I could be killed because of my wife.

12 Besides, she really is my sister. We both have the same father but not the same mother, so I married her.

13 When Elohim sent me wandering from my father's house, I asked her to do me a favor. Wherever we were, she was to say that I was her brother."

14 Abimelech took sheep, cattle, and servants, and he gave them to Abraham. He also returned Abraham's wife Sarah to him.

15 Abimelech said, "Travel through my whole land. Settle wherever you choose."

16 To Sarah he said, "I am giving your 'brother' a thousand pieces of silver as payment to you and all who are with you for the violations that have been done to you. This will settle all claims against me."

17 Abraham prayed to Elohim, and Elohim healed Abimelech, as well as his wife and his female servants, so that they would be able to have children. **18** Adonai had made all the women in Abimelech's house infertile, because of what he intended to do to Abraham's wife Sarah.

21

At last Adonai remembered Sarah and His promise to her. **2** Sarah became pregnant, and she gave birth to Abraham's son in his old age, at the exact time that Elohim had promised him. **3** Abraham named his son Isaac, [the son] to whom Sarah had just given birth. **4** When his son Isaac was eight days old, Abraham circumcised him, just as Adonai had commanded.

Isaac Is Born   *5ᵗʰ Aliyah*

5 Abraham was a hundred years old when his son Isaac was born. **6** Sarah said, "Adonai has made me laugh. All who hear about it will laugh with me." **7** She said, "Who would even have suggested to Abraham that Sarah would be nursing children? But here I have given birth to a son in my old age!"

8 The child grew up and was no longer nursed. Abraham made a great feast on the day that Isaac was three years old. **9** But Sarah saw that Hagar's son was being cruel to Abraham. **10** So Sarah said to Abraham, "Drive away Hagar and her son. The son of Hagar will not share your inheritance with my son Isaac!" **11** This troubled Abraham very much because it involved his son Ishmael.

12 But Elohim said to Abraham, "Do not be upset about Hagar and her son. Do everything that Sarah tells you to do. It is only through Isaac that your descendants will gain nationhood. **13** But I will also make Hagar's son into a nation, because he is your child."

14 Abraham got up early in the morning. He took bread and a leather bag filled with water, and gave it to Hagar, who placed it on her shoulder. He sent Hagar and the boy away. She left and wandered in the desert around Beer-sheva. **15** When the water in the bag was used up, she lay the boy under a shady bush. **16** She walked away, and sat down facing the boy, and she said, "I cannot bear to see my boy die." She sat there facing Ishmael, and wept out loud.

17 Elohim heard the boy crying. Elohim's angel called Hagar from above and said to her, "Hagar, do not be afraid. Elohim has heard the boy's cries. **18** Go and hug your son and comfort him. Keep watch over him, for I will make his descendants into a great nation."

19 Then Elohim opened her eyes, and she saw a well of water. She went and filled the leather bag with water and gave the boy some to drink. **20** Adonai watched over the boy. The boy grew up and lived in the desert, where he became an expert hunter. **21** He lived in the Paran Desert, and his mother found him a wife in Egypt.

A Peace Treaty   *6ᵗʰ Aliyah*

22 Around that time, Abimelech and his general, Pikhol, spoke to Abraham, saying, "We are aware that Elohim helps you in everything that you do. **23** Now swear to me in Elohim's name that you will not deal falsely with me, or with my children, or with my grandchildren. Show me and my people the same friendship that I have shown to you."

24 "I swear," replied Abraham.

25 Abraham then complained to Abimelech about the well that Abimelech's servants had taken over from Abraham's servants.

26 Abimelech said, "I have no idea who could have done such a thing. You never told me. I heard nothing about the problem until today."

27 Abraham then took sheep and cattle and gave them to Abimelech, and the two of them made a treaty.

28 Abraham then gathered seven sheep and put them aside. **29** Abimelech asked Abraham, "What is the meaning of these seven sheep?" **30** "Take these seven sheep from me," replied Abraham. "This gift will be my proof that I dug this well."

31 Since then the area has been called Beer-sheva (The Well of the Seven) because the two made peace there and **32** made a treaty in Beer-sheva. Abimelech and his general, Pikhol, then left, and they returned to the land of the Philistines.

33 Abraham planted a tamarisk tree in Beer-sheva, and there he prayed to Adonai, Creator of the Universe. **34** Abraham lived in the land of the Philistines for a long time.

Sacrifice Your Son   *7ᵗʰ Aliyah*

22 After these events, Elohim tested Abraham's faith. He said, "Abraham!" And Abraham replied, "*Hineni, here I am.*" **2** Elohim said, "Take your only son Isaac, the one you love, and go away to the region of Moriah. And sacrifice him as an offering on one of the mountains that I will show you."

3 Abraham got up early and saddled his donkey.

He took two servants and his son Isaac with him. He cut wood for the fire and set out, heading for the place that Adonai had told him.

4 On the third day, Abraham looked up and saw the place from afar.

5 Abraham said to his two servants, "Remain here with the donkey. Isaac and I will go farther, and after we worship we will return to you."

6 Abraham placed the wood on the shoulders of his son Isaac, while he carried the fire and the slaughter knife, and the two of them walked together. **7** Isaac said to Abraham, "Father!" And Abraham answered, "*Hineni!* Here I am."

Isaac said, "Here are the fire and the wood. But where is the lamb for the sacrifice?"

8 Abraham replied, "My son, Elohim will provide a lamb for the offering."

The two of them continued walking together. **9** Finally they came to the place chosen by Elohim. Abraham built the altar there and arranged the wood. He then tied up his son Isaac, and placed him on the altar on top of the wood.

10 Now Abraham reached out and took the slaughter knife in his hand. **11** At that moment, Adonai's angel called to him from heaven and said, "Abraham! Abraham!" And Abraham answered, "*Hineni!* Here I am."

12 The angel said, "Do not harm your son. Do not do anything to him. For now I know that you have complete faith in Elohim. You have not even withheld your only son from Him."

13 Abraham looked up and saw a ram caught by its horns in a bush. He went and took the ram and sacrificed it in his son's place. **14** Abraham named the place Adonoy Yir'eh (Adonai Will See). Today it is called B'har Adonai Yerah (He Will Be Seen on Adonai's Mountain).

15 Adonai's angel called to Abraham from heaven a second time, **16** and said, "Adonai declares, 'I have sworn that because you performed this deed, and did not even hold back your beloved son, **17** I will bless you greatly, and make your descendants as many as the stars of the sky and the sand on the seashore. Your descendants shall conquer their enemies.

18 All the nations of the world shall be blessed because of your descendants—all because you obeyed me.'"

19 Abraham returned to his servants and they went back to Beer-sheva. Abraham remained in Beer-sheva.

The Children of Nachor   *Maftir*

20 After this, Abraham received a message: "Milcah has given birth to children by your brother Nachor:

21 Utz, his first-born; Buz, his brother; Kemuel, father of Aram; **22** Kesed, Chazo, Pildash, Yidlaf, and Bethuel.

23 Bethuel has a daughter, Rebecca."

Milcah gave birth to eight sons by Abraham's brother Nachor. **24** Nachor's second wife was named Reumah. She too had children: Tevach, Gacham, Tachash, and Ma'akhah.

Chayay Sarah חַיֵּי שָׂרָה
THE LIFE OF SARAH

23 Sarah lived to be 127 years old. **2** Sarah died in Kiryath Arba, also known as Hebron, in the land of Canaan. Abraham came to mourn Sarah and to cry for her.

3 When Abraham rose from mourning, he spoke to the citizens of Heth. **4** "I am a stranger and a visitor among you," he said. "Please sell me a piece of land for a burial place so that I can bury my dead wife here."

5 The people of Heth replied to Abraham, saying to him,

6 "My lord, listen to us. You are a prince of Adonai among us. Choose our best burial place to bury your wife. No one among us will refuse you a piece of land to bury your wife."

7 Abraham then rose, and he bowed down to the citizens of Heth. **8** He said to them, "If you really want to help me bury my dead, please speak up for me to Ephron son of Zohar. **9** Let him sell me the Cave of Machpelah, which he owns, at the end of his field. Let him sell it to me for its full price, as a burial place for my family."

10 Ephron was sitting among the people of Heth. Ephron the Hittite answered Abraham in the presence of the people of Heth, so that everyone who came to the city gate could hear. **11** "No, my lord," he said. "Listen to me. I will give you the field and the cave that is there. Here, in the presence of my countrymen, I have given you the Cave of Machpelah. Bury your dead."

12 Again Abraham bowed down before the people. **13** He spoke to Ephron so that all the people could hear. "Please listen to me," he said. "I will pay you for the field. Take the money from me, so I can bury my dead there."

14 Ephron replied to Abraham, **15** "My lord, listen to me. What is 400 silver coins worth of land between friends? Go ahead and bury your dead."

16 Abraham understood what Ephron meant. Abraham weighed out for Ephron the amount of silver that had been decided in the presence of the citizens of Heth. Abraham paid 400 coins of silver.

Abraham Buys the Cave
of Machpelah   *2ⁿᵈ Aliyah*

17 Abraham bought Ephron's field in Machpelah facing Mamre. It became Abraham's legal property. The property included the field, the cave, and every nearby tree. **18** It became Abraham's property, and all the people of Heth were eyewitnesses. **19** Abraham then buried his wife Sarah in the Cave of Machpelah, which is near Mamre, which is also known as Hebron, in the land of Canaan.

20 This is how the field and its cave, purchased from the people of Heth, became the uncontested legal property of Abraham as a burial site.

24 Abraham was very old, and Adonai had blessed Abraham with everything. **2** One day Abraham spoke to his trusted servant, who was in charge of all that he owned; he said,

3 "Promise me and swear to Adonai, Creator of heaven and earth, that you will not choose a wife for my son from among the Canaanite girls where I live. **4** Instead, you must go to my homeland, to my relatives' birthplace, and there find a wife for my son Isaac."

5 "But suppose the girl does not want to return with me to this land?" asked the servant. "Then shall I bring your son back to the land that you left?"

6 Abraham replied, "No you must never do that. Under no circumstances bring my son back there!

7 Adonai, the Creator of Heaven, sent me away from my father's house and the land of my birth. He spoke to me and promised me that He would give this land to my descendants. He will send His angel in front of you, and there you will surely find a wife for my son. **8** But if the girl does not want to return with you, then you will be freed of your promise. But no matter what, you must not bring my son back there!" **9** So the servant promised Abraham, his master, that he would follow his instructions.

Rebecca at the Well   *3rd Aliyah*

10 The servant then took ten of his master's camels and brought along some of the precious things that his master owned. He set off and traveled to Aram Naharayim, where Nachor, Abraham's brother lived.

11 When he arrived there, he made the camels rest on their knees outside the city, beside the well. It was in the evening, when women go out to draw water.

12 He prayed, "Adonai, Savior of my master Abraham: Be kind to me today, and also show kindness to my master Abraham. **13** I am now standing by a well, and the daughters of the townspeople are coming out to draw water. **14** If I ask a girl, 'Please let me have a drink from your jar,' and she replies, 'Yes, certainly drink, and I will also water your camels,' then she will be the one whom You have chosen for Your servant Isaac. If there is such a girl, I will know that You have kept Your promise to my master."

15 He had just finished speaking when Rebecca appeared. She was the daughter of Bethuel, the son of Milcah, the wife of Abraham's brother Nachor. Her water jar was on her shoulder. **16** Rebecca was beautiful, and she was untouched by any man. Rebecca went to the well and filled her jar, and started back.

17 At that moment the servant rushed toward her and said, "Please, let me have a drink of water from your jar."

18 Without hesitation she replied, "Drink as much as you want." She quickly lowered the jar and gave him a drink.

19 When he had finished drinking, she said, "Now let me bring some water for your camels, so they too can drink. **20** She quickly emptied her jar into the trough and ran to the well again to bring more water. She brought enough water for all his camels.

21 The man stood there silently staring at her, waiting and wondering if Adonai had miraculously made his journey successful.

22 When the camels had finished drinking, Abraham's servant took out a gold ring weighing half a shekel, and two gold bracelets weighing ten gold shekels, and gave them to her.

23 He then asked, "Whose daughter are you? Also tell me whether there is anyplace in your father's house for us to spend the night."

24 She replied, "I am the daughter of Bethuel, and my grandparents are Milchah and Nachor." **25** Then she said, "Of course, we have plenty of straw and feed, as well as a place for your people to spend the night." **26** The man bowed low and thanked Adonai.

The Mission Is Successful   *4ᵗʰ Aliyah*

27 He said, "Blessed be Adonai, Savior of my master Abraham, who has been kind to my master. Here I am, and Adonai has led me directly to the house of my master's family!"

28 The girl ran to her mother's home and told the woman what had happened.

29 Now Rebecca had a brother named Laban. He heard Rebecca, and he ran to the stranger at the well. **30** He had seen the ring, and the bracelets on his sister's arms, and had heard his sister Rebecca telling what the man had said to her. He rushed to the stranger, who was standing beside the camels near the well, **31** and said, "Come! You are a man blessed by Adonai! Why are you still standing outside? Come, I have a room for you, and I have prepared a place for the camels."

32 So the stranger came into the house and unloaded the camels. Laban gave the camels straw and feed, and brought water for the stranger and the men with him with which to bathe their feet. **33** But when the food was served, the stranger said, "I will not eat until I tell you the reason I came here." Laban replied, "Tell us your mission."

34 The stranger said, "I am Abraham's servant. **35** Adonai has blessed my master, and he is very rich. Adonai has given him many sheep and cattle, silver, gold, servants, camels, and donkeys. **36** In her old age my master's wife Sarah gave birth to a son. And my master has given him everything that he owns.

37 My master made me swear: 'Do not choose a wife for my son from among the daughters of the Canaanites, in whose land I live. **38** Instead, you must go to my father's house, to my family, and there you shall get a wife for my son.'

39 I said to my master, 'But what if the girl will not come back with me?' **40** He said to me, 'Adonai, will send His angel with you and make your mission successful. But you must find a wife for my son from my family and from my father's house.

41 There is only one way that you can be free of your promise. If you go to my family and they do not give you a girl, only then will you be released from your promise.'

42 Now today I came to the well, and I prayed, 'Adonai, Savior of my master Abraham, please make my mission that I have undertaken a success. **43** I will stand by the town well, and when a girl comes out to draw water, I will ask her, "Please let me drink some water from your jar." **44** If she answers, "Not only may you drink, but I will also draw water for your camels," then she is the wife chosen by Adonai for my master's son.'

45 Then, even before I had finished speaking to myself, Rebecca suddenly came by, carrying a water jar on her shoulder. As she went down to the well to fill her jar, I asked her, 'Please give me a drink.' **46** She immediately lowered her jar and said, 'Drink! I will also bring water for all your camels.' I took a drink, and she also brought water for all the camels.

47 I asked her, 'Whose daughter are you?' She replied, 'I am the daughter of Bethuel son of Nachor and Milcah.' I then put a ring on her nose, and bracelets on her arms. **48** I bowed low to Adonai. I blessed Adonai, Savior of my master Abraham, because He led me on the right path to find a wife for my master's son.

49 Now if you are willing to do what is kind and right for my master, please tell me. If not, say so, and I will then know my next step whether to go to the right or to the left."

50 Laban and Bethuel both spoke up. "We know that Adonai has purposely sent you here! We have no choice whether it is bad or good. **51** Rebecca is right here in front of you. Adonai has spoken; take her and go. Let her become the wife for your master's son."

52 When Abraham's servant heard these words, he bowed down to Adonai and thanked Him.

Rebecca Meets Isaac   *5ᵗʰ Aliyah*

53 The servant then brought out gifts of gold and silver jewelry, as well as articles of clothing, and gave them to Rebecca. He also presented gifts to her brother and mother. **54** Abraham's servants and his men then ate and drank, and they spent the night.

When they got up in the morning, the servant said, "It is time for us to go back to our master."

55 The girl's brother and mother replied, "At least allow her to remain with us for another week or ten days, and then she will be prepared to go."

56 "Do not make me stay any longer," said the servant. "Adonai has already made my mission a success. Let me leave, so that I can return to my master."

57 They replied, "In that case let's call Rebecca and ask her what she wants to do." **58** So they called Rebecca and asked her, "Are you willing to go with this man?" She replied "Yes, I will go."

59 So Rebecca and her servants left with Abraham's servant, and his men. **60** They blessed Rebecca and said to her, "You are our sister, may you become the mother of millions! And your ancestors triumph over all their enemies."

61 Rebecca and her servants mounted their camels and followed Abraham's servants. **62** Just at that moment Isaac was returning from Beer LaChai Ro'i, since he was then living in the Negev. **63** Toward evening Isaac decided to take a walk in the fields. He looked up and saw camels approaching.

64 When Rebecca looked up and saw Isaac, she stepped down from her camel. **65** She asked Abraham's servant, "Who is this man walking to meet us?"

Abraham's servant replied, "That is my master." Then Rebecca took her veil and covered her face.

66 The servant told Isaac everything that had happened to him. **67** Then Isaac brought the girl into his mother Sarah's tent, and he married Rebecca. She became his wife, and he loved her. She comforted Isaac for the death of his mother.

Abraham Dies   *6ᵗʰ Aliyah*

25
Abraham married another woman, whose name was Keturah. **2** She gave birth to Zimran, Yakshan, Medan, Midian, Yishbak, and Shuach.

3 Yakshan fathered Sheba and Dedan. The sons of Dedan were the Ashurim, Letushim, and Leumim **4** The sons of Midian were Eiphahl, Epher, Enoch, Avidah, and Elda'ah.

All these children were Keturah's descendants.

5 Abraham left everything that he owned to Isaac. **6** To the sons of the concubines, Abraham also gave gifts. Then, while he was still alive, he sent them to the East, far away from his son Isaac.

7 This is the history of Abraham's life. He lived a total of 175 years. **8** Abraham breathed his last and died at a ripe old age. **9** His sons Isaac and Ishmael buried him in the Cave of Machpelah, in the field of Ephron son of Zohar the Hittite, which borders Mamre. **10** The field that Abraham bought from the children of Heth is where Abraham and his wife Sarah were buried.

11 After Abraham died, Adonai blessed Isaac, his son. Isaac now lived near Beer LaChai Ro'i.

The History of Ishmael   *7ᵗʰ Aliyah*

12 This is the history of Ishmael, son of Abraham, whom Hagar the Egyptian, Sarah's slave, bore to Abraham:

13 These are the names of Ishmael's sons in order of their birth: Nebayoth, Ishmael's first-born, Kedar, Adbiel, Mibsam, **14** Mishma, Duma, Masa, **15** Chadad, Tema, Yetur, Nafish, and Kedmah.

Ishmael Dies   *Maftir*

16 Ishmael's sons founded towns and villages. They became the founders of twelve tribes named after them. **17** This is the history of Ishmael's life. He lived a total of 137 years. and died.

18 His descendants lived in the area from Havilah to Shur, which borders on Egypt, all the way to Assyria. They were always fighting one another.

THE HISTORY OF ISAAC

19 These are the chronicles of Isaac son of Abraham: Abraham was Isaac's father. **20** When Isaac was forty years old, he married Rebecca, daughter of Bethuel the Aramaean of Padan Aram and sister of Laban the Aramaean.

21 His wife Rebecca could have no children, and Isaac pleaded with Adonai for her sake. So Adonai answered his prayer, and Rebecca became pregnant. **22** But the twins inside her fought, and when this occurred, she asked, "Why is this happening to me?" She went to seek an answer from Adonai. **23** Adonai said to her, "Two competing nations are in your body. One nation will be stronger than the other. The descendants of the older son will serve the descendants of the younger son. "

24 Rebecca gave birth to twins.

25 The first one that came out was covered with red hair. So they named him Esau. **26** The second twin that came out was holding on to his brother Esau's heel (*akav*). So Isaac named him Jacob. Isaac was sixty years old when Rebecca gave birth to Esau and Jacob.

27 The boys grew up. Esau became a skilled hunter, a man of the field. Jacob was a quiet man who remained at home. **28** Isaac favored Esau and enjoyed eating Esau's wild game, but Rebecca favored Jacob. **29** Once Jacob was cooking a stew, when Esau came home exhausted from the hunt. **30** So Esau said to Jacob, "I'm famished. Give me some of that red stuff that you are cooking." This is how Esau earned his other name, Edom (Red). **31** Jacob replied, "First sell me your birthright." **32** Esau exclaimed, "I'm about to die of hunger! What good is a birthright to me now?"

33 Jacob answered, "Swear to me right now that the birthright belongs to me." So Esau swore and sold his birthright to Jacob. **34** Then Jacob gave Esau bread and some of the red lentil stew. Esau ate it, drank, got up, and left, not caring that he had rejected the birthright.

26

Once again there was a famine in the land, just like the first famine in the time of Abraham: Isaac went to Abimelech, king of the Philistines, in Gerar.

2 Adonai appeared to Isaac and said, "Do not go down to Egypt. Stay here in this land that I am going to give you.

3 Continue to live in this land. I will protect you and bless you, and I will give all of this land to your descendants. I will keep the promise that I made to your father Abraham. **4** I will make your descendants as numerous as the stars of the sky, and give them all these lands. All the nations on earth will be blessed because of your descendants. **5** I will do this because Abraham obeyed Me and My commandments, and My decrees, and My laws."

Isaac and Abimelech   *2nd Aliyah*

6 So Isaac settled in Gerar. **7** When the residents asked about his wife, he told them that she was his sister. He was afraid to say that she was his wife, because Rebecca was beautiful, and they would have killed him because of her.

8 Once, after Isaac had been there for some time, Abimelech, king of the Philistines, was looking out the window, and he saw Isaac embracing his wife Rebecca.

9 Abimelech summoned Isaac and asked, "Is Rebecca your wife? Why did you tell me that she is your sister?"

Isaac answered, "I was afraid that I would be murdered because of her."

10 "What have you done to us?" exploded Abimelech. "One of my people could easily have molested your wife! You would have made us commit a terrible crime!"

11 Abimelech announced to all his people. "Whoever dares to harm this man or his wife shall die." **12** Isaac farmed in the area. That year he harvested a hundred times more than he planted because Adonai had blessed him.

The Quarrels Over the Wells   *3rd Aliyah*

13 This was the beginning of his wealth. He continued to prosper until he became extremely wealthy. **14** He had flocks of sheep, herds of cattle, and many servants. The Philistines became jealous of him. **15** They filled up all the wells that his father's servants had dug while Abraham was still alive. **16** Abimelech said to Isaac, "Leave us; you have become too wealthy for us." **17** Isaac left the area and settled in the Gerar Valley. **18** He opened the wells that had been dug in the days of his father Abraham, which had been closed up by the Philistines after Abraham's death. He gave them the same names that his father had given them.

19 Isaac's servants again dug in the valley and found a new well, overflowing with fresh water. **20** The shepherds of Gerar quarreled with Isaac's shepherds, claiming that the water was theirs. Isaac named the well Esek (Challenge) because the shepherds had challenged him.

21 Isaac's shepherds then dug another well, and again the shepherds harassed them. So Isaac named the well Sitnah (Harassment).

22 He then moved away from there and dug another well. This time it was not challenged, so he named it Rehovot (Wide Spaces). "Now at last Adonai will grant us wide open spaces," he said. "We can be prosperous in this land."

Isaac and Abimelech Make a Treaty   *4th Aliyah*

23 From there, Isaac went to Beer-sheva. **24** That night Adonai appeared to him and said, "I am Adonai of your father Abraham. Do not be afraid, for I am with you. I will bless you and give you very many descendants because of My promise to your father Abraham."

25 Isaac built an altar and worshipped Adonai. He settled there, and his servants dug a well in the area.

26 Abimelech from Gerar, along with a group of friends and his general, Pikhol, came to Isaac. **27** Isaac asked, "Why have you come to me? You hate me, and you drove me away!"

28 They replied, "We have seen that you are blessed by

Adonai. We propose that we make a treaty between us, **29** that just as we did not touch you, you will do no harm to us. We will not harm you, and you will not harm us. We will leave you in peace."

The Well at Beer-sheva   *5th Aliyah*

30 Isaac prepared a feast for them, and they ate and drank. **31** They arose early in the morning and exchanged promises. Isaac then said goodbye and they left in peace.

32 On that very same day, Isaac's servants came and told him about the well they had been digging. They announced, "We have found water!" **33** Isaac named the well Shevah. The city is therefore called Beer-sheva (Well of the Seven) to this very day.

34 When Esau was forty years old, he married Judith, daughter of Beeri the Hittite, and Basemath, daughter of Elon the Hittite. **35** His Hittite wives made life bitter for Isaac and Rebecca.

27

Isaac had grown old and his eyesight was almost gone. He called for his elder son, Esau, and said, "My son." Esau answered, "Yes, father, I am here."

2 "I am old, and soon I will die. **3** Take your bow and arrows, and go out into the field and get some deer meat.

4 Make it into a tasty dish, the way I like it, and bring it to me to eat. Afterwards I will give you the blessing of the first-born."

5 Rebecca had secretly been listening while Isaac spoke to Esau. Esau went out to the field to hunt for a deer and bring it home for Isaac.

6 Rebecca said to her son Jacob, "I just heard your father speaking to your brother Esau. He said, **7** 'Bring me some deer meat and cook it for me. After I eat I will bless you with Adonai's blessing before I die.' "

8 Rebecca continued, "Now, my son, listen to me. Follow my instructions carefully. **9** Go to the herd and choose two lambs. And I will prepare it just the way your father likes. **10** Then you must bring it to your father, so that he will eat it and bless you before he dies."

11 Jacob replied, "But my brother Esau is hairy. I am smooth-skinned.

12 Suppose my father touches me. He will immediately know that I am not Esau! I will earn a curse instead of a blessing!"

13 Rebecca said, "My son, let any curse on you be on me. Listen to me. Go, and do what I said."

14 Jacob went and brought the lambs that his mother had requested. She took the lambs and cooked them, using the same tasty recipe that Jacob's father liked.

15 Rebecca then took some of Esau's clothing and put them on her younger son, Jacob. **16** She also covered Jacob's arms and the hairless parts of his neck with the lambskins.

17 Rebecca gave her son Jacob Isaac's favorite food and the bread she had baked. **18** He approached his father and said, "Father, I am here." Then Isaac asked, "Who are you, my son?"

19 "It is I, Esau, your first-born," said Jacob. "I have done as you asked me. Sit up, and eat the deer meat, so that you can give me your special blessing."

20 Asked Isaac, " My son, how did you find the deer so quickly?"

Jacob answered, "Adonai was with me."

21 Jacob replied, "Then come closer to me. Let me touch you, my son. I must be sure that you are really Esau."

22 Jacob came close, and Isaac touched him. He said,

> "The voice is the voice of Jacob,
> but the hands
> are the hands of Esau."

23 He did not recognize him because Jacob's arms were hairy just like those of his brother Esau.

24 Suddenly Isaac again asked, "Are you really my son Esau?"

Jacob answered, "I am."

25 Isaac then said, "Serve me the food. I will eat the deer meat that you hunted and then I will give you my blessing."

Jacob served the food, and Isaac ate. Then Jacob brought Isaac some wine, and he drank it.

26 His father Isaac said to him, "My son, come closer and kiss me."

27 Jacob approached and kissed him. Isaac smelled the aroma of his clothing.

Isaac said,

> "My son's aroma
> is like the perfume of a field
> blessed by Adonai.

Isaac Blesses Jacob   *6ᵗʰ Aliyah*

> **28** "May Elohim
> grant you the dew of heaven
> and the richness of the earth
> and much grain and wine.
> **29** Nations will serve you;
> and people will bow down to you.
> You will be the leader of your brothers;
> And your mother's children
> will bow down before you.
> Those who curse you
> will be cursed,
> and those who bless you
> will be blessed. "

30 As soon as Isaac had finished blessing Jacob, his brother Esau returned from the hunt. **31** He too prepared Isaac's favorite food and brought it to his father. Esau said, "My father, get up and eat your favorite food so that you can give your blessing."

32 Isaac asked, "Who are you?"

Esau replied, "I am your first-born, Esau."

33 Isaac began trembling. "Then who just served me my favorite dish? I ate it all before you came, and I blessed him. The blessing must remain his."

34 When Esau heard his father's words, he broke out into a loud scream. Esau pleaded, "Father, bless me too."

35 Isaac said, "Your brother came with trickery and he has taken your blessing."

36 Esau said, "No wonder you named him Jacob (Ya'akov)! He tricked (*akav*) me behind my back (*akav*) twice. First he stole my birthright, and now he has taken my blessing!"
Esau pleaded, "Haven't you saved a blessing for me too?"

37 Isaac answered, "I have declared that he will be the leader of all his brothers, and I have assured him an abundance of grain and wine. Now what kind of blessing can I give you?"

38 Esau said to his father, "There must be at least one blessing that you have for me? Father, please bless me too!" Esau raised his voice and began to cry. **39** His father Isaac then said,

"Your home will be in fertile places,
they will be watered by dew of heaven.
40 But you shall live by your sword.
You will serve your brother,
but then you will throw off his yoke
and finally be free."

41 Esau hated Jacob because of the blessing that his father had given him. He said to himself, "The days of mourning for my father will be over soon; then I will be able to kill my brother Jacob."

42 When Rebecca heard of Esau's plan, she sent word to her younger son, Jacob. "Your brother Esau is planning to kill you," she said. **43** "My son, listen to me; escape to my brother Laban in Haran. **44** Stay with him until your brother's anger is gone. **45** When your brother has calmed down and has forgotten what you have done to him, I will send word and call you home. Why should I lose both of my sons?"

46 Rebecca said to Isaac, "I am sick and tired of those Hittite women. I'd rather die than see Jacob married to a Hittite girl."

28 Isaac summoned Jacob and gave him his blessing and a warning. "Do not marry a Canaanite girl," he said. **2** "Go to Padan Aram, to the house of your mother's father, Bethuel, and marry a daughter from your uncle Laban's family.

3 El Shaddai will bless you and give you many children. You will grow into a great nation. **4** He will grant Abraham's blessing to you and your descendants, and you will rule over the land that Elohim gave to Abraham, where you had lived only as a foreigner."

Jacob Goes to Padan Aram   *7th Aliyah*

5 Isaac then sent Jacob on his way. Jacob headed toward Padan Aram, to Laban son of Bethuel the Aramaean, the brother of Rebecca, Jacob and Esau's mother.

6 Esau saw that Isaac had blessed Jacob and sent him to Padan Aram to find a wife, with the warning, "Do not marry a Canaanite girl."

Esau Marries the Daughter of Ishmael   *Maftir*

7 Esau was aware that Jacob had obeyed his father and mother and had gone to Padan Aram. **8** Esau understood that his father, Isaac, detested the Canaanite girls.

9 Therefore Esau went to Ishmael and married Machlath, daughter of Abraham's son Ishmael, a sister of Nebayoth, in addition to his other wives.

Vayetze וַיֵּצֵא
JACOB SET OUT

10 Meanwhile, Jacob left Beer-sheva and set out for Haran.
11 He came to a camping place and, because the sun had already set, spent the night there. He took some stones, placed them at his head as a pillow, and lay down to sleep.

12 He had a dream and saw a ladder standing on the ground, with its top way up in the sky. He saw Elohim's angels climbing up and down on it. **13** Suddenly he saw Adonai standing beside him.

Adonai said, "I am Adonai, Lord of your father Abraham, and Lord of Isaac. I will give to you and your descendants the land upon which you are lying. **14** Your descendants will be as numerous as the dust of the earth. Your descendants will cover the earth from the west to the east, to the north and to the south. Every family on earth will be blessed because of you and your descendants. **15** Be assured that I am with you. I will protect you wherever you go and bring you back to this land. I will be with you until I have fully kept My promise to you."

16 Jacob woke up from his dream. He said "Adonai is truly in this place, but I did not know it." **17** He was frightened. And he exclaimed, "This is an awe-inspiring place. It must be Elohim's temple. It is the gate to heaven!"

18 Jacob rose up early in the morning and took the stones that he had placed under his head. He built them into a pillar and poured oil on top of it. **19** He made a pillar with the stones and named the place Adonai's Temple (*Beth El*). The town's former name had been Luz.

20 Jacob made a vow, saying, "If Elohim will be with me, if He will protect me on the journey that I am undertaking, if He gives me food to eat and clothing to wear, **21** and if He brings me back in peace to my father's house, then I will dedicate myself totally to Elohim. **22** These stones that I have set up as a pillar will become a temple to worship Elohim. Everything that You give me, I will offer a tenth to charity."

Rachel Meets Jacob   *2ⁿᵈ Aliyah*

29 Jacob set out and traveled toward the land of the Kedemites, the people of the East. **2** From a distance he saw a well. Three flocks of sheep were lying beside it. The mouth of the well was covered with a large, heavy stone. **3** When all the flocks came together there, the shepherds would roll the heavy stone from the top of the well and water the sheep. Then they would replace the stone on the well.

4 Some shepherds were already there, and Jacob asked, "Brothers, where are you from?"

They answered, "We are from Haran."

5 Jacob said, "Do you know Nachor's grandson, Laban?" and they answered, "Of course! We all know him."

6 Again Jacob asked, "Is he doing well?"

They answered, "Well enough! Here is his daughter Rachel, coming with Laban's sheep."

7 Then Jacob said, "It's still the middle of the day, too early to bring the flocks together. Why not water the sheep and let them go on grazing?" **8** They answered, "We can't until all the shepherds have come together. Only then will we be able to roll the stone from the mouth of the well. Only then will we able to water the sheep."

9 He was still speaking with the shepherds when Rachel appeared with her father's sheep. **10** As soon as Jacob saw his cousin Rachel, who was with his uncle Laban's sheep, he stepped forward and single-handedly rolled the stone from the top of the well and watered his uncle Laban's sheep. **11** Then Jacob kissed Rachel and began to cry. **12** He told her that he was Rebecca's son, and was related to her father. She quickly ran to tell her father the news.

13 When Laban heard that Jacob had arrived, he ran to greet him. He hugged and kissed him, and brought him home. Jacob told Laban everything that had happened to him. **14** Laban said, "Just think, you are my own flesh and blood." Jacob remained with him for a month. **15** Laban then said to Jacob, "Just because you are my close relative, does that mean you must work for me for nothing? Tell me what you want to be paid."

16 Laban had two daughters. The older one's name was Leah, and the younger one was called Rachel. **17** Leah had beautiful eyes, while Rachel was shapely and pretty.

Jacob Marries Leah and Rachel   *3ʳᵈ Aliyah*

18 Jacob fell in love with Rachel. Jacob said, "I will work for you seven years for Rachel, your younger daughter."

19 Laban replied, "I would rather give her to you than to any other man. You can stay with me."

20 For seven years Jacob worked for Rachel. But he loved her so much that it seemed like no more than a few days. **21** At the end of seven years Jacob said to Laban, "My time is up. Give me my bride so we can be married."

22 Laban invited all of his neighbors and made a wedding feast. **23** In the evening, he took his veiled older daughter, Leah, and in the darkness brought her to Jacob, and Jacob slept with her.

24 Laban gave his servant Zilpah to his daughter Leah to be her handmaid.

25 In the morning, Jacob discovered that he had married the older daughter, Leah. He angrily said to Laban,

"How could you do this to me? Why did you cheat me? Didn't I work for you for Rachel?" **26** Laban answered, "In our country it is the custom for the older to marry before the younger. We never give a younger daughter in marriage before the first-born. **27** But wait until the wedding celebrations for Leah are over. Then I will also give you my younger daughter, Rachel, in return for your serving me for another seven years."

28 Jacob agreed and finished the week of celebration for Leah. Laban then gave his daughter Rachel to Jacob as a wife.

29 Laban also gave his servant Bilhah as a handmaid to his daughter Rachel.

30 Jacob also married Rachel, and he loved Rachel more than Leah. He worked for Laban for another seven years.

31 And Adonai saw that Jacob did not love Leah and He made her fertile while Rachel was childless. **32** Leah became pregnant and gave birth to a son. She named him Reuben (Look at My Son), for she said, "Adonai has looked at [i.e., seen my troubles]. Now my husband will love me."

33 She became pregnant again and had a son. "Adonai heard that I was unloved," she said, "and He gave me this son also." She named the child Simeon (Hearing). **34** Leah became pregnant again and had another son. "Now my husband will become attached [*lavah*] to me," she said, "because I have given him three sons." Jacob therefore named the child Levi (Attachment).

35 Leah became pregnant again and had another son. She named the child Judah (Praised be Adonai). She then stopped having children.

30 When Rachel realized that she could not give birth to children, she became jealous of her sister and said to Jacob, "Give me children or I will die! "

2 Jacob became angry with Rachel. He said, "Can I take the place of Elohim? It is He who has made you childless." **3** Rachel said, "Here is my handmaid Bilhah. Sleep with her and let her give birth to children for me. Then I will also have a son through her." **4** So she gave her handmaid Bilhah to Jacob as a wife. **5** Bilhah became pregnant and gave birth to Jacob's son. **6** Rachel said, "Elohim has judged [*dan*] me and heard my prayer. He has finally given me a son!" She therefore named the child Dan.

7 Once again Rachel's handmaid Bilhah became pregnant and had a second son with Jacob. **8** Rachel said, "I have wrestled with my sister [*naphtuley*], but I have finally won." So she named the child Naphtali (Champion).

9 Leah realized that she no longer could have children. She gave her handmaid Zilpah to Jacob as a wife. **10** Leah's handmaid Zilpah bore Jacob a son. **11** Leah exclaimed, "Good luck [*gad*] has come!" So she named the child Gad.

12 Leah's handmaid Zilpah gave birth to a second son to Jacob. **13** Leah said, "It's my happiness [*asher*]. Women will consider me happy!" She named the child Asher.

Reuben and the Love Flowers   *4ᵗʰ Aliyah*

14 During the wheat harvest Reuben took a walk, and he found some love flowers in the field. He brought them to his mother Leah.

Rachel said to Leah, "Please give me some of your son's love flowers."

15 Leah angrily said, "Isn't it enough that you have stolen my husband? Now you even want to steal my son's love flowers!"

Rachel replied, "All right, I will allow Jacob to sleep with you tonight in exchange for your son's love flowers."

16 That evening, when Jacob came home from the field, Leah went out to meet him and she said, "Tonight you will sleep with me. I have paid for your services with my son's love flowers." So Jacob slept with her that night.

17 Elohim heard Leah's prayer, and she became pregnant, and she gave birth to a fifth son. **18** Leah said, "Elohim has given me my reward [*sachar*] because I have given my handmaid to my husband." She named the child Issachar.

19 Again Leah became pregnant, and she gave birth to a sixth son. **20** "Elohim has given me a wonderful gift [*zeved*]," said Leah. "Now let my husband make his permanent home [*zevul*] with me." She named the child Zebulun (*Zevulun*).

21 Leah then had a daughter, and she named her Dinah.

22 Elohim remembered Rachel. He heard her prayer, **23** and she became pregnant and gave birth to a son. She said "Adonai has taken away [*asaf*] my sorrow." **24** She named the child Joseph (*Yosef*), saying, "May Adonai grant another [*yosef*] son to me."

25 After Rachel had given birth to Joseph, Jacob said to Laban, "It is time for me to leave. I would like to return to my homeland. **26** Let me have my wives and children, since I have earned them by working for you, and I will leave. You are well aware that I have repaid you by my labor."

27 Laban replied, "Haven't I earned your friendship? I have learned from a fortune-teller that it is because of your presence that Adonai has blessed me."

Jacob and Laban Come to an Agreement
                                                               5ᵗʰ Aliyah

28 Laban said, "Just tell me how much I owe you. Name your price and I will pay it!"

29 Jacob replied, "You know how hard I worked for you, and how your flocks increased because of me. **30** You had very little before I came, and now your flocks have increased and become very large. Adonai blessed you with my coming. But now I must do something for my own family."

31 Laban asked, "How much should I pay you?" Jacob said, "Do not pay me, just do one thing for me. I will stay and tend your herds and give them the best care. **32** Just let me go through all your flocks with you today and remove every lamb that is spotted or speckled and every sheep that has dark markings and every goat that is speckled or spotted. Those kinds of animals will be my wages. **33** As a sign of my honesty, I will let you inspect all the animals that I have taken as my pay. If you find in my possession any goat that is not spotted or speckled, or any sheep without dark markings, then you will know that I have stolen them from you."

34 Laban replied, "Just as you have said. It's a deal." **35** That day, Laban removed the speckled and streaked male-goats, and all the spotted and speckled female-goats. He also removed every sheep with dark markings. Those animals he gave to his sons. **36** Laban then moved away from Jacob by the distance of a three-day journey. Jacob was left tending Laban's remaining flocks.

37 Jacob took branches of fresh poplar, almond, and plane trees. He peeled the branches and made white stripes by removing part of the bark.

38 He set up the wooden rods that he peeled facing the animals near the watering troughs where the flocks came to drink. They usually mated where they came to drink. **39** The animals mated in the presence of the rods, and they gave birth to ringed, spotted, and speckled animals.

40 Jacob separated the newborn animals. He made the animals in Laban's flocks mix with the spotted ones and all those with dark markings. Jacob did not allow his own flocks to mix with Laban's flocks.

41 Whenever the stronger females mated, Jacob placed the striped rods before their eyes at the troughs, so that they mated facing the rods. **42** But when the sheep were weak, he did not place the striped rods in front of them. The weak animals went to Laban, while Jacob got the stronger ones.

43 As a result Jacob became very wealthy. He owned many servants, sheep, goats, camels, and donkeys.

31

Soon Jacob began to hear that Laban's sons were complaining, "Jacob has stolen everything that belongs to our father. He has become rich by stealing our father's property!" **2** Jacob saw that Laban was acting very cold toward him.

3 Adonai said to Jacob, "It is time for you to go back to your birthplace in the land of your fathers. I will be with you all the way."

4 Jacob then sent for Rachel and Leah to come to the field where he was with the flock. **5** He said, "Your father is angry at me. He is not treating me in the same friendly way as he used to. But the Elohim of my father has been with me.

6 You know how hard I worked for your father.

7 Your father cheated me and broke his agreement about my wages at least ten times, but Elohim would not let him cheat me. **8** If he said, 'Your pay will be speckled ones,' then all the animals gave birth to speckled ones. When he said, 'Spotted ones will be yours,' then all the animals gave birth to spotted ones. **9** It was Adonai who took away your father's herds and gave them to me. **10** One day during the mating season, I suddenly had a vision. I saw the male sheep mating with the ringed, spotted, and speckled sheep. **11** Then an angel called me in Elohim's name, 'Jacob!'—and I replied, 'Yes, here I am.'

12 The angel said, 'Look, and you will see that the male sheep that are mating with the female sheep are ringed, speckled, and streaked. I have seen what Laban is doing to you. **13** I am the Elohim of Beth El, where you set up a pillar and made an agreement with Me. Now get up and leave this land. Return to the land where you were born.' "

14 Both Rachel and Leah spoke up. "We will inherit nothing from our father's wealth. **15** He treats us like strangers! He has sold us and spent our bridal money! **16** Everything that Elohim has taken from our father actually belongs to us and our children. So go ahead and do what Elohim told you to do."

Rachel Steals Laban's Idol   *6ᵗʰ Aliyah*

17 So Jacob put his children and wives on camels and began the journey. **18** He took all his livestock, and took everything that he had earned, including everything that he had bought in Padan Aram, and set off to return to his father, Isaac, in the land of Canaan.

19 While Laban was away, shearing his sheep, Rachel stole the idols that belonged to her father.

20 Jacob secretly left Laban the Aramaean. **21** He left with everything he owned, and crossed the Euphrates River, in the direction of the Gilead Mountains.

22 Three days later, Laban learned that Jacob had fled. **23** He took along his relatives and chased after Jacob for seven days and finally caught up to him in the Mountains of Gilead.

24 That night Elohim appeared to Laban the Aramaean and said, "Be very careful; do not harm or bless or curse Jacob." **25** Laban caught up to Jacob, who had pitched his tents on a hill, while Laban stationed his relatives on Mount Gilead. **26** Laban said to Jacob, "How could you do this thing to me? You went behind my back and stole my daughters away as if they were prisoners of war! **27** Why did you have to leave so secretly? You went behind my back and told me nothing! I would have sent you off with singing and music, with drum and harp! **28** You didn't even let me kiss my grandchildren and daughters goodbye.

What you did was very foolish. **29** I have it in my power to destroy you. But Elohim spoke to me last night and said, 'Be very careful of what you say about Jacob.' **30** I am aware that you are homesick for your parents. But why did you have to steal my idols?"

31 Jacob spoke up. "I left secretly because I was afraid of you. I thought that you might take your daughters away from me by force. **32** However, if you find your idols here, I will punish the person who stole them. Let all our close relatives here be witnesses. If you can find anything here belonging to you, you can take it back." Jacob did not realize that Rachel had stolen the idols.

33 Laban searched the tents of Jacob, Leah, and the two handmaids, but he found nothing. When he left Leah's tent, he went into Rachel's tent. **34** Rachel had taken the idols and hid them inside a camel cushion on which she was sitting. Laban searched the entire tent and found nothing. **35** Then Rachel said to her father, "Do not be angry with me. I cannot get up for you because I am not feeling well." Laban searched, but he did not find the idols.

36 Jacob became very angry, and he argued with Laban. "Have I committed a crime? What terrible thing did I do, that you came chasing me like this? **37** You searched all my belongings. What did you find that is yours? Put it right here, in front of our relatives. Let them decide which of us is right! **38** I worked for you twenty years! During that time, your sheep and goats never lost their young. Never once did I ever take a ram from your flocks as food. **39** I never brought you a goat or a sheep that had been killed by a wild animal. I took the blame on myself. You made me responsible for it whether it was stolen by day or at night.

40 By day I sweated in the scorching heat, and at night I froze in the cold. **41** I have worked for twenty years—fourteen years for your two daughters, and six years for some of your flocks. During this time you reduced my wages ten times!

42 If the Elohim of my fathers—the Elohim of Abraham and the Elohim of Isaac—had not been with me, you would have sent me away empty-handed! But Elohim saw my hard work, and last night He came to a decision!"

Jacob and Laban Make a Treaty   *7th Aliyah*

43 Laban interrupted Jacob. "Leah and Rachel are my daughters! The children are my grandchildren! The flocks are my flocks! All that you see is mine! As for my daughters . . . what can I do for them today? Or for the children they have borne? **44** Now come on! Let's you and I make a treaty; let us make a peace treaty between us."

45 Jacob took a large stone and set it up it as a pillar.

46 He said to his relatives, "Gather stones!" They took stones and made a large mound. Jacob and Laban and all the relatives then ate a meal of peace beside the large mound.

47 Laban called it Yegar Sahadutha (Witness Mound), but Jacob named it Gal'ed (Witness).

48 Laban said, "This mound shall be a witness between you and me today." That is why it is called Gal'ed. **49** "And let the pillar be called Mitzpah [Watchpost] because Elohim will keep watch between us when we are out of each other's sight.

50 If you mistreat my daughters, or marry other women, I may learn about it, but you must always realize that Elohim is the Witness between you and me."

51 Laban then said to Jacob, "Here is the mound, and here is the pillar that I have set up between us. **52** The mound and pillar shall be witnesses. I will not cross over to attack you and you will not cross over to attack me. We must never break the treaty between us. **53** May the Elohim of Abraham, the Elohim of Nachor, and the Elohim of their fathers be our judge." Jacob made a promise to the Elohim of his father Isaac.

54 He then made a sacrifice, and invited his relatives to eat with him. They ate and spent the night on the hill.

Jacob Camps at Machanayim   *Maftir*

32 The next morning Laban got up early and kissed his grandchildren and daughters goodbye. He then blessed them and left to return home.

2 Jacob also continued on his journey, and he met angels of Elohim. **3** When Jacob saw them, he said, "This is Adonai's camp." He named the place Machanayim (Twin Camps).

Vayishlach וַיִּשְׁלַח
JACOB SENDS MESSENGERS

4 Jacob sent messengers ahead of him to his brother Esau, to Edom's Field in Seir. **5** He instructed them to deliver the following message to his brother:

"Greetings to my brother Esau. Your humble servant Jacob says: I have stayed with Laban and have delayed my return for a long time. **6** I have acquired cattle, donkeys, sheep, servant-girls, and am now sending word to you to welcome me with friendship."

7 The messengers returned to Jacob with an answer: "We met your brother Esau, and he is heading toward you, and he has 400 men with him."

8 Jacob was very frightened, so he divided the people, the sheep, the cattle, and the camels with him into two camps. **9** He said, "If Esau comes and attacks one camp, at least the other camp will escape."

10 Jacob prayed, "Elohim of my grandfather Abraham and Elohim of my father Isaac. You Yourself told me, 'Return to the land where you were born, and I will help you.' **11** I do not deserve all of the kindness and faith that You have shown me. When I left home, I crossed the Jordan. I was alone, with only my shepherd's staff, and now I have grown into two camps. **12** I pray, save me from the anger of my brother—from the hand of Esau. I am afraid of him, for he can come and kill my whole family. **13** You once promised, 'I will make things go well for you, and make your descendants as many as the sand grains of the sea, which are too many to count.'"

Jacob Sends Gifts to Esau   *2nd Aliyah*

14 After spending the night there, Jacob assembled a gift for his brother Esau. **15** The gift consisted of 200 female goats, 20 male goats, 200 lambs, 20 rams, **16** 30 nursing camels with their young, 40 cows, 10 bulls, 20 female donkeys, and 10 male donkeys.

17 Jacob put a servant in charge of each herd. He said to his servants, "Move on ahead of me. Make a space between the two herds."

18 He instructed the first group: "When my brother Esau meets you, he will ask, 'To whom do you belong? Where are you going? Who owns all of these animals?' **19** You must reply, 'They belong to your brother Jacob. It is a gift to his brother. Jacob is following right behind us.' "

20 Jacob gave the same instructions to the second group, to the third, and to all who followed the herd. **21** "You must all say the same thing: 'Your brother Jacob is right behind us.' " Jacob said to himself, "I will quiet him with the gifts that are being sent ahead, and then I will meet him face to face. Hopefully, he will forgive me."

22 Jacob sent the gifts ahead of him, and spent the night in the camp. **23** In the middle of the night, Jacob got up and took his two wives, his two handmaids, and his eleven sons, and sent them across the Jabbok River. **24** After he sent them across, he also sent across all his possessions.

25 Jacob remained alone, when suddenly a stranger appeared and wrestled with him until dawn. **26** When the stranger saw that he could not defeat Jacob, he struck Jacob's thigh. Jacob's hip joint became dislocated as he wrestled with the stranger.

27 The stranger said, "Let me leave! Dawn is breaking." Jacob answered, "I will not let you leave unless you bless me."

28 The stranger then asked, "What is your name?" and Jacob answered, "My name is Jacob."

29 "Your name will no longer be Jacob, it is now Israel [*Yisrael*] because you have struggled with angelic beings and you have been victorious."

30 Jacob asked, "Please tell me your name." The stranger replied, "You must not ask my name." Then he blessed Jacob.

Jacob Wrestles with an Angel   *3rd Aliyah*

31 Jacob named the place Peniel (Divine Face). He said, "I have seen Elohim face to face, and my life has been spared."

32 As he left Peniel the sun rose and shone on him. And he was limping because of his dislocated thigh.

33 Today the Children of Israel do not eat the meat that is attached to the hip joint. This is because the stranger dislocated Jacob's thigh.

33

Jacob looked up, and in the distance he saw Esau approaching with 400 men. He divided the children among Leah, Rachel, and the two handmaids. **2** He placed the handmaids and their children in front, Leah and her sons behind them, and Rachel and Joseph last. **3** Jacob went ahead of them, and he bowed seven times as he approached his brother.

4 Esau ran to meet them. He hugged Jacob and kissed him. They both wept.

5 Esau looked up and saw the women and children, and he asked, "Who are these to you?"

Jacob replied, "They are the children with whom Elohim has blessed me."

Jacob and Esau Reconcile   *4th Aliyah*

6 Then the handmaids approached, along with their children, and the women bowed. **7** Then Leah and her children also approached and bowed. Finally, Joseph and Rachel came forward and bowed.

8 "What were the herds and the people that came to greet me?" asked Esau. "It was my gift to you," Jacob replied.

9 Esau said, "My brother, I have plenty. Let what is yours remain yours."

10 "Please, I beg you!" said Jacob. "If you have forgiven me, please accept this gift from me. After all, you have received me so favorably that seeing your face again is like seeing the face of Elohim. **11** Please accept my welcoming gift exactly as it has been brought to you. Adonai has been kind to me, and I have all I need." Jacob urged him, and Esau finally accepted it.

12 "Let's get going and move on," said Esau. "I will lead the way in front of you."

13 "My brother," replied Jacob, "As you can see, the children are weak, and I have responsibility for the young sheep and cattle. If they are driven hard for even one day, many of the sheep will die. **14** Please move ahead of me. I will lead my group slowly at their own pace, and the pace of the children. I will eventually meet you in Seir."

15 Esau said, "At least let my people help and protect you." Jacob replied, "What for? Just let me remain on friendly terms with you."

16 So on that day, Esau started back to Seir. **17** Jacob moved to Sukkoth. There he built a house for himself and made booths for his livestock. He therefore named the place Sukkoth (booths).

18 Jacob arrived safely at the city of Shechem, which is in the land of Canaan, when he returned from Padan Aram, and he made his camp outside the city.

19 Jacob bought a piece of open land for 100 silver coins from the sons of Hamor, chief of Shechem, upon which he set up his tent. **20** He erected an altar there and named it El Elohey Yisrael (Adonai Is Israel's Lord).

Dinah Is Raped   *5ᵗʰ Aliyah*

34 Leah's daughter, Dinah, went out to visit some of the girls who lived nearby. **2** Shechem, son of the chief of the region, Hamor the Hivite, saw her, and he raped her.

3 Hamor fell in love with Jacob's daughter, Dinah, and tried to win her affections. **4** Shechem said to his father, Hamor, "I would like to marry Dinah."

5 Jacob learned that his daughter Dinah had been raped. At that time Jacob's sons were in the field with the livestock, and Jacob did not tell them anything.

6 Meanwhile, Shechem's father, Hamor, came to speak to Jacob about the problem. **7** In the meantime Jacob's sons returned from the field. When they learned what had happened, the men became very angry. Shechem had committed a crime by raping Jacob's daughter. Such a criminal act could not be tolerated.

8 Hamor tried to reason with them. He said, "My son Shechem is truly in love with your daughter. Allow him to marry her. **9** Intermarry with us. Our sons will marry your daughters, and our daughters will marry your sons.

10 You will be able to live among us, and our land will be open to you. Settle down, and purchase land among us."

11 Shechem also spoke to Dinah's father and brothers. "I will do anything to regain your respect. I will give you whatever you ask. **12** Set the bridal payment and gifts as high as you like—I will gladly give whatever you demand of me. Just let me have Dinah as my wife."

13 When Jacob's sons replied to Shechem and his father, Hamor, they had a different idea, for they were speaking to the one who had raped their sister Dinah.

14 They said, "We cannot allow our sister to marry an uncircumcised man. It would be a disgrace to us. **15** The only way we can agree is if you will circumcise every male among you. **16** Only then can we give you our daughters and take your daughters for ourselves. Only then will we be able to live together with you and become as a single nation. **17** But if you do not agree to be circumcised, we will take our sister and go."

18 Their terms seemed fair to Hamor and his son Shechem. **19** Because Shechem loved Jacob's daughter, he lost no time and accepted the terms. He was the most respected person in his father's house.

20 Hamor and his son Shechem went to the city gate and spoke to the citizens of the city. **21** They said, "These men are our friends. Allow them to live on the land and earn a living from it. There is more then enough space for them. We will marry their daughters, and they will marry ours. **22** But only if we meet one of their conditions will they agree to live among us and become one nation. Every male among us must first be circumcised, just as they are circumcised. **23** After all, their livestock, their possessions, and their animals will eventually be ours. Let us agree to their condition and live with them."

24 So all the people who came out to the city gate agreed with Hamor and his son Shechem. All the males allowed themselves to be circumcised.

25 On the third day, when the men were in deep pain, Dinah's brothers Simeon and Levi took their swords and sneaked into the city and killed every male.

26 They also killed Hamor and his son Shechem, and rescued Dinah from Shechem's house. Then they returned to the camp.

27 Jacob's sons went and plundered the city that had disgraced their sister. **28** They took the sheep, cattle, donkeys, and whatever else was in the city and in the fields. **29** They also took the women and children as captives. They took everything from the houses, plundering the city's wealth.

30 Jacob said to Simeon and Levi, "You have given me a bad reputation among the Canaanites and Perizzites who live in the land. I have only a few men. In revenge they can band together and attack us, and our family will be wiped out."

31 The sons replied, "Should we have allowed them to treat our sister like a prostitute?"

35 Elohim said to Jacob, "Rise up and go up to Beth El. Stay there and erect an altar to Me, the Elohim who appeared to you when you were escaping from your brother Esau."

2 Jacob said to his family and everyone with him, "Get rid of the idols you have. Purify yourselves and change your clothes. **3** We are going up to Beth El. There I will erect an altar to Elohim, who answered my prayers in my time of trouble, and who has watched over me on every journey I have ever taken."

4 The family members gave Jacob all their idols, even the rings from their ears. Jacob buried them under a tree near Shechem.

5 Jacob and his family began their journey, and terror from Elohim spread through all the cities in the region, and they were afraid to attack them.

6 Jacob and all the people with him arrived at Luz, now called Beth El, meaning "House of El."

7 Jacob built an altar there and named the place El Beth El (Elohim in Beth El) because it was the place where Elohim had appeared to him when he was escaping from his brother Esau.

8 Rebecca's nurse, Deborah, died, and she was buried in the valley of Beth El, under the oak. It was named Alon Bakhuth (Weeping Oak).

9 When Jacob returned from Padan Aram, Elohim once again appeared and blessed him. **10** Elohim said to him,

> "Your name is now Jacob.
> But your name from now on
>   will not be Jacob;
>   you will also have Israel as a name."

Elohim named him Israel.

11 Elohim said to him,

> "I am El Shaddai, Elohim the Almighty,
>   be fruitful and increase.
> A nation and even many nations
> will come into existence because of you.
> Kings will be among your descendants.

The Monument at Beth El   *6th Aliyah*

> **12** "I will grant you the land
> that I promised to Abraham and Isaac;
>   I will also give the land

to your descendants
who will follow you."

13 Elohim left Jacob in the place where He had spoken to him. **14** Jacob set up a stone pillar in the place where Elohim had spoken to him. Then he poured oil on it.

15 Jacob named the place where Elohim had spoken to him Beth El (Elohim's Temple).

16 They then left Beth El and marched toward Ephrath, where Rachel began to give birth. Rachel had great difficulty giving birth. **17** The midwife said to her, "Don't be afraid. You will have a son." **18** As Rachel was dying, she named the child Ben-oni (Son of My Sorrow). But his father called him Benjamin (Son of My Strong Right Hand).

19 Rachel died and was buried on the road to Ephrath, now called Bethlehem. **20** Jacob set up a monument over her grave. It is the same monument that marks Rachel's grave to this very day.

21 Israel traveled on, and he set up his tent near Migdal Eder (Herd Tower). **22** While Jacob was living in the area, Reuben went and disturbed the sleeping arrangements of Bilhah, his father's concubine. Jacob had twelve sons. **23** The sons of Leah were Reuben, Jacob's first-born, Simeon, Levi, Judah, Issachar, and Zebulun. **24** The sons of Rachel were Joseph and Benjamin.

25 The sons of Rachel's handmaid Bilhah were Dan and Naphtali. **26** The sons of Leah's handmaid Zilpah were Gad and Asher. These are the sons born to Jacob in Padan Aram.

27 Jacob came to his father Isaac in Mamre, at Kiryath Arba, now called Hebron, where Abraham and Isaac had lived. **28** Isaac lived to be 180 years old. **29** He died at a ripe old age. His sons, Esau and Jacob, buried him.

36 This is the history of Esau, also known as Edom. **2** Esau married girls from the daughters of the Canaanites. His wives were Adah, daughter of Elon the Hittite, and Oholibamah, daughter of Anah, daughter of Ziv'on the Hivite. **3** He also married Basemath, daughter of Ishmael and sister of Nebayoth.

4 Adah gave birth to Esau's son Eliphaz.

Basemath gave birth to Reuel.

5 Oholibamah gave birth to Yeush, Yalam, and Korach. These are Esau's sons who were born in the land of Canaan. **6** Esau took his wives, his sons, his daughters, all the members of his household, his livestock, and all the wealth that he had accumulated in the land of Canaan, and he moved away from his brother Jacob. **7** He did so because they had too many animals and not enough grass for both of their herds. **8** Esau moved to the hill country of Seir. There Esau's descendants became the nation of Edom.

9 This is the history of Esau, the ancestor of the nations of Edom who lived in the hill country of Seir:

10 These are the names of Esau's sons:

Eliphaz, son of Esau's wife Adah;

Reuel, son of Esau's wife Basemath.

11 The sons of Eliphaz were Teman, Omar, Czefo, Gatam, and Kenaz. **12** Timna became the second wife of Esau's son Eliphaz, and she gave birth to Eliphaz's son Amalek. All these children were the descendants of Esau's wife Adah.

13 These are the sons of Reuel: Nachath, Zerach, Shamah, and Mizzah. These are the descendants of Esau's wife Basemath.

14 These are the sons of Esau's wife Oholibamah, daughter of Anah, daughter of Ziv'on: By Esau she gave birth to Yeush, Yalam, and Korach.

15 These are the *alufim* (tribal chiefs) among the children of Esau:

The sons of Esau's first-born, Eliphaz, were: Aluf Teman, Aluf Omar, Aluf Zefo, Aluf Kenaz, **16** Aluf Korach, Aluf Gatam, Aluf Amalek. These were the alufim from Eliphaz in the land of Edom. The above were descendants of Adah.

17 These are the alufim among the children of Esau's son Reuel: Aluf Nachath, Aluf Zerach, Aluf Shamah, Aluf Mizzah These are the alufim from Reuel in the land of Edom. The above were descendants of Esau's wife Basemath.

18 These are the sons of Esau's wife Oholibamah: Aluf Yeush, Aluf Yalam, Aluf Korach. These are the alufim from Esau's wife Oholibamah, daughter of Anah.

19 These are the sons of Esau, and these are their alufim. They are also known as Edom.

The Descendants of Seir   *7ᵗʰ Aliyah*

20 These are the sons of Seir the Horite, native to the land of Seir: Lotan, Shoval, Ziv'on, Anah,

21 Dishon, Ezer, Dishan. These were the alufim of the Horites, the descendants of Seir in the land of Edom.

22 The sons of Lotan were Hori and Hemam. Lotan's sister was Timna.

23 These are the sons of Shoval: Alvan, Manachath, Ebhal, Zefo, and Onam.

24 These are the children of Ziv'on: Ayah and Anah. Anah was the one who discovered the hot springs in the desert when he was tending the donkeys for his father, Ziv'on.

25 These are the children of Anah: Dishon and Oholibamah, daughter of Anah.

26 These are the sons of Dishon: Hemdan, Eshban, Yithran, and Keran.

27 These are the sons of Ezer: Bilhan, Zaavan, and Akan.

28 These are the sons of Dishan: Utz and Aran.

29 These are the alufim of the Horites: Aluf Lotan, Aluf Shoval, Aluf Ziv'on, Aluf Anah, **30** Aluf Dishon, Aluf Etzer, Aluf Dishan. These are tribes of the Horites according to their alufim in the land of Seir.

31 These are the kings who ruled the land of Edom before there were any Israelite kings:

32 Bela son of Beer was king of Edom, and Dinhava was the name of his capital.

33 Bela died, and Yovev son of Zerach from Botzrah became king.

34 Yovav died, and Husham from the land of the Temanites became king.

35 Husham died, and Hadad son of Badad, who defeated Midian in the field of Moab, became king. The name of his capital was Avith.

36 Hadad died, and Samlah of Masrekah became king.

37 Samlah died, and Shaul from Rechovoth Hanahar (Rechovoth on the River) became king.

38 Shaul died, and Baal Hanan son of Akhbor became king.

39 Baal Hanan son of Akhbor died, and Hadar became king. The name of his capital was Pau. His wife's name was Meheitaval daughter of Matred, daughter of Me-Zahav.

The Tribes of Esau   *Maftir*

40 These are the names of the tribes of Esau, according to their families who lived in places named after them:

the tribe of Timna,
the tribe of Alvah,
the tribe of Yetheth,
41 the tribe of Oholibamah,
the tribe of Elah,
the tribe of Pinon,
42 the tribe of Kenaz,
the tribe of Teman,
the tribe of Mibtzar,
43 The tribe of Magdiel,
the tribe of Iram.

These are the tribes of Esau, who lived in places named after them. This is how Esau was the ancestor of the Edomites.

Vayeshev וַיֵּשֶׁב

JACOB IN CANAAN

37 Now Jacob settled in the land of Canaan where his father had lived.

2 This is the history of Jacob: Joseph was seventeen years old, and as a young man, he tended the sheep with his brothers, the sons of Bilhah and Zilpah, his father's wives. Joseph tattled to his father about his brothers.

3 Israel loved Joseph more than any of his other sons, because Joseph was the child of his old age. He made Joseph a colorful jacket. **4** When his brothers saw that their father loved Joseph more than all of them, they began to hate him. They could not say a friendly word to him.

5 Once Joseph had a dream, and when he told it to his brothers, they hated him even more. **6** He said to them, "Listen to the dream I had. **7** We were binding sheaves in the field, when my sheaf suddenly stood up and your sheaves formed a circle around my sheaf, and they bowed down to it."

8 The brothers angrily replied, "So you want to be our king? Do you intend to rule over us?" Because of his dreams and his attitude, they hated Joseph even more.

9 Joseph had another dream and once again told it to his brothers. "I just had another dream. The sun, the moon, and eleven stars all bowed down to me."

10 When he told his dream to his father and brothers, his father was angry at him and said, "What kind of dream did you have? Do you expect me, your mother, and your brothers to bow down to you?"

11 His brothers became very jealous of him, but his father silently thought about its meaning.

Joseph Finds His Brothers   *2nd Aliyah*

12 Joseph's brothers left to graze their father's sheep in Shechem. **13** Israel said to Joseph, "Your brothers are grazing the sheep in Shechem. I would like you to go and see if they are well." "I'm ready," replied Joseph.

14 "Bring me a report and see how your brothers and the sheep are doing," said Israel.

Israel sent Joseph from the Hebron Valley to Shechem.

15 A villager found him wandering in the fields. "What are you looking for?" asked the villager.

16 Joseph replied, "I'm looking for my brothers. Perhaps you can tell me where they are grazing their sheep."

17 "They have already left this area," said the villager. "I heard them planning to move to Dothan." Joseph followed after his brothers and found them in Dothan. **18** They saw him in the distance, and they began plotting to kill him.

19 They said to one another, "Here comes the dreamer! **20** This is our chance! Let's kill him and throw his body into one of the wells. We can tell our father that a wild animal ate him. Then we'll see what will come of his fancy dreams!"

21 Reuben heard them and decided to save Joseph. He said to them, "Let's not kill our brother!"

22 Reuben tried to talk sense to his brothers. He said, "At least don't kill him. You can throw him into this well, but do not harm him." He planned to secretly save Joseph and bring him back to his father.

Joseph Is Sold   *3rd Aliyah*

23 When Joseph came to his brothers, they stripped him of the colorful jacket that he was wearing. **24** They picked him up and threw him into the well. The well was empty; there was no water in it.

25 Then the brothers sat down to eat. In the distance they saw an Ishmaelite caravan coming from Gilead. The camels were carrying spices, balsam, and resin to sell in Egypt.

26 Judah said to his brothers, "What will we gain if we kill our brother and cover up his death? **27** Let's sell him to the Ishmaelites and not harm ourselves with his blood. After all, he's our brother, he is our own flesh and blood." The brothers reluctantly agreed with Judah.

28 The merchants turned out to be Midianite traders. The brothers pulled Joseph out of the well and sold him to the merchants for twenty pieces of silver. The Midianites intended to bring Joseph to Egypt.

29 Later, when Reuben returned to the well, Joseph was no longer there. Reuben tore his clothes in anger and grief. **30** He returned to his brothers and cried, "Joseph is gone! Now what can I do?" **31** The brothers took Joseph's jacket, and they killed a goat and dipped the jacket in the blood. **32** Then they sent the blood-soaked jacket to their father. When the brothers returned they said to Jacob, "Can you identify the jacket? Is it Joseph's jacket?"

33 Jacob immediately recognized it. He cried, "It is Joseph's jacket. A wild animal must have eaten him! My Joseph has been torn to pieces!" **34** Jacob tore his robes in grief and put on sackcloth and mourned for a long time. **35** His sons and daughters tried to comfort him. He cried, "I will go down to my grave mourning for my son." He wept for his son as only a father could.

36 In Egypt the Midianites sold Joseph to Potiphar, one of Pharaoh's officers, a captain of the guard.

Judah and Tamar   *4ᵗʰ Aliyah*

38 About this time, Judah moved away from his brothers. He became friends with a man from Adullam by the name of Hirah. **2** There Judah met the daughter of a merchant named Shua. He married her, and **3** she became pregnant and gave birth to a son. He named the child Er. **4** She became pregnant again, and had another son. She named him Onan. **5** She gave birth for the third time and again gave birth to a son. She named him Shelah. Judah was in Keziv when she gave birth to Shelah.

6 Judah arranged a marriage for Er, his first-born, and the bride's name was Tamar. **7** Judah's first-born, Er, was evil in the eyes of Adonai. And Adonai made him die. **8** Judah said to Onan, "According to the law you must marry your brother's wife. In this way you will then raise children and keep your brother's name alive." **9** However, Onan realized that the children would not carry his name, so whenever he slept with his brother's wife, he let his seed go to waste so as not to have children that did not belong to him. **10** What he did displeased Adonai, and He also made Onan die.

11 Then Judah said to his daughter-in-law Tamar, "You can live as a widow in your father's house until my son Shelah is old enough to marry you." He said that to her because he was afraid that Shelah would also die like his brothers. So Tamar left and lived in her father's house.

12 A long time passed, and Judah's wife, the daughter of Shua, died. When Judah stopped mourning, he went to supervise his sheep-shearers in Timna, together with his friend, Hirah the Adullamite. **13** Someone told Tamar that her father-in-law had gone to Timna to shear his sheep. **14** So she took off her widow's robe and disguised herself with a veil. Then she sat at the entrance of Eynayim, which was on the road to Timna. Tamar was angry because she saw that Shelah had grown up and she had not been called to marry him.

15 Judah saw her, and because she was disguised, he thought that she was a prostitute. **16** So he stopped, not realizing that she was his own daughter-in-law. He said, "Hello, I would like to sleep with you." She replied, "How much will you pay me if I sleep with you?" **17** He answered, "I will send you a goat from the flock."

She said, "You must give me something to make sure

that you will keep your promise." **18** "What do you want?" he asked. "Your ring, your jacket, and the walking stick in your hand," she replied.

He gave them to her and he slept with her and she became pregnant. **19** She got up and removed her veil and put her widow's robe back on.

20 As soon as Judah returned home, he sent the young goat with his friend the Adullamite to get back the ring, the jacket, and the walking stick from the woman, but his friend could not find her. **21** His friend Hirah asked the local people, "Where is the prostitute that used to sit near the side of the road in Eynayim?"

"There was no prostitute here," they replied.

22 Hirah returned to Judah and said, "I couldn't find the woman. The local men said that they never saw a prostitute there."

23 Judah replied, "Let her keep the things. We don't want to look like fools. I tried to send her the goat, but you couldn't find her."

24 Three months later, Judah was told, "Your daughter-in-law has been behaving like a prostitute. She has become pregnant and has no husband."

"In that case take her out and have her burned," said Judah.

25 As she was being dragged out, she sent the ring, jacket, and walking stick to her father-in-law with a message: "The man who made me pregnant is the owner of these articles." When Judah came to see her, she said, "Can you identify these objects. Who is the owner of this seal, this coat, and this staff?"

26 Judah immediately recognized them. "She is more in the right than I am!" he said. "She did it because I refused to marry her to my son Shelah." **27** When her time came, she gave birth to twins. **28** As she was in labor, one of the twins put out an arm. The midwife grasped it and tied a red ribbon on it. She announced, "This one came out first."

29 But he pulled his hand back, and then his brother emerged. She said, "You have pushed [*peretz*] yourself out." So Judah named the child Peretz.

30 Then his brother with the ribbon on his hand was born. Judah named him Zerach (Brightness).

Joseph Is Sold   *5th Aliyah*

39 Joseph was brought down to Egypt, and Potiphar, one of Pharaoh's Egyptian officers, the captain of the guard, bought him from the Midianites who had brought him there. **2** Adonai watched over Joseph and made him very successful. Soon he was working in his master's own house. **3** His master realized that Adonai was with Joseph and that Adonai brought success to everything Joseph did.

4 Joseph impressed his master and before long was appointed his master's personal servant. His master put him in charge of his household, giving him responsibility for everything he owned. **5** Soon his master had put him in charge of his household and possessions. Adonai blessed Potiphar because of Joseph. Adonai blessed everything the Egyptian owned in his house and in his fields.

6 Potiphar put all his family affairs in Joseph's hands except for the food he himself ate. He did not concern himself with anything Joseph did. Meanwhile, Joseph grew to be a handsome young man.

Potiphar's Wife   *6th Aliyah*

7 Soon Potiphar's wife took a liking to Joseph. She begged, "Sleep with me!"

8 Joseph refused. He explained to his master's wife, "My master does not even know what I do in the house. He has entrusted me with everything he owns. **9** No one in this house has more authority than I have. He has not held back anything at all from me, except for you—his wife. How could I do such a great wrong? It would be a sin before Elohim!"

10 Every day she propositioned Joseph, but he would not pay attention to her. He did not even stand close to her or spend time near her.

11 One day, Joseph came to the house to do his work. None of the household servants were inside. **12** The woman grabbed him by his cloak. She begged, "Make love to me!" Joseph ran away, leaving his cloak in her hand.

13 When Potiphar's wife realized that he had left his cloak in her hand and fled, **14** she called her household servants and screamed, "Be my witnesses! My husband brought us a Hebrew man to insult us! He tried to rape me, but I screamed as loud as I could! **15** When he heard me scream and call for help, he ran outside and left his cloak with me!"

16 She kept Joseph's cloak with her until her husband came home, **17** then she told him the same story. "The Hebrew slave that you brought us came and molested me! **18** When I screamed and called for help, he escaped, leaving his cloak with me!"

19 When her husband heard his wife's story about what Joseph had done, he became very angry.

20 Joseph's master had him arrested and thrown into the jail where the king's prisoners were kept. **21** But Adonai was with Joseph, and the warden took a liking to him. **22** In time, the warden put all the prisoners in the jail under Joseph's supervision. Joseph took care of everything.

23 The warden did not have to worry about anything under Joseph's care. Adonai was with Joseph, and Adonai made him successful in everything he did.

The Dream of the Two Prisoners 7th *Aliyah*

40 Some time later, the Egyptian king's cup-bearer and the chief baker offended their master, the king of Egypt. **2** Pharaoh was angry at his two officials, the chief wine steward and the chief baker, **3** and he had them arrested. They were put in the same jail where

Joseph was imprisoned. **4** They remained in jail for a long time, and the captain of the guards assigned Joseph to care for them.

5 One night, the two of them had dreams. The king's cup-bearer and baker, who were imprisoned in the dungeon, each had a dream that seemed to have a special meaning. **6** When Joseph came to them in the morning, he saw that they were worried. **7** Joseph tried to find out what was bothering Pharaoh's officials who were his fellow prisoners. He asked, "Why are both of you so sad today?"

8 They replied, "We each had a dream, and there is no one here to tell us what they mean."

Joseph replied, "Interpretations are Elohim's business. If you wish, you can tell me about your dreams."

9 The cup-bearer told his dream to Joseph. He said, "In my dream I saw a grapevine right in front of me. **10** The vine had three branches. As soon as its buds formed, its blossoms bloomed and its clusters ripened into grapes. **11** I was holding Pharaoh's cup in my hand. I took the grapes and squeezed them into Pharaoh's cup. Then I placed the cup in Pharaoh's hand."

12 Joseph said to him, "This is what your dream means: The three branches are three days. **13** In three days, Pharaoh will pardon you and give you back your position. You will continue to put Pharaoh's cup in his hand, just as you did before.

14 Please, when things go well for you, just remember that I was in jail with you. Do me a favor and say something nice about me to Pharaoh. Perhaps you will be able to free me from jail. **15** I was kidnapped from the land of the Hebrews and did not deserve to be thrown in jail."

16 The chief baker saw how well Joseph was able to interpret the first dream. He said to Joseph, "I too saw myself in my dream. There were three baskets of fine white bread on my head. **17** In the top basket, there were all kinds of baked goods that Pharaoh likes to eat. But birds were eating it from the basket on my head!"

18 Joseph replied, "This is what your dream means: The three baskets are three days. **19** In three days, Pharaoh will cut off your head! He will hang you from a tree and the birds will eat your flesh."

The Cup-Bearer Forgets Joseph   *Maftir*

20 Pharaoh's birthday came three days later, and he made a party for all his officials. At that time he sent for the chief cup-bearer and the chief baker. **21** He returned the wine steward to his position, and he was again allowed to set the cup in Pharaoh's hand. **22** The chief baker was hanged, just as Joseph had predicted.

23 However, the wine steward did not remember Joseph. He forgot all about him.

Miketz מִקֵּץ
TWO YEARS LATER

41 Two years later, Pharaoh had a dream. He dreamed that he was standing near the Nile River, **2** when suddenly seven strong, healthy cows came up from the Nile and grazed in the grass. **3** Then another seven, thin, bony cows came up from the Nile and stood next to the strong cows already on the river bank. **4** The thin, bony cows ate up the seven strong healthy, fat cows. Then Pharaoh woke up.

5 Pharaoh fell asleep again and had a second dream. He saw seven large, golden ears of corn growing on a single stalk.

6 Then, suddenly, another seven ears of thin and burnt corn grew up behind them. **7** The seven thin ears swallowed the seven large ears of corn. Pharaoh woke up and realized that it had been a dream.

8 In the morning Pharaoh was very worried, so he sent for his magicians and the wise men of Egypt. Pharaoh told them his dreams, but no one could interpret them for Pharaoh.

9 Then the chief wine steward spoke to Pharaoh. "Today I must recall my sins. **10** Pharaoh was angry at me, and he put me under arrest in the jail of the captain of the guard, along with the chief baker. **11** One night we each had a dream that had its own special meaning.

12 There was a young Hebrew man with us, a slave of the captain of the guard. We told him our dreams, and he interpreted them. He told each of us the meaning of our dreams, **13** and things worked out exactly as he said they would. I was restored to my position, while the baker was hanged."

14 Pharaoh sent messengers to bring Joseph to the palace. They rushed him from the jail. Joseph shaved and changed his clothes, and then appeared before Pharaoh.

Pharaoh's Dream
2nd Aliyah

15 Pharaoh said to Joseph, "I had a dream, and there is no one who can interpret it. I have heard that when you hear a dream, you can explain it."

16 Joseph replied to Pharaoh, "It is beyond my own power. But Elohim will tell me what Pharaoh's dream means."

17 Pharaoh told his dream to Joseph: "In my dream, I was standing on the bank of the Nile River. **18** Suddenly, seven fat, healthy cows came up from the Nile and grazed in the grass. **19** Then, just as suddenly, seven other cows, very thin and bony, came up after them. I never saw such bony cows anywhere in Egypt.

20 The thin and bony cows ate up the seven healthy cows.

21 They were completely swallowed by the thin cows, but the cows looked just as bony as they had at first. Then I woke up.

22 Then I had another dream. There were seven full, golden ears of corn growing on one stalk. **23** Suddenly, seven other ears of corn grew behind them. The second ones were thin and burnt. **24** The thin ears of corn swallowed up the seven full ears of corn.

I told my dream to the magicians, but none of them could interpret it for me."

25 Joseph said to Pharaoh, "Pharaoh's two dreams have a single meaning. Elohim has mercifully revealed to Pharaoh what He is about to do. **26** The seven healthy cows and the seven full ears of corn are both seven years. It is one dream.

27 The seven thin, bony cows and the seven thin, burnt ears of corn are also seven years, but seven years of famine.

28 It is just as I have told Pharaoh. Elohim has mercifully shown Pharaoh what He is about to do. **29** During the coming seven years, there will be a great abundance of food all over Egypt. **30** But these seven years will be followed by seven years of famine, when all the surplus in Egypt will disappear. The famine will devastate the land. **31** The coming famine will be so great that there will be no way of telling that there once was a surplus of food in the land.

32 The reason that Pharaoh had the same dream twice is that the event has already been decided by Elohim, and He will soon make it happen.

33 Now Pharaoh must find a man of wisdom and put him in charge of a national food program for Egypt.

34 Pharaoh must appoint officials over the land. A rationing system will have to be set up in Egypt during the seven years of abundance by collecting one-fifth of all the crops.

35 Let the officials collect all the food during these coming years of plenty, and let them store the grain under Pharaoh's control. The food will be kept in each of the cities under guard. **36** The food will be held in storage when the seven famine years come to Egypt. In that way Egypt will survive the famine."

37 Pharaoh and all his advisers realized that it was an excellent plan.

38 Pharaoh said to his advisers, "Is there any other person who has Elohim's spirit in him as this man does?"

Joseph Becomes Second to Pharaoh   *3rd Aliyah*

39 Pharaoh said to Joseph, "Since Elohim has revealed His plans to you, obviously there is no one as wise as you. **40** You shall be in charge of the project, and food will be distributed to my people only by your orders. Only I will outrank you."

41 Pharaoh then formally declared to Joseph, "I am putting you in charge of food for the entire land of Egypt."

42 Pharaoh took his ring off his own finger and put it on Joseph's finger. He dressed Joseph in the finest linen garments and put a gold chain around his neck. **43** Joseph rode in the second royal chariot, and wherever he went they announced, "Kneel down! Make way for Joseph." Joseph was put in charge of all the food in Egypt.

44 Pharaoh said to Joseph, "I am Pharaoh. Without your permission, no man will lift a hand or foot anywhere in Egypt."

45 Pharaoh renamed Joseph Tzaphnath Paaneach. He gave him Asenath, daughter of Poti Phera, the priest of On, as a wife. **46** Joseph was thirty years old when he was elevated as second to Pharaoh.

Joseph left Pharaoh's court and made an inspection tour of the entire land of Egypt. **47** During the seven years of abundance, the land of Egypt produced tons of grain. **48** Joseph collected the food during the seven years of abundance and stored the food in the granaries. The food growing in the fields around each city was put inside warehouses in each of the cities. **49** Joseph stored so much grain, it was like the sand of the sea. They had to give up counting it, because there was too much.

50 Before the famine years came, Joseph fathered two sons with his wife Asenath, daughter of Poti Phera, priest of On.

51 Joseph named the first-born Manasseh "because Elohim has made me forget [*nasheh*] all my troubles—and even my father's house." **52** He named his second son Ephraim, "because God has made me fruitful [*p'ri*] in the land of my suffering."

The Brothers Come to Egypt   *4th Aliyah*

53 Just as Joseph had predicted, the seven years of abundance that Egypt was enjoying finally came to an end. **54** The seven years of famine then began; there was famine in every other land, but in Egypt there was plenty of food. **55** After a while even Egypt began to feel the famine, and the people cried out to Pharaoh for food. Pharaoh announced to all Egypt, "Go to Joseph. You must do whatever he tells you."

56 The famine spread over the entire region. Joseph opened all the storehouses, and he sold food to the Egyptians. But still the famine grew even worse in Egypt. **57** The famine was also becoming more severe in the entire region, and people from all the surrounding countries came to Egypt to buy food from Joseph.

42 Jacob found out that there was food in Egypt, and he said to his sons, "Why are you sitting around doing nothing?

2 I have heard that there is food in Egypt. Go there and buy food so we can live and not starve to death."

3 Joseph's ten brothers went to buy food in Egypt.
4 But Jacob would not send Joseph's younger brother,
Benjamin, along with the others because he was afraid
that something might happen to him.

5 Israel's sons were among the many who came to buy
food because of the severe famine in Canaan. **6** Joseph
was like a governor over the land, since he was the
only one who distributed food to all the people. When
Joseph's brothers arrived, they bowed to him.

7 As soon as he saw them, Joseph recognized his
brothers. But he acted like a stranger and spoke
harshly to them. Joseph asked, "Where are you from?"
"We are from the land of Canaan, we have come to
buy food," they replied.

8 Joseph recognized his brothers, but they did not
recognize him. **9** He remembered what he had
dreamed about them years before. "You are spies!"
he shouted at them. "You have come to see where
Egypt can be attacked."

10 "No, my lord!" they replied. "We are your servants
who have come only to buy food. **11** We are all the
sons of the same man. We are honest men. We are
not spies."

12 "That is not so!" answered Joseph. "You have
come to see where Egypt can be attacked."

13 They pleaded, "We are twelve brothers, we are
the sons of one father who is in Canaan. Right now
our youngest brother is with our father, and one
brother is dead."

14 Joseph insisted, "I still say that you are spies.
15 There is only one way to find out who you really
are. I swear by the life of Pharaoh that you will not
leave this place unless your youngest brother comes
here. **16** Let one of you return and bring your brother.
The rest of you will remain here in jail. That way I
will find out if you are telling the truth. If not, I will
know that you are spies." **17** Joseph had them put

under guard for three days. **18** On the third day, Joseph said to them, "I respect Adonai, and if you do as I say, you will live.

Benjamin Is Brought to Joseph   *5ᵗʰ Aliyah*

19 "We will find out if you are really telling the truth. I will hold only one of you under arrest. The rest can go and bring food to your starving families. **20** But you must bring your youngest brother here, and only then will I be convinced that you are telling the truth. Then you will not be put to death." The brothers agreed. **21** But they said to one another, "We deserve to be punished because of what we did to our brother Joseph. We allowed him to suffer, and when he begged us we refused to listen. That is why these great troubles have come upon us now."

22 Reuben interrupted them and said, "Didn't I tell you not to commit the crime against the boy? You wouldn't listen. That is why we are now being punished."

23 Meanwhile, the brothers did not realize that Joseph was listening and understood them, because they had spoken to him only through a translator. **24** Joseph left them and wept. When he returned, he spoke to them harshly. He had Simeon taken away and put in chains while they watched.

25 Joseph gave orders that when their bags were filled with grain, each one's money should also be returned in his sack. They were also to be given extra food for the return journey. This was done. **26** The brothers then loaded the food they had bought on their donkeys, and they left.

27 When they camped for the night, one of the brothers opened his sack to feed his donkey. He saw his money at the top of his sack. **28** He called to his brothers, "My money has been returned! It's in my sack!"

Mystified, they said to each other, "What is this terrible calamity that Elohim has brought upon us?" **29** When they returned to their father, Jacob, in the land of Canaan, they told him everything that had happened to them. **30** They said, "The man who was the governor spoke harshly to us, and he accused us of spying on the land. **31** We said to him, 'We are honest men. We have never been spies. **32** We are twelve brothers, all of the same father. One of us is dead, and the youngest is now with our father in Canaan.'

33 The man who was the governor of the land said to us, 'I have a way of knowing if you are honest. Leave one of your brothers with me, and take all the food that you need for your hungry families, and return.

34 Bring your youngest brother back to me, and only then will I know that you are honorable men, and not spies. After that I will return your brother back to you, and you will be able to move freely about Egypt.' "

35 When they began emptying their sacks, they found each one's money was in his sack. The brothers and their father saw the money-bags, and they were frightened.

36 Their father, Jacob, said to them, "You are making me lose my children. Joseph is gone! Simeon is gone! And now you want to take Benjamin!"

37 Reuben tried to reason with his father. "If I do not bring Benjamin back to you," he said, "you can put my two sons to death. Let him be my responsibility, and I will bring him back to you."

38 "My son will not go with you!" thundered Jacob. "His brother is dead, and he is all I have left. If something should happen to him along the way, you will bring me down to the grave!"

43 The famine became worse in Canaan. **2** When they had used up all the food that they had brought from Egypt, Jacob said to the brothers, "Go back and get us some food."

3 Judah tried to reason with his father. He said, "The man warned us, 'Do not appear before me unless your brother is with you.' **4** If you agree to send our brother with us, we will go and get you food. **5** But if you will not send him, we cannot go. The man told us, 'Do not appear before me unless your brother is with you.'"

6 Israel said, "Why did you do such a terrible thing to

me, telling the man that you had another brother?"

7 The brothers replied, "The man kept asking us about our family. He asked, 'Is your father still alive? Do you have another brother?' We simply answered his questions. How were we to know that he would demand that we bring our brother to Egypt?"

8 "Send the boy with me," said Judah to his father, Israel. "Let us get moving. Let us and our children live and not die. **9** I will be responsible for Benjamin. If I do not bring him back, you can blame me as long as I live. **10** If we had not wasted so much time, we could have been to Egypt and back twice by now!"

11 Their father Israel said to them, "If that's the way it must be, this is what you must do. In your baggage take some of Canaan's special delicacies, perfumes, honey, and some spices, pistachio nuts, and almonds. **12** Take along twice as much money, so that you will be able to return the money that was put in your sacks by mistake.

13 Take your brother with you. Go and return to the man. **14** May El Shaddai (Elohim Almighty) grant that the man have pity on you and release your brothers Simeon and Benjamin. If I must lose my children, then I am prepared to lose them."

15 The brothers took the gifts and also brought along twice as much money as was needed. They set out with Benjamin and returned to Egypt. Once again they stood before Joseph.

Joseph Inquires About Jacob   *6th Aliyah*

16 When Joseph saw Benjamin, he said to his chief servant, "Bring these men to my palace. Prepare some food. These men will be eating lunch with me."

17 The servant did as Joseph said, and he escorted the brothers to Joseph's palace. **18** When the brothers realized that they were being brought to Joseph's palace, they became terrified. They said, "We are being brought here because of the money that was put back in our sacks the last time. We will be arrested and our donkeys will be confiscated, and we will be taken as slaves."

19 When they reached the entrance to Joseph's palace, they spoke to the chief servant. **20** "We specially came down to Egypt just to buy food. **21** Then, when we stopped for the night, we opened our sacks, and each man's money was at the top of his sack. It was our own money, in its exact weight. We have brought that money back with us. **22** We have also brought along more money to buy food. We do not know who put the money back in our sacks!"

23 The servant replied, "As far as you are concerned, everything is fine. Do not be afraid! The Elohim you and your father worship must have put a hidden gift in your sacks. I received your money in full." With that, he brought Simeon out to them.

24 The chief servant brought the brothers into Joseph's palace. He gave them water to bathe their feet, and brought food for their donkeys. **25** They readied their gifts to give to Joseph at noon, since they had heard that they would be eating with Joseph.

26 When Joseph came home, they presented him with the gifts they had brought and they bowed down to him.

27 He greeted them and asked, "Is your old father well? Remember, you told me about him. Is he still alive?"

28 They replied, "Our father is well and he is still alive." As in the dream of years before, they bowed their heads to Joseph.

29 Joseph looked up and saw his brother Benjamin, his mother's son. He said, "Is this your youngest brother, about whom you told me?" To Benjamin he said, "May Elohim be gracious to you, my boy."

The Missing Cup   *7ᵗʰ Aliyah*

30 Joseph rushed out because he was overcome with emotion, and he began to cry. He went to another room and there he controlled himself. **31** Joseph rinsed his face and returned, controlling his emotions. He said to his servants, "Serve the meal."

32 Joseph was served by himself, and the brothers by themselves. The Egyptians who were eating with them could not eat with the Hebrews, since this was against their custom.

33 When the brothers were seated before Joseph, they were placed in order of age, from the oldest to the youngest. The brothers eyed each other in amazement. **34** Joseph sent them delicacies from his table, giving Benjamin five times as much as the others. They feasted and drank with him.

44 Joseph gave his chief servant special instructions. He said, "Fill the men's sacks with as much food as they can carry. Put each man's money at the top of his sack. **2** And put my silver cup and his money at the top of the sack of the youngest brother." The servant did exactly as Joseph instructed him.

3 Early in the morning, the brothers saddled their donkeys and went on their way. **4** The brothers had just left the city and had not gone far when Joseph said to his servants, "Chase after those men. Catch up with them and say to them, 'Why did you repay good with evil? **5** You took my master's personal cup that he drinks from and uses for predicting the future. You have committed a terrible crime.' "

6 The servant caught up with the brothers and repeated Joseph's exact words to them. **7** They said to him, "How can you say such things to us? We would never have done such an evil thing.

8 After all, we returned the money we found at the top of our sacks—all the way from Canaan. How could we steal silver or gold from your master's house? **9** If any of us has it in his possession, that person shall die and you can take the rest of us for slaves."

10 The servant replied, "I'll do what you said, but only the one who has the cup will be enslaved. The rest of you will be free."

11 The brothers quickly lowered their sacks, and they all opened their sacks. **12** The servant carefully inspected each of the sacks, beginning with the oldest and ending with the youngest. The silver cup was found in Benjamin's sack. **13** The brothers ripped their clothes in despair. Then each one reloaded his donkey, and they returned to the city.

Elohim Has Uncovered Our Guilt *Maftir*

14 Joseph was still there when Judah and his brothers returned to the palace. They threw themselves on the ground before him.

15 Joseph said to them, "What are you trying to do? Don't you know that a person like me has a special way of discovering the truth?" **16** Judah replied, "What can we say to my lord? How can we prove our innocence? Elohim has uncovered our guilt. Let us be your slaves, especially the one who took the cup." **17** Joseph said, "Only the one who took the cup shall be my slave. The rest of you can return to your father in peace."

Vayigash וַיִּגַּשׁ
JUDAH AND JOSEPH

18 Judah went up to Joseph and said, "Your Highness, please let me say something to you. Do not be angry with me, even though you have as much power as Pharaoh.

19 You asked if we still had a father or another brother.

20 We told you, 'We have a father who is very old, and the youngest brother is the child of his old age. He had a brother who died, and he is the only one of his mother's children still alive. He is our father's favorite.' **21** You said to us, 'Bring him to me, so I can see him with my own eyes.'

22 We told you, 'The boy cannot leave his father,' because if he left him, our father would die. **23** But you replied, 'If your youngest brother does not come, do not show your faces to me again.'

24 We returned to our father and told him what you said.

25 Our father told us to go back and buy some food. **26** We replied, 'We cannot go. We can only go if our youngest brother is with us. If he is not with us, we are forbidden to show our faces.'

27 Our father said, 'You know that my wife Rachel gave birth to two sons. **28** One is dead, and I believe that he was torn to pieces by wild animals. I have seen nothing of him ever since.

29 Now you want to take Benjamin from me too! If something were to happen to him, you will have brought me down to the grave.'

30 How can I return to our father if the boy is not with us? His life depends upon the boy!

Joseph Reveals His Identity   *2ⁿᵈ Aliyah*

31 "When he sees that the boy is not with us, he will die! I will have brought our father's life down to the grave.

32 As a guarantee I pledged to my father and I said, 'If I do not bring him back to you, you can blame me for the rest of my life.'

33 Please now, let me remain as your slave in place of the boy.

Let the boy return home with his brothers! **34** I cannot return to my father if the boy is not with me. I cannot bear to see my father suffer!"

45

Joseph could not control his emotions. Since his servants were present, he cried out, "Everybody out! Everyone leave my presence!" He wanted to be alone when he revealed himself to his brothers. **2** He began to cry with such loud sobs that the Egyptians throughout the palace could hear his cries. The news of these strange events quickly reached Pharaoh's palace. **3** Joseph said to his brothers, "I am Joseph! Is my father still alive?"

His brothers were amazed and speechless.

4 Joseph said to his brothers, "Please, come close to me."

When they came closer, he said, "Yes, I am Joseph your brother! You sold me to Egypt. **5** Don't worry or feel guilty because you sold me. Elohim is the one who sent me ahead of you to save your lives! **6** There has been a famine in the land for two years, and for another five years no one will be able to plow or harvest grain. **7** Elohim has sent me ahead of you to make sure that you survive and keep you alive through this miraculous event.

Joseph Sends for Jacob   *3rd Aliyah*

8 "It is not you who sent me here, but Elohim. He has made me the governor of the entire country. **9** Hurry, return to my father and give him my message: Your son Joseph says, 'Elohim has made me a governor in Egypt. Come down to me immediately.

10 You and your children, and your grandchildren, and your sheep, and your cattle, and all that you own will be able to live close to me in the land of Goshen. **11** There I will care for you, since there will still be another five years of famine. I do not want you and your family and all that is yours to go hungry.' "

12 Then Joseph said, "You and my brother Benjamin can see with your own eyes that I am really Joseph. **13** Tell my father all about my high position in Egypt and everything that you saw. You must hurry and bring my father to me."

14 With that, Joseph fell on the shoulders of his brother Benjamin, and he wept with joy. Benjamin also wept on Joseph's shoulders. **15** Joseph hugged all his brothers, and they all wept. After that, the brothers talked with Joseph.

16 The news quickly spread to Pharaoh's palace that Joseph's brothers had arrived. Pharaoh and his advisers were pleased by the news.

17 Pharaoh told Joseph to tell his brothers, "This is what you must do: Load your donkeys and return to Canaan. **18** Bring your father and your families, and come and live with me. I will give you the most fertile land in Egypt. You shall eat the best of the land.

Jacob's Family Comes to Egypt   *4ᵗʰ Aliyah*

19 "Now I want you to do the following: Bring wagons from Egypt for your small children and wives, and also use them for your father. Come, **20** and do not be concerned about your belongings, for the best of Egypt will be yours."

21 Israel's sons agreed to do all that Pharaoh instructed. Joseph gave them wagons, and he also supplied them with food for the journey. **22** He gave each of his brothers new clothes. However to Benjamin he gave 300 pieces of silver and five sets of new clothing.

23 As a present Joseph sent his father ten male donkeys loaded with Egypt's finest delicacies, and ten female donkeys loaded with grain, bread, and food for his father's journey.

24 Then he sent his brothers on their way. As they were leaving, he wished them "A safe and pleasant journey!"

25 From Egypt the brothers headed northward, and they returned to their father Jacob in Canaan. **26** They excitedly told Jacob, "Joseph is still alive. He is the governor of all Egypt." Jacob's heart skipped a beat, for he could not believe the news. **27** They repeated everything that Joseph had said to them. When Jacob saw the wagons that Joseph had sent to transport him to Egypt, he felt much better.

Jacob Journeys to Egypt 5th Aliyah

28 Israel said, "It must be true. My son Joseph is alive! I must go and see him before I die!"

46 Israel assembled all his possessions and began the journey to Beer-sheva. There he brought sacrifices to the Elohim of his father Isaac. **2** That night Elohim spoke to Israel and said, "Jacob! Jacob!"

Jacob answered, "Yes, here I am."

3 Elohim said, "I am the Elohim of Isaac your father. Do not be afraid to go down to Egypt, for it is there that I will make you into a great nation. **4** I will go down to Egypt with you, and I will also bring your descendants back again. You will die in Egypt, and Joseph will be at your deathbed."

5 Jacob and his sons set out from Beer-sheva. They brought their father, their children, and their wives on the wagons that Pharaoh had sent to carry them. **6** They brought their livestock and all the possessions that they had acquired in Canaan. Jacob came to Egypt with all his sons **7** and grandsons. He also brought his daughters and his granddaughters to Egypt with him.

8 These are the names of the Israelites, the descendants of Jacob, who came to Egypt:

Reuben was Jacob's first-born. **9** Reuben's sons were Enoch, Palu, Hezron, and Carmi.

10 Simeon's sons were Yemuel, Yamin, Ohad, Yakhin, and Zohar, as well as Shaul, the son of a Canaanite woman.

11 Levi's sons were Gershon, Kehath, and Merari.

12 Judah's sons were Er, Onan, Shelah, Peretz, and Zerah, but Er and Onan died in Canaan. The sons of Peretz were Hezron and Hamul.

13 Issachar's sons were Tolah, Puvah, Yov, and Shimron.

14 Zebulun's sons were Sered, Elon, and Yachleel.

15 All the above were from the sons that Leah gave birth to Jacob in Padan Aram, in addition to Jacob's daughter, Dinah. All of his descendants through Leah, including his sons and daughters, totaled thirty-three.

16 Gad's sons were Zifon, Hagi, Shuni, Ezbon, Eri, Arodi, and Areli.

17 Asher's sons were Imnah, Ishvah, Ishvi, and Beriah, also their sister Serach. The sons of Beriah were Hever and Malkiel.

18 These sixteen were the descendants of Jacob through Zilpah, whom Laban gave to his daughter Leah.

19 The sons of Jacob's wife Rachel were Joseph and Benjamin.

20 In Egypt, Joseph's wife Asenath, daughter of Poti Phera, priest of On, gave birth to Manasseh and Ephraim.

21 Benjamin's sons were Bela, Bekher, Ashbel, Gera, Naaman, Echi, Rosh, Muppim, Huppim, and Ard.

22 These fourteen were the descendants of Jacob and his wife Rachel.

23 Dan's son was Hushim.

24 Naphtali's sons were Yachtzeel, Gum, Yezer, and Shilem.

25 These seven were the descendants of Jacob through Bilhah, the servant whom Laban gave to his daughter Rachel.

26 All the blood descendants who came to Egypt with Jacob were sixty-six, not counting the wives of Jacob's sons. **27** Joseph's sons, born to him in Egypt, added another two persons. In total, all of the people in Jacob's family who came to Egypt now added up to seventy.

The Children of Israel
Settle in Goshen

28 Jacob sent Judah ahead of him to make preparations in Goshen. When they arrived in the Goshen district, **29** Joseph himself harnessed his chariot and went to Goshen to greet his father Israel. When they met, they embraced each other and wept with joy. **30** Israel said to Joseph, "Now I can die; I have seen you in person and know that you are still alive."

31 To his brothers and his father's family, Joseph said, "I will go and tell Pharaoh, 'My brothers and my father's family have come to me from Canaan. **32** These men are shepherds. They have brought with them sheep, their cattle, and all their possessions.'

33 When Pharaoh summons you and asks, 'What is your occupation?' **34** you must say, 'We and our fathers have been shepherds all our lives.'

In this way you will be able to settle in the district of Goshen, since shepherds are forbidden in other parts of Egypt."

47 Joseph went to see Pharaoh. He said, "My father and brothers have come from Canaan, along with their sheep, their cattle, and all their belongings. They wish to settle in Goshen." **2** From among his brothers, he selected five men and introduced them to Pharaoh.

3 Pharaoh asked Joseph's brothers, "What are your occupations?"

They replied to Pharaoh, "We are shepherds, just like our fathers before us.

4 We have come to live in your land, because there is a strong famine in Canaan and there is no grass for our flocks. If you permit us, we would like to live in the district of Goshen."

5 Pharaoh said to Joseph, "Your father and brothers have come to you. **6** The land of Egypt is open to them. Settle your father and brothers on the most fertile land. Let them live in the district of Goshen. If there are capable men among them, appoint them to be in charge of my cattle."

7 Joseph brought Jacob, his father, and introduced him to Pharaoh. Jacob blessed Pharaoh. **8** Then Pharaoh asked Jacob, "How old are you?"

9 Jacob replied, "I have lived 130 difficult years. I will not live as long as my ancestors did during their journeys through life." **10** With that, Jacob again blessed Pharaoh and left.

Joseph Saves Egypt   *7th Aliyah*

11 Joseph found fertile land for his father and brothers to live on. As Pharaoh had ordered, Joseph gave them fertile land in the area around Rameses. **12** Joseph provided all the needs of his father, his brothers, and all his father's family.

13 Meanwhile, the famine was very severe, and there was no bread anywhere. The people of Egypt and Canaan became weak with hunger. **14** Joseph collected all the money that was in Egypt and Canaan in payment for the food the people were buying. Joseph brought all the money to Pharaoh's palace.

15 When their money ran out, people from all over the land of Egypt came to Joseph and complained, "Give us bread! Why should we die just because we have no money?"

16 Joseph replied, "Bring your livestock. If you have no more money, I will give you food in exchange for your animals."

17 From then on they brought their livestock to Joseph, and Joseph gave them bread in exchange for horses, flocks of sheep, herds of cattle, and donkeys. All through that year Joseph gave them bread in exchange for their livestock.

18 The next year they again came back to Joseph and pleaded, "Your Highness, we haven't held anything back from you. Our money and our stock of animals are used up; now there is nothing left for you except our bodies and our land. **19** Why should we die before your very eyes? Buy our bodies and our land in exchange for bread. We will become Pharaoh's slaves, and let our land also be his. Just give us enough food. Let us live and not die! Let the land not be devastated."

20 So Joseph bought up all the farmland in Egypt for Pharaoh. Every farmer in Egypt sold his field because the famine was too much for them, and all the land became Pharaoh's property. **21** Joseph transferred the people from the farms to the cities. **22** But Joseph did not buy the lands of the priests, because they were given food by Pharaoh.

23 Joseph said to the people, "I have bought your bodies and your land for Pharaoh. Now I will give you seeds so that you can plant your fields. **24** When you harvest your crops, you will have to give a fifth of them to Pharaoh. You can keep the other four parts, as seed for your fields, and as food for your families."

Do Not Bury Me in Egypt   *Maftir*

25 They gratefully exclaimed. "You have saved our lives; we will gladly be Pharaoh's slaves."

26 Joseph passed a law that one-fifth of whatever grew on the farmland of Egypt belonged to Pharaoh. Only the priestly lands did not belong to Pharaoh.

27 Meanwhile, the tribes of Israel lived in the land of Egypt, in the district of Goshen. They bought land there, and their numbers increased very rapidly.

Vayechi וַיְחִי
JACOB'S LAST DAYS

28 Jacob lived in Egypt for seventeen years. And he died at the age of 147 years.

29 Israel felt that he would soon die, so he called for his son Joseph, and said to him, "If you really love me, swear to me that you will not bury me in Egypt.

30 Bury me with my fathers. Carry me out of Egypt, and bury me with my ancestors."

Joseph replied, "I swear to do as you wish." **31** Joseph swore to his father, and from his bed Israel nodded his thanks to Joseph.

48 Some time later Joseph was told that his father was very sick. Joseph took his two sons, Manasseh and Ephraim, along with him and went to see his father. **2** When Jacob was told that Joseph was coming to him, Israel gathered his strength and sat up in bed to greet them.

3 Jacob said to Joseph, "El Shaddai (Elohim Almighty) once appeared to me in Luz, in the land of Canaan. He blessed me **4** and said to me,

'I will give you a large family.
They will grow into a mighty nation.
I will give this land to you
and to your descendants forever.'

5 Joseph, your two sons who were born to you in Egypt before I came here shall be considered as my own. Ephraim and Manasseh shall be just like Reuben and Simeon to me. **6** Any children who are born later shall be considered yours. They shall inherit only through their older brothers, Ephraim and Manasseh.

7 When I was coming from Padan, your mother Rachel died. It was in Canaan, a short distance before we got to Ephrath. I buried her there along the road to Ephrath, which is now called Bethlehem."

8 Israel, who was almost blind, asked, "Who are these youngsters?"

9 Joseph replied to his father, "They are the sons that Elohim gave me here." Jacob said "Please bring them close to me. I will give them a blessing."

Jacob Blesses Ephraim and Manasseh   *2nd Aliyah*

10 Israel was almost blind and could hardly see. So Joseph brought his sons near to him. Israel kissed them and hugged them. **11** Israel said to Joseph, "I never thought to see your face again. But now Elohim has even let me see your children."

12 Joseph brought the boys close to his father, and he bowed down to Jacob.

13 Joseph then took the two boys. He placed Ephraim to Israel's left, and Manasseh he placed to Israel's right. He then brought them close to Israel. **14** With his right hand Israel reached out and put it on Ephraim's head even though he was the younger son. He put his left hand on Manasseh's head. Jacob purposely crossed his hands, even though Manasseh was the first-born.

15 Jacob gave Joseph a blessing. He said,

> "The Elohim whom my ancestors,
> Abraham and Isaac, worshipped
> is the Elohim who has been
> my Shepherd all my life.
> **16** He sent an angel to deliver
> me from all evil.
> May He bless these boys,
> and let them preserve my name,
> and the names of my ancestors,
> Abraham and Isaac.
> May Ephraim and Manasseh increase
> and became a powerful nation."

Jacob Prophesies the Future   *3rd Aliyah*

17 When Joseph saw that his father had put his right hand on

Ephraim's head, he was upset. He tried to lift his father's hand from Ephraim's head and put it on Manasseh's. **18** Joseph said, "No, father, that's not the way it should be done. Manasseh is the first-born. Put your right hand on his head."

19 His father refused and said, "My son, I know what I am doing.

> The older one, Ephraim,
> will become a nation.
> He will attain greatness.
> But his younger brother, Manasseh,
> will become even greater,
> and his descendants
> will become many mighty nations."

20 Jacob blessed them on that day. He said, "In time to come, the children of Israel will use both of you as a blessing. They will say,

> 'May Elohim make you like
> Ephraim and Manasseh.'"

He purposely put Ephraim before Manasseh.

21 Israel said to Joseph, "I am dying. Elohim will be with you, and He will bring you back to the land of your fathers. **22** In addition to what your brothers will share, I will give you an extra share. I give you the city of Shechem, which I conquered from the Amorites."

Jacob Blesses His Sons   *4ᵗʰ Aliyah*

49 Jacob called his sons together. When they came, he said,

> "Gather around me,
> and I will prophesy
> what will happen in the future.
> **2** Come and listen, sons of Jacob;
> listen to your father, Israel.
> **3** Reuben, you are my first-born,
> my strength and the child of my youth,

you are first in rank and first in power.

4 But because you were wild as stormy water,
you will no longer be first.
Because you moved your father's bed,
and committed a dishonorable act.

5 Simeon and Levi are a pair,
men of violence and weapons.

6 I will never be part of your evil.
In anger you have killed men
and abused animals.

7 Cursed be your anger,
for it is cruel.
I will scatter your descendants
among the tribes of Israel.

8 Judah, your brothers will praise you.
Your strength will defeat your enemies;
your father's sons shall bow to you.

9 Judah, you are like a young lion
that has eaten its victims;
you crouch like a fierce lion.
No one will dare challenge you.

10 The power will not depart from Judah,
and not from your descendants.
Nations will obey you
until the final peace comes.

11 You tie your donkey with a single grapevine,
you wash your clothes in wine,
your cloak in the juice of grapes.

12 Your eyes sparkle like wine,
your teeth are whiter than milk.

13 Zebulun, you will live along the seashore;
your land will be a harbor for ships;
your border shall extend as far as Sidon.

14 Issachar, you are like a strong donkey,
lying down among the sheep.

15 When the resting place is good,
and the land is pleasant,

you will accept the load,
and work like a slave.
16 Dan, you will judge your people,
just like the other tribes of Israel.
17 Dan, you will be like a snake on the road,
a poisonous viper on the path,
that bites a horse's heel,
so that the rider falls backward.
18 I pray that Adonai will help you.

Jacob Blesses Gad, Asher, Naphtali, and Joseph   *5ᵗʰ Aliyah*

19 "Raiders shall attack Gad,
but you will rise and defeat them.
20 Asher, you will produce the richest foods,
fit for a king's table.
21 Naphtali, you are like a free-running deer
with beautiful children.
22 Joseph, you are like a fruitful vine
near a fountain,
with branches spreading over the wall.
23 Enemies will attack you
and will make you their target.
24 But you will remain strong,
with steadfast arms.
From Jacob's Champion,
the Shepherd of Israel.
25 The El of your father will help you,
and Shaddai will bless you,
with blessings from heaven above,
and blessings of water below.
26 May your father's blessing,
added to the blessing of my parents,
last as long as the eternal hills.
May blessings circle Joseph's head,
The leader of his brothers.

Jacob's Final Instructions   *6ᵗʰ Aliyah*

27 "Benjamin is like a hungry wolf.
He devours his enemies in the morning,
and divides his prey in the evening."

28 All of these sons became the twelve tribes of Israel, and this is what their father said to them when he blessed them. He gave each one of his sons a special blessing.

29 Jacob then gave his sons his final instructions. He said, "I am going to die. Bury me with my fathers, in the cave in the field of Ephron the Hittite.

30 It is the Cave of Machpelah, near Mamre, in the land of Canaan. Abraham bought the field from Ephron the Hittite as a burial place. **31** This is where my grandfather Abraham and his wife Sarah are buried; this is where my father Isaac and his wife Rebecca are buried; and this is where I buried Leah. **32** It is the field and the cave that Abraham legally bought from the children of Heth."

33 Jacob finished his instructions to his sons. He took his last breath and died.

50 Joseph hugged his father and kissed him. **2** Joseph then ordered the morticians to embalm his father. **3** It took forty days to embalm Jacob. All of Egypt mourned Jacob for seventy days.

4 When the period of mourning for Jacob ended, Joseph spoke to Pharaoh's close advisers and said, "Please do me a favor, give my personal message to Pharaoh:

5 'My father made me swear and said, "I am dying. You must bury me in the grave that I prepared for myself in the land of Canaan." Please allow me to go north and bury my father, and then I will return.'"

6 Pharaoh said, "Go bury your father, just as you swore to him."

7 Joseph headed north to bury his father, and with him went all of Pharaoh's counselors as well as all the leaders of Egypt. **8** All of Joseph's household, his brothers, and his father's family also went. They left their small children, their sheep, and their cattle behind in Goshen. **9** A troop of horsemen accompanied the funeral cortege.

10 They came to Gorèn Ha'atad, meaning The Threshing Floor of Atad on the bank of the Jordan, and there they held a great religious funeral. Joseph observed a seven-day mourning period for his father. **11** When the Canaanites living in the area saw the mourning, they said, "Egypt is in deep mourning here." The place on the bank of the Jordan was therefore called Avel Mitzraim (Egypt's Mourning).

12 Jacob's sons did as he had instructed them. **13** His sons carried him to Canaan, and they buried him in the Cave of Machpelah, near Mamre. This is the field that Abraham bought for a burial property from Ephron the Hittite.

14 After he buried his father, Joseph returned to Egypt along with his brothers and everyone who had gone with him to his father's burial. **15** Joseph's brothers began to be afraid. They said, "What if Joseph is still angry at us? He is sure to pay us back for all the evil we did him."

16 So they sent a message to Joseph: "Before your father died, **17** he told us what to say to you. He said, 'Forgive the crime and the sin your brothers committed against you.' Now we ask you to forgive the terrible wrong that we have done."

When Joseph heard the message he wept.

18 His brothers then came and threw themselves at his feet and cried. "Here!" they said, "We are your slaves!" **19** Then Joseph said to them, "Do not be afraid. I cannot change what Elohim did. **20** You tried to harm me, but Elohim made it come out good. He brought me to Egypt so that I could save you and the lives of our families.

Joseph at Peace
with His Brothers   *7ᵗʰ Aliyah*

21 "Don't worry. I will provide for you and your children," he assured them and made peace with them.

22 Joseph and his father's family continued to live in Egypt. He lived to be 110 years old.

Joseph Dies   *Maftir*

23 Joseph lived to see Ephraim's grandchildren, and the children of Manasseh's son Makhir.

24 Joseph said to his family, "I am dying. Elohim will remember you and bring you out of Egypt to the land that He swore to give to our ancestors Abraham, Isaac, and Jacob."

25 Then Joseph made the sons of Israel swear, "When Elohim comes to lead you back to Canaan, you must bring my body out of Egypt." **26** Joseph died at the age of 110 years. He was embalmed and buried in a coffin in Egypt.

סֵפֶר שְׁמוֹת
THE BOOK OF SHEMOT

Masoretic Torah Notes

Here is a list of some of the Masoretic notes for the Book of Shemot.

1.   The Book of Shemot contains 1,209 verses.
2.   The Book of Shemot contains 40 chapters.
3.   The Book of Shemot contains 11 sidrot.

These are the sidrot in the Book of Shemot.

סֵפֶר שְׁמוֹת

THE BOOK OF SHEMOT

The Hebrew name for the second of the Five Books of Moses is Shemot. It comes from the book's second word in Hebrew, shemot, meaning "names." The Greek name of the book is Exodus, meaning "the road out."

The book of Shemot recounts a great variety of important events that lead up to the Exodus from Egypt under the charismatic leadership of Moses. The book of Shemot can be divided into four scenarios.

The first section (1:1–15:21) deals with the miraculous deliverance from Egyptian slavery.

Toward the end of the history related in the book of Bereshit, there was a famine in Canaan, so Jacob (Israel) sent his sons to Egypt to purchase food. There they met their long-lost brother, Joseph, and he brought Jacob and the families of his brothers to live in Egypt. The Israelites lived and prospered there until, after 270 years, a new Pharaoh arose "who did not know Joseph."

The new Pharaoh declares, "The Israelites are becoming too numerous and are a danger to us. We must find a way to deal wisely with them" (1:9–10). He "deals wisely" with the Israelites by enslaving and oppressing them. Adonai sends Moses to free the Israelites from slavery. After nine disastrous plagues, Pharaoh begs the Israelites to leave Egypt. But then he changes his mind, so Adonai sends the tenth plague and all the first-born Egyptian males and animals die. During the plague the holiday of Passover is established and the Israelites make a miraculous escape by crossing the Sea of Reeds.

The Egyptian experience was a decisive factor in the development of Israel as a nation. The purpose of the Exodus was not merely to free a group of slaves but to create a holy nation bound to Adonai. Thus the second scenario (15:22–18:27)

171

finds the Israelites camped at the foot of Mount Sinai, where they enter into a covenant with Adonai.

After forty days on Mount Sinai, Moses returns with the Ten Commandments (20:2–14). These include rules about the observance of Shabbat, the existence of Adonai, reverence for parents, and prohibitions of murder, theft, false testimony, and adultery. The awestricken Israelites pledge, "We will obey all of Adonai's laws and commandments" (19:8). During this period Adonai miraculously provides food for the Israelites by sending them manna and quail.

The third scenario (19:1–24:18) deals with a series of laws and commandments (mitzvot) that transform the Israelites into a holy nation. The commandments sealed the covenant between Israel and Adonai. They dictated Israel's social and ethical behavior and provided for the welfare of the disadvantaged.

Moses is a man of iron who endures constant challenges yet manages to mold a mass of slaves into a strong and God-fearing nation. He faces an endless struggle with rivals who are jealous of his power. Korach and his followers challenge the authority of Moses. Aaron, in a moment of weakness, allows himself to be influenced by backsliders who have lost confidence in Moses and persuade him to build the golden calf. At key moments, many Israelites of weak faith want to return to Egypt because they miss the food there.

The fourth section (25:1–29:46) describes the Meeting Tent and its furnishings and the building of the Holy Ark under the supervision of Betzalel. The priesthood is established under the leadership of Aaron, the first high priest.

The fifth and last section (30:1–40:38) contains a great variety of instructions and laws: instructions for the High Priest, laws for offerings, furnishings for the Meeting Tent, priestly clothing, and instructions for setting up the Meeting Tent.

Shemot שְׁמוֹת
THESE ARE THE TRIBES

1 These are the names of Israel's sons who came to Egypt with him, each with his own family: **2** Reuben, Simeon, Levi, Judah, **3** Issachar, Zebulun, Benjamin, **4** Dan, Naphtali, Gad, and Asher. **5** The total number of Jacob's direct descendants, including Joseph, who were in Egypt was seventy.

6 Joseph, his brothers, and everyone else in that generation died. **7** The Israelites were fertile and their numbers increased. They became so numerous that Egypt was overrun with them.

8 A new king came to power who no longer remembered how Joseph had saved Egypt. **9** He inflamed his people and said, "The Israelites are becoming too numerous and are a danger to us. **10** We must find a way to deal wisely with them. If we don't, they will increase too much, and if a war breaks out they will join our enemies and fight against us, and drive us from our own country."

11 So the Egyptians appointed taskmasters over the Israelites with orders to crush them with hard labor. The Israelites were forced to build the storehouse cities of Pithom and Ra'amses for Pharaoh. **12** However, the more the Egyptians mistreated them, the more the Israelites increased. **13** The Egyptians forced the Israelites into slavery so as to break their resistance. **14** They made the lives of the Israelites bitter with hard work, making cement and bricks, and doing all kinds of farm labor. The goal was to physically break them.

15 The king of Egypt called the Hebrew midwives, Shifra and Puah. **16** He said to them, "When you help the Hebrew women give birth, if the baby is a boy, kill it; but if it is a baby girl, let it live."

17 The midwives respected Elohim and disobeyed the Egyptian king. They allowed the baby boys to live.

Moses Is Born

2nd Aliyah

18 The king of Egypt summoned the midwives and angrily demanded, "Why did you disobey me? Why did you deliberately let the baby boys live?"

19 The midwives, Shifra and Puah, replied, "The Hebrew women are not like the Egyptians. They are very healthy. They give birth before we even get to them."

20 Elohim blessed the midwives, and the Israelites continued to increase. **21** And because the midwives feared Elohim, He gave them many children of their own.

22 Pharaoh then ordered his people: "You must throw every newborn baby boy into the Nile, but every girl shall be allowed to live."

2 In this time of trouble, a man and a woman of the tribe of Levi married. **2** The woman became pregnant and gave birth to a son. The child was very healthy and beautiful, and the mother managed to keep him hidden for three months. **3** When she could no longer hide him, she wove a basket of reeds and waterproofed it with tar and pitch. Then, tearfully, she placed the child in it. She put the basket in the reeds on the edge of the Nile. **4** Miriam, the baby's sister, secretly watched from a distance to see what would happen to her brother.

5 At that moment Pharaoh's daughter came to bathe in the Nile, while her maids walked along the edge of the river. The princess saw the basket in the reeds and sent her servant to bring the basket to her. **6** When the princess opened the basket and heard the baby begin to cry, she took pity on it. She said, "It is one of the Hebrew babies."

7 The baby's sister approached and said to Pharaoh's daughter, "Shall I find a Hebrew woman to nurse the child for you?"

8 "Yes, go," replied Pharaoh's daughter. The young girl went and brought the baby's own mother.

9 Pharaoh's daughter said to the mother, "Take this baby and nurse it for me, and I will pay you." The mother took her own child and nursed it for the princess.

10 When the child was old enough, the mother brought him to Pharaoh's daughter. She adopted him as her own son and named him Moses (Moshe) because, she said, "I took [*mashe*] him from the water."

Moses in Midian   *3rd Aliyah*

11 When Moses became an adult, he began to be interested in the Hebrews, and he saw how they had to labor as slaves. One day he saw an Egyptian taskmaster kill one of his fellow Hebrews. **12** Moses was very angry. When he thought no one was watching, he killed the Egyptian and buried his body in the sand.

13 The next day Moses went out and saw two Hebrew men fighting. Moses asked one of them, "Why are you beating your brother?" **14** The man replied, "Who appointed you our prince and judge? Do you mean to kill me just as you killed the Egyptian?"

Moses became frightened. He said to himself, "Everyone knows what I did." **15** Soon Pharaoh heard that Moses had killed an Egyptian. He ordered Moses arrested and put to death. But Moses fled from Pharaoh and escaped to the land of Midian.

When he reached Midian, Moses sat down to rest near a well. **16** The priest of Midian had seven daughters, who came every day to draw water for their flock. Just as they were starting to fill the troughs to water their father's sheep, **17** other shepherds began to chase them away. Moses stepped up and helped them and then watered their sheep.

18 When they returned home, their father, Reuel, asked them, "Today you came home early. How did you water the sheep so fast?" **19** They answered, "An Egyptian stranger defended us from the shepherds. He also drew water for us and helped water our sheep."

20 The priest asked his daughters, "And where is the stranger now? Why did you leave him at the well? Find him, and invite him to eat with us."

21 Moses decided to live with Reuel and work for him. Reuel gave Moses his daughter Tzipporah as a wife. **22** When she gave birth to a son, Moses named him Gershom, because, he said, "I have been a foreigner (*ger*) there (*shom*) in a strange land."

23 Years passed, and the king of Egypt died. The Israelites were still suffering under their burden of slavery. They cried out for deliverance from their slavery, and their pleas rose up to Adonai. **24** Adonai heard their cries, and He remembered His covenant with Abraham, Isaac, and Jacob. **25** Adonai saw the Israelites and realized that it was time to rescue then.

The Burning Bush   *4ᵗʰ Aliyah*

3 One day Moses was pasturing the sheep of his father-in-law Yitro, priest of Midian. He drove the flock to the edge of the desert and came to the mountain of Adonai near Sinai.

2 An angel of Adonai appeared to Moses in the midst of a fire, in the heart of a thorn-bush. As Moses looked, he saw that the bush was on fire but was not being burned up. **3** Moses thought to himself, "I must get closer and find out why the bush does not burn."

4 When Adonai saw that Moses was coming too close, He called from the heart of the bush. He called, "Moses, Moses!" Moses replied, "Yes, I am here."

5 Adonai said, "Do not come any closer. Remove your sandals. You are standing on holy ground."

6 Adonai continued and said, "I am the Elohim of your father, the Elohim of Abraham, the Elohim of Isaac, and the Elohim of Jacob."

Moses was afraid to look at the Divine, so he hid his face.

7 Adonai said, "I have seen the suffering of My people in Egypt. I have heard their cries because of the cruelty of the slave masters. **8** I have decided to rescue them from Egypt's cruelty. I will bring them to their own land, to a land flowing with milk and honey, the territory of the Canaanites, Hittites, Amorites, Perizzites, Hivites, and Jebusites.

9 At this moment the cries of the Israelites have reached me. I see, as well, the torture which Egypt is inflicting on them. **10** I am sending you to Pharaoh. Now go, and lead My people, the Israelites, out of Egypt."

11 Moses said to Adonai, "Who am I that I should go to Pharaoh? How can you expect me to lead the Israelites out of Egypt?"

12 Adonai replied, "Have faith, because I will be with you. And this will be your sign that it was I who sent you to lead My people out of Egypt. When you are free, all of you will return to this mountain in Sinai." **13** Moses said to Elohim, "If I go to the Israelites and say, 'Your fathers' Elohim sent me to you,' and they ask me, 'What is His name?' what should I answer them?"

14 Adonai replied to Moses, "*Ehyeh Asher Ehyeh*" (I Will Be Who I Will Be). Adonai then explained, "This is what you must say to the Israelites: '*Ehyeh* [I Will Be] sent me to you.'"

15 Then Adonai said to Moses, "You must say to the Israelites, 'The Adonai of your ancestors, the Adonai of Abraham, Isaac, and Jacob, sent me to you.' This is My eternal name, and this is how I am to be remembered for eternity.

I Will Bring You Out of Egypt   *5th Aliyah*

16 "Go, assemble the leaders of Israel, and say to them, 'The Adonai of your fathers appeared to me—the Adonai of Abraham, Isaac, and Jacob. He said, "I am aware of what is happening to you in Egypt. **17** I promise that I will bring you out of the slavery of Egypt, to a land flowing with milk and honey, to the land of the Canaanites, Hittites, Amorites, Perizzites, Hivites and Jebusites."'

18 They will believe what you say. Then you and the leaders of Israel will go to the king of Egypt. You must tell him, 'Adonai of the Hebrews has met with us. Now we petition that you allow us to take a three-day journey into the desert, to worship Adonai.'

19 I know that the Egyptian king will not allow you to leave unless he is forced to do so. **20** Then I will show my power and punish Egypt with miraculous deeds. Only then will Pharaoh let you go free.

21 I will see that the Egyptians treat you well, and when you finally leave, you will not go empty-handed.

22 Every Hebrew woman should ask for articles of silver and gold, as well as clothing, from her neighbors. In this way the Egyptians will pay you reparations for your (210) years of slavery."

4 Once again Moses asked, "But will the Hebrews believe me? They will not listen to me. They will say, 'Elohim never appeared to you.' "

2 Adonai asked Moses, "What is that in your hand?"
Moses answered, "A walking staff."

3 "Now throw your staff on the ground."
When Moses threw it on the ground, it turned into a snake, and Moses was frightened.

4 Then Adonai said to Moses, "Reach out and grab the snake by its tail." When Moses reached out and grabbed the snake, it turned back into a walking staff.

5 Adonai said, "Do this and they will believe that Elohim appeared to you. The Elohim of their ancestors, the Elohim of Abraham, Isaac, and Jacob."

6 Once again Adonai said to Moses, "Now put your hand inside your robe."
Moses put his hand in his robe. When he removed it, it was leprous and as white as snow.

7 Adonai said, "Now put your hand in your robe again."
Moses put his hand back into his robe, and when he removed it his skin was as healthy as before.

8 Adonai said, "If they did not believe you, and did not pay attention to the first miraculous sign, then they will surely believe the second sign.

9 And if they do not believe these two miracles, then take some water from the Nile River and pour it onto the ground. The clear water that you took from the Nile will turn into blood on the ground."

10 Now Moses pleaded with Adonai. "Adonai, I beg you, I am not a man of words. I never was, and I am not now. I find it difficult to speak because I have a speech defect."

11 Adonai replied, "Who makes people speak? Who makes a person deaf? Who gives a person sight or makes him blind? I do. **12** Now go! I will be with you and will teach you what to say."

13 Moses pleaded, "Adonai, I beg you! Please send some-one else."

14 Adonai was angry with Moses. He said, "Is Aaron the Levite your brother? I know that he is a good speaker. He is coming to meet you, and when he sees you, he will be happy. **15** You will tell him to speak for you, and you will put the right words in his mouth. I will be your mouth and his mouth, and I will direct you what to say. **16** He will be your spokesman. He will speak to the people for you, and you will be his guide. **17** Make sure you take your staff with you, in order to perform the miracles with it."

Moses Leaves Midian   *6ᵗʰ Aliyah*

18 With that Moses left and returned to his father-in-law, Yitro. Moses said to him, "I must leave and return to my people in Egypt, to see how they are getting along."

Yitro said to Moses. "Go in peace."

19 While Moses was still in Midian, Adonai said to him, "It is now safe to return to Egypt. The Egyptians who wanted to kill you have died."

20 Moses took his wife and sons, mounted them on a donkey, and set out to return to Egypt. He took the miraculous walking staff in his hand.

21 Adonai instructed Moses, "On your way back to Egypt, keep in mind the miraculous powers that I have taught you. Use them before Pharaoh. However, I will make him stubborn, and he will refuse to allow the Israelites to leave.

22 Then you must say to Pharaoh, 'This is what Adonai says:

Israel is My son, My first-born. **23** Let My son go to worship Me. If you refuse to let them leave, I will kill your first-born son.'"

24 Moses and his family came to a place where they camped for the night. Adonai confronted Moses and wanted to punish him because he had not circumcised his son Gershom. **25** His wife, Tzipporah, took a knife and circumcised her son. She said to the child, "Now you are safe because you are circumcised." **26** After that Adonai did not punish Moses. **27** Now Adonai said to Aaron, "Go and meet Moses in the wilderness." Aaron went, and when he met Moses near the Mountain of Elohim, he hugged him.

28 Moses repeated to Aaron everything that Adonai had told him about his mission, as well as the miracles that He had instructed him to perform.

29 Moses and Aaron went to Egypt, and they assembled all the leaders of Israel. **30** Aaron repeated everything that Adonai had told Moses and performed the miracles before the people. **31** The people believed that Adonai had visited them and had seen their misery. They bowed their heads and prayed.

Let My People Go   7*th* *Aliyah*

5 Then Moses and Aaron went to Pharaoh and said, "This is what Adonai demands: Let My people go, so that they can worship Me in the wilderness."

2 Pharaoh replied, "Who is Adonai that I should obey Him and let the Israelites go? I do not know Adonai. Nor will I allow the Israelites to leave."

3 "The Adonai of the Hebrews has revealed Himself to us," said Moses and Aaron. "Please allow us to take a three-day journey into the wilderness to worship Adonai. Otherwise He will punish us."

4 The Egyptian king shouted, "Moses and Aaron, why do you bother the people when they are working? Go away and mind your own business!"

5 Pharaoh said, "The slaves are increasing, and you want to stop them from their work!"

6 That very day, Pharaoh met with his slave masters and the Hebrew foremen. He said, **7** "From now on, do not supply the slaves with straw for bricks as before. Let them find and gather their own straw. **8** However, they must still produce the same amount of bricks. Do not reduce the quota. They are lazy, and that is why they want to go to worship Adonai. **9** Increase the workload for the men, and make sure they do it. Then they will stop paying attention to what Moses and Aaron tell them."

10 The slave masters and foremen went out and told the Hebrews, "Pharaoh has ordered us to stop supplying you with straw. **11** From now on you must go and find your own straw wherever you can find it. But remember, you must still produce the same amount of bricks as before."

12 The Israelites scattered all over Egypt to find straw for the bricks. **13** The slave masters brutally said to them, "You must make the same number of bricks as before."

14 The Israelite foremen, whom Pharaoh had appointed, were whipped. They were told, "Yesterday and today you did not complete your quota of bricks." **15** The Israelite foremen complained to Pharaoh, "Why are you punishing us? **16** You no longer give us straw, but we are told to make bricks. We are the ones being whipped, but it is the fault of your slave masters." **17** Pharaoh angrily replied, "You are all lazy! You say you want to sacrifice to Elohim, but it is just an excuse. **18** Now go! Enough talk! We will not give you any straw, but you must still produce the same amount of bricks."

19 The Israelite foremen realized that they were in serious trouble. Clearly there was no chance of the daily brick quota being reduced.

20 When they left Pharaoh, the foremen met Moses and Aaron, who were waiting for them. **21** They said, "May Adonai punish you. You have destroyed our influence with Pharaoh and his advisers. You have given them an excuse to kill us."

Pharaoh Will Drive Them Out of Egypt   *Maftir*

22 Moses returned to Adonai and said, "Adonai, why have you punished Your people? Why did You send me? **23** Ever since I first went to Pharaoh to speak in Your name, he has become more cruel. You have done nothing to save Your people."

6 Elohim said to Moses, "Soon I will show you how I will punish Pharaoh. He will gladly let them go. In fact he himself will drive them out of Egypt."

Va'era וָאֵרָא
ADONAI REVEALS HIMSELF

2 Adonai spoke to Moses and said to him, "I am Adonai.
3 I appeared to Abraham, Isaac, and Jacob as El Shaddai, but I did not reveal to them My name Adonai. **4** I established My covenant with them and promised to give their descendants the land of Canaan, where they lived as foreigners. **5** I have heard the suffering of the Israelites, whom the Egyptians have enslaved, and I have remembered My covenant.

6 Moses, I command you to assure the Israelites that I will free them from forced labor in Egypt, and that I will liberate them with power and great miracles.

7 Tell them, I will adopt you as My people, and Elohim will always be with you. Know that I, Adonai, will bring you out from under the Egyptian slavery. **8** I will bring you to the land that I swore I would give to Abraham, Isaac, and Jacob. I will give it to you as your own. I am Adonai."

9 Moses told all of this to the Israelites, but because they were demoralized by hard work, they refused to listen to him.

10 Adonai spoke to Moses, saying, **11** "Go back again and speak to Pharaoh, king of Egypt, and tell him to let the Israelites leave Egypt."

12 Then Moses spoke and said, "Now even the Israelites will not listen to me. How can I expect Pharaoh to listen to me? Besides, I have a problem speaking clearly."

13 Adonai then spoke to both Moses and Aaron. He told them what to say to Pharaoh, king of Egypt, demanding that he let the Israelites leave Egypt.

The Ancestors of the Tribes of Israel *2nd Aliyah*

14 These are the ancestors and families of the tribes of Israel. The sons of Israel's first-born, Reuben, were Hanoch, Pallu, Hezron, and Carmi. Their descendants became the tribe of Reuben. **15** The sons of Simeon were Yemuel, Yamin, Ohad, Yakhin, and Zochar, as well as Saul, son of the Canaanite woman. Their descendants became the tribe of Simeon.

16 According to their family records, these are the descendants of Levi. Gershon, Kehoth, and Merari are the names of Levi's sons. Levi lived to be 137 years old.

17 The descendants of Gershon were Livni and Shimi.

18 The descendants of Kehoth were Amram, Izhar, Hebron, and Uzziel. Kehoth lived to be 133 years old.

19 The descendants of Merari were Machli and Mushi.

These are the families of Levi and their descendants.

20 Amram married Jochebed, and she gave birth to Aaron and Moses. Amram lived to be 137 years old.

21 The sons of Izhar were Korach, Nefeg, and Zikri.

22 The sons of Uzziel were Mishael, Eltzafan, and Zithri.

23 Aaron married Elisheva, Nachshon's sister, daughter of Aminadav. She gave birth to Nadav, Abihu, Eleazar, and Ithamar.

24 The sons of Korach were Assir, Elkanah, and Aviasaf. These descendants became the Korachites.

25 Eleazar, Aaron's son, married one of the daughters of Putiel, and she gave birth to Pinchas.

The above are the ancestors of the Levite clans listed according to their families.

26 This is the family tree of Moses and Aaron, to whom Adonai said, "Bring the Israelites out of Egypt." **27** Moses and Aaron were the ones who spoke to Pharaoh, king of Egypt, for permission to lead the Israelites out of Egypt.

28 Yet on that day in Egypt, Adonai spoke only to Moses.

Pharaoh Refuses for the Second Time *3rd Aliyah*

29 Adonai said to Moses, "I am Adonai. Tell Pharaoh, king of Egypt, everything that I tell you." **30** Then Moses said, "Adonai, I do not have the confidence to speak. Pharaoh will never listen to me because I do not speak well."

7 Then Adonai said to Moses, "Watch! I will make you seem like a god to Pharaoh; Aaron, your brother, will be your prophet, and he will speak for you.

2 You must repeat everything that I tell you, and then

your brother Aaron will repeat it to Pharaoh. Then Pharaoh will allow the Israelites to leave Egypt.

3 I will make Pharaoh stubborn, and then you will have the opportunity to show My miraculous signs and wonders in Egypt. **4** Even then Pharaoh will refuse to listen to you. Then I will show My power against Egypt. With powerful acts and deeds, I will bring My armies—My people, the Israelites—out from Egypt. **5** When I show My power and bring the Israelites out from among them, Egypt will be certain that I am Adonai." **6** So Moses and Aaron did exactly as Adonai had instructed them.

7 When they confronted Pharaoh, Moses was eighty years old, and Aaron was eighty-three years old.

The Staff Turns into a Snake   *4th Aliyah*

8 Adonai said to Moses and Aaron, **9** "When Pharaoh speaks to you, he will ask you to prove who you are by performing a miraculous sign. You, Moses, must then tell Aaron to take your walking staff and throw it down in front of Pharaoh. It will became a snake."

10 So Moses and Aaron went to Pharaoh. They did exactly as Adonai had instructed them. Aaron threw his staff down before Pharaoh, and it became a snake.

11 Pharaoh summoned his wise men and magicians. The magicians were able to do the same thing with their mumbo-jumbo. **12** Each magician threw down his staff, and they all turned into snakes. Then Aaron's staff swallowed up their staffs. **13** But Pharaoh remained stubborn, and just as Adonai had predicted, he refused to listen to them. **14** Adonai said to Moses, "Pharaoh is still stubborn and refuses to let the people leave.

15 In the morning meet Pharaoh when he goes down to the Nile. Hold in your hand the staff that was changed into a snake.

16 Say to him: 'Adonai has sent me to you with this message: "Let My people leave, so they can worship me in the wilderness. So far, you have not listened to us. **17** Now Adonai says:

By this miracle you will surely find out that I am Adonai. I will strike the water of the Nile with the staff in my hand, and the waters will turn into blood. **18** The fish in the Nile will die, and the river will become polluted, and the Egyptians will have to stop drinking water from the Nile.'" **19** Adonai said to Moses, "Tell Aaron to take your staff and point it toward the waters of Egypt—over their rivers, their canals, their reservoirs, and every place where water is stored—and the water shall turn into blood. There will be blood throughout all Egypt, even in the wooden barrels and stone pots."

20 Moses and Aaron did exactly as God had commanded. Aaron raised the staff and struck the Nile in the presence of Pharaoh and his officials. The waters of the Nile were changed into blood.

21 The fish in the Nile died, and the river smelled so bad that the Egyptians were no longer able to drink its water. There was blood throughout the land.

22 However, when the magicians of Egypt were able to produce the same effect with their magic, Pharaoh continued to be stubborn, just as Adonai had predicted, and he refused to listen to Moses and Aaron. **23** Pharaoh turned around and returned to his palace. Even this miracle did not impress him.

24 Since they could not drink any water from the river, the Egyptians dug wells close to the Nile for fresh drinking water.

25 After Adonai struck the Nile, it remained polluted for seven full days.

26 Now Adonai said to Moses, "In My name, go to Pharaoh and say to him: 'Let My people leave so they can worship Me. **27** If you refuse, I will flood the land of Egypt with frogs. **28** The Nile will swarm with frogs, and when they emerge, they will jump into your palace, into your bedroom, and even into your bed. They will also be inside the homes of your leaders and people, even in your ovens and your bread-making bowls. **29** When the frogs emerge, they will jump and hop all over you, your people, and your leaders.'"

8 Adonai said to Moses, "Tell Aaron to point the staff at the rivers, canals, and reservoirs, and he will make frogs swarm all over Egypt." **2** Aaron extended his staff over the waters of Egypt, and the frogs jumped out and covered Egypt.

3 The magicians were also able to produce even more frogs, which blanketed Egypt. **4** Pharaoh hurriedly summoned Moses and Aaron, and said, "Pray to Adonai! Please ask him to remove the frogs from me and my people. Then I will let the Hebrews leave to worship Adonai." **5** Moses replied, "Test me. Tell me exactly when I should remove the frogs from you and your homes and return them to the Nile."

6 Pharaoh begged, "Please remove them tomorrow!"

And Moses replied, "Just as you say. Now you will know that there is none like Adonai.

Frogs and Lice   *5ᵗʰ Aliyah*

7 "The frogs will disappear from your houses, your leaders, and your people. They will remain only in the Nile."

8 Moses and Aaron left Pharaoh, and Moses pleaded with Adonai to remove the frogs He had brought upon Pharaoh. **9** Adonai did just as Moses requested, and the frogs in the houses, courtyards, and fields died. **10** The Egyptians shoveled them into big piles, and the land of Egypt stank.

11 When Pharaoh saw that the frogs were gone, he once again became stubborn, and again would not listen to them, just as Adonai had predicted.

12 Adonai said to Moses, "Tell Aaron to raise his staff and strike the dust of the earth. It will turn into lice that will infest all of Egypt."

13 Aaron did this. He raised his hand with his staff and struck the dust of the earth. Suddenly the lice appeared, attacking humans and animals. All over Egypt, the dust turned into lice. **14** The magicians tried to produce lice with their mumbo-jumbo, but they could not. Meanwhile, the lice attacked and itched the Egyptians and their animals. **15** The Egyptians said it must be the finger of Elohim. Still Pharaoh remained stubborn and, just as Adonai had predicted, refused to listen. **16** Adonai said to Moses, "Get up early in the morning, and meet Pharaoh when he goes down to the Nile. In My name say to him: 'Let My people go and worship Me. **17** If you do not let My people leave, I will send swarms of wild animals to attack you, your leaders, your people, and your homes. The houses of Egypt, and even the ground upon which they stand, will be filled with wild animals.

18 On that day, I will isolate the district of Goshen, where the Israelites live, so that there will not be any wild animals there. Then you will realize that I, Adonai, am right here in Egypt.

Cattle Plague and Boils   *6th Aliyah*

19 "'I will separate My people from your people. This miracle will take place tomorrow.'"

20 Adonai did this, and huge packs of wild animals attacked the palaces of Pharaoh and his officials. Throughout all Egypt, the land was devastated by the animals.

21 Pharaoh hastily summoned Moses and Aaron and begged, "Leave! You have permission to worship Adonai here in Egypt."

22 "That is not acceptable," replied Moses. "What we will sacrifice to Adonai is holy to the Egyptians. We cannot sacrifice the sacred animal of the Egyptians in their presence, because they will kill us. **23** What we must do is make a three-day journey into the desert. There we will be able to worship Adonai, just as He wants us to."

24 "I will allow you leave," said Pharaoh, "as long as you do not go too far away. You can sacrifice to Adonai in the desert. But remember to pray for me!"

25 Moses replied, "When I leave your presence, I will pray to Adonai. Tomorrow the animals will disappear from Pharaoh, his servants, and his people.

But let Pharaoh never again deceive us by refusing to let the people sacrifice to Adonai."

26 Moses left Pharaoh and prayed to Adonai.

27 Adonai did just as Moses requested. Adonai caused the animals to leave Pharaoh, his servants, and his people. Not a single one remained. **28** But once again Pharaoh became stubborn and would not allow the Israelites to leave.

9 Once again Adonai told Moses to go to Pharaoh and, in the name of Adonai, say to him, "Let My people leave to worship Me.

2 If you refuse to let them leave, and continue holding them, **3** the power of Adonai will strike your livestock in the field. Your horses, donkeys, camels, cattle, and sheep will die from a very deadly epidemic.

4 Once again Adonai will separate Israel's livestock from Egypt's livestock. Not a single animal belonging to the Israelites will die. **5** Adonai has announced that the plague will begin the very next day." **6** The next day, all the cattle in Egypt began to die, but not a single one of the Israelite animals died. **7** Pharaoh investigated and discovered that not a single one of the Israelites' animals had died. But Pharaoh remained stubborn and still would not let the people leave.

8 Then Adonai said to Moses and Aaron, "Take a handful of ashes and throw it up in the air in front of Pharaoh's eyes. **9** It will spread out like dust all over Egypt, and when it touches a man or a beast, it will cause a rash and boils will break out." **10** So they took some ashes and stood before Pharaoh. Moses threw the ashes up in the air, and they caused boils in people and animals. **11** Even the magicians were too sick to stand before Moses because of the boils, since the boils attacked the magicians as well as every other living thing in Egypt. **12** This time Adonai made Pharaoh even more stubborn. Just as Adonai had predicted, this time too Pharaoh refused to listen to the warning of Moses and Aaron. **13** Adonai told Moses to get up early in the morning and stand before Pharaoh, and say to him in the name of Adonai, "Let My people go, so that they can worship Me.

14 This time, I am going to send a plague against your

whole land. It will infect your leaders and your people, and prove that there is no one as powerful as Me in all the world.

15 I could have killed you and your people with the epidemic. **16** But I let you survive to demonstrate My power to you and to the whole world.

The Plague of Hail   *7ᵗʰ Aliyah*

17 "But now you are still enslaving my people, refusing to let them leave. **18** Tomorrow at this time I will bring a very powerful hailstorm. Never before, since the day it was founded, has Egypt suffered such a hailstorm. **19** Quick! Warn the people to shelter their livestock and everything else you have in the field. Any person or animal who remains outdoors and does not find shelter will be crushed by the hail and will die."

20 Some of the Egyptians believed Adonai, and they brought their slaves and livestock indoors. **21** But those who did not fear Adonai's warning left their slaves and livestock in the field.

22 Now Adonai said to Moses, "Raise your hand toward the sky, and hail will fall over Egypt. It will fall on people and animals and on all the growing things throughout Egypt."

23 So Moses raised his staff toward the sky, and Adonai sent a hailstorm with thunder and lightning. Adonai sent a hailstorm all over the land of Egypt. **24** There was hail, with flashes of lightning. It was the heaviest Egypt had experienced since it was founded. **25** Throughout all Egypt, the hail killed every human and animal that was outdoors. The hail destroyed all the outdoor plants, and smashed every tree in the fields.

26 Only in Goshen, where the Israelites lived, was there no hail.

27 Pharaoh hurriedly summoned Moses and Aaron. He said to them, "This time it is my fault. Adonai is right! I and my people are wrong! **28** Please pray to Adonai for me. There has been enough of this thunder and hail. I will let you leave. You will not be stopped again."

29 Moses said to Pharaoh, "When I leave the city I will raise my hands to Adonai. Then the thunder will stop, and there will be no more hail. By this sign you will understand that the whole world belongs to Adonai.

30 I am aware that you and your subjects still do not fear Adonai. **31** All your flax and barley plants have been destroyed, since the barley was ripe, and the flax was full-grown. **32** But the wheat and spelt seeds have not been destroyed, since they are still in the ground."

Pharoah Remains Stubborn   *Maftir*

33 Moses left Pharaoh and went out of the city. Just as soon as he raised his hands up to Adonai, the thunder and the hail and rain stopped. **34** But when Pharaoh saw that there was no longer any rain, hail, or thunder, he and his officials continued their stubborn behavior. **35** Just as Adonai had predicted, Pharaoh continued to be stubborn and did not let the Israelites leave.

Bo בֹא

GO AND WARN PHARAOH

10 Adonai said to Moses, "Go to Pharaoh! I have made him and his advisers stubborn, so that I will be able to demonstrate my miraculous powers to them. **2** Now you will be able to tell your children and grandchildren how I performed miracles among them and how I proved that I am Adonai."

3 Moses and Aaron went to Pharaoh and said to him in the name of Adonai, "How long will you refuse to submit to Me? Let My people leave to worship Me. **4** If you refuse to let My people leave, tomorrow I will cover Egypt with locusts. **5** They will cover every visible spot of land, so that you will not be able to see the ground, and they will devour everything that remained after the hail. They will eat every tree in the land. **6** They will overrun your palaces and the houses of your leaders. Never did your fathers and your fathers' fathers see so many locusts." With that, Moses turned his back and left Pharaoh.

7 Pharaoh's officials said to him, "How long will you allow the Israelites to be a problem to us? Let the Israelites go and allow them to worship Adonai. Don't you see that Egypt is being ruined?"

8 Moses and Aaron were brought back to Pharaoh. He said, "All right! Go worship Adonai. But I must know exactly who will be going."

9 Moses replied, "Young and old alike will go. We will take our sons and our daughters, our sheep and our cattle. For us it is a festival in honor of Adonai."

10 Pharaoh replied, "You will need Adonai to be with you if you intend to leave with your children! I know that you are looking for trouble. **11** No, I will not permit it! If that's what you really want, only the males may go and worship Adonai." With that, Pharaoh threw them out of the palace.

Locusts and Darkness   *2nd Aliyah*

12 Adonai said to Moses, "Raise your hand toward Egypt to bring the locusts over Egypt. They will eat whatever growing things still remain in the land after the hail."

13 Moses raised his hand over Egypt, and all that day and night Adonai sent an east wind to blow over Egypt. When morning came, the east wind had brought the locusts.

14 The locusts swarmed all over Egypt. It was a terrible plague. In Egyptian history, there had never been such a plague of locusts.

15 The locusts covered the entire surface of the land, making the earth look black. They ate all the plants on the ground and all the fruit on the trees, and anything that had survived the hail. Throughout all of Egypt nothing green remained on the trees and plants.

16 Pharaoh hurriedly called for Moses and Aaron and said, "I have committed a sin against you and Adonai. **17** Forgive me just this one more time. Pray to Adonai, I beg you! Just take this plague away from me!"

18 Moses left Pharaoh and prayed to Adonai. **19** So Adonai sent a very strong west wind, and it carried away the locusts and drowned them in the Sea of Reeds. Not a single locust remained in all of Egypt. **20** But once again, Adonai made Pharaoh stubborn, and he would not allow the Israelites to leave.

21 Adonai said to Moses, "Raise your hands toward the sky, and darkness will cover Egypt. The darkness will be very strong." **22** So Moses raised his hand toward the sky, and there was a deep darkness all over Egypt, which lasted for three days. **23** People could not see each other, and no one left his home for three days. Where the Israelites lived, however, there was light.

Pharaoh's Last Chance   *3rd Aliyah*

24 Once again Pharaoh called for Moses, and said, "Go! Worship Adonai! You can go, and even your children can go with you. Just leave your sheep and cattle behind."

25 Moses replied, "No! You have to provide us with sacrifices and burnt offerings so that we can offer them to Adonai. **26** Our own livestock must also go along with us. Not a single animal can be left behind. We must take them to worship Adonai, since we will not know how to worship Adonai until we get there."

27 Again Adonai made Pharaoh stubborn, and he refused to allow the Israelites to leave. **28** Pharaoh shouted at Moses, "Leave my presence! Don't dare show your face to me again. The moment you appear before me, you will die!"

29 Moses replied, "Just as you say. I will never see your face again."

11 Adonai said to Moses, "There is one more plague that I will send against Pharaoh and Egypt. After that, he will let you leave this place. When he lets you leave, he will actually drive you out of here. **2** Now speak to the people quietly, and let each man request from his friends gold and silver articles. Let every woman make the same request of her friends."

3 The Israelites were respected by the Egyptians. Moses was also admired, both by Pharaoh's officials and the Egyptian people.

Death of the First-born   *4ᵗʰ Aliyah*

4 Moses said to Pharaoh in the name of Adonai, "About midnight I will pass over Egypt. **5** Every first-born in Egypt will die, from the first-born of Pharaoh sitting on his throne, to the first-born of the slave girl. Every first-born animal will also die. **6** There will be a great cry of mourning throughout all Egypt. Never before has there been so much sadness, and never again will it happen. **7** Among the Israelites, however, not even a dog will bark. Then you will know that Adonai has made a miraculous distinction between the Egyptians and the Israelites.

8 Then all your leaders will come and bow down to Me. They will beg, 'Please leave! You and all your followers!' Only then will I leave." Moses left Pharaoh in great anger.

9 Adonai said to Moses, "Pharaoh will still not listen to you, so I will have to perform more miracles in Egypt."

10 Moses and Aaron had performed all these wonders before Pharaoh. Yet because Adonai had made Pharaoh stubborn, he would not allow the Israelites to leave Egypt.

12

Adonai said to Moses and Aaron: **2** "This month (Nisan) shall be the first month of the year to you. **3** Speak to the community of Israel, saying: 'On the tenth of this month, every person must choose a lamb for each family. **4** If the family is too small for a whole lamb, then they and a neighbor can share a lamb together. **5** You must choose a healthy, one-year-old male lamb or goat. **6** Watch over it until the fourteenth day of this month.'

Then, in the evening, the entire community of Israel shall slaughter their sacrifices.

7 They must take the blood and smear it on the two doorposts and the beam above the door of the house where they will eat the sacrifice. **8** You must eat the sacrificial meat during the night, roasted over a fire. Eat the roasted meat as a sandwich with matzah and bitter herbs.

9 Do not eat it raw or boiled in water, but only roasted over a fire, and include all of it. **10** Do not leave anything over until morning. Whatever is left over that night must be burned in fire.

11 You must eat it in your marching clothes, with your shoes on your feet, and your walking staff in your hand, and you must eat it quickly, for it is the Passover offering to Adonai.

12 On that night I will pass over Egypt, and I will strike down every first-born in Egypt, man and beast. I will punish all the gods of Egypt. I alone am Adonai.

13 The blood on the doorposts will be a sign where you are staying. I will see the blood and pass over that home. There will be no deadly plague among the Hebrews when I punish Egypt.

14 This day will be one that you will long remember. You must observe it as a festival to Adonai in every generation, and you must celebrate it as a law forever. **15** You must eat matzot for seven days. On the first day, you must clean your homes and remove all leaven. Whoever eats leaven from the first day until the seventh day will be cut off from the community. **16** The first day and the seventh day shall also be a sacred holiday. No work shall be done on these two days. The only work that you may do is the preparation of food so that everyone will be able to eat.

17 You shall observe the Festival of Matzot, for on this very day I brought your people out of Egypt. In every generation you must carefully observe this festival.

18 From the fourteenth day of the month of Nisan in the evening, until the night of the twenty-first day of the month, you must eat matzot. **19** During these seven days, no leaven shall be found in your homes. If someone eats any leaven during this period, he shall be cut off from the community of Israel. It is a law for the stranger as well as for Israelites. **20** It is forbidden to eat anything leavened. Wherever you live, you must eat matzot."

The First Passover   *5ᵗʰ Aliyah*

21 Moses gathered the leaders of Israel and said to them, "Assemble the people and tell them to choose a lamb for each of their families, for the Passover sacrifice.

22 Also, take a bunch of hyssop plants and dip it into the blood that is in a basin. Smear the blood on the beam of the door and the two doorposts. Remember, none of you is allowed out of the door of your house until morning.

23 Adonai will then pass over and punish Egypt. When He sees the blood above the door and on the two doorposts, Adonai will pass over that door and not let the plague strike your houses.

24 You must observe this custom as a law for you and your descendants forever.

25 When you come to the land that Adonai will give you, you must also keep this custom. **26** When your children ask, 'Why are you observing this custom?' **27** you must answer, 'It is the Passover service to Adonai. When He struck the Egyptians, He passed over the houses of the Israelites in Egypt, and spared our families.' "
The people bowed their heads and worshipped.

28 The Israelites did as Adonai had instructed Moses and Aaron. They did it exactly.

The Final Plague   *6ᵗʰ Aliyah*

29 At the stroke of midnight Adonai killed every first-born in Egypt, from the first-born of Pharaoh, who ruled the country, to the first-born of the prisoner in jail, as well as every first-born animal.

30 Pharaoh, along with all his officials and all the rest of Egypt, stayed up that night. There was much mourning because there was not a single Egyptian house where there were no dead.

31 Pharaoh sent for Moses and Aaron during the night and pleaded, "Get moving! You and the Israelites, get out from among my people! Go! Worship Adonai just as you demanded! **32** Take your flocks and your cattle and leave us. Go! But as you leave, bless me!"

33 The Egyptians also urged the Israelites to hurry and leave Egypt. They kept crying, "If you don't leave us, we will all surely die!"

34 The Hebrews took their unleavened dough, which had not had time to rise. They wrapped the bread bowls of unleavened dough with robes and carried them on their shoulders.

35 The Israelites also did as Moses had suggested. They asked for silver and gold articles and clothing from the Egyptians.

36 Adonai made the Egyptians respect the Israelites, and they gladly granted their requests. In this way the Israelites were paid reparations for their (210) years of slavery in Egypt.

37 That night the Israelites marched from Ra'amses toward Sukkot. There were about 600,000 adults besides the children. **38** Many non-Israelites left with them. There were also many sheep and cattle.

39 When the Israelites stopped, they baked the unleavened dough, which had not risen, into matzah cakes. They had been driven out of Egypt, and there had been no time for the dough to rise, and no time to prepare any other food for the journey.

40 The Israelites had lived in Egypt for 430 years.

41 At the end of the 430 years, the children of Israel left Egypt in broad daylight. **42** The last night in Egypt was the night of freedom in which Adonai saved the Israelites. This event was a night for the Israelites to remember for all generations.

43 Adonai said to Moses and Aaron, "This is the law of the Passover offerings: No foreigner may eat it. **44** If a person purchases a slave and circumcises him, then the slave can eat it. **45** No foreigners or hired workers may eat the Passover sacrifice.

46 The whole lamb must be eaten by a single group at once. Do not take any of its meat out of the house. Do not break any of its bones.

47 The entire community of Israel must celebrate this festival at the same time. **48** When a stranger joins you and wants to celebrate the Passover with you, then each male must be circumcised. Only then may he join in the observance and be counted as if he had been born an Israelite. But no uncircumcised man may eat the sacrifice. **49** This law applies to the native-born Israelite and to the stranger who settles among you."

50 All the Israelites did exactly as Adonai had instructed Moses and Aaron. **51** On that very day, Adonai led the Israelites out of Egypt tribe by tribe.

Remember the Exodus   *7ᵗʰ Aliyah*

13 Adonai spoke to Moses: **2** "Dedicate to Me every first-born among the Israelites. Both man and beast are Mine."

3 Moses said to the people, "Remember this day on

which you left Egypt, the land of slavery, when Adonai brought you out of Egypt with a show of force. Always remember that no leaven may be eaten during this festival.

4 You were freed on this day in the month of Aviv (Nisan).

5 A time will come when Adonai will bring you to the land of the Canaanites, Hittites, Amorites, Hivites, and Jebusites, which he swore to your ancestors that He would give you—a land flowing with milk and honey. There too you will have to observe this festival in this way. **6** For seven days eat matzot, and make the seventh day a festival to Adonai. **7** Since matzot must be eaten for these seven days, no leaven may be seen in your possession. No leaven may be seen in all your territories.

8 On that day, you must explain to your children, 'It is because of what Adonai did for me when I left Egypt.'

9 These words shall be a sign on your arm and a reminder in the center of your head. Adonai's teaching will then be in your mouth: that it was with a show of strength that He brought you out of Egypt.

10 You must observe this law at the same time each year.

11 The time will come when Adonai will have brought you to the land of the Canaanites, which He promised you and your ancestors. **12** There you will also bring to Adonai every first-born. All first-born males belong to Adonai.

13 Every first-born donkey must be bought back with a sheep. If it is not bought back, you must kill it. You must also buy back every first-born among your sons.

If Your Childs Asks   *Maftir*

14 "Your child should later ask, 'Why do you observe this custom?' You must answer him, 'Adonai brought us out of Egypt, the place of slavery, with a show of power. **15** When Pharaoh stubbornly refused to let us leave, Adonai killed all the first-born in Egypt, both man and beast.

That is why we sacrifice to Adonai all the male first-born animals, and buy back all the first-born of our sons.'

16 These words shall also be a reminder on your arm and a sign in the center of your head. We do this because Adonai brought us out of Egypt with a show of strength."

Beshallach בְּשַׁלַּח
THE ISRAELITES LEAVE EGYPT

17 When Pharaoh finally allowed the Hebrews to leave, Adonai did not lead them through the land of the Philistines even though it was the shorter route. Adonai realized that if the people met with armed resistance, they would become discouraged and return to Egypt. **18** Therefore Adonai led the people on a roundabout route, through the desert to the Sea of Reeds. The Israelites were well armed when they left Egypt.

19 Moses remembered and took Joseph's body with him. Joseph had made the Israelites swear, saying, "Adonai will remember you, and then you must bring my body with you out of Egypt."

20 The Israelites marched from Sukkot and camped in Etham, at the edge of the wilderness.

21 By day Adonai guided them with a pillar of cloud. By night a pillar of fire guided them with light. In this way they were able to move forward by day and by night. **22** The pillar of cloud by day and the pillar of fire at night were never out of sight.

14 Adonai spoke to Moses, saying, **2** "Speak to the Israelites and tell them to turn back and march to Pi-hahiroth (Freedom Valley), between Migdal and the sea, before Baal-zephon, meaning Lord of the North. **3** In this way Pharaoh will think that the Israelites are lost and trapped in the wilderness.

4 One last time I will make Pharaoh stubborn, and he will chase after you. I will be victorious over Pharaoh and his entire army, and once again Egypt will realize that I am Adonai." The Israelites did as they had been instructed.

5 When the king of Egypt learned that the Israelites were escaping, Pharaoh and his officials again changed their minds, and said, "Look what we have done. How could we have freed the Israelites from doing our work?"

6 Pharaoh harnessed his chariot and alerted his troops to go with him. **7** He mobilized 600 chariots with armed troops, as well as the rest of the chariot corps of Egypt, with supporting cavalry. **8** Adonai again made Pharaoh, king of Egypt, stubborn, and he pursued the Israelites. Meanwhile, the Israelites were leaving in triumph.

Do Not Be Afraid   *2nd Aliyah*

9 The Egyptians caught up to the Israelites while they were camping by the sea, at Pi-hahiroth opposite Baal-zephon. All of Pharaoh's chariots, cavalry, and infantry were there.

10 As Pharaoh's army approached, the Israelites looked up and saw the Egyptians marching after them, and the Israelites were very frightened.

The Israelites cried out to Adonai. **11** They complained to Moses, "Aren't there enough graves for us in Egypt? Why did you have to bring us out here to die in the wilderness? How could you do such a thing to us, bringing us out of Egypt? **12** Didn't we tell you in Egypt to leave us alone and let us slave for the Egyptians? It would have been better to be slaves in Egypt than to die here in the wilderness!"

13 Moses replied to the people, "Do not be afraid. Be strong, and you will see that Adonai will rescue you. Today you see the Egyptians, but you will never see them again. **14** Adonai will fight your battle, and you will not even lift a finger."

Crossing the Sea of Reeds   *3rd Aliyah*

15 Adonai said to Moses, "Why are you wasting My time by crying to Me? Speak to the Israelites, and tell them to start moving. **16** Raise your staff and stretch your hand over the sea, and you will split the sea, and the Israelites will be able to pass over to dry land.

17 I will make the Egyptians stubborn so that they will chase after you. In this way I will defeat Pharaoh and his entire army, his chariot corps, and his cavalry. **18** When I have defeated Pharaoh, his chariot corps, and his cavalry, then the Egyptians will know that I am Adonai."

19 An angel of Adonai had been in front of the Israelite camp, and now the angel moved behind it. The pillar of cloud shifted from in front of them and now stood behind them. **20** It stood between the Egyptian and Israelite camps. That night there was cloud and darkness, and no one could see. All that night the Egyptians and the Israelites could not see each other.

21 Then Moses raised his hand over the Sea of Reeds. During that whole night, Adonai drove back the sea with a powerful east wind, which drove back the waters till the sea bed became dry land. The waters in the sea were split. **22** The Israelites marched into the dry land in the sea bed. There was a wall of water on their right and a wall of water on their left. **23** The Egyptians chased after the Israelites. All of Pharaoh's horses, chariot corps, and cavalry drove into the middle of the sea. **24** In the morning Adonai struck the Egyptian army with a pillar of fire and cloud. The Egyptian army panicked. **25** The chariot wheels became stuck in the mud of the sea bed and they could hardly move. The Egyptians shouted, "Let us get away from the Israelites, for Adonai is fighting for them against us!"

The Song of Victory   *4ᵗʰ Aliyah*

26 Now Adonai said to Moses, "Raise your hand toward the sea. The walls of water will break and rush back over the Egyptians and drown their chariots and cavalry."

27 Just as the sun rose, Moses raised his hand toward the sea, and the walls of water broke and flooded back to their usual place. The Egyptians tried to escape the rushing waters, but they were drowned in the middle of the sea. **28** The waters rushed back and completely covered the cavalry and chariots. Of all Pharaoh's army that chased after the Israelites into the sea, not a single man remained alive.

29 Meanwhile, the Israelites had marched in the midst of the sea on dry land. There was a wall of water on their right and a wall of water on their left.

30 On that day, Adonai freed the Israelites from Egypt. From the dry land on the other side, the Israelites saw the Egyptians dead in the sea. **31** When the Israelites saw the mighty power that Adonai had displayed against Egypt, they were in awe of Adonai. They believed in Adonai and in his servant Moses.

15 Moses and the Israelites sang this song to Adonai:

"I will sing to Adonai for His great victory,
Horse and rider He has thrown into the sea.
2 Adonai is my strength and my song,
He is my deliverer;
Adonai is mine, I will adore Him.
I will praise the Adonai of my ancestors.
3 Adonai is the Master of war,
Adonai is His name.
4 Pharaoh's chariots and army
He has thrown into the sea;
The best of his officers
Were drowned in the sea.
5 The waters of the deep covered them;
They sank to the bottom
Like a stone.
6 Adonai, Your right hand
Is awesome in power;
Adonai, Your right hand
Crushes the enemy.
7 In triumph
You shattered Your enemies;
You sent forth Your anger;
It burned them like dried straw.
8 At the blast of Your breath
The waters became tall like towers.
Flowing waters stood tall like a wall.
The waters of the deep
Froze in the heart of the sea.
9 The enemy said, 'I will pursue;
I will catch them, I will divide their riches,
I will satisfy my hunger.

I will draw my sword;
My hand will destroy them.'
10 But You made Your wind blow;
The sea drowned them.
They sank like lead
In the mighty waters.
11 Adonai, no one is like You among the powerful.
There is no one so majestic in holiness as You.
You are awesome, doing wonders.
12 You just raised Your right hand,
and the earth swallowed them.
13 With love, You led Your people,
You freed them with might,
You led them to Your holy shrine.
14 Nations heard and trembled;
Terror crippled the Philistines;
15 The leaders of Edom panicked;
The bravest of Moab trembled;
The people of Canaan melted with fear.
16 Fear and terror overcame them
Because of the strength of Your arm.
They were motionless like stone
Till Your people crossed the sea,
Till the people You saved passed over.
17 You will bring them
and plant them on Your mountain,
In the sanctuary of Adonai
Which You have established.
18 Adonai will rule for ever and ever."

19 This song was sung when Pharaoh's army, along with his chariot corps and cavalry, marched into the sea, and Adonai made the sea return and cover them, while the Israelites walked on dry land in the midst of the sea.
20 Aaron's sister, Miriam the prophetess, took a tambourine, and all the women followed her with drums and dancing.

21 Miriam led them in the response:

> "Sing to Adonai
> for His great victory,
> Horse and rider
> He has thrown into the sea."

22 Moses led the Israelites away from the Sea of Reeds, and they marched into the wilderness of Shur. They marched for three days in the wilderness but could not find any water. **23** Finally they came to Marah, but they could not drink any of the water. The water was bitter [*marah*], and that is why the place was called Marah.

24 The people complained to Moses. They cried, "What can we drink?"

25 Then Moses asked Adonai, and He showed him a certain bush; Moses threw it into the water, and the water became drinkable.

It was there at Marah that Adonai gave them rules and laws to test their faith in Him. **26** He said, "If you obey Adonai and do what is right in His sight, carefully obeying all His commandments and keeping all His laws, then I will not afflict you with any of the diseases that I sent on Egypt. I am Adonai who heals you."

The Oasis of Elim   *5ᵗʰ Aliyah*

27 From Marah they marched to Elim, an oasis where there were twelve springs of water and seventy date palms. They camped near the water.

16 From Elim the entire community of Israel marched to the wilderness of Sin, which is between Elim and Sinai. They arrived on the fifteenth of the second month after they had left Egypt.

2 There in the desert, the entire Israelite community began to complain against Moses and Aaron. **3** The Israelites said to them, "We would have been better off if we had died by the hand of Adonai in Egypt! At

least there we could smell pots of meat and stuff ourselves with bread! But you had to bring us into this
desert and starve our whole community to death!'"

4 Then Adonai said to Moses, "I will make bread rain
down for you from the sky. Everyone must go out
and gather just enough for each day. I will test them
to see whether or not they obey My instructions.
5 On Friday, they will have to gather twice as much
as they gather every other day."

6 Moses and Aaron said to the Israelites, "By evening
you will realize that it was Adonai who brought you
out of Egypt; **7** and in the morning, you will see
Adonai's presence. He has heard your complaints,
which are against Him, and not against us."

8 Moses said, "In the evening, Adonai will give you
meat to eat, and in the morning, there will be
enough bread to fill your stomachs. Adonai has
heard your complaints, which are really against Him.
Who are we? Your complaints are not against us, but
against Adonai!"

9 Moses said to Aaron, "Tell the entire Israelite community to assemble before Adonai, for He has heard
their complaints."

10 As Aaron spoke to the Israelite community, they
turned toward the desert and saw Adonai's divine
light shining in the clouds.

Manna and Quail   *6ᵗʰ Aliyah*

11 Adonai spoke to Moses, saying,
12 "I have heard the complaints of the Israelites. Reassure
them and say, 'In the evening you will have meat to eat, and
in the morning you will have your fill of bread. Then you will
know that I am Adonai.' "

13 That evening, a flock of quail flew in and covered the
camp. Then, in the morning, there was a layer of dew around
the camp. **14** When the layer of dew evaporated, there were

tiny balls covering the surface of the desert. It looked like frost on the ground.

15 The Israelites looked at it, and they had no idea what it was. They asked each other, "*Man-hu?*" (What is it?). Moses said to them, "This is the bread that Adonai is giving you to eat.

16 Adonai has instructed that each person is to gather only as much as each person needs. There will be an omer (2 quarts) for each person."

17 When the Israelites did so, some gathered more and some gathered less.

18 But when they measured the manna with an omer, the one who had gathered more did not have any extra, and the one who had gathered less did not have too little. Each one had gathered exactly enough to eat.

19 Moses warned them, "Do not leave any manna over until the morning."

20 Of course some people did not listen to Moses and left a portion for the morning. It became smelly and filled with worms. Moses was angry with those Israelites.

21 Each morning the people gathered as much as they could eat. Then, when the sun became hot, the manna melted.

22 When Friday came, they gathered a double portion of manna, four omers for each person. The leaders of the community were puzzled. They asked Moses, "Why did this happen?"

23 Moses explained, "This is what Adonai has said: 'Tomorrow is a day of rest, Adonai's holy Sabbath. Bake what you want to bake, and cook what you want to cook today. Whatever is left over, carefully set it aside until morning.'"

24 The next morning, as Moses had instructed, they saved the food until Saturday, and it was not smelly, and there were no worms in it.

25 Moses instructed them, "Eat it today, for today is Adonai's Sabbath. Today you will not find any manna in the field.

26 On the six weekdays you are to gather this food, but the seventh day is the Sabbath, and on that day there will not be any manna."

27 Nevertheless, some people went out to gather manna on Saturday, but they did not find anything.

28 Adonai said to Moses, "Say to the Israelites: 'How long will you refuse to observe My commandments and My laws?'

29 They must understand that Adonai has given them the Sabbath, and that is why He sent you food for two days on Friday. On the Sabbath you must all remain at home, and no one is to gather manna on Saturday."

30 And so the Israelites rested on Saturday. **31** The Israelites called the food manna. It looked like coriander seeds, except that it was white, and it tasted like honey bread.

32 Moses said, "This is what Adonai has commanded: Fill an omer measure with the manna as a sacred reminder for your descendants. Then they will be able to see the food that I fed you in the desert when I brought you out of Egypt."

33 Moses said to Aaron, "Take a jar and fill it with two quarts of manna. Set it before Adonai as a sacred reminder for your descendants."

34 Just as Adonai commanded Moses, Aaron later set the jar of manna before the Ark of the Covenant as a sacred reminder.

35 The Israelites ate the manna for forty years, until they came to a fertile land. The Israelites ate manna until they reached the land of Canaan, where there were growing things to eat.

36 An omer (two quarts) is a tenth of an ephah.

Water from the Rock at Horeb   *7ᵗʰ Aliyah*

17 According to Adonai's plan, the entire Israelite community marched from the wilderness of Sin until they reached Rephidim. When they arrived, there was no water for the people to drink. **2** Once again the Israelites complained to Moses. "Give us water to drink!"

Moses asked, "Why are you complaining to me? You are just wearing out Adonai's patience."

3 Because of the lack of water, the people were suffering from thirst, and they began grumbling against Moses. Their leader shouted, "Why did you bring us out of Egypt? Do you want to make me, my children, and my cattle die of thirst?"

4 Moses pleaded, "Adonai, what shall I do with these people? Before long they will stone me!"

5 Adonai said to Moses, "Take the staff with which you struck the Nile and, with the leaders of Israel, march in front of the people. **6** I will stand beside you on the rock at Horeb. Strike the rock, and water will stream out of it for the people to drink." Moses did this in the presence of the leaders of Israel.

7 Moses named the place Massah and Merivah (Testing and Quarreling) because the people had tested and quarreled with Adonai, and because they had asked, "Is Adonai going to take care of us, or is He against us?"

8 Now the army of Amalek came and attacked the Israelites in Rephidim.

9 Moses instructed Joshua, "Select fighters, and prepare them to battle against Amalek. Tomorrow, I will station myself on top of the hill with the staff of Adonai in my hand."

10 Joshua did as Moses had told him. He and his warriors battled Amalek. Meanwhile, Moses, Aaron, and Hur had climbed to the top of the hill.

11 As long as Moses held his hands outstretched, Israel won, but as soon as he let his hands down, the battle turned against Israel.

12 When the hands of Moses became tired, they took a stone and placed it so that he could sit. Aaron and Hur each supported one of Moses' arms so that they remained outstretched until sunset. **13** As a result Joshua was able to defeat Amalek and his allies.

I Will Destroy Amalek   *Maftir*

14 Adonai instructed Moses, "Record this as a permanent reminder, and carefully repeat it to Joshua. I will totally wipe out the memory of Amalek from under the heavens." **15** Moses built an altar there, and he named it Adonai Nissi (Adonai Is My Banner). **16** He said, "Adonai has sworn that in every generation He will battle against Amalek."

Yitro יִתְרוֹ

YITRO, FATHER-IN-LAW OF MOSES

18 Yitro, the sheikh of Midian and Moses' father-in-law, heard about the miracles that Adonai had performed for Moses and the Israelites when He brought them out of Egypt. **2** So Yitro brought Tzipporah, the wife of Moses, and her two sons, who had earlier been sent home. **3** The name of the first son was Gershom, because Moses had declared, "I was a foreigner [*ger*] there [*shom*] in a foreign land." **4** The name of the second son was Eliezer, because "My father's *El* [Elohim] was my helper [*ezer*] and rescued me from Pharaoh's vengeance."

5 Yitro, accompanied by Moses' wife and sons, came to the wilderness, where Moses was camped, near the mountain of Elohim.

6 He sent word to Moses: "I, your father-in-law Yitro, with your wife and your two sons, am on my way to see you."

7 Moses went out to meet his father-in-law and greeted him by bowing and hugging him. They asked about each other's health and went into a tent to talk. **8** Moses told his father-in-law everything that Adonai had done to Pharaoh in Egypt to free Israel, as well as all the problems they had experienced, and how Adonai had saved them from their troubles. **9** Yitro was happy for all the good things Adonai had done for Israel by rescuing them from Egypt. **10** Yitro said, "Blessed be Adonai, who rescued you from the power of Egypt and from Pharaoh. **11** Now I know that Adonai is greater than any other deity. Despite all their schemes, He defeated them." **12** Yitro brought sacrifices to Adonai. Aaron and the leaders of Israel shared the sacrificial meal with Moses' father-in-law in the presence of Adonai.

Moses the Judge   *2nd Aliyah*

13 The next day, as usual, Moses went out to judge the people. They surrounded Moses from morning to evening.

14 When Moses' father-in-law saw that Moses was doing this for the people all by himself, he said, "Why are you the only judge? Why do you sit all by yourself while people crowd around you from morning until evening?"

15 Moses replied to his father-in-law, "The people come to me and ask Adonai's advice. **16** Whenever they have a dispute, they come to me, and I settle the problems between them, and I also teach them Elohim's rules and laws."

17 Moses' father-in-law said to him, "What you are doing is not right. **18** The responsibility will exhaust you and will harm the nation. You are going to wear yourself out. You cannot do it all alone.

19 Now listen to me. Let me give you some advice, and may Elohim be with you. You must continue to be the representative who brings the people's problems to Elohim. **20** Explain the rules and laws to the people. Show them the right path to take, and the rules to follow.

21 But most important, find among the people capable, honest men who hate injustice and fear Adonai. Appoint them as leaders of thousands, leaders of hundreds, leaders of fifties, and leaders of tens.

22 Let them regularly judge the people. Have them bring you all the important cases, but let them judge the minor cases by themselves. In this way, they will share the burden, and make things easier for you. **23** If you follow this advice, and Elohim agrees, then you will be able to survive. The entire nation will be able to reach their goal in peace."

Moses Takes Yitro's Advice   *3rd Aliyah*

24 Moses took his father-in-law's advice and followed all of his suggestions. **25** Moses picked capable people from all the tribes of Israel, and he appointed them as chiefs over the people, leaders of thousands, leaders of hundreds, leaders of fifties, and leaders of tens. **26** They regularly dispensed justice, bringing the difficult cases to Moses, and settling the simple cases by themselves.

27 After a while Moses let his father-in-law return to his home-land in Midian.

A Kingdom of Priests   *4th Aliyah*

19 Exactly three months after the Israelites left Egypt, on the first day of the month (Sivan), they arrived in the wilderness of Sinai. **2** They left Rephidim and entered the wilderness of Sinai, camping in the wilderness, at the base of the mountain.

3 Moses went up to meet Adonai. Adonai called to him from the mountain and said, "This is what you must say to the family of Jacob, the Israelites: **4** 'You witnessed what I did in Egypt, and how I carried you on wings of eagles and brought you to Me. **5** Now, if you will obey Me and keep My covenant, you shall be My special treasure among all the nations of the world. **6** You will be a kingdom of priests and a holy nation to Me.' These are the exact words that you must repeat to the Israelites."

Israel at Sinai   *5th Aliyah*

7 Moses came down the mountain and assembled the leaders of the people and repeated to them everything Adonai had said to him.

8 In one loud voice, all the people answered and said, "Everything that Adonai has spoken, we will do."

Moses reported the Israelites' reply to Adonai.

9 Adonai said to Moses, "I will return to you in a thick cloud, so that all the people can hear when I speak to you. Then they will completely trust you forever."

Then Moses repeated the people's response to Adonai.

10 Adonai said to Moses, "Go to the people, and sanctify them today and tomorrow. Tell them to clean their clothes. **11** Tell them to be ready for the third day, because on that day Adonai will come down upon Mount Sinai, as everyone will see.

12 Set a boundary line for the people, and warn them not to climb the mountain, or even come close. Anyone touching the mountain will die. **13** You will not have to touch him, for he will be stoned or shot by an arrow. Neither man nor beast will be allowed to live. Only when a long blast is sounded on the shofar will they be allowed to climb the mountain."

14 Moses went down to the people from the mountain. He sanctified them, and they purified themselves and their clothing. **15** Moses said to the people, "Prepare yourselves for three days. Do not go near a woman."

16 On the third day, there was thunder and lightning in the morning, and a heavy cloud covered the mountain, and there was a loud shofar blast. All the Israelites trembled. **17** Moses led the people from the camp toward the Divine Presence. They stood frozen at the foot of the mountain.

18 Now Mount Sinai was covered in smoke because of the Presence that had come down on it. Adonai was in the fire, and smoke rose up like the smoke from a furnace. The whole mountain quaked violently. **19** Then there was a loud shofar blast. Moses spoke, and Elohim answered.

The Ten Commandments   *6th Aliyah*

20 Then Adonai came down to the top of Mount Sinai, and He called Moses to climb up to the peak. Moses climbed up. **21** Adonai said to Moses, "Go back and warn the people not to cross the boundary line to see the Divine, because they will die. **22** Even the priests, who usually come near Adonai, must sanctify themselves, or else Adonai will destroy them."

23 Moses protested to Adonai "The people cannot climb Mount Sinai, because You have already warned them to set a boundary line around the mountain and declare it holy."

24 So Adonai said to him, "Go down and return with Aaron. However, the priests and the other people must not cross the boundary line to go up to Adonai. If they do, He will punish them." **25** Moses went down to the people and told them what Adonai had said.

20 Elohim gave the Israelites these Ten Commandments:

The First Commandment

2 I am Adonai, who brought you out of Egypt, from the land of slavery.

The Second Commandment

3 You shall not have any other gods except Me. **4** Do not make any carved statues or pictures of anything in the heavens above, or on the earth below, or in the water below. **5** Do not bow down to such idols or pray to them. I, Adonai, am jealous, and I demand total loyalty. As for My enemies, I will remember the sins of the fathers up to the third and fourth generations. **6** But for those who love Me and keep My commandments, I will show them kindness for thousands of generations.

The Third Commandment

7 Do not misuse the name of Adonai. He will not allow anyone who misuses His name to go unpunished.

The Fourth Commandment

8 Remember to observe the Sabbath and keep it holy. **9** You shall do all your regular work during the six days of the week. **10** But the seventh day is the Sabbath to Adonai, your Lord. Do not do any kind of work. This includes you, your son, your daughter, your slave, your maid, your animal, and the strangers in your country. **11** It was during the six weekdays that Adonai created the cosmos, which includes planet earth, the sea, and everything that is in them, but He rested on the Sabbath. Therefore Adonai blessed the Sabbath and made it holy.

The Fifth Commandment

12 Honor your father and your mother. If you do, you will live long on the land that Adonai is giving you.

The Sixth Commandment

13 You must not murder.

The Seventh Commandment

You must not commit adultery.

The Eighth Commandment

You must not steal.

The Ninth Commandment

You must not act as a false witness against your neighbor.

The Tenth Commandment

14 You must not be jealous of your neighbor's wealth. You must not be jealous of your neighbor's wife, his slave, his maid, his ox, his donkey, or anything belonging to your neighbor.

The Israelites Are Awed   *7ᵗʰ Aliyah*

15 When the Israelites heard the sounds, and saw the flames, and heard the blast of the shofar, and saw the mountain smoking, they trembled with fear and kept their distance. **16** They said to Moses, "You teach us what Adonai said, and we will listen and do. But don't let Adonai speak with us any more, for if He does we will die." **17** Moses assured the people, "Have no fear. Elohim only came to show you His power. From now on you will obey Him and you will not sin."

18 The people kept far away while Moses entered the cloud where Elohim was.

I Will Bless You   *Maftir*

19 Adonai said to Moses: "This is what you must tell the Israelites: You were witnesses that I spoke to you from heaven.

20 Remember, do not make a statue that represents Me. Do not make silver or gold statues for yourselves.

21 Make a simple earthen altar for Me. On it you can sacrifice your burnt offerings and your peace offerings, your sheep and your cattle. Wherever you build a sanctuary, I will come and bless you.

22 When you build a stone altar for Me, do not build it out of stone that has been cut by metal. If you use metal on your altar, it will not be holy. **23** Do not build My altar with steps, for someone might look up and see your nakedness."

Mishpatim מִשְׁפָּטִים
THESE ARE THE LAWS

21 These are the laws that the Israelites must obey.
2 If you buy a Hebrew slave, he shall serve for six years, but in the seventh year he is to be set free without paying for his freedom. **3** If he was unmarried when he entered slavery, he shall leave by himself. However, if he was a married man, his wife must leave with him.

4 But if his master gives him a wife, and she gives birth to sons or daughters, the woman and her children shall remain her master's property. The slave must leave by himself.

5 If the slave on his own says, "I like my master, and my wife and my children; I do not wish to go free," **6** then his master must bring him to court, and stand the slave next to a door or doorpost, and then his master must pierce his earlobe with an awl. Then the slave shall serve his master forever.

7 If a man sells his daughter as a maidservant, she shall not be released the same way as the male servants. **8** If she displeases her master, then he should allow her to be redeemed. Since he is considered to have broken the agreement with her, he does not have the right to sell her to anyone else.

9 If the master chose her as a bride for his son, she must be treated exactly the same as any free girl.

10 Also, if the master marries another wife, he must not reduce her allowance or clothing or shelter rights. **11** If he fails to provide these three things to the slave girl, then she shall be free without any payment.

12 If one person deliberately strikes another and the victim dies, the murderer must be put to death.

13 If he did not deliberately plan to kill his victim, but it happened accidentally, then I will provide a refuge where the killer can find safety.

14 If a person intentionally plots to kill his neighbor, then you must drag him even from My altar to put him to death.

15 Anyone who deliberately harms his father or his mother must be put to death.

16 If someone kidnaps and sells another person, and is found with the victim, then the kidnapper shall be put to death.

17 Whoever insults his father or mother must be put to death.

18 When two people fight, and one hits the other with a stone or with his fist, and the victim does not die but is bedridden, **19** and later gets up and can walk under his own power, then the one who struck him must not be punished. But he must pay for the victim's loss of earning power, and must also pay for his medical expenses.

Injuries and Penalties   *2nd Aliyah*

20 If a man hits his male or female slave with a stick, and the slave dies, the death must be avenged.

21 However, if the slave lives for a day or two, then his death shall not be avenged, because he is his master's property.

22 When two men fight and accidentally harm a pregnant woman and cause her to miscarry, but there is no fatal injury to the woman, then the guilty party must pay a monetary penalty. The woman's husband must sue, and the amount will be determined by the court.

23 However, if the woman is fatally injured, then he must pay full compensation for her life.

24 Compensation must be paid for the loss of an eye, a tooth, a hand, or a foot. **25** Compensation must also be paid for a burn, a wound, or a bruise.

26 If a person strikes his male or female slave in the eye and blinds it, he shall set the slave free in compensation for the loss of his eye.

27 And if he knocks out the tooth of his male or female slave, he must set the slave free in payment for the tooth.

28 If an ox injures a man or woman, and the victim dies, the ox must be stoned to death, and its flesh must not be eaten. The owner of the ox shall not be punished.

29 However, if the ox had a history of hurting people, and the owner was warned and failed to take precautions, and it kills a person, then the ox must be stoned, and its owner, too, must be put to death.

30 As a redemption for his life, an atonement fine can be imposed, and he must pay a redemption for the lost life.

31 The same law also applies if the ox injures a young boy or a young girl.

32 But if the ox injures a male or female slave, its owner must give thirty silver coins to the slave's master, and the bull must be stoned.

33 If a person digs a hole in the ground, or opens a hole, and does not cover it, and an ox or a donkey falls into it, **34** the person responsible for the hole must pay the full value of the animal to its owner, and the dead animal becomes his property.

35 If a person's ox injures the ox of another person, and it dies, they must sell the live ox and share the money received for it. They shall also share the dead animal.

36 But if the ox was known to injure people on previous occasions, and its owner did not control it, he must pay the full price for the dead ox. The dead animal still remains the property of its owner.

37 If a person steals an ox or a sheep and then kills it and sells it, he must be fined five oxen for each stolen ox, and four sheep for each sheep.

22 If a thief is caught in the act of breaking in, and is struck and killed by the owner, it is not considered an act of murder.

2 However, if it is broad daylight when the thief breaks in and is struck and killed, the one who killed the thief is a murderer.

Every thief must make full restitution. If he does not have the means, he must be sold into servitude to pay for what he has stolen.

3 If the stolen animal is found in his possession, and it is an ox, a donkey, or a sheep, he must repay double.

Crimes and Damages   *3rd Aliyah*

4 If a person lets his animal loose so that it grazes in someone else's field, he must pay for the damages to the field or vineyard.

5 If fire breaks out and spreads to weeds, so that it burns stacks of grain, then the one who started the fire must pay for the damages.

6 When a person entrusts money or goods to someone for safekeeping, and they are stolen from the house of that person, then if the thief is caught, the thief must repay double the amount. **7** But if the thief is not found, the owner of the house shall be brought to court and he must swear that he did not steal the property given into his care.

8 In every case in which an ox, a donkey, a sheep, a garment, or anything else is lost, and witnesses testify that it was seen, the claims of both parties must be brought to the court. The guilty person must pay double damages to the other.

9 If one person asks another to watch a donkey, an ox, a sheep, or any other animal, and it dies or is hurt or is stolen, without any eyewitnesses, **10** then the case between the two must be decided by taking an oath to Adonai. If the person watching the animal did not make use of the other's property, the owner must take his word, and the person watching the animal need not pay.

11 However, if it was stolen from the keeper, then he must repay the animal's owner.

12 But if the animal was killed by a wild beast and the keeper can prove it, he need not pay for the dead animal.

13 If a person borrows an animal from another, and it becomes injured or dies while the owner is not with the borrower, then the borrower must make full payment.

14 But if the owner was present with him, then the borrower need not make any payments. If the animal was hired, the loss is guaranteed by the rental price.

15 If a man sleeps with a virgin who is not engaged to anyone, he must pay a dowry and must marry her. **16** If her father refuses to let him marry her, then he must pay the father the usual dowry money for virgins.

17 Do not allow a witch to live.

18 Whoever has sexual relations with an animal must be put to death.

19 Whoever worships any god other than Adonai must be condemned to death.

20 Do not abuse a foreigner or oppress him, for you must remember that you were foreigners in Egypt.

21 Do not abuse a widow or an orphan. **22** If you abuse them, and they cry to Me for help, I will hear their cry.

23 And then I will hear and I will punish you, so that your wives are widowed, and your children are orphaned.

24 When you lend money to the poor among you, do not threaten him for repayment. And do not take interest from him.

25 If you accept your neighbor's garment as security for a loan, you must return it to him before the sun goes down.

26 Remember, this is his only warm covering for his body. How can he sleep without his covering? If he cries out to Me, I will listen, for I am merciful.

Authority and Justice   *4th Aliyah*

27 You must not curse the judge. You must not curse a leader of your people. **28** You must bring your offerings of newly ripened produce and your agricultural offerings on time. You shall redeem the first-born of your sons.

29 You must also redeem your first-born ox and sheep. It must remain with its mother for seven days, but on the eighth day you must give it to Me.

30 You are My holy people. You must not eat the flesh of a torn animal killed in the field by a wild beast. Let the dogs eat it.

23

You must not listen to false rumors.

You must not cooperate with a wicked person and become a false witness.

2 You must not join a mob to do evil.

You must not lie in court to deny justice.

A court case must be decided by a majority.

3 Do not slant your testimony to favor the poor man in his lawsuit.

4 If you come across your enemy's ox or donkey that has wandered away, you must bring it back to him.

5 If you see an overloaded donkey that belongs to someone who hates you, you may not want to help him unload it, but nevertheless you must do so.

Keep Away from Evil   *5ᵗʰ Aliyah*

6 You are not permitted to treat someone unfairly in a lawsuit simply because he is poor.

7 Keep far away from accusing anyone falsely.

Do not kill a person who is innocent or one who has been found innocent by a court.

But take care not to allow a guilty person to escape punishment.

8 You shall not accept bribes. Bribery blinds your fairness and destroys the words of an honest person.

9 You shall not oppress a foreigner. You know how it feels to be a foreigner, for you were foreigners in the land of Egypt.

10 Plant your land for six years and harvest its crops. **11** But during the seventh year, let the land rest. This will allow the poor among you to glean from your fields, and whatever is left over can be eaten by the wild animals. The same rule applies to your vineyard and your olive grove.

12 Work on the six weekdays, but you must stop and rest on Saturday. In this way your donkey and ox will be able to rest, and your servants and the foreigner will also be reinvigorated.

13 Be sure to obey all My instructions. Do not mention the name of any other god. Their names must never pass your lips.

14 Three times each year bring a sacrifice to Me.

15 Observe the Festival of Matzot (Passover). You must eat matzot for seven days, as I commanded you, during the set time in the month of Aviv, because this was the time when you left Egypt.

You must not come to me empty-handed without a sacrifice!

16 You must observe the Festival of Harvest (Shavuot) and bring Me the first fruits of what you have planted in the field.

Also observe the Festival of Ingathering (Sukkot) at the end of the year, when you gather what you have grown from the field.

17 Three times each year, every man in Israel must appear before Adonai, Master of the universe!

18 Do not offer the blood of My Passover offering in the presence of matzot.

Do not keep the fat of the festival sacrifice to remain overnight until morning.

19 Bring the best of your first fruits to the House of Adonai. You must not cook your goat in its mother's milk.

My Angel Will Protect You   *6th Aliyah*

20 Be aware that I will send an angel to safeguard you on your journey and bring you to the land I have prepared for you.

21 Be respectful to the angel and listen to his advice.

Do not defy him, for he is My messenger. He will not forgive your disobedience.

22 But if you listen to him and do everything I say, then I will be an enemy to your enemies.

23 My angel will go before you and lead you to the lands of the Amorites, Hittites, Perizzites, Canaanites, Hivites, and Jebusites, and I will destroy them. **24** You must not bow down to their gods and worship them. You must not follow the evil customs of these nations. You must smash their idols and destroy their sacred pillars.

25 You must worship Adonai, and He will bless you with food and with drink. I will remove sickness from among you.

In the Land of Israel

26 No woman in your land will suffer miscarriages or remain childless. I will give you long, healthy lives.

27 I will confuse the enemies who stand in your path, and they will be terrified of Me; I will make your enemies turn and run away in a panic.

28 I will send deadly hornets ahead of you to drive out the Hivites, Canaanites, and Hittites from your path.

29 I will not drive them out in just one year; otherwise the land will be deserted and the wild animals will become too numerous for you to control. **30** Little by little I will drive out the inhabitants and give you the opportunity to increase in numbers and fully occupy the land.

31 I will establish your borders from the Sea of Reeds to the Mediterranean Sea, from the desert to the river. I will defeat the inhabitants, and you will drive them before you.

32 Do not make a peace treaty with these nations or with their gods. **33** Do not allow them to live in your land, because they will then make you sin against Me. You may even end up worshipping their gods, and it will be a disaster for you.

24 Adonai said to Moses, "Come up to Me along with Aaron, Nadab, and Avihu, and seventy of the leaders of Israel. All of you must worship at a distance. **2** Only Moses shall approach Me. The others must not come close, and the people are not allowed to go up to the mountain with him."

3 Moses came and repeated to the people all of Adonai's teachings and laws. The Israelites responded with a single voice: "We will treasure and obey every word that Adonai has spoken."

4 Then Moses wrote down all of Adonai's words. He rose up early the next morning and built an altar at the foot of the mountain, along with twelve stone pillars, one for each of the twelve tribes of Israel. **5** He sent the first-born young men from among the Israelites, and they sacrificed oxen as burnt offerings and peace offerings to Adonai.

6 Moses took half the blood of these offerings and poured it into large bowls; the other half he sprinkled on the altar.

7 He took the Book of the Covenant and read it to the people. They replied, "We will faithfully do and obey all that Adonai has commanded."

8 Then Moses took the rest of the blood and sprinkled it on the people. He said, "This blood confirms the covenant that Adonai has made with you regarding all of these laws."

9 Moses, along with Aaron, Nadav and Avihu, and the seventy leaders, went up the mountain, **10** and there they saw a vision of Adonai, and under his feet there was a floor decorated with sapphire jewels as clear as the heavenly skies. **11** Adonai did not harm the leaders of the Israelites. They had a vision of Elohim, and they celebrated and they ate and drank.

12 Adonai said to Moses, "Come up to Me, to the mountaintop, and wait there until I give you the stone tablets, the Torah and the commandments that I have written for you to teach the people."

13 Moses and his assistant, Joshua, set out and ascended the Mountain of Adonai. **14** Moses said to the leaders, "Wait for us here until we return to you. Aaron and Hur will remain with you. Anyone who has a problem can consult with them."

On Top of Mount Sinai   *Maftir*

15 As soon as Moses reached the mountaintop, a cloud covered the mountain. **16** Adonai's glorious presence rested on Mount Sinai, and for six days it was covered by the cloud. On the seventh day, Adonai called to Moses from the midst of the cloud.

17 To the Israelites, the appearance of Adonai on the mountaintop was like a brilliant flame. **18** Moses climbed up to the mountaintop and disappeared into the cloud, and Moses remained on the mountain for forty days and forty nights.

Terumah תְּרוּמָה
OFFERINGS FOR THE TEMPLE

25 Adonai spoke to Moses, saying, **2** Speak to the Israelites, and have each one bring Me a gift. Accept the gifts from everyone who wants to give willingly. **3** The gifts that you accept from them shall consist of the following: gold, silver, copper, **4** blue wool, dark red wool, and crimson wool, linen, goats' hair, **5** tanned rams' skins, dyed blue sealskins, acacia wood, **6** olive oil for the lamp, spices for the anointing oil and the sweet-smelling incense, **7** and onyxes and other precious stones for the ephod and breastplate.

8 The Israelites shall make Me a Tabernacle in which I will live among them.

9 Make the Tabernacle and all its furnishings according to the construction plan that I am showing you.

10 Make an ark of acacia wood, 3.5 feet long, 2.25 feet wide, and 2.25 feet high. **11** Cover it with a layer of pure gold on the inside and the outside, and make a gold molding all around the top.

12 Cast four gold rings for the ark, and attach them on its four corners, and attach two rings on one side, and attach two on the other side. **13** Make two carrying poles of acacia wood and coat them with a layer of gold. **14** Fit the poles into the rings on the sides of the ark, so that the ark can be carried with them. **15** The poles must remain in the rings and not be removed.

16 Inside the ark place the engraved tablets with the Ten Commandments that I will give you!

Make the Ark   *2ⁿᵈ Aliyah*

17 Make a golden cover for the ark out of pure gold. Make it 3.75 feet long and 2.25 feet wide. **18** Make two golden cherubs, hammering them out from one piece of gold, and place them on the two ends of the cover.

19 Put one cherub on one end, and one cherub on the other. Make the cherubs from the same piece of gold as the cover on its two ends. **20** The cherubs shall spread their wings outward so that their wings shield the cover. The cherubs shall face one another and downward toward the cover of the ark.

21 Set the ark cover on top of the ark after you put the Ten Commandments that I will give you into the ark.

22 There I will meet with you and speak to you from the ark cover, from between the two cherubs that are on the ark. This is how I will pass along My instructions for the Israelites.

23 Make a table out of acacia wood, 3 feet long, 1.5 feet wide, and 2.25 feet high. **24** Cover it with pure gold, and make a gold rim all around it. **25** Make a 3-inch-wide rim around the edge of the table, and put a gold molding on the rim.

26 Make four gold rings for the table, and set the rings on the four corners next to the four legs. **27** The rings shall be close to the frame; they will hold the poles with which the table is carried. **28** Make the poles of acacia wood, and cover them with a layer of gold. The poles will be used to carry the table.

29 For the table make bread pans, ladles, incense bowls, and gold pitchers for pouring the liquid offerings.

30 The showbread shall be placed before Me at all times on this table.

Make a Menorah   *3rd Aliyah*

31 Make a menorah out of pure gold. The entire menorah— its base, stem, decorative cups, buds, and flowers—must be hammered out of a single piece of gold.

32 Six branches shall extend from its sides, three branches of the menorah on one side and three branches on the other side. **33** Each branch shall hold one embossed cup, as well as a bud and a flower. All six branches extending from the menorah's stem must be the same.

34 The center of the menorah shall be decorated with four embossed cups along with its buds and flowers. **35** A bud shall serve as a base for each pair of branches extending from the center. All six branches extending from the center must be the same. **36** The buds and branches must all be a part of the menorah. They shall all be hammered out of a single piece of pure gold.

37 Make seven lamps for the menorah. The lamps are to be attached in such a way as to shine toward the center of the menorah. **38** The tongs and the ash shovels for the menorah shall also be made out of pure gold.

39 The menorah, including all its parts, will require an ingot of pure gold weighing 75 pounds.

40 Carefully observe the model that you will be shown on the mountain, and make the menorah exactly the same.

26 Construct the Tabernacle out of ten large tapestries woven of fine linen with blue, purple, and scarlet wool, with a pattern of cherubs woven into them. **2** Each of the ten hanging tapestries shall be 42 feet long and 6 feet wide. Make each tapestry the exact same size. **3** The first five tapestries shall be sewn together, and the second five tapestries shall also be sewn together. **4** Sew loops of blue wool at the edge of the last tapestry of the first group. Do the same on the edge of the last tapestry of the second group. **5** Sew fifty loops on the edge of one tapestry, and fifty loops on the edge of the tapestry in the second group. The two sets of loops shall be made so that the loops are exactly opposite one another.

6 Make fifty golden fasteners: The fasteners will join together the two groups of tapestries so that the Tabernacle will be one piece.

7 Weave goats' wool into sheets to cover the roof of the Tabernacle. Weave eleven such sheets. **8** Each sheet shall be 45 feet long and 6 feet wide. Make sure that all eleven sheets are exactly the same size. **9** Sew together the first five sheets, and sew together the remaining six sheets. Half of the sixth sheet shall hang over the front of the Tabernacle.

10 Sew fifty loops on the edge of the last sheet of the first group, and sew fifty loops on the edge of the last sheet of the second group. **11** Make fifty copper fasteners. Put the fasteners in the loops, and join the sheets together, making the Tabernacle into one piece. **12** Hang the remaining extra half of this sheet over the back of the Tabernacle.

13 The extra 18 inches on both sides of the tent will hang down over the sides of the tapestries of the Tabernacle to cover them on both sides.

14 Make the roof for the tent out of tanned rams' skins. Above the rams' skins add the tanned waterproof blue sealskins.

Make the Frames   *4ᵗʰ Aliyah*

15 Out of acacia wood make upright frames for the Tabernacle. **16** Each frame shall be 15 feet long and 2.25 feet wide.

17 Each frame shall have two matching square pegs carved out at the bottom. All the frames for the Tabernacle must be made exactly the same way.

18 Make twenty frames for the southern side of the Tabernacle. **19** Set forty silver bases under the twenty frames—two bases under each frame, one for each peg.

20 For the northern side of the Tabernacle, set the twenty frames **21** and the forty silver bases with two sockets under each and every frame.

22 Make six frames for the western side of the Tabernacle, **23** and place an extra frame at the corners. All the frames must be exactly next to each other on the bottom. **24** Every pair must be joined together evenly on top with a square ring making a single unit. This shall also be done with the two frames at the two corners.

25 On the western side there will be a total of eight frames and sixteen silver bases, two bases under each and every frame.

26 Make crossbars out of acacia wood. There shall be five for the frames of the first side of the Tabernacle to the south.

27 There shall also be five for the frames of the second side to the north, and five for the frames of the Tabernacle on the western wall. **28** The center crossbar shall go through the middle of the frames, from one end of the Tabernacle to the other. **29** Cover the frames with a layer of gold. Also make gold rings on the frames to hold the crossbars. The crossbars shall also be covered with a layer of gold.

30 You will then be ready to set up the Tabernacle exactly as you were shown on the mountain.

The Partition   *5ᵗʰ Aliyah*

31 Weave a cloth partition out of blue, purple, and scarlet wool, woven together with fine linen. Cherubs shall be woven into it so that they can be seen on both sides. **32** Hang it on four gold-covered acacia pillars fitted with gold hooks. The pillars shall be set in four silver sockets.

33 Place the cloth partition directly under the fastenings holding the tapestries together.

In the space behind this curtain you will place the ark. The curtain will serve as a partition between the sanctuary and the Holy of Holies. **34** Put the cover on the ark in the Holy of Holies.

35 Place the table outside the curtain, near the northern wall of the Tabernacle. The menorah shall be opposite the table, near the southern wall of the Tabernacle.

36 Weave a screen for the entrance of the tent out of blue, purple, and scarlet wool, and twined linen. It shall be embroidered work. **37** Make five acacia pillars to hold the screen. Cover the pillars with a layer of gold and attach golden hooks to them. Cast five copper bases for the pillars.

The Altar   *6ᵗʰ Aliyah*

27 Build the altar out of acacia wood. The altar shall be square, 7.5 feet by 7.5 feet, and 4.35 feet tall. **2** Make horns on all four sides of the altar. Then cover the altar with a layer of copper.

3 Make pails to remove the ashes, as well as shovels,

basins, hooks, and fire pans for the altar. All these altar instruments must be made of copper.

4 Make a grating out of copper net to go around the altar. Fasten four copper rings on the four corners of the grating. **5** Put the grating below the decorative border of the altar, extending downward until the middle of the altar.

6 Make carrying poles for the altar from acacia wood covered with a layer of copper. **7** Insert the poles into the rings so that the poles will be secured on both sides of the altar when it is carried.

8 Make the hollow altar out of boards. Make it exactly like the model you were shown on the mountain.

Make the Enclosure   *7ᵗʰ Aliyah*

9 Make the enclosure for the Tabernacle in this manner: On the southern side will be hangings made of woven linen. It shall be 150 feet long **10** and shall have twenty pillars and twenty copper bases. The hooks and clasps for the pillars shall be made of silver. **11** The same shall be done on the northern side. The curtain hangings shall be 150 feet long, with twenty pillars and twenty copper bases, with silver hooks and clasps for the pillars. **12** The width of the curtain hangings at the western end of the enclosure will be 75 feet, and it shall have ten pillars and ten bases.

13 The width of the enclosure at its eastern end shall also be 75 feet. **14** The curtains on one side of the entrance shall be 22 feet long, with three pillars and three bases. **15** On the other side, the curtain shall also be 22 feet long, with three pillars and three bases.

16 The entrance of the courtyard shall be covered with a 30-foot embroidered drape made of blue, purple, and scarlet wool together with woven linen. It shall have four pillars and four bases.

The Courtyard   *Maftir*

17 All the pillars of the courtyard will have silver rings, silver clasps, and copper bases.

18 The courtyard shall be 150 feet long and 75 feet wide. The pillars holding the hangings of woven linen shall be 7.5 feet high, and their bases shall be made of copper.

19 All the tools used to make the Tabernacle shall be made out of copper. The pegs for the Tabernacle and all the pegs for the courtyard shall also be made of copper.

Tetzaveh תְּצַוֶּה
INSTRUCT THE ISRAELITES

20 Moses, you must instruct the Israelites to bring clear illuminating oil, made from crushed olives, to keep the menorah constantly burning. **21** Aaron and his sons shall care for the burning lamps from evening until morning in the presence of Adonai, in the Meeting Tent, outside the cloth partition that conceals the ark. It is a permanent rule for all time that this oil shall be given by the Israelites.

28 Ordain your brother Aaron and his sons Nadav, Avihu, Eleazar, and Ithamar from among the Israelites, and bring them close to you so that Aaron and his sons can serve Me as priests.

2 Make sacred garments that will add dignity and honor for your brother Aaron. **3** Find talented weavers and tailors to make Aaron's garments. These special garments will be used to ordain Aaron and make him a priest to serve Me.

4 These are the garments that they shall make: a breastplate, an ephod, a robe, a knitted tunic, a headdress, and a sash. They will be designed as sacred garments for Aaron and his sons so that they will be able to officiate as priests before Me.

5 The skilled workers shall embroider the gold thread, the blue, purple, and scarlet wool, and the fine linen. **6** The embroiderer shall make the ephod out of gold thread, blue, purple, and scarlet wool, together with fine twined linen. **7** Make two attached shoulder pieces at its two corners, and attach them to the ephod. **8** Make the sash the same way as the ephod. Weave it out of gold thread, blue, purple, and scarlet wool, and fine linen.

9 Take two onyx stones and engrave them with the names of Israel's sons. **10** There shall be six names on one stone, and six names on the second stone, inscribed in the order of their birth. **11** The names of

Israel's sons shall be inscribed by a skilled engraver, like the engraving on a signet ring.

Mount these stones in gold settings. **12** Attach the two stones on the two shoulder pieces of the ephod as a reminder of Israel's history. Aaron shall carry the engraved names on his two shoulders as a remembrance before Adonai.

Make a Judgment Breastplate   *2nd Aliyah*

13 Make gold settings. **14** Also make matched chains of pure gold, braided like cord. Attach the braided chains to the settings on the shoulders of the ephod.

15 Make a judgment breastplate. It shall be embroidered like the ephod. Make it out of gold thread and blue, purple, and scarlet wool, and fine linen.

16 When folded over, it shall be 9 inches long and 9 inches wide.

17 Set it with four rows of mounted, precious jewels.

The first of these rows shall contain a ruby, an emerald, and a topaz.

18 The second row: carnelian, sapphire, and a diamond.

19 The third row: amber, agate, and jasper.

20 The fourth row: beryl, onyx, and amethyst.

All of these stones shall be mounted in gold settings.

21 The twelve stones shall contain the names of the twelve sons of Israel. Each one's name shall be engraved as on a signet ring, to represent one of the twelve tribes.

22 For the breastplate make matched chains out of pure gold, braided like cords. **23** Make two gold rings for the breastplate, and attach them to the two upper corners of the breastplate.

24 Attach the two gold braids to the two rings on the two corners of the breastplate.

25 Attach the two chains on the two corners to the two settings; then attach them to the two shoulder pieces of the ephod, toward the front.

26 Make two gold rings, and attach them to the two lower corners of the breastplate, toward the inside of the ephod. **27** Make another two gold rings, and attach them to the bottoms of the two shoulder pieces, toward the front, above the ephod's sash. **28** Attach the lower rings of the breastplate to the lower rings of the ephod with a cord of blue wool.

29 In this way, when Aaron comes into the sanctuary, he will carry the names of Israel's sons on the judgment breastplate over his heart. It will be a constant reminder to Adonai of His people.

30 Place the Urim and Thumim in the judgment breastplate, over Aaron's heart, whenever Aaron enters into the presence of Adonai. He must always carry the judgment-making device for the Israelites at all times when he enters Adonai's presence.

Make a Robe   *3ʳᵈ Aliyah*

31 Make the robe that is worn under the ephod out of blue wool. **32** It shall have an opening for the head in the middle, and this opening shall have a woven border all around it, so that it does not tear. **33** Fasten pomegranates made of blue, purple, and scarlet wool on the bottom of the robe, all along its lower border, and put gold bells in between the pomegranates. **34** There shall be a gold bell and a pomegranate, a gold bell and a pomegranate, all around the lower edge of the robe. **35** Aaron is to wear this robe whenever he officiates at a divine service. The tinkling of the bells will be heard when he enters Adonai's sanctuary, and when he goes out, to ensure that he does not die.

36 Make a medallion of pure gold, and engrave on it, in the same manner as a signet ring, the words "Holy to Adonai." **37** Attach a cord of blue wool to it, so that it can be worn at the front of the headdress.

38 This medallion shall be worn on Aaron's forehead. Thus Aaron will carry the medallion that removes sin from the sacred offerings that the Israelites bring as holy gifts. It shall always be on Aaron's forehead when he makes the offerings of the Israelites acceptable before Adonai.

39 Weave the tunic out of linen. Also make the headdress and the embroidered sash out of linen.

40 Make tunics and sashes for Aaron's sons. Also make digni-
fied and beautiful headdresses for them.

41 Clothe Aaron and his sons in these garments. Then anoint
and ordain them to serve as priests before Me.

42 Make linen undergarments for them, reaching from their
hips to their thighs.

43 Aaron and his sons must wear all these garments whenever
they enter the Meeting Tent or offer sacrifices on the altar, in
the sanctuary; otherwise they will have committed a sin and
they will die. For all time, this shall be a law for Aaron and his
descendants after him.

Ordain Aaron and His Sons   *4th Aliyah*

29 Moses, this is what you must do to ordain Aaron and
his sons as priests to Me.

Take a young bull, two perfect rams, **2** loaves of
unleavened bread, unleavened loaves mixed with
olive oil, and flat matzot brushed with olive oil. All
the loaves must be made of fine wheat flour.

3 Place all the loaves in a basket, and present them
in the basket along with the young bull and the two
rams.

4 Bring Aaron and his sons to the door of the
Meeting Tent, and cleanse them with water.

5 Clothe Aaron in the tunic, the ephod's robe, the
ephod, and the breastplate, and bind him with the
ephod's sash.

6 Then place the headdress on Aaron's head, and
attach the sacred medallion to the headdress.

7 Take the holy anointing oil, and pour a little on
Aaron's head. **8** Next, clothe Aaron's sons in their
linen tunics, **9** sashes, and headdresses.

You shall ordain Aaron and his sons as priests, and
their descendants shall be priests forever.

10 Bring the young bull before the Meeting Tent, and
have Aaron and his sons place their hands on the
bull's head.

11 Then slaughter the bull at the door of the Meeting

Tent. **12** With your finger, smear some of the bull's blood onto the horns of the altar. Pour the remaining blood at the base of the altar.

13 Remove all the organs of the bull and burn them on the altar.

14 Burn the bull's flesh, outside the camp, as a sin offering.

15 Have Aaron and his sons place their hands on the head of the first ram. **16** Then slaughter the ram, and sprinkle its blood on all sides of the altar. **17** Cut the ram into pieces and cleanse the internal organs and legs. Place them near the head and the other body parts. **18** Burn all the parts of the ram on the altar as a burnt offering to Adonai. This offering will be a sign of faith in Adonai.

The Wave Offering   *5ᵗʰ Aliyah*

19 Take the second ram, and have Aaron and his sons place their hands on its head. **20** Slaughter the ram, and place a drop of its blood on the right earlobes of Aaron and his sons, as well as on their right thumbs and right big toes. Sprinkle the remaining blood on all sides of the altar.

21 Collect the blood that is on the altar, and together with the anointing oil, sprinkle it on the garments of Aaron and his sons. This will ordain Aaron and his sons and their garments.

22 Burn the organs of the second ram, as an ordination offering.

23 Take one flat unleavened loaf of bread, one loaf of oil bread, and one flat cake from the basket of unleavened bread that is before Adonai.

24 Put all these items into the hands of Aaron and his sons, and have them offer them as a wave offering before Adonai.

25 Then take these items and burn them on the altar as a fragrant burnt offering to Adonai. This offering will be a sign of faith in Adonai.

26 Remove the breast of Aaron's dedication ram, and wave it before Adonai as a wave offering. Moses, afterwards you may keep that portion for yourself.

27 Dedicate the breast that was offered as a wave offering and the hind leg of the wave offering from the ram of ordination. **28** It shall be a law for all times that the breast and the thigh shall be a gift offering for Aaron and his sons from the Israelites, taken from their peace offerings to Adonai.

29 Aaron's sacred garments shall be preserved and passed down to his descendants so they can be ordained in them.

30 The descendant who takes Aaron's place in the Meeting Tent must first put on these garments for seven consecutive days before performing the divine service in the inner sanctuary.

31 Take the rest of the dedication ram and cook its flesh in a sacred area. **32** Then Aaron and his sons shall eat the rams' meat and the bread from the basket near the door of the Meeting Tent. **33** They are the only ones permitted to eat the meat and bread used to make atonement in the dedication ceremony. These offerings are sacred and must not be eaten by nonpriests. **34** You must burn any meat or bread of the dedication offering that is left over until morning. Since it is holy, it must not be eaten.

35 Do exactly as I have instructed you to ordain Aaron and his sons. The ordination ceremony shall take seven days.

36 Each day you shall sacrifice a young bull as a sin offering to make atonement. Afterwards you shall purify the altar by sprinkling it with oil. **37** For seven days, you shall purify the altar and sanctify it, making the altar very holy. Anyone who touches the altar will be sanctified.

The Sacrifices   *6ᵗʰ Aliyah*

38 This is what you must sacrifice on the altar:

Sacrifice two lambs each day. **39** The first lamb shall be sacrificed in the morning, and the second lamb in the late afternoon.

40 Offer two quarts of fine flour mixed with one quart of olive oil, and a liquid offering of wine, with the first lamb. **41** In the late afternoon, sacrifice the second lamb along with a meal offering and a liquid offering like the one offered in the morning. It shall be a fragrance offering to Adonai. **42** There shall be a daily burnt offering throughout the generations. It shall be offered to Adonai at the entrance of the Meeting Tent, the place where I will meet with the people and also speak to you. **43** It is there that I will meet with the Israelites, and the Tabernacle will be sanctified by My presence. **44** I will sanctify the Meeting Tent and the altar, and I will also sanctify Aaron and his sons, so that they will become priests and serve Me. **45** I will live among the Israelites. **46** They will know that I, Adonai, liberated them from Egypt so that I could live among them. I am Adonai.

The Incense Altar
7th Aliyah

30 Make an altar of acacia wood on which to burn incense.

2 Make it square, 18 inches long and 18 inches wide, and 36 inches tall, with horns at the corners. **3** Cover it with a layer of pure gold, on its top, its sides all around, and its horns. Make a gold molding all around the altar.

4 Attach two gold rings under the altar's molding on its two opposite sides. These rings will hold the carrying poles.

5 Make the carrying poles from acacia wood and cover them with a layer of gold.

6 Set the incense altar in front of the cloth curtain concealing the ark—before the cloth curtain where I will meet with you.

7 Each morning Aaron will burn incense on this altar when he cleans the lamps.

The Atonement Sacrifices
Maftir

8 Aaron shall also burn incense in the evening when he lights the lamps. In every generation, at all times, there must be incense before Adonai.

9 Do not burn any foreign incense on it. And do not offer any animal sacrifice, meal offering, or liquid offering on it.

10 Once each year Aaron shall sanctify the horns of the altar. Once each year, throughout the generations, he shall sanctify the altar with the blood of the sin sacrifice. This altar is the most holy to Adonai.

Ki Tissa כִּי תִשָּׂא
TAKE A CENSUS

11 Adonai spoke to Moses, saying:

12 Whenever you take a census of the Israelites, each one that is counted shall donate a ransom offering to Adonai for his life, so that they will not be stricken by the plague when they are counted.

13 Every person included in the census must pay a half-shekel (one-fifth of an ounce of silver), as measured by the sanctuary weight standard, whereby a shekel is twenty gerahs. The half-shekel must be given as a donation to Adonai.

14 Every man over twenty years of age shall be included in the census and must give this donation to Adonai. **15** The rich may not give more than a half-shekel, and the poor may not give less. It is an offering to Adonai to atone for your lives.

16 You will take this atonement money from the Israelites and use it for constructing the Meeting Tent. It will be a reminder for the Israelites before Adonai to atone for their lives.

17 Adonai spoke to Moses, saying:

18 Make a copper washbasin with a copper base. Put it between the altar and the Meeting Tent, and fill it with water for cleansing.

19 Aaron and his sons must cleanse their hands and feet in this washbasin. **20** They must cleanse themselves with the water in the washbasin before entering the Meeting Tent or approaching the altar to perform a divine service to Adonai. **21** They must first cleanse their hands and feet, or they will die. This shall be a law for Aaron and his descendants for all time, throughout the generations.

22 Adonai spoke to Moses, saying, **23** You must collect the following spices: 12 pounds of pure myrrh, 6 pounds of cinnamon and 6 pounds of aromatic cane, **24** and 12 pounds of cassia, all measured by the sanctuary weight standard along with a gallon of olive oil.

25 Blend it into the sacred anointing oil. It must be blended by a skilled perfumer into the sacred anointing oil.

26 Then use it to anoint the Meeting Tent, the ark, **27** the table and all its utensils, the menorah and its utensils, the incense altar, **28** the sacrificial altar and all its utensils, the washbasin and its base. **29** You will sanctify them, making them holy, so that anything touching them also becomes holy. **30** You must also anoint Aaron and his sons, ordaining them as priests to serve Me.

31 And you shall speak to the Israelites and tell them, "This shall be the sacred ordaining oil to serve Me for all generations. **32** Do not pour it on the skin of any unauthorized person, and do not make any of it for your own use. It is holy, and it must remain sacred. **33** If a person blends the same mixture, or puts it on an ordinary person, he shall be cut off from his people."

34 Adonai instructed Moses: Take aromatic spices, such as balsam, onycha, galbanum, and an equal amount of frankincense. **35** Let a master perfumer blend the mixture into a holy incense. **36** Grind it finely, and place it before the ark in the Meeting Tent where I meet with you. This shall be holy to you.

37 Do not blend the same incense for your own personal use. It must remain sacred to Adonai. **38** If a person blends it to enjoy its fragrance, he shall be cut off from his people.

31 Adonai spoke to Moses, saying: **2** I have chosen Betzalel son of Uri, son of Hur, of the tribe of Judah. **3** I have filled him with a special spirit, with wisdom, understanding, and knowledge, and with skills to perform all types of craftsmanship. **4** He will be able to create plans as well as work in gold, silver, and copper, **5** cut stones to be set, carve wood, and do other work.

6 As his assistant I have assigned Oholiav son of Achisamakh of the tribe of Dan. Besides this, I have also granted wisdom to every talented Israelite.

They will construct everything that I have ordered: **7** the Meeting Tent, the ark, the ark cover to go on it, all the utensils for the tent, **8** the table and its utensils, the pure gold menorah and all its utensils, the incense altar, **9** the sacrificial altar and all its utensils, the washbasin and its base, **10** the packing cloths, the sacred garments for Aaron the priest, the garments that his sons wear to serve as priests, **11** the anointing oil, and the incense for the sanctuary. Now they will have the skills to follow all My instructions. **12** Adonai instructed Moses **13** to speak to the Israelites and say to them:

You must observe My Sabbaths. This is a sign between Me and you throughout the generations, to make you realize that I, Adonai, have made you holy. **14** Therefore observe the Sabbath as something sacred. Anyone who does not observe the Sabbath shall be cut off from his people, and therefore anyone violating the Sabbath shall be put to death. **15** Do your work during the six weekdays, but observe the Sabbath as holy to Adonai. Whoever works on the Sabbath shall be put to death.

16 The Israelites shall observe the Sabbath eternally throughout the generations. **17** It is a sign between Me and the Israelites that during the six weekdays Adonai created planet Earth and the rest of the universe, but on the Sabbath He stopped working and rested.

The Golden Calf   *2nd Aliyah*

18 When Adonai finished speaking to Moses on Mount Sinai, He gave him two tablets. They were stone Ten Commandments tablets, written by the finger of Adonai.

32 Meanwhile, the people saw that Moses was taking a long time to come down from the mountain. They gathered around Aaron and demanded, "Make us a god to lead us. Moses, the man who brought us out of Egypt, has disappeared. We have no idea what happened to him."

2 Aaron replied, "Remove the rings from the ears of your wives and children and bring them to me."

3 All the people removed their earrings and brought them to Aaron. **4** He melted the golden rings, and someone molded them into a golden calf. Some of the people said, "This is the god who brought us out of Egypt."

5 When Aaron saw the mood of the people, he built an altar before the golden calf. Aaron said, "Tomorrow there will be a festival to Adonai."

6 Early the next morning, the people sacrificed burnt and peace offerings. The Israelites sat down and feasted, and then they began to dance. **7** Adonai said to Moses, "Hurry! Go down, for the Israelites whom you brought out of Egypt, they have abandoned My teachings and are acting like wild people. **8** They have so quickly abandoned the laws that I ordered them to follow, and they have made themselves a golden calf. They have worshipped and sacrificed to it, boasting, 'This is the god of Israel, who brought us out of Egypt.' "

9 Adonai said further to Moses, "I have closely watched the people, and they are a rebellious, stubborn bunch.

10 Now do not try to stop Me when I become angry and destroy them. Then I will make you, Moses, and your descendants into a great nation."

11 Moses began to plead and beg Adonai. He said, "Adonai, why are You angry against the people whom You freed from Egypt with Your great power and miracles?

12 Do You want the Egyptians to say that You deliberately took them out to kill them in the mountains and erase them from the face of the earth? Turn back Your anger, and do not punish the Israelites.

13 Remember Your promises to Abraham, Isaac, and Jacob. You swore, and promised that You would make their descendants as numerous as the stars of the sky and give them the land You promised, so that they would be able to live in it forever."

14 Adonai relented and postponed the punishment He had planned.

15 Moses went down the mountain holding the two stone tablets with the Ten Commandments. They were two stone tablets written on both sides, with the writing visible from either side. **16** The tablets had been made by Adonai, and Adonai Himself had written on them.

17 When Joshua heard the sound of the people partying, he said to Moses, "It sounds as though there is a battle going on in the camp!"

18 Moses replied,

> "It is not a song of victory,
>   nor the sound of defeat.
>   That I hear
>   It is just plain singing."

19 As Moses approached the camp and saw the golden calf and the dancing, he lost his temper and threw down the Ten Commandments that were in his hands, shattering them. **20** He removed the golden calf that the people had made, and melted it in fire, and ground it into a fine powder. He mixed the powder in water, and made the Israelites drink the mixture.

21 Now Moses angrily said to Aaron, "How could you have permitted the people to commit such a great sin?" **22** Aaron replied, "Do not be angry, my lord, but you must be aware that the people have evil in their blood. **23** They insisted and said to me, 'Make a god to lead us, since the man who took us out of Egypt has disappeared.' **24** When I asked them, 'Who has gold to contribute?' they willingly took off their gold jewelry and gave it to me. I threw the gold jewelry into the fire and out came a golden calf."

25 Moses realized that the people were out of control: Aaron had been unable to restrain them, and they were a danger to those who would try to control them.

26 Moses stood up at the camp's entrance and shouted, "Whoever is on Adonai's side, join me!" All the Levites immediately gathered around him.

27 Moses said to them, "This is what Adonai says: Let each man buckle on his sword, and go from one end of the camp to the other. Let each one execute all the idol worshippers, even his own brother, close friend, or relative." **28** The Levites did as Moses ordered, and about three thousand Israelites were killed.

29 Moses said, "Today, Adonai has ordained you with a special blessing as a nation dedicated to Adonai. At Adonai's command you have been willing to kill your own sons and brothers."

30 The next day, Moses said to the people, "You have committed a terrible sin. Now I will return to Adonai and try to gain forgiveness for your crime."

31 Moses returned to Adonai and said, "The people have committed a terrible sin by making the golden calf. **32** Please forgive their sin. If not, You can erase me out of the future You have written."

33 Adonai replied to Moses, "I will erase from My history those who have sinned against Me. **34** Now go; you still have to lead the people to the land I have given to you. I will send My angel to lead you. But when I make My final decision, I will take their sin into account."

35 Then Adonai sent a plague among the Israelites because of the golden calf Aaron had made.

33 Now Adonai said to Moses, "You and the people you took out of Egypt will have to leave this place and go to the land I swore to give to Abraham, Isaac, and Jacob and to their descendants. **2** I will send an angel ahead of you, and I will drive out the Canaanites, Amorites, Hittites, Perizzites, Hivites, and Jebusites. **3** It is a land flowing with milk and honey. However, I will not go with you, since they are a stubborn people, and I may be tempted to destroy them along the way." **4** When the Israelites heard this disastrous news, they began to mourn, and they stripped the jewelry from their clothes.

5 Adonai told Moses to say to the Israelites, "You are a stubborn people. In just one second I can completely destroy you. Now remove your jewelry and I will think about how to punish you."

6 After that warning at Mount Horeb, the people no longer wore their jewelry.

7 Now Moses took his personal tent and set it up outside the camp. He called it the Meeting Tent. Anyone who wanted to consult Adonai would go to the Meeting Tent outside the camp.

8 Whenever Moses went out to his tent, all the people would stand at attention, watching Moses until he entered his tent. **9** Whenever Moses went into his tent, a pillar of cloud would descend and stand guard at the tent's entrance, and there Adonai would speak to Moses. **10** When the people saw the pillar of cloud standing at the entrance of the tent, they would stand and bow toward the entrance of his tent.

11 There Adonai would speak to Moses face to face, just as a person speaks to a close friend. Afterwards Moses would return to the camp. But his assistant, Joshua son of Nun, remained in the tent.

Moses Asks for Guidance   *3ʳᵈ Aliyah*

12 Moses said to Adonai, "You told me to lead the Israelites to the Promised Land, but You did not tell me who You would send with me. You also said that You specially chose me because You are pleased with me. **13** Now, if You are really pleased with me, guide me so that I will know how to continue pleasing You. And remember that this nation of Israel is Your people."

14 Adonai replied, "I will go and lead you."

15 Moses said, "If You are not going to accompany us personally, do not make us leave this place. **16** Unless You accompany us, no one will even know that I and Your people have pleased You. How will anyone know that we are different from any nation on the face of the earth?"

No Human Will Ever See My Face   *4th Aliyah*

17 Adonai said to Moses, "You have pleased Me, and I chose you by name. I will fulfill your request." **18** Moses begged, "Please let me see Your Holy Presence."

19 Adonai replied, "I will make My Presence pass before you, and I will reveal the meaning of My Holy Name to you, and I will have mercy and show kindness to anyone I choose."

20 Adonai explained, "You will not see My face. No human can see Me and remain alive."

21 Then Adonai said to Moses, "However, I have a safe place on the rocky mountain where you can stand. **22** When My Presence passes by, I will place you in a crack in a rock and cover you with My hand. This will protect you from My power when I pass by. **23** Then I will remove My protective power, and you will have a vision of My back. My face itself, however, will not he seen."

The Second Ten Commandments   *5th Aliyah*

34 Adonai said to Moses, "Carve two tablets of the Ten Commandments, just like the first ones. I will write on those tablets the same commandments that were on the first tablets, the ones you shattered. **2** Be ready to climb Mount Sinai in the morning and stand waiting for Me on the mountaintop. **3** Allow no person to climb up with you, and let no one else on the entire mountain. Even the cattle and sheep must not graze close to the mountain."

4 Moses carved two stone tablets like the first. Early in the morning, as Adonai had commanded him, he climbed Mount Sinai, carrying the two stone tablets. **5** Adonai descended in a cloud, and stood there near Moses.

6 Adonai passed before Moses and proclaimed,

"I am Adonai, Adonai.
merciful and kind, am I
I am slow to anger, overflowing with love and truth.
7 I show love for thousands of generations,
I forgive sin and rebellion,
But I do not forgive those who are guilty.
I remember the sins of the parents,
And I will punish the children and grandchildren
up to the third and fourth generation."

8 Moses immediately bowed his head and worshipped.

9 He said, "Adonai, if You are pleased with me, come among us. This nation may be stubborn, but please forgive our sins and errors, and make us Your special people."

Do Not Trust the Inhabitants   *6ᵗʰ Aliyah*

10 Adonai said, I will make a covenant with the Israelites and will perform miracles that have never been done before among any nation. All the Israelites with you will see the miracles that I, Adonai, will perform.

11 Listen carefully to what I am telling you today. I will drive out the Amorites, Canaanites, Hivites, Perizzites, Hittites, and Jebusites before you. **12** Never make a treaty with the people who live in the land where you are going, because they will trap you. **13** You must destroy their altars, smash their sacred pillars, and cut down their goddess Asherah trees. **14** Do not worship any other gods, because I, Adonai, demand exclusive worship.

15 You must not make a treaty with the people who live in the land. They will invite you to pray and sacrifice to their gods, and you will end up eating their sacrifices. **16** Then you will allow their daughters to marry your sons, and when their daughters worship their gods, they will lead your sons to follow their religion.

17 Do not make idols of any kind.

18 Observe the Festival of Matzot. You must eat matzot for seven days, just as I have commanded, at the designated time in the month of Aviv. It was in the month of standing grain that you left Egypt.

19 The first-born is Mine. You must separate the males of the first-born cattle and sheep from all your livestock.

20 The first-born of a donkey can be redeemed with a sheep, and if it is not redeemed, you must kill it. You must also redeem every first-born of your sons.

Do not appear in My Tabernacle empty-handed.

21 You may work on the six workdays, but on Saturday you must stop working and stop plowing and reaping.

22 Observe the Festival of Shavuot, of the first fruits of your wheat harvest. Also keep the Harvest Festival (Sukkot) at the turn of the year.

23 Three times each year all your males must appear before Adonai.

24 When I drive out the other nations and enlarge your boundaries, no one will attack your land when you appear before Adonai three times each year.

25 Do not slaughter the Passover sacrifice with leaven. Do not allow the meat of the Passover sacrifice to remain until morning.

26 Bring the best of the first fruits of your crops to the Temple of Adonai.

Do not boil a goat in the milk of its mother.

Moses Returns from Mount Sinai   *7th Aliyah*

27 Adonai said to Moses, "I want you to write these words down, since it is with these words that I have made a covenant between you and Israel."

28 Moses stayed on the mountain for forty days and forty nights without eating or drinking. Adonai wrote the words of the Ten Commandments on the two tablets of stone.

29 Moses came down from Mount Sinai with the two tablets of the Ten Commandments. As Moses descended from the mountain, he did not realize that his face was glowing because Adonai had spoken to him.

30 When Aaron and all the Israelites saw that the face of Moses was glowing with a brilliant light, they were afraid to approach him.

31 Moses called them, and when Aaron and the community leaders came to him, Moses spoke to them.

32 Afterwards all the Israelites came, and Moses relayed the instructions Adonai had given him on Mount Sinai.

Moses and His Veil   *Maftir*

33 When Moses finished speaking with them, he placed a veil over his face.

34 Whenever Moses went to speak with Adonai, he would remove the veil until he was ready to leave. Then he would go out and speak to the Israelites, and tell them what he had been commanded. **35** The Israelites could see that the face of Moses was glowing brilliantly. Moses would then replace the veil over his face until he once again went in to speak to Adonai.

Vayakhel וַיַּקְהֵל

MOSES ASSEMBLES THE ISRAELITES

35 Moses assembled the entire Israelite community and said to them, "These are the laws that Adonai has commanded you to observe:

2 You may do work during the six workdays, but Saturday must be kept holy as a Sabbath of rest. Whoever does any work on that day shall be put to death. **3** Wherever you live, do not light a fire on the Sabbath."

4 Moses continued and said, "This is the law that Adonai has commanded:

5 Collect gifts among yourselves as an offering to Adonai. Any person who willingly feels like giving an offering to Adonai can bring any of the following: gold, silver, copper, **6** blue wool, purple wool, wool dyed scarlet, fine linen, goats' wool, **7** tanned rams' skins, dyed blue sealskins, acacia wood, **8** oil for the menorah, aromatic spices for the anointing oil and perfume incense, **9** as well as onyxes and other precious jewels for the ephod and the breastplate.

10 Every skilled person can volunteer and help make everything that Adonai has commanded:

11 The Tabernacle with its tent, roof, clasps, frames, crossbars, and pillars; **12** the ark and its carrying poles, the ark cover, the cloth partition; **13** the table along with its carrying poles, all its utensils and the showbread; **14** the menorah with its utensils, lights, and illuminating oil; **15** the incense altar and its carrying poles; the anointing oil, the perfumed incense, the curtain for the entrance to the Tabernacle; **16** the sacrificial altar with its carrying poles and all its utensils; the washbasin, **17** the curtains for the enclosure, its frames and its bases, the curtain for the entrance to the enclosure, **18** the pegs for the tent, the pegs for the enclosure, the tying ropes; **19** the packing cloths for sacred use, the sacred garments for Aaron the priest, and the garments that his sons will wear during the services in the Tabernacle."

Gifts for the Tabernacle   *2nd Aliyah*

20 The entire Israelite community left Moses. **21** And everyone who was willing to volunteer came forward. Each person who wanted brought an offering to Adonai for the construction of the Meeting Tent and all its furnishings, and for the sacred garments.

22 The men and the women, and all who wanted to, brought offerings of bracelets, earrings, rings, and ornaments, all made of gold. They presented their gold offerings as wave offerings to Adonai.

23 Every person who had blue wool, purple wool, scarlet wool, fine linen, goats' wool, tanned rams' skins or blue-dyed sealskins, brought them. **24** Those who offered silver or copper brought it as a divine offering, and everyone who had acacia wood that could be used for the Tabernacle also brought it.

25 Every skilled woman who could sew brought spun yarn of blue wool, purple wool, scarlet wool, and woven linen.

26 Highly skilled women also spun the goats' wool.

27 The tribal leaders brought onyxes and other precious jewels for the ephod and the breastplate. **28** They also brought aromatic spices and olive oil for the menorah, the anointing oil, and the perfumed incense.

29 Every man and woman willingly brought offerings to Adonai to complete all the tasks Adonai had commanded through Moses.

Betzalel the Architect   *3rd Aliyah*

30 Moses said to the Israelites, "Adonai has chosen Betzalel son of Uri, grandson of Hur, from the tribe of Judah, **31** and has filled him with a divine spirit of wisdom, understanding, knowledge, and a talent for all types of craftsmanship. **32** He will be the architect, and he will also create artistic objects of gold, silver, and copper, **33** cut precious jewels, and do carpentry and other skilled work.

34 Adonai has also given Oholiav son of Achisamakh, of the tribe of Dan, the ability to teach others. **35** Adonai has granted them a talent for all types of craftsmanship, to weave materials, to embroider patterns with blue, red, and crimson wool, and to weave fine linen. These experts will be able to perform and do all the necessary planning and work.

36 Betzalel, Oholiav, and every other skilled individual to whom Adonai has granted the wisdom and understanding to know how to do all the work necessary for the sacred task shall carry out all that Adonai has commanded."

2 Moses summoned Betzalel, Oholiav, and all the other skilled individuals upon whom Adonai had bestowed a natural talent, and who volunteered to dedicate themselves to completing the task. **3** They took from Moses all the materials that the Israelites had brought to complete the sacred task.

Meanwhile, the Israelites continued bringing more gifts.

4 The craftsmen engaged in the sacred work **5** complained to Moses, "The people are bringing much more than is needed to complete the work that Adonai commanded to do."

6 So Moses made an announcement in the camp, "Let no man or woman bring any more contributions for the Tabernacle." The people stopped bringing, **7** because there was more than enough materials for all the work that had to be done.

Erecting the Tabernacle   *4ᵗʰ Aliyah*

8 The most talented craftsmen worked on the Tabernacle itself, which consisted of ten tapestries made of woven linen, with blue, purple, and scarlet wool, embroidered with cherubs. **9** All the tapestries were the same size: 42 feet long and 6 feet wide.

10 The first five tapestries and the second five tapestries were sewn together. **11** Loops of blue wool were sewn on the edge of the last tapestry of the first group of five, and loops were also sewn on the second group of tapestries.

12 The fifty loops on the first set of tapestries and the fifty loops on the edge of the second set of tapestries were exactly opposite each other. **13** Fifty gold fasteners were made to join the two sets of tapestries together to make the Tabernacle into a single unit.

14 They wove eleven sheets of goats' wool to cover the roof of the Tabernacle. **15** All the sheets were the same size: 45 feet long and 6 feet wide.

16 Five sheets were sewn together to form one group, and six to form the second group.

17 Fifty loops were sewn on the last sheet of the first group, and another fifty loops on the edge of the last sheet of the second group. **18** They also made fifty copper fasteners to join the sheets together and make it into a single unit.

19 They made the roof for the Tabernacle out of tanned rams' skins, and another roof above it out of blue-dyed sealskins.

Making the Frame   *5ᵗʰ Aliyah*

20 They made the upright frames for the Tabernacle out of acacia wood. **21** Each frame was 15 feet long and 2.25 feet wide, **22** with two matching square pegs on the bottom. All of the Tabernacle's frames were made exactly the same.

23 They made twenty frames for the southern wall of the Tabernacle, **24** with forty silver bases to go under the twenty frames. There were two bases under each frame, one base under each of the two square pegs at the bottom of each frame. **25** They also made twenty frames on the second wall of the Tabernacle to the north, **26** along with forty silver bases, two bases under each frame's two pegs.

27 They made six frames for the western wall of the Tabernacle, **28** and two frames for the corners of the Tabernacle. **29** At the bottom, all the frames were joined next to one another on top, every pair was joined with a square ring. The two frames on the two corners were also joined together with a square ring.

30 On the western side, there was a total of eight frames, along with sixteen bases, two bases for each frame.

31 They made five crossbars of acacia wood for the first wall of the Tabernacle to the south, **32** a second set of five crossbars for the second wall of the Tabernacle to the north, and five similar crossbars for the western wall of the Tabernacle. **33** The middle crossbar was made to go through the center of the frames from one end to the other.

34 They covered the frames with a layer of gold. They also made the rings that would hold the crossbars out of gold, and they covered the crossbars with a layer of gold.

35 They made the cloth partition out of blue, purple, and scarlet wool and woven linen, embroidered with cherubs. **36** They made four acacia poles to hold it, covering the poles with a layer of gold with gold hooks attached. They also cast four silver bases for these poles.

37 They made an embroidered curtain for the entrance to the tent out of blue, purple, and scarlet wool and woven linen. **38** There were five poles to support it, along with gold hooks, caps, and bands. There were five copper bases for these poles.

37

Betzalel made the ark of acacia wood: 3.5 feet long and 2.25 feet wide, and 2.25 feet high. **2** He covered it with a layer of pure gold on the inside, and made a gold molding for it all around. **3** He cast four gold rings for its four corners, two rings for one side, and two for the other.

4 He made carrying poles of acacia wood and covered them with a layer of gold. **5** Then he fitted the carrying poles into the rings on the sides of the ark, so that it could be carried with them.

6 He made a pure golden cover, 3.75 feet long and 2.25 feet wide. **7** He hammered two golden cherubs from the two ends of the cover. **8** The cherubs were made from the same piece of gold as the cover, one cherub on one end, and the second cherub on the other end. **9** The cherubs had their wings stretched outward so as to shield the ark cover with their wings. The cherubs faced each other, with their faces turned downward toward the cover of the ark.

10 He made the table out of acacia wood, 3 feet long, 18 inches wide, and 2.25 feet high. **11** He covered the table with a layer of pure gold. **12** He made a 3-inch-wide gold rim for it and placed the gold rim on the frame.

13 He cast four gold rings for the table, attaching the rings on the corners of its four legs. **14** The rings were close to the frame and were able to hold the poles used to carry the table. **15** He made acacia poles to carry the table, and covered them with a layer of gold.

16 Out of pure gold he made pans to go on the table, bread pans, bowls, ladles, and jars, and side frames to serve as dividers for the bread.

Making the Menorah   *6ᵗʰ Aliyah*

17 He made the menorah out of pure gold, hammering the menorah, with its base, stem, decorative cups, buds, and flowers, out of a single piece of gold.

18 Six branches extended from the menorah's sides, three branches on one side, and three branches on the other. **19** There were three embossed cups, a bud, and a flower on each branch. All six branches extending from the menorah were exactly the same.

20 The menorah's stem had four embossed cups, along with its own buds and flowers. **21** There was a bud at the base of each of the six branches extending from the center. **22** The buds and branches were all made from the same golden ingot as the menorah itself. The menorah was hammered from a single ingot of pure gold.

23 He made the menorah with seven lamps. He also made its wicks, the tongs, and the ash shovels out of pure gold. **24** The menorah and all its parts were made from a talent of gold weighing 75 pounds.

25 He constructed the incense altar of acacia wood, 18 inches square and, including its horns, 3 feet high. **26** He covered its top, its walls, and its horns with a layer of pure gold, and made it a gold rim all around.

27 He made two rings for the altar below its rim on its two opposite sides, so as to hold the poles with which the altar was carried. **28** He made the carrying poles out of acacia wood and covered them with a layer of gold. **29** Using the skills of a perfumer, he blended the sacred anointing oil and the pure perfume incense.

Making the Altar   *7ᵗʰ Aliyah*

38 He made the sacrificial altar out of acacia wood, 7.5 feet square and 4.5 feet high. **2** He made horns on all four corners as part of the altar, and then covered the entire altar with a layer of copper.

3 He made all the altar's utensils, pots, shovels, basins, hooks, and fire pans. They were all made out of copper.

4 He made a grating out of copper mesh, and placed it below the altar's border, and extended it downward to the middle of the altar. **5** He cast four rings on the copper screen to hold the carrying poles. **6** He made acacia carrying poles and covered them with a layer of copper.

7 He inserted the carrying poles into the rings on the altar's corners, so that it could be carried. He constructed the altar as a hollow structure made out of boards.

8 He made the copper washbasin and its copper base from the mirrors of the women workers at the entrance of the Meeting Tent.

9 He made the enclosure for the Tabernacle. On the southern side, the woven linen hangings were 150 feet long; **10** the hangings were supported by twenty poles, with twenty copper bases and silver pole hooks and bands.

11 On the northern side, it was also 150 feet long, supported by twenty poles, with twenty copper bases and silver pole hooks and bands. **12** On the western side, the curtains were 75 feet long supported by ten poles, with ten bases and silver pole hooks and bands.

13 The eastern side was also 75 feet wide. **14** The hangings on one side of the enclosure were 22.5 feet long, supported by three poles with three bases.

15 The hangings on the other side of the enclosure's entrance were also 22.5 feet wide, supported by three poles with three bases.

16 The enclosure's hangings were all made of woven linen. **17** The bases for the poles were made of copper, while the pole hooks and bands were made of silver. All the enclosure's poles also had silver caps, and the poles themselves were covered with silver.

The Entrance Curtain   *Maftir*

18 The curtain for the entrance to the enclosure was embroidered out of blue, purple, and scarlet wool, together with woven linen. It was 30 feet long and 7.5 feet high, just like the other hangings of the enclosure. **19** It was supported by four poles, having four copper bases, and silver hooks, caps, and bands.

20 The pegs used for the Tabernacle and the surrounding enclosure were all made of copper.

Pekuday פְּקוּדֵי

THE INVENTORY OF THE TABERNACLE

21 This is the inventory of the construction materials used to build the Tabernacle. Moses directed the Levites to assemble the quantities, and Ithamar, the son of Aaron, recorded the numbers. **22** Betzalel son of Uri, grandson of Hur, from the tribe of Judah, used these materials to construct everything that Adonai had commanded Moses. **23** His assistant was Oholiav son of Achisamakh, from the tribe of Dan, who was a skilled carpenter, and also was an expert in embroidering with blue, purple, and scarlet wool, and fine linen.

24 All the gold was used in the work to complete the sacred task. The amount of gold donated as a wave offering weighed 2,200 pounds by the sanctuary weight standard.

25 The silver census money collected from the community weighed 7,545 pounds by the sanctuary weight standard. **26** This total consisted of a third of an ounce of silver for each of the 603,550 men over twenty years old included in the census.

27 The 7,500 pounds of silver were used to cast the bases for the sanctuary and the cloth partition. There were a total of one hundred bases, 75 pounds for each base. **28** The hooks, clasps, and hoops for the pillars were made out of the remaining 45 pounds of silver

29 The copper donated as a wave offering weighed 5,310 pounds. **30** It was used to make the bases for the entrance to the Meeting Tent and the copper altar along with its copper screen and all the altar's utensils, **31** the bases for the surrounding enclosure, the bases for the enclosure's entrance, the pegs for the Tabernacle, and the pegs for the surrounding enclosure.

39 They made the packing cloths for sacred use from the blue, purple, and scarlet wool.

They also made the sacred garments for Aaron, just as Adonai had commanded Moses.

The Ephod and the Breastplate *2nd Aliyah*

2 He wove the ephod out of gold thread, blue, purple, and scarlet wool, and woven linen. **3** They hammered out thin sheets of gold and cut them into threads, which were woven into the blue, purple, and scarlet wool, and the fine linen. The ephod was made as an embroidered brocade.

4 They made shoulder pieces for the ephod and attached them to the two corners. **5** The ephod belt was made in the same way, out of gold thread, blue, purple, and scarlet wool, and woven linen. It was made exactly as Adonai had commanded Moses.

6 They prepared two onyx stones to be placed in gold settings. The stones were engraved with the names of Israel's sons. **7** He set them in the shoulder pieces of the ephod as a remembrance for Israel's sons. It was completed exactly as Adonai had commanded Moses.

8 The breastplate was embroidered, just like the ephod. It was also made from gold thread, blue, purple, and scarlet wool, and woven linen. **9** The breastplate was square when folded over. It was 18 inches long when folded over, and 18 inches wide.

10 The breastplate was decorated with four rows of precious jewels:

The first row: ruby, emerald, topaz.

11 The second row: amber, sapphire, jasper.

12 The third row: amber, agate, jasper.

13 The fourth row: beryl, onyx, amethyst.

14 Each of the jewels was engraved with the name of one of Israel's sons. Twelve names were engraved. There was one engraved jewel for each of the tribes.

15 Matched braided chains of pure gold were attached to the breastplate. **16** They made two gold settings and two gold rings, and they placed the two rings on the breastplate's two upper corners. **17** The two gold braids were then attached to the two rings on the breastplate's corners.

18 The two braids on the two corners were attached to the two gold settings on the shoulder pieces of the ephod.

19 They made two gold rings and placed them on the breastplate's two lower corners, on the inside edge of the ephod. **20** They made two gold rings and placed them on the bottoms of the ephod's two shoulder pieces toward the front, near where they were attached, above the ephod's belt. **21** The rings on the breastplate were fastened to the rings of the ephod with a cord of blue wool, so that the breastplate would remain above the ephod's belt. Thus the breastplate could not be detached from the ephod.

All this was done exactly as Adonai had commanded Moses.

The Robe and the Ephod   *3rd Aliyah*

22 He made the robe for the ephod, weaving it completely out of blue wool. **23** The robe's opening was in the middle, with a border all around so that it would not tear.

24 On the skirt of the robe, they made pomegranates out of blue, purple, and scarlet wool. **25** They made pure gold bells and placed the bells between the pomegranates. The bells were all around the bottom of the robe between the pomegranates. **26** There was a bell and a pomegranate, a bell and a pomegranate, all around the bottom of the robe. It was specially made for the holy service, just as Adonai had commanded Moses.

27 They made the robes for Aaron and his sons by weaving them out of fine linen.

28 They made the linen headdresses and linen undergarments for Aaron and his sons.

29 They embroidered the belt from woven linen and blue, purple, and scarlet wool.

It was all done exactly as Adonai had commanded Moses.

30 They made a sacred medallion out of pure gold. It was engraved with the words "Holy to Adonai." **31** They put a cord of blue wool on the medallion so that it could be worn at the front of the headdress. Everything was done exactly as Adonai had commanded Moses.

32 All the work on the Meeting Tent was completed. The Israelites did all the work exactly as Adonai had instructed Moses.

Moses Inspects the Tabernacle   *4th Aliyah*

33 Moses inspected the entire Tabernacle. He checked the Meeting Tent with its equipment, its fastenings, frames, crossbars, pillars, and bases; **34** the roof of tanned rams' skins and the roof of blue-dyed sealskins, the cloth curtain; **35** the ark and its carrying poles, the ark cover, **36** the table and its equipment, the showbread, **37** the pure gold menorah along with its prescribed lamps, all its utensils, and the illuminating oil; **38** the golden altar, the anointing oil, the perfumed incense, the curtain for the Meeting Tent; **39** the copper altar with its carrying poles and all its equipment; the washbasin and its base; **40** the hangings for the enclosure, its poles and bases, the curtain for the entrance to the enclosure, its tying ropes and pegs, all the equipment used in the service in the Meeting Tent, **41** the packing cloths for sacred use, the sacred garments for Aaron the priest, and the garments that his sons would wear to serve in the Tabernacle.

42 The Israelites performed all the work exactly as Adonai had instructed Moses.

43 When Moses saw that all the work had been done exactly as Adonai had ordered, he blessed the craftsmen.

Erect the Meeting Tent   *5th Aliyah*

40 Adonai spoke to Moses, saying:
2 "You shall erect the Meeting Tent on the first day of the first month [Nisan]. **3** Put the ark in it and enclose the ark with the cloth partition. **4** Bring in the table and set the menorah on it and light its lamps. **5** Place the gold incense altar directly in front of the ark, and then set up the curtain at the entrance of the Tabernacle.

6 Place the sacrificial altar in front of the entrance of the Meeting Tent. **7** Then place the washbasin between the Meeting Tent and the altar, and fill it with water. **8** Set an enclosure all around it, and hang the curtain over the entrance to the enclosure.

9 Take the holy anointing oil, and anoint the Tabernacle and everything in it. This will sanctify all the equipment.

10 Anoint the sacrificial altar and all its equipment. In this way you will sanctify the altar, and it will become holy.

11 Anoint the washbasin, and make it holy.

12 Bring Aaron and his sons into the Meeting Tent, and have them cleanse themselves. **13** Then have Aaron put on the sacred garment, and anoint him, and ordain him as a priest to serve Me.

14 Clothe Aaron's sons in their robes. **15** Then anoint them, just as you anointed Aaron, their father, so that they will become priests to serve Me. This anointing ceremony will ordain them and their descendants as priests throughout all the generations to come."

16 Moses did everything exactly as Adonai had instructed him.

The Tabernacle Is Erected   *6ᵗʰ Aliyah*

17 The Tabernacle was erected in the first month of the second year of the Exodus, on the first of the month.

18 Moses supervised the erection of the Tabernacle. He helped by setting up the bases, placing the frames in them, and fastening them together with the crossbars. He helped to set up the pillars.

19 He helped spread the tent over the Tabernacle, and placed the roof of the tent over it. It was all done exactly as Adonai had commanded Moses.

20 He took the tablets of the Ten Commandments and placed them in the ark. He then inserted the carrying poles into the ark, and set the cover on top of the ark.

21 He brought the ark into the Tabernacle, and set up the cloth partition so that it shielded the ark. Everything was done exactly as Adonai had instructed Moses.

22 He also helped place the table in the Meeting Tent outside the cloth curtain, on the northern side of the Tabernacle.

23 Then he placed the showbread on the table before Adonai. It was done exactly as Adonai had commanded Moses.

24 He placed the menorah in the Meeting Tent next to the table, on the southern side of the Tabernacle. **25** Moses then lighted the menorah before Adonai. Everything was done exactly as Adonai had instructed Moses.

26 Moses helped place the golden altar in the Meeting Tent in front of the cloth partition. **27** Then he burned perfumed incense on it. Everything was done exactly as Adonai had commanded Moses.

The Curtain and the Altar   *7ᵗʰ Aliyah*

28 He hung the curtain over the entrance of the Tabernacle.

29 Then he helped place the sacrificial altar in front of the entrance of the Meeting Tent Tabernacle, and he sacrificed the burnt offerings and the meal offerings on it. It was all done exactly as Adonai had commanded Moses.

30 He set the washbasin between the Meeting Tent and the altar, and he filled it with water for cleansing.

31 Moses, Aaron, and Aaron's sons cleansed their hands and feet in it. **32** They would cleanse themselves in this way whenever they entered the Meeting Tent or offered sacrifice on the altar.

Everything was done exactly as Adonai had instructed Moses.

33 He set up the enclosure surrounding the Tabernacle and altar, and he placed the curtain over the entrance of the enclosure. At last, Moses completed all the work that Adonai had entrusted to him.

The Cloud and the Fire   *Maftir*

34 The cloud covered the Meeting Tent when Adonai's glory filled the Tabernacle. **35** Moses could not enter the Meeting Tent once the cloud rested on it and Adonai's glory filled the Tabernacle.

36 Whenever the cloud lifted up above the Tabernacle, it signaled that the Israelites could move on.

37 When the cloud did not rise, they would not begin their march until it lifted. **38** Adonai's cloud covered the Tabernacle by day, and the fire by night. The clouds by day and the fire by night led the Israelites in all their journeys.

סֵפֶר וַיִּקְרָא

THE BOOK OF VAYIKRA

Masoretic Torah Notes

Here is a list of some of the Masoretic notes for the Book of Vayikira.

1. The Book of Vayikra contains 859 verses.
2. The Book of Vayikra contains 27 chapters.
3. The Book of Vayikra contains 10 sidrot.

These are the sidrot in the Book of Vayikra.

סֵפֶר וַיִּקְרָא

THE BOOK OF VAYIKRA

The Hebrew name for the third book of the Torah is Vayikra. The title is taken from the book's opening word, which means "and Adonai called." The Greek name of the book is Leviticus, meaning "about the Levites."

The book of Vayikra is a manual for living a holy and ethical life. The key phrase is found in (11:45):

*I am holy,
And therefore you must make yourselves holy.*

Here the people of Israel are commanded by Adonai to observe the commandments and thereby enrich their lives and make the world a better place in which to live.

The first eight chapters (1:1–8:35) deal with the sacrifices, followed by the installation of Aaron and his descendants into the priesthood.

The second section (9–15) alerts the Israelites to problems of health and hygiene and specifies which foods are permitted and which forbidden to be eaten.

The third section (16–20) contains the Holiness Code and sets the rules of conduct that Jews must practice to live a holy life.

The fourth section (21–26) includes instructions for celebrating Shabbat and the festivals, some of which are tied to seasons, harvests, and historical events. The theme for Rosh HaShanah and Yom Kippur is teshuvah—*a time for forgiveness.*

Vayikra is the source (25:10) of the quotation inscribed on the Liberty Bell:

Proclaim liberty throughout all the land
unto all the inhabitants thereof.

For the former slaves, the book of Vayikra was a road map for living a holy life in the midst of an idol-worshipping society. In reality, Adonai was preparing the Israelites for a military and spiritual clash with forces that would test their commitment to ethics and morality.

Vayikra וַיִּקְרָא

ADONAI SPOKE TO MOSES

1 Adonai spoke to Moses from the Meeting Tent and said: **2** Speak to the Israelites, and give them the following instructions: When a person presents an animal as an offering to Adonai, he must bring it from the bulls, sheep, or goats.

3 If the sacrifice is a burnt offering, a healthy male bull must be taken from the herd. He must bring it to the entrance of the Meeting Tent, so it can be presented before Adonai. **4** He shall place his hands on the head of the offering, and it will be accepted as his substitute and make atonement for him.

5 The young bull should be slaughtered. Then Aaron's sons, the priests, shall present the blood, by sprinkling it on all four sides of the altar that is at the entrance of the Meeting Tent.

6 Then the burnt offering should be skinned and cut into pieces. **7** Aaron's sons shall build a wood fire on the altar, **8** and arrange the body parts on top of the altar fire. **9** First the inner organs and legs must be cleansed with water. Then the priest shall burn the parts of the animal on the altar as a complete burnt fire offering to Adonai. This burnt offering is a thank you gift to Adonai. **10** If the burnt offering is a sheep or a goat, it must be a healthy male animal. **11** It shall be slaughtered on the northern side of the altar, and the priests who are Aaron's descendants shall sprinkle its blood on all sides of the altar. **12** Then the offering shall be cut into pieces, and the priest shall arrange all the body parts on top of the wood on the altar fire.

13 The organs and feet shall first be cleansed with water, and then the priest shall burn them on the altar. This offering is a thank you gift to Adonai.

Procedures for the Grain Offering *2nd Aliyah*

14 Should the burnt offering be a turtle dove or a pigeon, **15** the priest shall bring it to the altar and remove its head and burn it on the altar. Then he shall drain the bird's blood and sprinkle the blood against the wall of the altar.

16 Then he shall remove the bird's neck and its feathers and throw them into the ashes, to the east of the altar.

17 The priest shall then burn the bird on the altar. This burnt offering is a thank you gift to Adonai.

2 If anyone presents a grain offering to Adonai, it must consist of the finest flour; he shall mix it with olive oil and place frankincense upon it.

2 Then he shall bring it to the priest, and he shall take a handful of the flour and oil, and all the frankincense. The priest shall burn this small portion on the altar as a fire offering. This fire offering is a thank you gift to Adonai.

3 The remainder of the grain offering shall belong to Aaron and his descendants as their food. This is a holy part of the fire offerings to Adonai.

4 If he brings a grain offering that was baked in an oven, it must be made of unleavened flour mixed with olive oil, or unleavened matzot spread with olive oil.

More Grain Offerings *3rd Aliyah*

5 If the offering is fried, it shall be made of unleavened flour mixed with olive oil.

6 It should be broken into small pieces, and olive oil poured on them. It should be treated like any other grain offering.

7 If the offering is cooked in a pot, it shall be made of flour with olive oil.

8 Any type of grain offering that is brought must be presented to the priest and brought to the altar. **9** Then the priest will remove a token portion from the grain offering and burn it on the altar. This offering is a thank you gift to Adonai.

10 The remainder of the grain offering belongs to Aaron and his descendants as their food. This part is the most holy because it is a portion from Adonai's fire offering.

11 Do not offer any grain offering that is made with leavened dough, because neither yeast nor honey is acceptable as a fire offering to Adonai. **12** Although you may bring them as a first-fruit offering to Adonai, they must not be offered on the altar.

13 Every grain offering must be seasoned with salt. Always add salt to your grain offering because it will remind you of Adonai's covenant. Do not forget to add salt to all your animal sacrifices.

14 When you present an offering from the first grain harvest, bring it from freshly picked roasted kernels of barley.

15 Pour olive oil and frankincense on it, just as for any other grain offering. **16** And offer it as a grain offering to Adonai. The priest shall then burn a token portion taken from the barley grain, olive oil, and frankincense.

Procedures for the Peace Offerings   *4ᵗʰ Aliyah*

3 If the sacrifice is a peace offering taken from the cattle herd, it can be either a healthy male or a healthy female. **2** He shall place his hands on the head of the animal, and have it slaughtered at the entrance of the Meeting Tent. Then a priest, one of Aaron's descendants, shall sprinkle its blood on all four sides of the altar.

3 A peace offering that is presented as a fire offering to Adonai must include the fat around the internal organs. **4** The two kidneys and the liver must also be removed. **5** The priest shall burn all of these parts on the altar, as a burnt offering on the wood fire. This fire offering is a thank you gift to Adonai. **6** If the sacrifice is a peace offering to Adonai, you may present a healthy male or female goat or sheep. **7** If you bring a sheep as a gift, you shall present it before Adonai.

8 He shall place his hands on the head of the animal and have it slaughtered at the entrance of the Meeting Tent. The priests, Aaron's descendants, shall then sprinkle its blood on all four sides of the altar.

9 Parts of the peace offering shall be presented as a fire offering to Adonai. The peace offering shall not include the fat.

10 The kidneys and the liver must also be removed. **11** The priest shall burn the parts on the altar, to be consumed as a fire offering to Adonai. This offering is a thank you gift to Adonai.

12 If the sacrifice is a goat, **13** he shall place his hands on its head and have it slaughtered at the entrance of the Meeting Tent. The priests, Aaron's descendants, shall then sprinkle its blood on all four sides of the altar.

14 As part of his fire offering to Adonai, he shall present the fat that covers the internal organs. **15** The kidneys and the liver shall also be removed. **16** The priests shall burn these parts on the altar as a fire offering to Adonai. This offering is a thank you gift to Adonai. Remember that all the fat belongs to Adonai. **17** No matter where you may live, it shall be a law for all your generations that you must not eat any fat or blood that is usually sacrificed.

When a High Priest Sins   *5th Aliyah*

4 Adonai told Moses **2** to speak to the Israelites and tell them the following:

This is the law when a person accidentally commits a sin by violating one of Adonai's commandments.

3 If a High Priest accidentally commits a sin and brings guilt on the whole community, he shall bring a healthy young bull as a sin offering to Adonai. **4** He shall bring the bull to the entrance of the Meeting Tent and place his hands on the bull's head. Then he shall slaughter the bull before Adonai.

5 Then the priest on duty shall take some of the bull's blood and bring it into the Meeting Tent. **6** The priest shall dip his finger into the blood and sprinkle it seven times toward the Holy Ark that is behind the cloth partition in the sanctuary. **7** The priest shall smear some of the blood on the horns of the incense altar, which is in the Meeting Tent. He shall then sprinkle some of the blood at the base of the sacrificial altar, which is at the entrance of the Meeting Tent. **8** The priest shall remove all the fat from the sin offering.

9 The two kidneys and the liver shall also be removed. **10** All these are the same as the parts removed from the peace offering. The priest shall burn them on the sacrificial altar.

11 He shall take the bull's skin and all its flesh **12** and remove them to a clean place outside the camp, where the altar's ashes are thrown. They shall be burned on a wood fire in the place where the ashes are thrown.

13 If the entire community of Israel accidentally commits an error, even though the people were unaware that they had violated one of Adonai's commandments, they are still guilty. **14** When the sin they have committed becomes known, the congregation must bring a young bull as a sin offering and present it at the entrance of the Meeting Tent.

15 The elders of the community shall place their hands on the bull's head, and it shall be slaughtered before Adonai. **16** Then a priest shall bring some of the bull's blood into the Meeting Tent. **17** He shall dip his finger into the blood and sprinkle it seven times toward the Holy Ark, which is behind the cloth partition. **18** He shall then smear some of the blood on the horns of the incense altar, which stands before Adonai in the Meeting Tent. The remainder of the blood must be poured at the base of the sacrificial altar, which is in front of the entrance of the Meeting Tent.

19 The priest shall then remove all of the fat and burn it on the altar, **20** and do exactly the same with this bull as he did with the bull that was sacrificed as a sin offering for the anointed priest. In this way the priest will make atonement for the community, and they will be forgiven.

21 The priest shall take the bull outside the camp and burn it just as he burned the first bull. This is the sin offering for the entire community of Israel.

22 If a leader accidentally commits a sin and violates one of Adonai's commandments, then he is guilty. **23** When he becomes aware of the sin he has committed, he must bring a healthy male goat as his sacrifice. **24** He shall place his hands on the goat's head and have it slaughtered as a sin offering in the same place where the burnt offering is slaughtered. **25** Then the priest, with his finger, shall smear some of the blood of the sin offering on the horn of the sacrificial altar. The rest of the blood shall be poured out at the base of the sacrificial altar.

26 All the animal's fat shall be burned on the altar, just like the fat of the peace offerings. In this way the priest will make atonement for the leader, and he will be forgiven.

Sin Offerings for Israelites   *6ᵗʰ Aliyah*

27 If an ordinary Israelite accidentally commits a sin by violating one of Adonai's commandments, he is guilty.

28 When he is made aware of the sin he has committed, he must bring a healthy female goat as a sacrifice for the sin he has committed. **29** He shall place his hands on the head of the sin offering, and the goat shall be sacrificed in the same place as the burnt offerings.

30 The priest, with his finger, shall smear some of the goat's blood on the horns of the sacrificial altar and spill the rest of the blood at the base of the altar.

31 He shall remove all the fat, just as he did with the fat of the peace offering, and the priest shall burn it on the altar. This offering is a thank you gift to Adonai. In this way the priest will make atonement for the individual, and he will be forgiven.

32 If anyone brings a sheep as a sin offering, he shall bring a healthy female animal. **33** He shall place his hands on the head of the sin offering and have it slaughtered in the same place that the burnt offerings were slaughtered.

34 The priest, with his fingers, shall take some of the blood of the sin offering and smear it on the horns of the sacrificial altar, and spill the rest of the blood at the altar's base. **35** He shall remove all the fat parts, just as he removed all the fat parts from the sheep offering brought as a peace offering, and shall burn them on the altar along with the fire offerings. In this way the priest will make atonement for the sin the person committed and he will be forgiven.

5 If a person has sworn an oath to give evidence in court about something that he witnessed or something that he knew, and then refuses to testify, he has committed a sin and should be punished.
2 A person is guilty if he touches anything unclean, whether it is a dead animal, either wild or domestic, or a dead creeping animal. He has, without realizing it, committed a sin.
3 If he comes in contact with any unclean waste from a human being, and accidentally forgets about it, he may later discover that he has committed a violation.
4 This is also true if a person makes a promise to do something good or bad and then forgets about the promise. In all of these cases, the person is considered guilty as soon as he becomes aware of what he has done.
5 In all of these cases he is guilty, and he must confess the sin he has committed.
6 He must also bring a guilt offering to Adonai for the sin he has committed. It must be a female sheep or goat, brought as a sin offering. The priest will then make atonement for the person's sin.
7 If he cannot afford a sheep, the guilt offering he presents to Adonai for his sin shall be two doves or two pigeons. One of them shall be a sin offering, and one of them shall be a burnt offering. **8** He shall bring them to the priest, who shall first offer a dove as the sin offering. He shall wring its neck without separating the head from the body. **9** He shall then spill some of the blood on the side of the altar, and the rest of the blood at the base of

the altar. The dove is the sin offering.

10 As the law requires, he shall also sacrifice a pigeon as a burnt offering. In this way the priest will make atonement for the sin the person committed, and he will be forgiven.

Sin Offerings

11 However, if the sinner is poor and cannot afford the two doves or two pigeons for the sacrifice, he can bring two quarts of fine flour as a sin offering. Since it is a sin offering, he shall not mix it with olive oil or frankincense.

12 He shall bring the flour to the priest, and the priest shall take a handful of flour as a token portion. He shall burn this token portion as a sin offering on the altar just like any other fire offering. **13** In this way the priest will make atonement for the person's sin, and he will be forgiven. Just as in the case of the grain offering, the unburned portions of these sacrifices shall belong to the priest.

14 Adonai spoke to Moses, saying: **15** If a person accidentally sins by taking something that is sacred to Adonai for his own personal use, he shall bring a healthy ram as his guilt offering to Adonai or pay the price for a ram having the same value in silver according to the sanctuary weight standard. **16** For taking something that was sacred, he must make full restitution, and add twenty percent of its value, and give the payment to the priest. In this way the priest will atone for him with the guilt offering of a ram, and he will be forgiven.

17 If a person, without knowing it, sins by violating one of Adonai's commandments, he is still responsible for his error. **18** He must bring a healthy ram to the priest as a guilt offering or pay the price for a ram in silver according to the sanctuary weight standard. The priest shall then make atonement for the accidental sin the person committed, and he shall be forgiven for the oversight. **19** It is a guilt offering that he has committed against Adonai.

20 Adonai said to Moses: **21** This is the law when a person sins and commits an offense against Adonai by lying to his neighbor about an article that was entrusted to him for safekeeping, or cheats on a business deal, or by robbery, or by withholding money, **22** or by finding a lost object and denying it. A person who swears falsely in any of these cases is considered to have sinned. **23** When he is judged guilty of such a sin, he must return the stolen article or money, the withheld funds, the article left for safekeeping, or the found article.

Offerings for Dishonesty   *Maftir*

24 For these or for anything else about which he swore falsely, he must repay the full amount plus twenty percent. On the day that he seeks atonement for his crime, he must repay the total amount to its rightful owner. **25** He must bring to the priest his sin offering of a healthy ram as a guilt offering or pay the price for a ram according to the sanctuary weight standard. **26** The priest shall make atonement for him before Adonai, and he will then be forgiven for any crime he has committed.

Tzav צַו

INSTRUCT AARON AND HIS SONS

6 Adonai spoke to Moses, telling him **2** to instruct Aaron and his sons.

The burnt offering must remain on the altar until morning, and the altar's fires must continue to burn all night. **3** Then the priest shall dress in his priestly garments and linen undergarments. He shall remove the ashes of the burnt offering, and pile them near the altar.

4 He shall then remove his garments and put on his everyday garments, and then move the ashes to a ritually clean place outside the camp.

5 The fire of the altar shall be kept burning, and each morning the priest shall add more wood to the fire. He shall arrange the burnt offerings on the wood and burn parts of the peace offerings. **6** In this way, the fire under the altar will never go out.

7 These are the rules of the grain offering that one of Aaron's descendants shall offer before Adonai, on the altar. **8** The priest shall take a handful of the flour and oil offering and all the frankincense that is on the offering. He shall burn this on the altar. This grain offering is a thank you gift to Adonai.

9 Aaron and his descendants shall then eat whatever remains of the grain offering. It must he eaten as unleavened bread in a holy place; therefore they must eat it in the courtyard.

10 It must not be baked as leavened bread. I have given them their portion of My grain offerings, and it is holy, just like the sin and the guilt offerings. **11** Only the males among Aaron's descendants are entitled to eat it. It is a law for all the generations that it be taken from Adonai's fire offerings. Anyone who touches it becomes holy.

The Offering of the High Priest 　　　*2ⁿᵈ Aliyah*

12 Adonai spoke to Moses, saying:

13 This is the offering that Aaron and his descendants must bring when one of them is anointed as High Priest. It shall consist of two quarts of fine flour, and it shall be a daily grain offering, with one quart in the morning and one quart in the evening.

14 It shall be prepared in a frying pan with olive oil and then baked. It is to be presented as a grain offering of broken pieces of bread. This offering is a thank you gift to Adonai.

15 For all time it is a law that the newly appointed priest chosen from Aaron's descendants shall offer it completely burned.

16 Every grain offering brought by a priest must be completely burned and must not be eaten.

17 Adonai spoke to Moses, saying: **18** Instruct Aaron and his descendants about the laws of the sin offering: The holy sin offering must be slaughtered before Adonai in the place where the burnt offering is slaughtered.

19 The priest who offers the sin offering may eat it. It must be eaten in a holy place, in the courtyard near the Meeting Tent.

20 Whatever touches the sin offering will become holy, and any blood that is sprinkled on a garment must be washed in a holy area.

21 The clay pot in which the offering is cooked must be broken, but if the offering is cooked in a copper pot, it must be scrubbed and rinsed with water.

22 Any priest may eat it, although it is holy.

23 But a sin offering whose blood is brought into the Meeting Tent for an atonement must not be eaten. It must be burned in fire.

7 This is the holy law of the guilt offering:

2 The guilt offering must be slaughtered in the same place that the burnt offering is slaughtered, and its blood must be sprinkled around the altar. **3** All the fat, **4** and the two kidneys, and the liver must be removed.

5 The priests must burn all these parts as a guilt offering on the altar, as a fire offering to Adonai.

6 Only the priests may eat the offering. It must be eaten in a holy place, because it is sacred. **7** The same law applies to the priest who makes the sin offering and the guilt offering. It shall belong to the priest who makes atonement with it.

8 The priest who offers a person's burnt offering can keep the skin of the burnt offering for himself.

9 Any of the leftover grain offering which is baked in an oven, pan fried, or deep fried shall also be given to the priest who offered it. **10** Every grain offering, whether mixed with olive oil or dry, shall be shared by Aaron's descendants.

The Peace Offerings   *3rd Aliyah*

11 These are laws of the kinds of peace offerings that are to be presented to Adonai.

12 A peace offering must be presented along with a variety of unleavened loaves mixed with olive oil, flat matzot with oil, and loaves made of fine flour mixed with oil. **13** The peace offering shall be presented with loaves of leavened bread.

14 One of each of the four breads shall be presented as an elevated gift to Adonai. The bread will then belong to the priest who sprinkles the blood of the sacrificed offering.

15 The flesh of the peace offering must be eaten on the same day that it is sacrificed. None of it may be saved until morning. **16** But if the offering is meant to fulfill a vow or a pledge, it can be eaten on the same day that it is sacrificed, and whatever is left over can be eaten the next day.

17 But any meat that is left over from the sacrifice on the third day must be burned in fire. **18** The sacrifice will not be acceptable if the person bringing the peace offering plans to eat it on the third day. It will have no holy value as a sacrifice. The person who eats it will be guilty of a sin.

19 Any sacrificial meat that comes in contact with something unclean must not be eaten; it must be burned in fire. As for the other meat, any ritually clean person may eat it. **20** But if a person who is in an unclean state eats the meat of a peace sacrifice that was presented to Adonai, he will no longer belong to the community of Israel. **21** Any person who comes in contact with something unclean, such as human waste, or with an unclean animal or any other unclean creature, and then eats the meat of Adonai's peace offering, that person will no longer belong to the community of Israel.

22 Adonai spoke to Moses, saying, **23** Tell the Israelites the following:

Do not eat any of the fat of an ox, sheep, or goat. **24** The fat of an animal that is not properly slaughtered or is found dead may be used for any purpose you see fit, as long as you do not eat it. **25** Anyone who eats the fat of any animal that has been offered to Adonai will no longer belong to the community of Israel.

26 No matter where you may live, you must not eat any blood from an animal or a bird. **27** Any person who eats blood will no longer belong to the community of Israel.

28 Adonai spoke to Moses, saying: **29** Speak to the children of Israel and tell them that anyone who brings a peace offering to Adonai must also bring a special offering to Adonai. **30** He must bring the fat as well as the breast, and he shall present the breast before Adonai.

31 The priest shall burn the fat on the altar, but the breast shall belong to Aaron and his descendants.

32 You shall give the right hind leg of your peace offerings as a gift to the priest. **33** Any descendant of Aaron who is permitted to sprinkle the blood and offer the fat of the peace offerings shall be given the right leg as his portion. **34** Because I have chosen the breast and the hind leg of the peace sacrifices as an elevated gift from the Israelite sacrifices to be forever set aside for the priests, I have given these parts to Aaron the priest and his descendants. It is the law for all time that these parts taken from the Israelites are to be given to the priests forever. **35** This is the portion of the fire offerings made to Adonai that shall be given to Aaron and his sons from the day they are ordained as priests to Adonai.

36 On the day they were ordained, Adonai commanded that the Israelites are to give them as their share the breast and the right leg.

This is an eternal law for every generation to come.

37 These are the laws of the burnt offering, the meal offering, the sin offering, the guilt offering, the ordination offering, and the peace offering. **38** Adonai gave these instructions to Moses on Mount Sinai, so that they would know how to present the sacrifices to Adonai in the wilderness of Sinai.

The Ordination of Aaron
and His Sons

4th Aliyah

8 Adonai spoke to Moses, saying: **2** Gather Aaron and his sons, and their garments, the anointing oil, the bull for the sin offering, the two rams, and the basket of unleavened bread. **3** Then assemble the entire community to meet at the entrance of the Meeting Tent.

4 Moses did as Adonai commanded, and the entire community gathered at the entrance of the Meeting Tent.

5 Moses said to the Israelites, "This is what Adonai has instructed me to do."

6 Moses presented Aaron and his sons, and cleansed them with water.

7 He clothed Aaron with the embroidered robe and the sash, and he put the robe of the ephod on him and fastened the ephod with its straps.

8 Then Moses strapped the breastplate to the ephod on Aaron and inserted the Urim and Thumim in the breastplate. **9** He put the headdress on Aaron's head and tied the sacred golden medallion on the front of the headdress. Moses clothed Aaron just as Adonai had commanded him.

10 Then Moses took the anointing oil and sanctified the Tabernacle and everything in it.

11 He sanctified the altar and sprinkled some of the oil on the altar seven times. He then sanctified the altar, all its utensils, as well as the washbasin and its base.

12 He poured anointing oil on Aaron's head, and he sanctified him.

13 Next Moses presented Aaron's sons, and he clothed them in robes, and tied them with sashes, and placed headdresses on them, just as Adonai had commanded Moses.

The First Ram of Ordination   *5th Aliyah*

14 Moses then presented a bull for the sin offering, and Aaron and his sons placed their hands on its head.

15 Moses slaughtered the bull and took some of the blood, and with his finger he smeared the blood on the horns of the altar to purify it. He poured the rest of the blood at the base of the altar to sanctify it so that atonement could be offered on it.

16 Moses took the fat, the liver, and the two kidneys, and burned them on the altar. **17** The rest of the bull—its skin, the meat, and the internal organs—he burned outside the camp. It was all done just exactly as Adonai had commanded Moses.

18 Next Moses presented a ram for the burnt offering, and Aaron and his sons placed their hands on its head. **19** Moses slaughtered it and sprinkled its blood on all sides of the altar.

20 He cut the ram into pieces, and Moses burned the fat, the head, and some of the cut pieces on the altar. **21** After that he washed the internal organs and legs with water. Then Moses burned the entire ram on the altar as a whole burnt offering. The fire offering was a thank you gift to Adonai. It was all done exactly as Adonai had commanded Moses.

The Second Ram of Ordination   *6th Aliyah*

22 Now Moses presented the second ram, which was the ordination ram. Aaron and his sons placed their hands on the head of the ram. **23** Then Moses slaughtered the ram and took some of its blood and smeared it on Aaron's right ear, and on his right thumb, and on his right big toe.

24 Next, Moses presented Aaron's sons, and he smeared some of the blood on their right ears, their right thumbs, and their right big toes. Moses also sprinkled some of the blood on all sides of the altar.

25 Moses took the fat, the liver, the two kidneys, and the right hind leg, **26** and on top of these, from the basket of unleavened breads, before Adonai, he placed a loaf of unleavened bread, a loaf of unleavened oil bread, and one thin loaf with olive oil.

27 Moses gave all these to Aaron and his sons, and he waved them as an offering before Adonai.

28 Then Moses took all the offerings from their hands, and he burned them on the altar. This ordination offering was a thank you gift to Adonai.

29 Now Moses took the breast of the ram and waved the offering before Adonai. This was Moses' own portion of the ordination ram. It was all done exactly as Adonai had commanded Moses.

Moses Sanctifies the Priestly Garments
7th Aliyah

30 Next Moses took the anointing oil, and some of the blood from the altar, and he sprinkled it on the garments of Aaron and his sons. This is how he sanctified the garments of Aaron and his sons.

31 Then Moses said to Aaron and his sons, "Cook the meat at the entrance of the Meeting Tent, and eat it there with the bread from the ordination basket, just as I commanded you. **32** Any of the meat or bread that is left over must be burned.

The Seven Days of Ordination
Maftir

33 "You must remain at the entrance of the Meeting Tent for seven days until the ordination ceremony is finished. **34** Adonai has commanded that the ceremony will take seven days to make atonement for you. **35** You must remain at the entrance of the Meeting Tent for seven days and nights, and do everything that Adonai demands of you. In this way you will remain alive." **36** Aaron and his sons obeyed everything exactly as Adonai had instructed Moses.

Shemini שְׁמִינִי
ON THE EIGHTH DAY

9 On the eighth day, Moses assembled Aaron, his sons, and the leaders of Israel.

2 He said to Aaron, "Choose a healthy young calf for a sin offering and a healthy ram for a burnt offering, and sacrifice them before Adonai. **3** Then speak to the Israelites, and tell them to choose five healthy animals: a goat for a sin offering, a young calf and a lamb for a burnt offering, **4** and a bull and a ram for peace offerings, and sacrifice them before Adonai along with a grain offering mixed with oil, because today Adonai Himself will appear to you."

5 The Israelites brought everything Moses requested to the entrance of the Meeting Tent, and the entire community gathered and stood before Adonai.

6 Then Moses said, "This is what Adonai has commanded. Do it exactly, and Adonai in His glory will appear to you."

7 Moses then told Aaron to approach the altar and present the sin offering and the burnt offering, to make atonement first for himself and for the people. He presented the people's offering to atone for them, just as Adonai had commanded.

8 Aaron once again approached the altar, and slaughtered the calf for the sin offering for himself.

9 Then Aaron's sons brought him some of the blood, and he dipped his finger in it. Aaron sprinkled some of the blood on the horns of the altar. He spilled the rest of the blood at the base of the altar.

10 He burned the fat, the kidneys, and the liver as a sin offering. It was all done exactly as Adonai had commanded Moses.

11 He then burned the meat and skin of the sin offering in fire outside the camp.

12 Aaron slaughtered the burnt offering, and Aaron's sons brought him some of the blood, and he sprinkled the blood on all sides of the altar. **13** Piece by piece they handed him the cut-up parts and the head for the burnt offering, and he burned them on the altar. **14** He washed the internal organs and the feet, and he burned them, too, on the altar as a burnt offering.

15 Next Aaron presented the offering of the Israelites. He took the goat that was the sin offering of the people and slaughtered it, and he prepared it as a sin offering, just like the first offering. **16** Then he brought the burnt offering and prepared it according to the law.

Adonai's Glory Is Revealed   *2nd Aliyah*

17 Then he brought the grain offering. He took a handful of fine flour and burned it on the altar. This was in addition to the regular morning grain offering

18 Next, he slaughtered the bull and the ram that were the people's peace sacrifice. Aaron's sons brought some of the blood to him, and he sprinkled it on all sides of the altar.

19 They also brought him the parts of the bull and ram: the fat, the kidneys, and the liver.

20 He placed the fat on top of the breasts of the animals, and burned the fat, kidneys, and liver on the altar. **21** Aaron waved the breasts and the right hind legs as an offering before Adonai. It was done exactly as Adonai had commanded Moses.

22 Then Aaron raised his hands over the people and blessed them. He stepped down from the altar where he had presented the sin offering, the burnt offering, and the peace offerings.

23 Moses and Aaron went into the Meeting Tent, and when they came out they blessed the people. And then the glory of Adonai was seen by all the Israelites.

Nadav and Avihu   *3rd Aliyah*

24 Fire blazed from Adonai and vaporized the burnt offering and the parts on the altar. When the people saw this, they raised their voices in prayer and bowed down.

10 Aaron's sons, Nadav and Avihu, each took his fire pan, placed burning coals in it, and sprinkled incense on the flames. They presented this before Adonai, but it was not an authorized fire that Adonai had commanded.

2 Flames of fire blazed down from Adonai and burned them up, and they died before Adonai.

3 Moses said to Aaron, "This is exactly what Adonai meant when he said,

'I will be holy
to those who worship Me;
to them I will show My glory.'"

Aaron remained speechless.

4 Then Moses summoned Mishael and Elzafan, the sons of Aaron's uncle Uzziel, and said to them, "Come and remove your cousins from inside the sanctuary and take their bodies outside the camp."

5 They came and dragged Nadav and Avihu by their robes outside the camp, as Moses had ordered.

6 Moses said to Aaron and his two remaining sons, Eleazar and Ithamar, "Do not mourn them by tearing your hair or your clothes; or Adonai will get angry and will also strike you, and you too will die. As far as your brothers are concerned, the entire community of Israel can mourn for them.

7 You are a priest, and you must not leave the entrance of the Meeting Tent, because Adonai's anointing oil is still on you, or else you will die."

They did as Moses commanded.

8 Adonai said to Aaron, **9** "Neither you nor your descendants may drink wine or any other alcoholic liquor when you enter the Meeting Tent, or you will die. This law must be observed for all coming generations. **10** If you are sober you will be able to tell the difference between the holy and the ordinary, and between honesty and dishonesty. **11** You will, moreover, be able to make correct legal decisions for the Israelites on all the laws that Adonai has taught Moses."

The Holy Service Is Finished   *4ᵗʰ Aliyah*

12 Then Moses spoke to Aaron and his surviving sons, Eleazar and Ithamar: "Take the remainder of the holy grain offering that has been presented to Adonai, and eat it unleavened near the altar. 13 Adonai has commanded that you must eat it in a holy place because it is the portion that has been given to you and your descendants.

14 Remember, the breast taken as a wave offering and the hind leg taken as an elevated gift are yours, and your sons and daughters may eat them. They are the portion from the peace sacrifices that has been given to you and your descendants.

15 The hind leg for the elevated gift, and the breast for the wave offering, shall be placed on top of the fat as a fire offering and are to be presented as a wave offering. The legs and the breast are designated as a gift for you and your descendants for all time, as Adonai has commanded."

Moses Forgives Aaron   *5ᵗʰ Aliyah*

16 When Moses asked about the goat for the sin offering, he was told that it had already been burned. Moses became angry at Aaron's sons, Eleazar and Ithamar. He said to them, 17 "Why didn't you eat the holy sin offering in a holy place? It was specially given you to remove the community's guilt and to atone before Adonai.

18 Since its blood was not brought into the inner sanctuary, you should have eaten it in a holy place, as I instructed you."

19 Their father Aaron answered Moses, "Today a tragedy happened and I lost my sons when they sacrificed their sin offering and burnt offering before Adonai. If I had eaten the sin offering today, would Adonai have been pleased with me?"

20 Moses sadly forgave Aaron when he heard his explanation.

The Dietary Laws   *6ᵗʰ Aliyah*

11 Adonai spoke to Moses and Aaron and told them:
2 Speak to the Israelites and instruct them:
These are the only land animals that you may eat:

3 You may eat any animal that has split hoofs and chews its cud.

4 However, you must not eat the following cud-chewing, hoofed animals.

You must not eat the camel, although it chews its cud, because it does not have a real hoof.

5 You must not eat the hare, even though it brings up its cud, because it too does not have a real hoof.

6 You must not eat the rabbit, even though it brings up its cud, because it does not have a true hoof.

7 You must not eat the pig, even though it has a true hoof, because it does not chew its cud.

8 You must not eat the flesh of any of these animals. And at no time shall you touch their carcasses, because they are unclean.

9 These are the creatures that live in the water that you may eat. You may eat any creature that lives in the water, in the seas or in the rivers, as long as it has fins and scales.

10 But all marine creatures that live in the seas and rivers and do not have fins and scales, whether they are small or large creatures which crawl in the water, must not be eaten.

11 They are forbidden to you. You must not eat their flesh. **12** Every creature in the water that has no fins and scales must not be eaten.

13 The following birds must not be eaten. These are the flying animals that you must avoid: the eagle, the vulture, the buzzard, **14** the kite and birds of the falcon family, **15** ravens of every kind, **16** the ostrich, the owl, the sea gull, and hawks of every kind, **17** the falcon, the cormorant, the ibis, **18** the marsh hen, the pelican, the magpie, **19** the stork and herons of every kind, the hoopoe, and the bat.

20 Every flying insect that uses four legs for walking shall not be eaten. **21** The only flying insects that you may eat are those with jointed legs extending above their feet, which they use to hop on the ground. **22** Among these are the various kinds of locusts, grasshoppers, and the cricket family.

23 All other flying insects with four feet must not be eaten.

24 Anyone who touches the bodies of dead animals will be unclean until evening. **25** Anyone dealing with their bodies must wash his clothes and remain unclean until evening. **26** Every animal that does not have cloven hoofs and does not chew its cud must not be eaten, and anyone touching its flesh shall become unclean.

27 Every four-footed animal that walks on its paws must not be eaten, and anyone touching their bodies shall be unclean until evening. **28** Anyone that carries their bodies must wash his clothing and then remains unclean until evening.

29 The following small animals that live on land must not be eaten: the weasel, the mouse, the rat, **30** the hedgehog, the chameleon, the lizard, the snail, and the mole.

31 These small animals must not be eaten; whoever touches them when they are dead shall remain unclean until evening.

32 When any of these dead animals falls on wooden dishes, clothing, leather goods, sackcloth, or any other article with which work is done, each item must be washed; it remains unclean until evening, and then becomes clean and usable.

Laws About Dead Animals   *7ᵗʰ Aliyah*

33 If a dead animal falls on the inside of a clay pot, anything inside it becomes unclean, and the pot shall be broken. **34** Any food soaked with water from the clay pot must not be eaten. Any liquid in the clay pot is also unclean.

35 Anything upon which a dead body falls is unclean; even an oven or a range becomes unclean, and must be destroyed.

36 The only thing that is always ritually clean is a body of water, either a well or a natural spring of water. Any other water that is touched by the dead body of any of these animals shall become unclean.

37 If a dead body falls on any planted seeds, they are still ritually clean. **38** But if the dead body falls on seeds that have been soaked in water, the seeds become unclean. **39** If any animal that you are permitted to eat dies naturally, then anyone touching its carcass shall be unclean until evening.

40 Anyone eating anything from a dead animal must wash his clothing, and then remains unclean until evening. Anyone who moves a dead animal must wash himself and his clothing, and also remains unclean until evening.

41 Every creature that crawls on the ground must not be eaten. **42** You must not eat any creature that crawls on its belly, or any animal with four or more feet that lives on land. All of these animals must not be eaten.

43 Do not make yourselves unclean by eating any of these creatures, or you will become unclean as they are.

44 I am Adonai;
I am holy,
and therefore you must
make yourselves holy.

Do not make yourself unclean by eating any of the small creatures that crawl on the earth.

The Israelites Must Be Holy   *Maftir*

45 I am Adonai,
I brought you out of Egypt
to be your Elohim.
Since I am holy,
you too must remain holy.

46 These are the laws about animals, birds, marine creatures, and creatures that creep on the ground. **47** I have given you these laws so that you can tell the difference between the unclean and clean animals, and between the animals that you may eat and those that you must not eat.

Tazria תַּזְרִיעַ
WHEN A WOMAN GIVES BIRTH

12 Adonai spoke to Moses, and told him to **2** inform the Israelites of the following laws:

When a woman becomes pregnant and gives birth to a boy, she is ritually unclean for seven days, just as she is unclean during the time when she has her period. **3** On the eighth day, the boy must be circumcised. **4** The woman must wait another thirty-three days until her blood is ritually clean. Until this cleansing period is complete, she must not touch anything holy and must not enter the sanctuary.

5 Every woman who gives birth to a girl is unclean for fourteen days, just as she is during her menstrual period. After that she shall have a waiting period of sixty-six days until her blood is ritually clean.

6 When her cleansing period either for a son or a daughter is completed, she shall bring to the priest, at the entrance of the Meeting Tent, a lamb for a burnt offering and a pigeon or a dove for a sin offering.

7 The priest shall offer the sacrifice before Adonai and atone for the woman, cleansing her of the blood coming from her womb. This law applies to a woman whether she gives birth to a boy or to a girl.

8 If the woman cannot afford a lamb, she can bring two doves or two pigeons, one for a burnt offering and one for a sin offering. Then the priest shall make atonement for her, and she shall be clean.

13 Adonai spoke to Moses and Aaron, saying:

2 If a person has a white sore or a rash, and it spreads on the skin of his body, and it is suspected of being leprosy, he must be brought to Aaron, or to one of Aaron's descendants.

3 A priest shall then examine the sores on the person's skin, and if the hairs on the sores have turned white, and the infection has penetrated under the skin, then it is a sign of leprosy. The priest who examines the infected area must declare the person unclean.

4 However, if there are white spots on the skin but they are only on the surface of the skin, and the hairs in the infected area have not turned white, then the priest shall quarantine the infected person for seven days. **5** On the seventh day the priest shall reexamine the person. If the sores have remained the same size, the priest shall quarantine the patient for another seven days.

Skin Diseases   *2nd Aliyah*

6 On the seventh day the priest shall reexamine him, and if the sores have healed and the infection has not spread, the priest shall announce that the person is healed, since it is just a plain white sore. The person must wash his clothing, and he is then clean.

7 However, if the white sores on the skin continue to spread and increase in size after they were examined by the priest, then the person must be reexamined by the priest.

8 If the priest determines that the rash on the skin has increased in size, he must pronounce him a leper.

9 When a person has a skin condition, he must be brought to a priest. **10** If the priest sees that there are large white sores on the skin, and some of the hairs have turned white, **11** the priest must declare leprosy. He must quarantine the person for further examination because he is obviously unclean.

12 These are the laws if the rash spreads and covers all of the skin of the infected person from head to foot, so that the priest can easily see it.

13 When the priest sees that the rash has covered all of the person's skin, he shall declare the infected person clean. As long as the skin has turned completely white, he is clean.

14 But if the sores came back and are filled with pus, the priest must rule that the person is unclean. **15** When the priest sees the undiscolored skin, he shall declare the person unclean.

The healthy skin is a sign of uncleanness, because it is leprosy.
16 But if the skin again turns white, the person must return to the priest. **17** When the priest determines that the infected area has healed completely and is white, the priest shall say to him, "You are cured."

Leprosy Disease   *3rd Aliyah*

18 These are the laws when an infection develops on a person's body and then heals. **19** If a white or red sore develops where the infection was, it must be shown to the priest. **20** The priest shall examine it, and if it appears to have penetrated under the skin and the hair has turned white, the priest must declare that the person has leprosy.

21 But if the priest examines the infection and does not see any white hair, and the infection has not penetrated the skin and it is a dull white, then the priest shall quarantine the person for seven days. **22** If the infection on the skin spreads during this time, the priest shall declare the person unclean, because it is leprosy.

23 However, if the infection does not spread and remains in the same place, it is scar tissue from the infection, and the priest shall declare the person clean.

Burns and Leprosy   *4th Aliyah*

24 These are the laws when a person has a burn on the body, and the burned area develops a red or white sore. **25** The priest shall examine it, and if the hair in the burned area has turned white, and the infection has penetrated under the skin, it is leprosy that is breaking out in the burned area. Since it is leprosy, the priest shall declare the person unclean.

26 But if the priest examines the area, and the burned area does not have white hair, and the infection has not penetrated under the skin, the priest shall quarantine the person for seven days. **27** At the end of seven days, the priest shall reexamine the skin. If the infection has increased in size, the priest shall declare the person unclean, since it is leprosy.

28 But if the burned area has not increased in size and the redness has faded, then it is just a scar because of the burn.

Since it is scar tissue from the burn, the priest shall declare the person clean.

Leprosy and Baldness   *5ᵗʰ Aliyah*

29 These are the laws if a man or a woman has an infection on the head or chin. **30** The priest shall examine the infection, and if it has penetrated the skin and blond hairs are found in the infected area, the priest shall declare the person unclean. Such an infection is a sign of leprosy on the head or chin.

31 If the priest examines the area, and the infection has not penetrated under the skin and does not have black hairs in it, the priest must quarantine the person with the infection for seven days. **32** On the seventh day, the priest shall again examine the area, and if the infection has not increased in size, and there is no blond hair in it, the infection has not penetrated under the skin. **33** In this case the person shall shave, but without shaving off the hair in the infected area. The priest shall then quarantine the person with the infection for a second seven-day period.

34 The priest shall reexamine the infection on the seventh day, and if the infected area with the fallen hair has not increased in size, or if the infection has not penetrated under the skin, the priest shall declare the person clean. The person must then wash his clothing, and he is clean.

35 But if the infection with the fallen hair continues to spread after he has cleansed himself, **36** the priest must reexamine the person again. If the bald patch has increased in size, the priest need not check for blond hairs, since the person is unclean.

37 However, if the infected bald patch remains the same size and the black hairs are growing back, then the infection has healed and the person is clean. The priest shall declare the person dean.

38 If a man's or woman's body breaks out with white spots, **39** the priest shall carefully examine the infected area. If the skin is just covered with dull white spots, it is a simple skin rash and the person is clean.

Unclean and Contagious   *6ᵗʰ Aliyah*

40 When a man loses the hair on his head and simply becomes bald, he is clean. **41** If he loses the hair near his face, it is just a sign of a receding hairline and he is clean.

42 But if he has a red infection on the bald spots and finds sores and swelling in the front or back of his head, it may be a sign of a skin disease. **43** The priest shall examine the reddish sores on his bald spots, and if he finds swelling around the sores it is leprosy.

44 The person is considered infected with leprosy, and he is unclean. Since he is unclean because of the infection on his head, the priest must declare him unclean.

45 A person who is a leper must tear his clothing and leave his hair uncut, and wherever he goes he must cover his head and must call out, "Unclean! Contagious! Unclean! Contagious!"

46 He shall be unclean as long as the disease lasts. Since he is unclean, he must be isolated and live outside the camp.

47 These are the laws when a garment contains a mildew infection. It can be woolen clothing, linen clothing, **48** wool yarn, or anything made of leather. **49** If a green or red discoloration appears in the cloth, leather, yarn, or any leather article, it may be a fungus infection, and it must be shown to the priest.

50 The priest shall examine the mildewed area and quarantine the infected article for seven days. **51** On the seventh day, he shall examine the affected area, and if the mold in the mildewed area has increased in size on the cloth, the yarn, or the article made from leather, then it is a fungus infection, and it is unclean. **52** The cloth, the yarn, whether wool or linen, or the leather article containing the fungus must be burned. Since it is a fungus infection, it must be burned in fire.

53 However, if, when the priest examines it, the mildew in the garment, the yarn, or the leather article has not spread, **54** the priest shall order that the mildewed article be scrubbed and quarantined for a second seven-day period.

Mildew Infections   *7ᵗʰ Aliyah*

55 After the mildew has been scrubbed and quarantined, the priest shall examine the article, and if the mildew has not changed in appearance or spread, then it is still unclean and must be burned.

56 If the priest examines the item after it has been scrubbed and quarantined, and the mold from the mildew has faded from the cloth, then he shall cut off the mildewed spot from the cloth, the leather, or the yarn.

Clean and Unclean   *Maftir*

57 But if the mildew reappears on the same cloth, yarn, or leather item, then it is infected, and the article having the mildew must be burned.

58 If the fungus mold is completely removed from the cloth, yarn, or leather article, and is then scrubbed and washed a second time, it is considered clean.

59 These are the laws for deciding whether cloth, leather items, or yarn are clean or unclean from fungus infections.

Metzora מְצֹרָע
THE LAWS OF LEPROSY

14 Adonai spoke to Moses, saying:

2 These are the instructions which must be followed when you think that the leper under the care of a priest has been cured.

3 The priest shall go outside the camp to examine the leper and check whether the leprosy has healed.

4 The priest shall conduct a cleansing ceremony for the person by taking two live clean birds, a piece of cedar wood, some red wool, and a hyssop branch.

5 The priest shall delegate another priest to slaughter a bird over a clay bowl filled with fresh spring water.

6 Then he shall take the second live bird and the piece of cedar wood, the red crimson wool, and the hyssop branch, and along with the live bird he shall dip the cedar, the wool, and the hyssop into the spring water mixed with the blood of the slaughtered bird. **7** The priest shall then sprinkle this mixture seven times on the person undergoing the cleansing from leprosy, thereby making him clean. When the ceremony is over, the priest shall release the living bird and let it fly away.

8 The person undergoing cleansing shall wash his clothing and shave off all the hair on his body. He shall then wash himself and in this way complete the first part of the cleansing. He may return to the camp, but he must remain outside his tent for seven days.

9 On the seventh day, the person shall once again shave off all the hair on his head, beard, eyebrows, and other body hair. He shall then wash his clothing and body, and then he is completely clean.

10 On the eighth day, he shall take two healthy rams, one healthy lamb, and three-fifths of a pint of fine flour mixed with olive oil as a meal offering, and three-fifths of a pint of olive oil. **11** The priest will then present the offering and the person undergoing cleansing before Adonai at the entrance of the Meeting Tent. **12** The priest shall take one ram with the olive oil and present it as a guilt offering. He shall offer them as a wave offering before Adonai.

Healed of Leprosy 2nd *Aliyah*

13 Then he shall slaughter the lamb in the same place where burnt offerings and sin offerings are slaughtered. This guilt offering is holy and is just like a sin offering to the priest.

14 The priest shall take some blood from the guilt offering and smear it on the right earlobe, right thumb, and right big toe of the person who is being cleansed.

15 The priest shall pour some of the olive oil into the palm of his own left hand. **16** Then he shall dip his right forefinger into the oil in his left hand, and with his finger sprinkle some oil seven times before Adonai. **17** The priest shall then smear some of the oil from his hand on the right earlobe, right thumb, and right big toe of the person undergoing cleansing, over the guilt offering's blood. **18** The priest shall pour the rest of the oil in his hand onto the head of the person that is being cleansed. In this way, the priest shall make atonement before Adonai for the healed person.

19 Then the priest shall sacrifice the sin offering and make atonement for the person being cleansed. After that, he shall slaughter the burnt offering, **20** and the priest shall present the burnt offering and the grain offering on the altar. In this way the priest shall make atonement for the person who is cured and is now ceremonially clean.

A Poor Person's Offering 3rd *Aliyah*

21 If the leper is poor, however, and cannot afford the two lambs, he can bring one lamb as a guilt offering—this shall be the wave offering to atone for him—and two quarts of the best flour mixed with olive oil as a grain offering, and three-fifths of a pint of olive oil. **22** In addition, he shall bring two doves or two pigeons, whichever he can afford, one for a sin offering and the other for a burnt offering.

23 On the eighth day, the person being cleansed shall bring the offering to the priest, at the entrance of the Meeting Tent, before Adonai. **24** The priest shall take the lamb for the guilt offering and the olive oil, and offer them as a wave offering before Adonai. **25** He shall slaughter the lamb as a guilt offering. The priest shall take the blood of the guilt offering and place it on the right earlobe, the right thumb, and the right big toe of the person undergoing purification.

26 The priest shall then pour some of the oil into the palm of his left hand. **27** Then he shall dip his right finger and sprinkle some of the oil from his left hand seven times before Adonai. **28** The priest shall place some of the oil from his hand on the right earlobe, right thumb, and right big toe of the person undergoing cleansing, right over the place where the blood of the guilt offering was put. **29** The priest shall pour the rest of the oil from his hand onto the head of the person undergoing cleansing. With all this he shall make atonement for the person before Adonai.

30 He shall then prepare one of the doves or pigeons, whichever the person was able to afford.

31 With this offering, the priest shall sacrifice one bird as a sin offering and one as a burnt offering, and then present it with the grain offering. In this way the priest shall make atonement before Adonai for the person undergoing cleansing.

32 These are the instructions for cleansing the person who has a skin disease and cannot afford to bring the usual sacrifice for his cleansing.

Mildewed Houses   *4ᵗʰ Aliyah*

33 Adonai spoke to Moses and Aaron, saying:

34 When you come to the land of Canaan, which I am giving you as a permanent possession, and I for some reason contaminate houses in the land you inherit, **35** the owner of such a house must go and tell the priest, "It looks to me as if there is mildew growing in my house."

36 The priest shall order that the house be completely emptied so that everything in the house will not become unclean. Only then shall a priest inspect the house.

37 The priest shall examine the mildew to see whether the streaks of the green or red fungus have penetrated into the wall.

38 If the fungus mold has grown into the wall, then the priest shall leave and stand outside the entrance of the house. The priest shall quarantine the house for seven days. **39** On the seventh day the priest shall return and check whether the mold on the wall of the house has spread.

40 If the fungus has grown, the priest shall order the owner to dump the infected stones in an isolated place outside the city.

41 Afterwards the owner shall scrape the inside of the house, especially around the mildewed area. The workmen doing the scraping shall dump the plaster and stones outside the city in an isolated place. **42** Then the owner shall replace the stones and replaster the entire house with new clay.

43 But if the stones have been removed and the house has been scraped and plastered, and the mildew comes back, **44** the priest shall return and reexamine the house. If the fungus mold has grown again in the house, then the whole house is unclean. **45** The priest must order the house completely torn down, and all the wood and stones and plaster from the house shall be moved outside the city to an isolated dump.

46 As long as the house is in quarantine, anyone entering the house will be unclean until evening. **47** If someone eats or sleeps in the house, he must wash both his body and his clothing. However, he must wash his clothing only if he has remained in the house long enough to eat a small meal.

48 When the priest returns at the end of the seven days, after the house has been replastered, and he sees that the mold has not reappeared in the house, then the fungus has gone away and the priest shall declare the house clean. **49** To cleanse the house, he shall take two birds, a piece of cedar wood, some red wool, and a hyssop branch.

50 He shall slaughter one bird over a clay bowl filled with fresh spring water. **51** And then he shall take the cedar wood, the hyssop, the red wool, and the live bird, dip them in the blood of the slaughtered bird and the fresh spring water, and sprinkle it on the house seven times.

52 He shall cleanse the house with the bird's blood and spring water, along with the live bird, cedar wood, hyssop, and crimson wool. **53** He shall then release the live bird in a field outside the city. This is how he shall make atonement for the house, and it is then clean.

Skin and Mildew Infections　　　*5ᵗʰ Aliyah*

54 These are the laws for dealing with skin diseases and mildew infections, **55** if mildew streaks appear on a garment or in a house, **56** and white sores or discolorations appear on the skin. **57** These instructions must be followed when dealing with skin diseases and mildew, and to tell when someone or something is clean or unclean. These are the laws dealing with skin infections.

15 Adonai spoke to Moses and Aaron, and told them **2** to speak to the Israelites and tell them the following: When a man has a pus discharge from his penis, this discharge can make him unclean. **3** He becomes unclean if his penis drips pus or if some of the pus is stuck to his body. These discharges make him unclean, so that **4** any bed the man with the discharge lies in becomes unclean, and any object he sits upon also becomes unclean. **5** Any person who lies in the man's bed must wash his clothing and his body, and then remains unclean until evening.

6 Anyone who sits on an object upon which the man with a discharge has been sitting must also cleanse his clothing and his body, and then remains unclean until evening.

7 If anyone touches the body of a person with a pus discharge, he must wash his clothing and his body, and then remains unclean until evening. **8** If the saliva of someone with a discharge is spat on a ritually clean person, that person must wash his clothing and his body, and remains unclean until evening.

9 Any saddle or seat upon which the person with the discharge sits is unclean. **10** Anyone who touches something that has been under a person with a discharge shall be unclean until evening. Anyone who carries such an object must cleanse his clothing and his body, and then remains unclean until evening.

11 If anyone touches a man with a discharge who has not immersed even his hands in water, that person must immerse his clothing and his body in water and then remains unclean until evening.

12 Any clay pot touched by a man with a discharge must be broken. Every wooden utensil must be washed.

13 Seven days after a person with a pus discharge gets well, he is to be considered clean if he washes himself and his clothing in a stream of spring water.

14 On the eighth day, he shall take two doves or two pigeons, and present them before Adonai at the entrance of the Meeting Tent, and he shall give the birds to the priest.

15 The priest shall present one bird as a sin offering and one as a burnt offering. In this way the priest will make atonement for the person before Adonai, cleansing him of his discharge.

Bodily Discharges   *6ᵗʰ Aliyah*

16 When a man has a discharge of semen, he must wash his entire body and remains unclean until evening.

17 If any semen comes in contact with an article of clothing or a leather item, it must be washed and remains unclean until evening.

18 If a woman has sexual intercourse with a man, both of them must wash and then remain unclean until evening.

19 Whenever a woman has her menstruation, she shall remain ritually unclean for seven days, and anyone touching her shall be unclean until evening.

20 When a woman is in her menstrual state, anything upon which she sits or lies becomes unclean, and anyone sitting or lying on it also becomes unclean.

21 Whoever lies on her bed must wash his clothing and his body, and then remains unclean until evening. **22** The same applies to anyone who touches anything upon which she has rested. He must wash his clothing and his body and remains unclean until evening. **23** If he touches anything that is on her bed or any other article upon which she rested, he is unclean until evening.

24 If a man has sexual intercourse with her and her menstrual discharge touches him, he shall be unclean for seven days, and any bed upon which he lies shall be unclean.

25 If a woman has a discharge of blood for a long time when it is not time for her monthly menstrual period, or if she has a discharge beyond the usual time of her period, then she is unclean, just as when she has her period.

26 Anything upon which she sits or rests during the time of her discharge shall be unclean just as it would be during her normal period. **27** Anyone touching these articles must wash his clothing and his body, and remains unclean until evening. **28** Seven days after the woman is rid of her discharge, she must undergo cleansing.

Atonement for an Unclean Discharge   *7ᵗʰ Aliyah*

29 On the eighth day, she shall take two doves or two pigeons and bring them to the priest at the entrance of the Meeting Tent. **30** The priest shall prepare one bird as a sin offering and the other bird as a burnt offering, and the priest shall make atonement for her before Adonai, cleansing her from her discharge.

Separate the Clean from the Unclean   *Maftir*

31 Now Moses and Aaron must separate the Israelites from things that make them impure so that they will not die by corrupting My Tabernacle that I have placed among them.

32 These are the laws for a man who is unclean because of a discharge of semen, **33** and for a woman who has her monthly period, and for a man who has a genital discharge or who has sex with a ritually unclean woman.

Achare Mot אַחֲרֵי מוֹת

THE DEATH OF AARON'S SONS

16 Adonai spoke to Moses right after the death of the two sons of Aaron who had disobeyed Adonai and brought an unauthorized offering. **2** Adonai said to Moses:

Tell your brother Aaron not to enter the Holy of Holies that is behind the curtain concealing the ark or else he will die, because I appear there in a cloud over the ark.

3 Before Aaron enters the inner sanctuary, he must bring a young bull for a sin offering and a ram for a burnt offering. **4** He must clothe himself in the white linen robe, his linen undergarments, his linen belt, and his headdress. These are sacred garments, and before putting them on he must cleanse himself.

5 The Israelite community shall bring him two goats for sin offerings, and one ram for a burnt offering.

6 First he shall ask forgiveness for himself and his family by presenting a bull for his own sin offering.

7 Then he shall take the two goats, and lead them before Adonai at the entrance of the Meeting Tent.

8 Aaron shall cast two lots for the two goats: one lot marked "For Adonai," and the other lot marked "For Azazel."

9 Aaron shall present the goat that was chosen by lot for Adonai so that it can be offered as a sin offering.

10 But the goat that was chosen by lot for the demon Azazel must remain alive, so that it will be able to remove the sins of the Israelites and send the sins to Azazel in the desert.

11 Aaron shall present his bull as a sin offering and ask forgiveness for himself and for his fellow priests. Then he shall slaughter his bull as a sin offering.

12 Next he shall take a fire pan filled with burning coals from the side of the altar that is before Adonai, along with two handfuls of perfume incense, and bring them both into the inner sanctuary behind the cloth partition.

13 There he shall sprinkle the incense on the coals, so that the smoke from the incense covers the ark and the Ten Commandments. If he follows My instructions, he will not die.

14 Aaron shall then take some of the bull's blood, and with his forefinger sprinkle drops of the blood seven times toward the ark.

15 Then he shall slaughter the goat as the people's sin offering, and bring its blood into the inner sanctuary behind the cloth curtain. Aaron shall do the same with this blood as he did with the bull's blood, and sprinkle it both above and below the ark.

16 With this offering, he will take away the sins of the Israelites for their rebellious acts and all their uncleanness.

He shall then perform exactly the same ritual in the Meeting Tent, which remains among the Israelites despite their misdeeds.

17 No one must be in the Meeting Tent from the moment that Aaron enters the sanctuary to make atonement until he leaves. In this way Aaron will remove the sins from himself, from his family, and from the entire Israelite community.

The Azazel Goat   *2ⁿᵈ Aliyah*

18 After leaving the tent, Aaron shall make atonement by smearing some of the blood from the bull and the goat on the horns of the altar.

19 With his finger he shall sprinkle the blood on the altar seven times, and it will completely cleanse the sins of the Israelites. **20** When he has finished making atonement in the inner sanctuary, in the Meeting Tent, and on the altar, he shall present the live goat.

21 Aaron shall place both of his hands on the head of the goat and confess all the sins of the Israelites, their rebellious acts and their sins. Then Aaron will select someone to lead the Azazel goat into the wilderness.

22 When the person frees the goat in the wilderness, all of the sins of the Israelites will be transferred to Azazel.

23 Next Aaron shall enter the Meeting Tent and remove the priestly garments that he wore when he entered the Holy of Holies and leave his sacred garments there. **24** Aaron shall then bathe in a sacred place, and dress in his regular clothing. Then he shall complete his own and the people's burnt offerings, thus atoning for himself and the people.

The Sabbath of Sabbaths   *3rd Aliyah*

25 Aaron shall also burn the fat of the sin offering on the altar. **26** The person who leads the goat to Azazel in the wilderness shall wash his clothing and body, and only then can he re-enter the camp.

27 The remains of the bull and the goat presented as sin offerings, whose blood was brought into the inner sanctuary to make atonement, must be taken outside the camp, where their skin, flesh, and organs shall be burned. **28** The person who does the burning shall wash his clothing and body, and only then can he return to the camp.

29 This shall be a permanent law for all time. Every year, on the tenth day of the seventh month [Tishri], you must spend the day fasting and not doing any work. This law is the same for Israelites and for the foreigner who lives among you. **30** On this day you will be cleansed of all your sins before Adonai. **31** From now on the Sabbath of Sabbaths will be, for Israelites, a day of fasting and resting. This is a law, and it must be observed each year.

32 A priest who is anointed and ordained as the new High Priest shall make atonement by wearing the sacred garments of white linen. **33** He shall make his atonement in the Holy of Holies, in the Meeting Tent, and on the altar. The atonement that he makes shall be for the priests and for the Israelites.

34 This shall be a law for all time for you, so that the Israelites once each year will be able to gain forgiveness for their sins. Moses later did exactly as Adonai had commanded him.

Official Sacrifices   *4ᵗʰ Aliyah*

17 Adonai spoke to Moses, and told him: **2** Speak to Aaron, his sons, and the other Israelites, and tell them that this is what Adonai has commanded:

3 If any Israelite sacrifices an ox, sheep, or goat to Adonai whether in or outside the camp, **4** but does not bring the sacrifice in person to the Meeting Tent, he is treated as a murderer. He shall be considered guilty of murder, and he must be driven out of the community.

5 The Israelites must take the sacrifices that they are now offering in the fields and bring them to Adonai, to the entrance to the Meeting Tent, and present them to the priest. They will be offered as peace offerings to Adonai. **6** The priest will sprinkle the blood against the altar at the entrance of the Meeting Tent and burn the fat as a thank you gift to Adonai.

7 The Israelites must no longer sacrifice to idols who tempt them to worship. This shall be a law for all the generations to come.

Do Not Eat Blood   *5ᵗʰ Aliyah*

8 Any person, whether an Israelite or a foreigner who lives among you, who wishes to offer a burnt offering or any of the sacrifices, **9** must bring it to the Meeting Tent to present it to Adonai. If he does not, he must be driven out of the community of Israel. **10** If any person, whether of the family of Israel or a foreigner who lives among you, eats blood, it will make Me angry, and that person must be outlawed from among his people. **11** Because the life-force of a living thing is in its flesh and blood, and that is why I have given you the blood of animals to sacrifice instead of your own lives.

12 Therefore I say to the Israelites, "Do not eat blood." A foreigner who lives among you must also not eat blood.

13 If any person, whether of the family of Israel or a foreigner who lives among you, hunts and kills an animal or a bird which one is permitted to eat, he must drain its blood and must bury the blood in the earth.

14 The existence of every living creature is in its blood. That is why I have warned the Israelites not to eat any blood, because the life-force of every creature is in its blood. That is why anyone who eats blood must be driven out of the community of Israel.

15 Any Israelite or foreigner who eats a creature that is permitted to be eaten but has died a natural death or was killed by beasts must wash his clothing and body. He shall remain unclean until evening. **16** If he does not wash his clothing and body, he will be held responsible for his sin.

18

Adonai spoke to Moses and told him: **2** Speak to the Israelites, and say to them:

I am Adonai.

3 You must not follow the customs of the Egyptians, among whom you once lived, and also do not follow the customs of the people of Canaan, where I will be bringing you. You must not imitate their way of life.

4 Obey My laws and carefully observe My commandments. I am Adonai. I require it.

5 If you observe My commandments and laws, then you will surely live a good life. I am Adonai. I require it.

Unlawful Sexual Acts   *6th Aliyah*

6 You must not proposition a relative to commit a sexual act. I am Adonai. I forbid it.

7 You must not commit a sexual act with your close relatives especially your mother.

8 You must not commit a sexual act with your father's wife.

9 You must not commit a sexual act with your sister. It makes no difference if she is your sister or your stepsister.

10 You must not commit a sexual act with the daughter of your son or daughter.

11 You must not commit a sexual act with the daughter of your father's wife. She is your sister, and you must not commit a sexual act with her.

12 You must not commit a sexual act with your father's sister. She is your father's relative.

13 You must not commit a sexual act with your mother's sister. She is your mother's relative.

14 You must not commit a sexual act against your father's brother by having sexual contact with his wife. She is your aunt.

15 You must not commit a sexual act with your daughter-in-law. She is your son's wife.

16 You must not commit a sexual act with your brother's wife.

17 You must not commit a sexual act by marrying a woman and her daughter. Do not even marry her son's daughter or her daughter's daughter. They are your relatives, and it is a sin.

18 You must not marry a woman and also marry her sister as long as the first wife is alive.

19 You must not sleep with a woman who is ritually unclean because of her menstruation.

20 You must not have sex with your neighbor's wife.

21 You must not allow any of your children to be sacrificed to the idol Molekh. I am Adonai. I require it.

You Must Observe My Laws   7ᵗʰ *Aliyah*

22 You must not practice homosexuality. It is a sin.

23 You must not perform any sexual act with animals, because it is unclean. Nor shall a woman have sexual contact with an animal. It is a sin.

24 You must not lower yourself into the gutter by imitating any of these sexual acts. It is because they engage in these evil practices that I am driving away the nations who stand in your way.

25 The land has become unclean, and so I must punish the people who live there. Soon the land will throw them out.

26 Every Israelite and every foreigner who settles among you must observe My rules and commandments and not perform any of these disgusting acts.

27 The nations who inhabited the land before you practice all these disgusting acts and have made the land unclean.

You Must Not Imitate Their Customs   *Maftir*

28 Do not imitate them, or I will throw you out of the land just as I will throw out the people who lived there before you.

29 Anyone who performs any of these degrading acts will be outlawed from his people.

30 Follow My commandments; do not imitate any of the disgusting customs that were practiced before you arrived, lest you be defiled by them. I am Adonai. I require it.

Kedoshim קְדוֹשִׁים
YOU MUST BE HOLY

19 Adonai spoke to Moses, and told him: **2** Speak to the Israelite community and say to them:

You must be holy, because I am Adonai and I am holy.

3 Every person must respect his mother and his father. You must observe the Sabbath as a day of rest. I am Adonai. I demand it.

4 You must not worship false gods, and you must not make idols of any kind. I am Adonai. I forbid it.

5 When you bring a peace offering to Adonai, you must do it willingly. **6** And you must eat it on the same day you sacrifice it or on the next day, but anything that is left over on the third day must be burned. **7** If any of the offering is eaten on the third day, it will be considered impure and I will reject it.

8 Whoever eats it will be punished, because he has desecrated that which is holy to Adonai. Such a person must be exiled from the community of Israel.

9 When you reap your grain harvest, leave some of the wheat at the edges of your fields, and do not pick up the loose stalks that have fallen to the ground.

10 You must not pick up the fallen bunches of grapes in your vineyards. And you must not pick up the loose grapes that have fallen to the ground in your vineyards. Leave it all for the poor and the stranger who lives in your midst. I am Adonai. I demand it.

11 You must not steal.

You must not cheat.

You must not lie to one another.

12 You must not swear falsely and use My name. If you do, you will bring shame to My name. I am Adonai. I forbid it.

13 You must pay your worker on time. You must not withhold the daily wages of your workers until morning. **14** You must not curse a deaf person. You must not trip a blind (handicapped) person. You must fear Adonai. I am Adonai. I require it.

You Must Not   *2nd Aliyah*

15 You must not interfere with justice. Do not favor the poor or show favoritism to the rich. You must judge people fairly.
16 You must not spread gossip.
You must not stand still if your neighbor's life is in danger. You must try to help. I am Adonai. I demand it.
17 You must not be jealous of your neighbor.
You must warn your neighbor if he does something wrong. You must not close your eyes to wrongdoing.
18 You must not hold a grudge against people.
You must love your neighbors as much as you love yourself. I am Adonai. I demand it
19 You must faithfully observe My commandments. You must not mate your cattle with other species.
You must not plant your fields with different kinds of seeds.
You must not wear clothing that contains a forbidden mixture of wool and linen (*shatnez*).
20 If a man sleeps with a slave woman who is engaged to another man, and she has not been given her freedom, she must be tried in court, but neither of them shall be put to death, because she was not free.
21 The man must bring a ram as his guilt offering to Adonai at the entrance of the Meeting Tent. **22** The priest shall make atonement for him before Adonai with the guilt ram for the sin that he committed. In this way he will gain forgiveness.

Forbidden Fruit   *3rd Aliyah*

23 When you enter into the Promised Land and plant new fruit trees, you must not eat the fruit for the first three years. Avoid the fruit as a forbidden growth.
24 In the fourth year, all of the fruits shall be holy and must be given to Adonai as a tithe.
25 In the fifth year, you may eat its fruit and in this way your crops will increase. I am Adonai.

26 You must not eat blood.

You must not consult witches or fortune-tellers.

You must not practice magic.

27 You must not cut off the hair on the sides of your head.

You must not clip off the edges of your beard.

28 You must not cut yourself when you are in mourning.

You must not make any tattoo marks on your body. I am Adonai. I forbid it.

29 You must not degrade your daughter and make her into a prostitute, because you will make the land immoral, and the land will be filled with evil.

30 You must observe the Sabbath and respect My sanctuary. I am Adonai. I demand it.

31 You must not consult fortune-tellers or oracles who falsely claim to talk to the dead.

I am Adonai. I forbid it.

32 Elderly people deserve respect. I am Adonai. This I expect.

Honest Weights and Measures   *4th Aliyah*

33 When a foreigner comes to live in your land, do not insult or discriminate against him. **34** The foreigner who becomes a citizen must be treated exactly the same as a native-born person. You must love him just as much as you love yourself. You must remember that you were once foreigners in Egypt. I am Adonai.

35 You must not use dishonest standards when measuring length, weight, or volume.

36 You must use an accurate scale, correct weights, and honest dry and liquid measuring cups.

I am Adonai, who took you out of Egypt. **37** Observe My rules and My commandments. I am Adonai. I require it.

Penalties for Disobeying Adonai   *5th Aliyah*

20 Adonai spoke to Moses, and told him: **2** Say the following to the Israelites:

Any person, whether an Israelite or a foreigner, who lives among you and sacrifices his children to the idol Molekh must be executed.

3 I will be angry at that person because he has sacrificed his children to Molekh. He has disregarded everything that is holy to Me and degraded My holy name. **4** If the people allow him to sacrifice his children and do not put him to death, **5** then I will act against that person and his family. I will outlaw him from among his people, together with everyone who follows him to worship Molekh.

6 I will be an enemy to any person who consults fortune-tellers or psychics and follows their advice. I will be angry at them and cut them off from the community. **7** You must sanctify yourselves and be holy, for I, Adonai, am holy.

You Must Obey My Commandments   *6ᵗʰ Aliyah*

8 You must observe all of My commandments, for I, Adonai, have made you holy.

9 Any person who curses his father or mother must be put to death. **10** If a man has sex with a married woman, and she is the wife of a fellow Israelite, both the man and the woman shall be sentenced to death.

11 If a man has sexual relations with his father's wife, he has committed a sin against his father. Both of them shall be sentenced to death.

12 If a man has sexual relations with his daughter-in-law, both of them must be sentenced to death, because they have committed a vulgar sin.

13 If a man has homosexual relations with another man, both of them have committed a vulgar sin. And both of them shall be sentenced to death.

14 It is a sin if a man marries both a mother and a daughter; all of them shall be punished.

15 If a man has sex with an animal, he must be put to death, and the animal must also be put to death.

16 If a woman has sex with an animal, both the woman and the animal shall be sentenced to death.

17 It is a disgrace if a man has sex with his sister or his step-sister, and both of them must be exiled from their people, because he has committed incest with his sister and must be held responsible.

18 If a man has intercourse with a woman during her menstrual period, he has committed a sexual offense with her. He has violated her body, and both of them shall be driven out of the community.

19 You must not have sex with your mother's sister, since this disgraces a blood relative, and both of them are guilty of a sin.

20 If a man has sexual relations with his aunt, he has dishonored his uncle. Both of them are guilty, and they will die childless.

21 If a man marries his brother's wife, he has committed a sin against his brother, and both the man and the woman will die childless.

22 You must observe all My commandments and laws and obey them, to ensure that the land you are going to inherit does not throw you out.

Do Not Follow Their Customs   *7th Aliyah*

23 You must not follow the customs of the nations that I am driving out before you, because they are completely immoral and I detest their customs.

24 As I have already said to you, "Conquer the land that I have promised to give you as an inheritance. It is a land flowing with milk and honey." I, Adonai, have chosen you from among all the other nations.

You Must Be Holy   *Maftir*

25 You must make a distinction between the clean animals and birds and the unclean animals and birds. Do not degrade yourselves by eating animals, birds, or other creatures that I have set apart for you as unclean. **26** You shall be holy to Me, for I, Adonai, am holy, and I have chosen you from among the nations to be My own.

27 Any man or woman who practices witchcraft or talks to the dead shall be put to death.

Emor אֱמֹר

SPEAK TO THE LEVITES

21 Adonai told Moses to speak to Aaron's descendants, the priests:

You must not make yourselves ritually unclean by contact with the dead, **2** unless it is a blood relative, such as a mother, father, son, daughter, or brother, **3** or an unmarried sister.

4 But you must not defile yourself even for a close married relative.

5 No priest shall shave off hair from his head, nor may they shave off their beards or mutilate themselves while in mourning.

6 They must be holy to Adonai, and not shame the name of Adonai. They must remain holy, because they present fire offerings to Adonai.

7 They must not marry an immoral woman. And they must not marry a woman who has been divorced. A priest must be holy to Adonai.

8 They must be treated with respect, because they present food offerings to Adonai. Priests must be holy because I am Adonai—I am holy, and I have made them holy.

9 The daughter of a priest who prostitutes herself has disgraced her father's position, and she must be put to death.

10 The High Priest who wears the special priestly garments must not go bareheaded or tear his garments in mourning.

11 The High Priest must never go near a dead body even if it is his father or his mother. **12** A High Priest must not leave the sanctuary to participate in a funeral, because he has been ordained and he will defile Adonai's sanctuary. I am God. I command it.

13 A High Priest must marry a virgin. **14** He must not marry a widow, a divorcee, or an immoral woman.

He may marry only a virgin from among the tribe of the Levites.

15 A High Priest must not dishonor his children because of the reputation of his wife.

He must do all this because I am Adonai, and I make him holy.

Priests with Defects   *2nd Aliyah*

16 Adonai spoke to Moses, and said to him:

17 Instruct Aaron as follows:

Any of your descendants who has a physical defect must not approach the altar to present a food offering to Adonai. **18** A priest with a physical defect must not offer sacrifices. Nor a priest who is blind, deformed, or disfigured. **19** Nor any priest with any other physical defect. **20** Nor a priest who has a skin disease and running sores.

21 A descendant of Aaron the priest who has a defect is not permitted to offer fire offerings to Adonai.

22 He may still, however, eat the food offerings from the holy and from the most holy.

23 A priest with a defect must not go behind the cloth partition in the sanctuary, and he must not approach the altar. He must not defile My holy sanctuary. I am Adonai, and I make it holy.

24 Moses instructed Aaron and his sons and all the Israelites.

22 Adonai spoke to Moses, and said:

2 Instruct Aaron and his sons to be careful how they handle the sacred offerings that the Israelites present to Me, to ensure that they do not desecrate My holy name. I am Adonai.

3 Remind them that if any of their descendants is in an unclean state when he presents the sacred offerings to Adonai, he shall be cut off spiritually from Me. I am Adonai.

4 A priest who is a leper or who has a discharge from his penis must not eat any sacred offerings until he has cleansed himself.

Any priest who touches a dead person or who has an emission of semen **5** or who has touched an unclean animal or an unclean person— **6** a priest who touches any of the above shall be unclean until evening, and he shall not eat any sacred offering until he has cleansed himself.

7 Then at sunset when he becomes ritually clean, he can eat the sacred offerings.

8 The priest must not eat any clean creature that has died from natural causes or has been killed by wild animals. It is forbidden because it will make him unclean. I am Adonai. I demand it.

9 The priests shall observe all My rules and not profane the sacred offering or they will die.

Remember: I am Adonai, and I make them holy.

10 A non-priest is never allowed to eat sacred offerings. Even if he lives with a priest or is hired by him, he is still not allowed to eat the sacred offering.

11 However, if a priest purchases a slave, then the slave may eat the sacred offering. A slave born in the house of a priest may also eat his food.

12 If a priest's daughter marries a non-priest, she can no longer eat the sacred food. **13** But if the priest's daughter has no children, or is widowed or divorced, she may return to her father's house with the same status as when she was a girl, and then she is permitted to eat her father's food.

No unauthorized person may eat the food offering.

14 If a person by mistake eats a sacred offering, he must pay the price of the food plus twenty percent and give it to the priest.

15 The priests shall not profane the sacred offerings which the Israelites give as gifts to Adonai by allowing non-priests to eat the sacred offerings.

16 If they eat the sacred offerings, they will be guilty of sin. I am Adonai, and it is I who make these offerings holy.

No Sacrifices with Defects   *3rd Aliyah*

17 Adonai spoke to Moses, and said to him: **18** Instruct Aaron and his sons and all the Israelites, and say to them:

These are the laws for any person, whether an Israelite or a foreigner who resides among you, who brings an animal to present as a burnt offering to Adonai to fulfill a promise or as a voluntary gift.

19 It must be a healthy male animal taken from the cattle, sheep, or goats. **20** An animal with a defect will not be acceptable.

21 When a person presents a peace offering of cattle or sheep to fulfill a promise or as a voluntary gift, it must be healthy to be acceptable. It shall not have any defect.

22 You must not offer Adonai an animal that has any physical defects or sores or skin diseases. You must not offer such an animal as a fire offering to Adonai.

23 An ox or a sheep that has an extra or a missing limb can be brought as an offering to the sanctuary. But no such animal is acceptable as a sacrifice on the altar.

24 You must not offer an animal that has a genital injury to Adonai. **25** You must not offer such animal even if it is presented by a gentile. Animals that have physical defects are not acceptable for sacrifice.

26 Adonai instructed Moses, and said:

27 When a bull, sheep, or goat is born, it must remain with its mother for seven days, but after the eighth day it is acceptable as a fire offering to Adonai.

28 You must not slaughter a female animal and its child on the same day, whether it is a bull, a sheep, or a goat.

29 When you bring a thanksgiving offering to Adonai, it must be properly sacrificed. **30** It must be sacrificed and eaten on the same day; leave nothing until the next morning. I am Adonai. I command it.

31 You must observe My commandments and faithfully keep them; I am Adonai.

32 Do not profane My holy name. I must be respected among the Israelites.

I am Adonai, and I am making you holy. **33** Remember: I, Adonai, brought you out of Egypt.
Remember: I am Adonai.

The Festivals   *4ᵗʰ Aliyah*

23 Adonai spoke to Moses, and said to him: **2** Instruct the Israelites and say to them:

These are the special times that you must celebrate as sacred holidays to Adonai. These are My special festivals:

3 During the six weekdays you may do your work, but the seventh day is the Sabbath, a day of rest. It is a sacred time to Adonai, and you shall do no work, no matter where you live; it is Adonai's Sabbath.

4 These are the festivals that you must celebrate as sacred holidays at their appointed times:

5 In the first month [Nisan], on the afternoon of the fourteenth day, you must sacrifice a Passover offering to Adonai. **6** Then, on the fifteenth of the month [of Nisan] you shall celebrate the Festival of Unleavened Bread, and you must eat matzot for seven days.

7 The first day shall be a sacred holiday, and you must not do any work.

8 Then for seven days you shall bring sacrifices to Adonai. The seventh day shall be a sacred holiday, and once again you must not do any work.

9 Adonai spoke to Moses, and told him to **10** instruct the Israelites and say to them:

When you enter the land that I am going to give you, and gather your harvest, you must bring an omer (two quarts) of barley grain from your first harvest to the priest. **11** He shall present it as a wave offering to Adonai. The priest shall present a wave offering from you on the day after the first Sabbath of the Passover holiday.

12 On the day you present the wave offering of an omer of barley grain you shall also present a healthy lamb as a burnt offering to Adonai. **13** The grain offering to Adonai shall consist of four quarts of barley grain mixed with olive oil. The liquid offering shall consist of one quart of wine.

14 Until the day that you bring this sacrifice to Adonai, you must not eat leavened bread or roasted grain or fresh grain. No matter where you live, this shall be a permanent law for all generations.

15 From the day following the Passover holiday, when you brought the omer as a wave offering, you shall count seven complete weeks **16** until the day after the seventh week; there shall be a total of fifty days. Then, on the fiftieth day (Shavuot), you shall present an offering of new grain to Adonai.

17 From wherever you live, you must bring two loaves of bread as a wave offering.
The loaves shall be made of four pounds of flour and shall be baked as leavened bread. This will be your first-harvest offering to Adonai.

18 With this bread, you shall present seven healthy lambs, one young bull, and two rams as a burnt offering. These, together with the grain and liquid offering, shall be presented as a thank you gift to Adonai.

19 You shall also present one goat as a sin offering, and two lambs as peace sacrifices. **20** The priest shall present them as wave offerings before Adonai with the loaves of bread which are baked with grain from the first-harvest offering. These offerings are sacred to Adonai and are a gift to the priest.

21 That same day shall be celebrated as a sacred holiday (Shavuot) on which no work shall be done. This is a permanent law and must be observed wherever you may live.

22 When you gather your harvest, you must not completely harvest the ends of your fields. Also, do not pick up the stalks of grain that have fallen to the ground. You must leave all of it for the poor and the stranger. I am Adonai. I command it.

Rosh Hashanah and Yom Kippur   *5ᵗʰ Aliyah*

23 Adonai spoke to Moses and said: **24** Instruct the Israelites and say: The first day of the seventh month [Tishri] shall be a day of complete rest. It is a sacred holiday of remembrance and shall be welcomed by sounding the shofar.

25 On this day (Rosh Hashanah) you must not do any work, and you must bring a fire offering to Adonai.

26 Adonai spoke to Moses, and said:

27 The tenth of the seventh month [Tishri] shall be celebrated as a Day of Atonement (Yom Kippur).

It is a sacred holiday, and you must fast and bring an offering to Adonai. **28** Do not do any work on this day; it is a Day of Atonement, when you ask Adonai to forgive your sins.

29 Anyone who does not fast on this day shall be cut off from his people. **30** And no one is to work on this day; I will punish any Israelite who works.

31 No matter where you may live, you must not do any work on Yom Kippur. This is a permanent law for all generations.

32 For you it is a Sabbath, a day of rest and of fasting. You must observe this holiday from the ninth day of the month of Tishri in the evening until the evening of the tenth.

The Festival of Sukkot   *6ᵗʰ Aliyah*

33 Adonai spoke to Moses and instructed him:

34 Speak to the Israelites, and say:

Beginning on the fifteenth of the seventh month [Tishri] you shall celebrate the Festival of Sukkot to Adonai for seven days. **35** On the first day of this sacred holiday you must not do any work. **36** For seven days, you must present offerings to Adonai.

The eighth day shall be a sacred holiday, and you shall bring an offering to Adonai. It is a time of complete rest, and you shall not do any work.

37 These are Adonai's special times, and they must be observed as sacred holidays. On these special festivals you must present burnt offerings, grain offerings, and liquid offerings, **38** in addition to Adonai's Sabbath offerings, and the pledges and the voluntary gifts that you offer to Adonai.

39 Remember: on the fifteenth of the seventh month [Tishri], when you begin to harvest the grain, you shall celebrate the Festival of Sukkot for seven days. The first day of Sukkot shall be a day of complete rest, and the eighth day shall also be a day of complete rest.

40 On the first day of Sukkot you must take a fruit of the citron tree (an *etrog*), a palm branch, myrtle branches, and willows that grow near the brook. You shall celebrate the Festival of Sukkot before Adonai for seven days.

41 During these seven days of each year, you shall observe the Festival of Sukkot.

42 All Israelites must live in thatched huts (*sukkot*) during these seven days. **43** In this way future generations will know that I made their ancestors live in huts when I brought them out of Egypt. I am Adonai.

44 This is how Moses instructed the Israelites to celebrate the festivals to Adonai.

The Golden Menorah   *7ᵗʰ Aliyah*

24 Adonai spoke to Moses, and told him to **2** instruct the Israelites to bring pure olive oil made from hand-crushed olives, to keep the golden menorah constantly burning.

3 Aaron and the priests shall keep the menorah continually lighted with the oil, before Adonai, from evening to morning, outside the cloth curtain in the Meeting Tent. This must be a permanent law for all your generations.

4 The priest must keep the lamps on the pure gold menorah burning before Adonai from morning to night.

5 You shall take the finest grade of flour and bake it into twelve loaves. Each loaf shall weigh about four pounds.

6 Arrange the loaves in two rows, six loaves to each row, and place them on a special table before Adonai. **7** Alongside each row place pure frankincense as a memorial portion that will be presented to Adonai.

8 Every Sabbath, fresh loaves shall be arranged before Adonai. Priests in every generation must continue to do this for the Israelites.

9 The bread shall be given to Aaron and his descendants, but since it is one of Adonai's fire offerings, it must be eaten in a sacred area. This is a permanent law.

10 An Israelite woman married an Egyptian man. Their son quarreled with an Israelite man **11** and cursed Adonai.

The people angrily brought him to Moses. His mother's name was Shelomith daughter of Divri, of the tribe of Dan. **12** They imprisoned him until Adonai would tell them what to do.

13 Finally Adonai spoke to Moses, and said:

14 "Take the man who cursed me out of the camp, and let witnesses who heard him curse Me place their hands on his head. Then the entire community shall put him to death.

15 Warn the Israelites and say:

Anyone who curses Adonai will bear his sin. **16** However, if someone deliberately curses the Holy Name YHVH, he shall be put to death.

It makes no difference whether he is a foreigner or an Israelite, he shall be put to death.

17 Anyone who murders someone must be put to death.

18 If someone kills an animal that belongs to someone else, he must pay the cost of the animal.

19 If someone deliberately injures his neighbor, whatever he has done to his neighbor must be done to him. **20** Full compensation must be paid for a fracture or the loss of an eye or a tooth. If someone causes an injury to another person, then the same injury shall be inflicted on him.

Equality Under the Law   *Maftir*

21 If someone kills an animal, he must pay for it, but if he kills a human being, he must be put to death. **22** There shall be equality under the law for both the foreigner and the native-born. I am Adonai. I command it."

23 After Moses explained all this to the Israelites, they took the man who had cursed Adonai out of the camp and executed him. Thus the Israelites did as Adonai had commanded Moses.

Behar בְּהַר

ON MOUNT SINAI

25 When Moses was on Mount Sinai, Adonai spoke to him and said:

2 Speak to the Israelites and say to them:

When you enter the land that I am giving you, you must allow the land to remain unused for a period of rest, a Sabbath to Adonai. **3** You may plant your fields, prune your vineyards, and harvest your crops for six years **4** but the seventh year shall be a Sabbath for the land. It is Adonai's Sabbath, during which you must not plant your fields, or prune your vineyards, **5** or harvest crops that grow by themselves, or gather the grapes on your vines, because it is a year of rest for the land.

6 While the land is resting, anything that continues to grow naturally may be eaten by you, by your slaves, and by your employees and hired workers who live with you.

7 The crops may also be eaten by your domestic cattle or by wild animals.

8 You must count seven Sabbath years seven times for a period of forty-nine years.

9 Then, in the forty-ninth year, on the tenth day of the seventh month [Yom Kippur], you shall blow a shofar.

10 You shall consecrate
the fiftieth year,
and proclaim liberty
for the slaves
in your land
in the Jubilee Year.

This is your Jubilee Year. This is the time when all family hereditary lands sold to others must be returned to the original families.

11 The fiftieth year shall also be a restful time for you. You must not plant or harvest crops that grow on their own, or gather grapes from unpruned vines during that year. **12** Since it is a holy Jubilee Year, you must eat only crops from fields that grow naturally by themselves.

13 In the Jubilee Year, every man shall return to his ancestral property.

The Jubilee Year   *2nd Aliyah*

14 When you buy or sell land to your neighbor, do not cheat each other. **15** Remember that you are buying the land only for the number of crops it will produce until the Jubilee Year. **16** He is selling you the land for a specified number of harvests. You can increase the price if it will be for many years, and lower it if only for a few years.

17 You must be fair and not take advantage and cheat one another. You must fear Adonai.

18 Observe My commandments and My laws. If you obey them, you will live securely in your land.

The World Belongs to Me   *3rd Aliyah*

19 The land will produce its crops, and you will eat your fill, and you will live in peace.

20 In the seventh year you may ask, "What will we eat during the Jubilee Year, since we are not allowed to plant or harvest crops?"

21 The answer is: I will send My blessings to your land in the sixth year, and the land will produce enough food to last for three years. **22** You will be eating your old crops, and when you plant after the eighth year, you will still be eating your old crops until the ninth year, when the new crops are ripe and ready to be harvested.

23 The world belongs to Me, and no land must be sold permanently, because as far as I am concerned, you are just my guests and tenants, **24** and therefore you must allow the redemption of all hereditary lands.

Redemption of All Hereditary Lands   *4ᵗʰ Aliyah*

25 If your relative becomes poor and sells some of his hereditary land, a close relative can redeem the land that has been sold. **26** If a man does not have anyone to help him redeem his land but later earns enough money to be able to buy it back, **27** the price for the land shall be based on the number of years until the next Jubilee Year. Then the original owner can return to his land.

28 However, if he does not have the money to redeem the land, then it shall remain with the buyer until the next Jubilee Year. Then the land will be released in that year, so that the original owner can return to his hereditary land.

Houses in Walled Cities   *5ᵗʰ Aliyah*

29 When a man sells a house in a walled city, he has only one full year to redeem it.

30 If the house in the walled city is not redeemed by the end of this year, it shall become the permanent property of the buyer and can be passed down to his descendants, and it is not released in the Jubilee Year.

31 But houses in unwalled villages shall be considered the same as open land. They must be returned to the original owner in the Jubilee Year.

32 The Levites shall always have the right to redeem the houses in the cities belonging to them. **33** If someone buys a house in one of their cities from a Levite, it must be released in the Jubilee Year, for the houses in the Levite cities are their hereditary property.

34 The open fields surrounding the Levite cities cannot be sold permanently, because it is their hereditary property.

35 When your neighbor becomes poor and is unable to support himself, you must help him to survive, whether he is a foreigner or an Israelite.

36 Do not take any interest from him. Fear Adonai, and allow him to live alongside you as your brother.

37 Do not take advantage of him and do not make him pay interest for your money, and do not sell him food at high prices. **38** I am Adonai, who brought you out of Egypt to give you the land of Canaan.

Redemption of the Poor   *6ᵗʰ Aliyah*

39 If your fellow Israelite becomes poor and sells himself to you, you must not treat him like a slave.
40 Treat him as an employee or a hired worker. He shall serve you only until the Jubilee Year. **41** Then he and his children shall be free to leave you and return to his family and his hereditary land.
42 Always remember that you are My servants whom I freed out of Egypt. Your fellow Israelites must not be sold in the market as slaves. **43** Do not mistreat or brutalize them, because you must show your respect for Adonai.
44 You can purchase male or female slaves from the nations around you. **45** You can also buy slaves from the foreigners who live among you, and from their families that are born in your land. These shall become your property. **46** They are property that you can pass down to your children, and they can be your slaves forever.
But as far as your fellow Israelites are concerned, you must not be cruel to them.

Israelite Slaves   *7ᵗʰ Aliyah*

47 If a foreigner becomes wealthy while your Israelite brother becomes poor and is sold to a foreigner who worships idols, he must be saved. **48** After he is sold, he must be redeemed by one of his close relatives— **49** his uncle or cousin, or the closest relative in his family. If he manages to earn enough money, he can redeem himself.
50 The price for his freedom shall be based on the number of years that remain until the Jubilee. **51** If there are still many years until the Jubilee, the freedom money he pays his purchaser shall be based on the amount of money for which he was sold and when he sold himself.
52 If only a few years remain until the Jubilee Year, he shall repay only a small amount.

In all cases he shall repay a sum of freedom money based on the number of years until the Jubilee Year.

53 Such a slave must be treated the same as an employee hired on a yearly basis. You must not allow his master to treat him cruelly.

54 If the slave is not freed by any of the above means, then he and his children shall be freed in the Jubilee Year.

Do Not Pray to Idols   *Maftir*

55 All this is because the Israelites are actually My slaves. They are My slaves because I brought them out of Egypt and saved them. I am Adonai.

26 You must not make idols. Do not carve stone idols or erect sacred pillars. Do not erect idols in your land and worship them. I am Adonai. I forbid it.

2 Observe My Sabbaths and respect My sanctuary. I am Adonai. I demand it.

Bechukkotai בְּחֻקֹּתַי
OBSERVE MY COMMANDMENTS

3 If you follow My laws and faithfully observe My commandments, **4** I will provide you with rain in season, so that your land will grow your crops and the trees will produce fruit. **5** Your harvest will be so plentiful that your threshing season will continue until your grape harvest, and your grape harvest will continue until planting time. You will have more than enough food, and you will live in safety in the land.

I Will Bless the Land   *2ⁿᵈ Aliyah*

6 I will bless the land with peace, so that you will be able to sleep without fear. I will remove the dangerous animals and protect your land from your enemies.

7 You will defeat your enemies and destroy them.

8 Only five of you will be able to defeat a hundred, and only a hundred of you will defeat ten thousand.

9 I will be kind to you, and your nation will grow and became numerous, and I will keep My promises to you.

You Will Be My People   *3ʳᵈ Aliyah*

10 Each year your barns will overflow with crops, and you will be forced to clear out the old crops because of the new. **11** I will establish My sanctuary among you, and I will never grow tired of you. **12** I will always dwell among you. I, Elohim, will be with you, and you will always be My people dedicated to Me.

13 I am Elohim. I rescued you from slavery in Egypt. I broke your chains and now you can live in dignity.

14 But if you do not listen to Me, and do not keep My commandments, **15** if you reject My laws, and do not observe My commandments, you will have broken My covenant with you.

16 Then I will turn around and do the same to you. I will punish you with terror and disease, and I will make your lives miserable. You will plant your crops in vain, because your enemies will eat them.

17 I will be angry at you and your enemies will defeat and rule over you. You will be frightened of your own shadows.

18 If you still disobey Me, I will increase the punishment for your sins seven times as much. **19** I will break your pride, and the skies will not produce rain, and your land will not yield any crops.

20 You will exhaust your strength in vain, since your land will not yield its crops, and the trees of the land will not produce fruit.

21 If you still do not listen to Me, I will again increase the punishment for your sins seven times over. **22** I will send wild beasts to kill your children and destroy your cattle, and I will decimate your population, so that the roads will be deserted.

23 If this punishment does not reform you, and you continue to ignore Me, **24** then I will ignore you, and I will again punish you for your sins seven times over. **25** I will send enemies against you because you broke My covenant, and you will hide in your cities. Then I will punish you with the plague, and your enemies will take you captive.

26 I will deprive you of your food supply so that ten women will have only enough flour to bake bread in one oven, and they will bring back only a few crumbs. There will not be enough to satisfy your hunger. **27** If you still do not listen to Me but remain hostile to Me, **28** then I will be hostile to you and will punish you seven times over for your sins. **29** You will be so hungry that you will eat the flesh of your sons and your daughters.

30 I will destroy your altars and smash your gods. I will pile your dead bodies around your broken idols.

I will despise you. **31** I will let your cities become desolate and ruin your sanctuaries. I will not accept your sacrifices.

32 I will devastate the land so that even your enemies who live there will be shocked at the devastation.

33 I will scatter you among the nations, and I will use my sword against you. Your land will be devastated, and your cities will be in ruins.

34 As long as the land remains desolate and you are in exile, the land will at last enjoy its missed Sabbaths. Then the land will finally rest and enjoy its sabbatical years.

35 As long as the land remains desolate, it will enjoy the sabbatical rest that you would not give it every seven years while you lived there.

36 In exile you will tremble at the sound of a rustling leaf, and you will run with fear and panic when no one is chasing you.

37 You will have no power to resist your enemies.

38 You will die among the foreign nations, and your enemies will destroy you.

39 Those who survive will rot away in enemy lands because of their sins. The survivors will realize that their existence is threatened because of their own sins and those of their ancestors. **40** Then they will finally confess their sins and the sins of their ancestors against Me. **41** Because of their sins I remained indifferent to them and exiled them into the land of their enemies. But when they ask for forgiveness, **42** I will keep my covenant with Abraham, Isaac, and Jacob and I will remember the land. **43** Now, the land will enjoy its rest while you are in exile. They will pay for their sins because they rebelled against Me and My laws.

44 Even when they are in exile in the land of their enemies, I will never completely reject them or destroy them and break My covenant with them, because I am Adonai, their protector.

45 I will remember My covenant with their ancestors when I, Adonai, brought them out of Egypt while the nations watched. I am Adonai.

46 These are the commandments and laws that Adonai gave to the Israelites at Mount Sinai by the hand of Moses.

Donations   *4th Aliyah*

27 Adonai spoke to Moses, and told him to **2** instruct the Israelites and say to them:

This is the law when an Israelite decides to honor a person by donating a sum of money to Adonai.

3 The donation for a male aged twenty to sixty years shall be fifty shekels according to the sanctuary weight. **4** For a woman, the donation shall be thirty shekels.

5 For a person between five and twenty, the donation shall be twenty shekels for a male and ten shekels for a female.

6 For a person between one month and five years old, the donation shall be five shekels for a male and three shekels for a female.

7 For a person over sixty years old, the donation shall be fifteen shekels for a man and ten shekels for a woman.

8 In the case of a person too poor to give the statutory donation, the priest will decide the amount. The priest shall make his decision on the basis of how much the person wishing to make the donation can afford.

9 If the donation is a healthy animal and it can be presented as a sacrifice to Adonai, then the gift to Adonai becomes holy.

10 The animal cannot be exchanged or replaced by a better animal or a worse animal. If the animal, nonetheless, is replaced, then both the substituted animal and the original animal shall become holy.

11 But if the donation is an unclean animal, it cannot be presented as a sacrifice to Adonai. In such cases the owner shall present the animal to the priest, **12** and the priest will determine its value.

13 If the owner wishes to redeem the animal, its value shall be set by the priest, and he shall add twenty percent to the donation.

14 If a person donates a house to Adonai, the priest shall set its value according to its condition. The value shall be determined by the priest. **15** If the person who donated his house wishes to buy it back, he must add twenty percent to its value, and then the house becomes his again.

Donations of Farmlands   *5ᵗʰ Aliyah*

16 If a man donates a field from his ancestral property to Adonai, its value shall be determined by the amount of seed required to plant it—fifty shekels for every ten bushels (*chomer*) of barley seed.

17 If this donation is made just after the Jubilee Year, the land is valued at its full price. **18** But if someone donates his field after the Jubilee Year, the priest shall determine its value on the basis of the number of years remaining until the next Jubilee Year.

19 If the person who donates his field wishes to buy it back, he must pay the full price plus twenty percent. **20** But if he does not buy back the field, or if the land is sold to someone else, it can no longer be bought back.

21 When the field is released in the Jubilee Year, it becomes holy and special to Adonai, and then becomes the hereditary property of the priest.

Forbidden Animals and Farmland   *6ᵗʰ Aliyah*

22 If someone donates a field to Adonai that he bought, and thus it is not his ancestral property, **23** the priest shall determine its value depending on the number of years remaining until the next Jubilee Year. On that day, he can buy back the land by donating the purchase price to Adonai. **24** In the Jubilee Year, the field shall return to its original owner.

25 Every monetary donation shall be set according to the sanctuary standard.

26 You cannot present first-born animals to Adonai, whether an ox, sheep, or goat, because these animals already belong to Adonai. **27** But if the first-born of a nonkosher animal is presented, it can be redeemed by paying its value plus twenty percent. If it is not redeemed, the priest can sell it.

28 However, anything a person owns, whether it is a slave, an animal, or his hereditary field, that has been forbidden (placed in *cherem*) shall be specially set apart for Adonai and must never be sold or redeemed. This is true of everything he owns. Everything that is specifically donated is holy to Adonai.

Tithes for Crops and Fruits   *7ᵗʰ Aliyah*

29 A person who has been condemned to death (placed in *cherem*) cannot be saved. He must be put to death.

30 One-tenth of the crops of the soil or the fruit of trees is set apart for Adonai. **31** If a person wishes to redeem his tithe, he must pay its market value plus twenty percent.

Tithes for Animals   *Maftir*

32 When you count your herds and flocks, you shall give every tenth animal to Adonai.

33 It makes no difference whether the animal is healthy or not. You must not substitute one animal for another. But if a substitution is made, then both the original animal and its replacement shall be holy and cannot be redeemed.

34 These are the commandments that Adonai gave Moses for the Israelites on Mount Sinai.

סֵפֶר בַּמִדְבָּר

THE BOOK OF BAMIDBAR

Masoretic Torah Notes

Here is a list of some of the Masoretic notes for the Book of Bamidbar.

1. The Book of Bamidbar contains 1,288 verses.
2. The Book of Bamidbar contains 36 chapters.
3. The Book of Bamidbar contains 10 sidrot.

These are the sidrot in the Book of Bamidbar.

סֵפֶר בַּמִּדְבָּר

THE BOOK OF BAMIDBAR

Bamidbar is the fourth of the Five Books of Moses. The Hebrew word bamidbar *means "in the wilderness," and this name was given to the book because it chronicles some of the things that happened to the Israelites during their forty years in the wilderness after leaving Egypt. The English name of the book, translated from the Greek, is Numbers. The book was given this name because it reports the details of a census in which Moses counted all the able-bodied men.*

The book of Bamidbar can be divided into five sections.

In the first section (1–10), Adonai tells Moses to take a census to determine the number of men aged twenty and above who are available for military service. The census shows that there were 603,550 able-bodied men. Adonai also tells Moses how to organize the tribal camps. The section ends with the celebration of the first Passover in the wilderness.

The second section (11–21) describes the hardships of life in the wilderness, the difficulties Moses faced as leader of the Israelites, and a series of rebellions against him and Adonai. The Israelites still have a slave mentality and are afraid to confront the inhabitants of Canaan even though Adonai has promised that they will be victorious. So Adonai punishes them and makes them wander in the wilderness for forty years until the generation of slaves dies out and a determined, desert-hardened new generation arises. The section ends with the Israelites camped near Pisgah.

The third section (22–25) starts with the conquest of the land east of the Jordan River. Balak, the king of Midian, realizes that he is too weak to defeat the Israelites, so he hires the prophet Balaam to curse them and weaken them. Adonai intervenes, and instead Balaam blesses the Israelites.

343

In the fourth section (26–34), the generation born in Egypt has passed away, and the new generation of tough, fearless Israelite warriors is confidently prepared to cross the Jordan and claim their heritage. Moses once again counts the Israelites, and he appoints Joshua ben Nun as his successor.

The book concludes (35–36) with a series of new laws.

Bamidbar describes a people with a slave mentality searching for strength and stability in the shifting sands of the desert. Adonai is aware of their fears and, like a loving father, He encourages and protects them until they have the ability to stand on their own feet. He knows that in time the Israelites will mature into a strong and powerful nation.

Bamidbar בְּמִדְבַּר

IN THE WILDERNESS

1 On the first day of the second month [Iyar], in the second year of the Exodus, Adonai spoke to Moses in the Wilderness of Sinai, in the Meeting Tent, saying:

2 Take a census of the entire Israelite community. Do it by their clans and families, and record the names of every male. **3** You and Aaron shall record every male over twenty years old who is fit for military service.

4 Choose one leader from each tribe to assist you.

5 These are the names of the leaders who will assist you: For Reuben, Elitzur son of Shedeur.

6 For Simeon, Shelumiel son of Zurishaddai.

7 For Judah, Nachshon son of Aminadab.

8 For Issachar, Nethanel son of Zuar.

9 For Zebulun, Eliav son of Helon.

10 For Joseph's two sons:

For Ephraim, Elishama son of Amihud.

For Manasseh, Gamliel son of Pedahzur.

11 For Benjamin, Avidan son of Gidoni.

12 For Dan, Achiezer son of Amishaddai.

13 For Asher, Pagiel son of Okhran.

14 For Gad, Eliassaf son of Deuel:

15 For Naphtali, Achira son of Eynan.

16 These are the leaders, the heads of their tribes and the leaders of the thousands of Israelites.

17 Moses and Aaron assembled the tribal leaders.

18 The leaders summoned the entire Israelite community on the first day of the second month [Iyar], and all the people registered according to their tribal families. All males over twenty years of age were registered by name.

19 Moses counted the Israelites in the Wilderness of Sinai just as Adonai had commanded him.

The Tribal Census   *2nd Aliyah*

20 According to the records of the tribe, the number of males over twenty years of age fit for military service **21** from the tribe of Reuben was 46,500 soldiers.

22 According to the records of the tribe, the number of males over twenty years of age fit for military service **23** from the tribe of Simeon was 59,300 soldiers.

24 According to the records of the tribe, the number of males over twenty years of age fit for military service **25** from the tribe of Gad was 45,650 soldiers.

26 According to the records of the tribe, the number of males over twenty years of age fit for military service **27** from the tribe of Judah was 74,600 soldiers.

28 According to the records of the tribe, the number of males over twenty years of age fit for military service **29** from the tribe of Issachar was 54,400 soldiers.

30 According to the records of the tribe, the number of males over twenty years of age fit for military service **31** from the tribe of Zebulun was 57,400 soldiers.

32 Among the two sons of Joseph, Ephraim and Manasseh: According to the records of the tribe, the number of males over twenty years of age fit for military service **33** from the tribe of Ephraim was 40,500 soldiers.

34 According to the records of the tribe, the number of males over twenty years of age fit for military service **35** from the tribe of Manasseh was 32,200 soldiers.

36 According to the records of the tribe, the number of males over twenty years of age fit for military service **37** from the tribe of Benjamin was 35,400 soldiers.

38 According to the records of the tribe, the number of males over twenty years of age fit for military service **39** from the tribe of Dan was 62,700 soldiers.

40 According to the records of the tribe, the number of males over twenty years of age fit for military service **41** from the tribe of Asher was 41,500 soldiers.

42 According to the records of the tribe, the number of males over twenty years of age fit for military service **43** from the tribe of Naphtali was 53,400 soldiers.

44 The following is the official count tabulated by Moses, Aaron, and the twelve tribal leaders of Israel:

45 The number of Israelite males according to their tribes, over twenty years old and all fit for military service **46** officially counted was 603,550 soldiers

47 However, the men from the tribe of Levi were not counted together with the other Israelites.

48 Adonai explained to Moses, saying:

49 Do not count the Levites together with the other Israelites. **50** Put the Levites in charge of the Tabernacle and all its furniture and equipment. They will carry the Tabernacle and all its furniture, and they will take care of it, and they will camp around the Tabernacle.

51 Whenever the Tabernacle is moved, the Levites shall take it down, and whenever it is to be erected they will assemble it. Any non-Levite who touches anything belonging to the Tabernacle shall die.

52 Whenever the Israelites halt, each tribe shall camp under its own tribal banner. **53** The Levites, however, must camp around the Tabernacle, to protect the Israelites from Adonai's anger. The responsibility of safeguarding the Tabernacle shall belong to the Levites.

54 The Israelites did everything exactly as Adonai commanded Moses.

The Order of the March   *3rd Aliyah*

2 Adonai spoke to Moses and Aaron and instructed them, saying: **2** Each Israelite tribe shall camp around its own tribal banner. Each of the tribal encampments shall be erected in a specified area around the Meeting Tent.

3 Three tribes shall camp to the east, in the direction of the sunrise, under the marching banner of Judah.

The leader of the tribe of Judah was Nachshon son of Aminadab. **4** His tribe enrolled 74,600 soldiers.

5 The tribe of Issachar shall camp near the tribe of Judah. The leader of the tribe of Issachar was Nethanel son of Zuar. **6** His tribe enrolled 54,400 soldiers.

7 The tribe of Zebulun camped near the tribe of Judah. The leader of the tribe of Zebulun was Eliav son of Helon. **8** His tribe enrolled 57,400 soldiers.

9 The total number of troops in Judah's part of camp was 186,400 soldiers. On the march, these three tribes will lead the way.

10 The three tribes under the marching banner of Reuben shall camp to the south.

The leader of the tribe of Reuben was Elitzur son of Shedeur. **11** His tribe enrolled 46,500 soldiers.

12 The tribe of Simeon shall camp near the tribe of Reuben. The leader of the tribe of Simeon was Shelumiel son of Zurishaddai. **13** The tribe of Simeon enrolled 59,300 soldiers.

14 The tribe of Gad shall camp near the tribe of Reuben. The leader of the tribe of Gad was Eliassaf son of Reuel. **15** The tribe of Gad enrolled 45,650 soldiers.

16 The total number of troops in Reuben's part of the camp was 151,450 soldiers.

On the march, these three tribes will be second in the line of march.

17 On the march, the Meeting Tent and the camp of the Levites shall march in the middle of the four groups. The people shall travel in the same order that they camp. Each person shall be in his place, under his own tribal banner.

18 The three tribes under the banner of Ephraim shall camp to the west. The leader of Ephraim was Elishama son of Amihud.

19 The tribe of Ephraim enrolled 40,500 soldiers

20 The leader of the tribe of Manasseh shall camp near the tribe of Ephraim. The leader of Manasseh's descendants was Gamliel son of Pedahzur. **21** The tribe of Manasseh enrolled 32,200 soldiers.

22 The tribe of Benjamin camped near the tribe of Ephraim. The leader of Benjamin's descendants was Avidan son of Gidoni. **23** The tribe of Benjamin enrolled 35,400 soldiers

24 The total number of troops in Ephraim's part of the camp totaled 108,100 soldiers.

On the march, these three tribes shall be third in line.

25 The three tribes under the marching banner of Dan shall camp to the north. The leader of the tribe of Dan was Achiezer son of Amishaddai. **26** The tribe of Dan enrolled 62,700 soldiers.

27 The tribe of Asher camped near the tribe of Dan. The leader of the tribe of Asher was Pagiel son of Okhran. **28** The tribe of Asher enrolled 41,500 soldiers.

29 The tribe of Naphtali camped near the camp of Dan. The leader of the tribe of Naphtali was Achira son of Eynan. **30** The tribe of Naphtali enrolled 53,400 soldiers. **31** The total number of troops in the camp of Dan was 157,600 soldiers.

On the march, their column shall be the last of the tribes.

32 This is the number of Israelite soldiers counted according to their tribes: the Israelite troops in all the tribal camps totaled 603,550 soldiers.

33 The Levites were not counted with the rest of the Israelites, just as Adonai had commanded Moses.

34 The Israelites did everything that Adonai had commanded Moses. They camped around their banners, in family groups and tribes.

Aaron's Family Tree   *4ᵗʰ Aliyah*

3 This is the family tree of Aaron and Moses on the day that Adonai spoke to Moses at Mount Sinai:

2 These are the names of Aaron's sons: Nadav the first-born, Avihu, Eleazar, and Ithamar. **3** These are the names of Aaron's sons, the anointed priests who were ordained to serve in the Tabernacle.

4 Nadav and Avihu died before Adonai when they presented an offering with unauthorized fire to Adonai in the Wilderness of Sinai. They had no children. During the lifetime of their father, Aaron, only Eleazar and Ithamar served as priests.

5 Adonai spoke to Moses, saying:

6 Assemble the tribe of Levi, and assign them to Aaron the priest, so that they can help him. **7** They will work for him and the entire Israelite community in the Meeting Tent, performing the sacred services.

8 They shall care for the furniture in the Meeting Tent on behalf of the Israelites, doing the holy work during the Tabernacle service.

9 Assign the Levites to Aaron and his descendants. And they will be their assistants.

10 Make Aaron and his descendants responsible for observing the priestly duties. Any nonpriest who tries to perform priestly duties shall die.

11 Adonai spoke to Moses, saying:

12 I have chosen the Levites from the other Israelites as substitutes for all the first-born among the Israelites; the Levites shall be Mine.

13 This is so because every first-born became Mine on the day I killed all the first-born in Egypt. I set apart for Myself every first-born in Israel, man and beast alike, and they shall remain Mine. I am Adonai.

The Census of the Levites   *5ᵗʰ Aliyah*

14 Adonai spoke to Moses in the Wilderness of Sinai and instructed him: **15** Count the Levites, family by family. Count every male over the age of one month.

16 At Adonai's command Moses counted them, just as he had been instructed.

17 Levi had three sons: Gershon, Kehoth, and Merari.

18 Gershon had two sons, Livni and Shimi, who were the heads of their families.

19 The four sons of Kehoth were Amram, Yitzhar, Hebron, and Uzziel, and they were the heads of their families.

20 Merari had two sons, Machli and Mushi, who were the heads of their families.

These are the three Levite families.

21 The Gershonites included the Livnite family and the Shimite family.

22 There were 7,500 Gershonites one month of age and older.

23 The Gershonite family shall camp to the west, behind the Tabernacle. **24** The leader of the Gershonites was Eliassaf son of Lael.

25 The descendants of Gershon shall be responsible for the Meeting Tent, the Tabernacle tapestries, the two roofs, the curtains in the entrance of the Meeting Tent, **26** the hangings at the entrance of the enclosure surrounding the Tabernacle, the altar, the ropes, as well as all the equipment used in the ceremonies.

27 The descendants of Kehoth comprised four families: the Amramite family, the Yitzharite family, the Hebronite family, and the Uzzielite family.

28 There were 8,600 males one month of age and older in the four Kehoth families.

They were responsible for all the holy articles in the sanctuary.

29 The family of Kehoth's descendants shall camp on the southern side of the Tabernacle. **30** The leader of the Kehothite family was Elzafan son of Uzziel.

31 They shall be responsible for the ark, the table, the golden menorah, the two altars, the holy utensils, the partition curtain, and all the equipment involving these items.

32 Eleazar son of Aaron the priest shall be the one in charge of the Levites' leaders. He shall be responsible for safeguarding the holy articles.

33 The descendants of Merari were the Machli family and the Mushi family.

34 There were 6,200 males one month of age and older in the Merari families.

35 The leader of the families of Merari was Zuriel son of Avichail. The family of the Merari shall camp on the northern side of the Tabernacle.

36 The responsibility of the descendants of Merari shall include the frames, crossbars, pillars, and bases of the Tabernacle, all its utensils, and the equipment for their use, **37** as well as the pillars, bases, pegs, and ropes of the surrounding enclosure.

38 Moses and Aaron and his sons shall camp to the east, in front of the Tabernacle, and they shall be responsible for the sanctuary on behalf of the Israelites.

Any unauthorized person who interferes or performs the duties of Moses and Aaron shall be put to death.

39 All the families of the tribe of Levi were counted, and there were 22,000 males more than one month old.

Census of the First-born   *6ᵗʰ Aliyah*

40 Moses and Aaron counted all the first-born male Levites who were over one month old and registered their names. **41** Adonai said, "The Levites are reserved for Me in place of all the first-born Israelite males. I will also accept the Levites' first-born animals in place of the Israelites' first-born animals." **42** Moses recorded all the first-born Israelite males, just as Adonai had commanded him.

43 All of the first-born males listed by name added up to 22,273.

44 Adonai spoke to Moses, and said, **45** "Take the Levites in place of all the first-born male Israelites. Also take the first-born livestock of the Levites in place of the first-born Israelite animals. The Levites shall be Mine. I am Adonai."

46 There were 22,273 first-born Israelites and 22,000 first-born Levites. **47** You must collect five pieces of silver from each of the 273 extra first-born Israelites.

48 Give the silver to Aaron and his sons as the redemption price for the extra 273 first-born Israelites.

49 Moses collected the redemption money for the extra first-born Israelites who had not been redeemed by the Levites. **50** The silver that he collected from the first-born Israelites weighed 34 pounds.

51 With Adonai's permission, Moses gave the silver for those who were redeemed to Aaron and his sons. It was all done exactly as Adonai had commanded Moses.

Duties of the Kehoth Family   7th *Aliyah*

4 Adonai instructed Moses and Aaron, saying:
2 Take a census of the Kehoth families of the tribe of Levi. **3** Count all the males from thirty to fifty years old who are able to work in the Meeting Tent.

4 The following will be the duties of the descendants of Kehoth in the Meeting Tent:

5 When the Israelites are ready to travel, Aaron and his sons shall take down the partition drape and use it to cover the ark, **6** and wrap a cover of blue-tanned sealskins over it, and on top of that a cloth of blue wool. They shall then insert its carrying poles into the rings.

7 Next they shall wrap blue cloth over the inner table. Then they shall set in place on it the bread forms, incense bowls, and covering side frames, so that the bread can constantly remain on the table. **8** Over it all, they shall place a red wool cloth, and cover it with a box made of blue-tanned sealskins. They shall then insert its carrying poles into the rings.

9 They shall take a cloth of blue wool and wrap the golden menorah lamp and its oil cups, wick tongs, and ash shovels and the oil containers for it.

10 The menorah and all its utensils shall be placed in a box made of blue-tanned sealskins, and placed on a carrying frame.

11 They shall wrap a blue wool cloth around the golden altar and cover it with a box made of blue-tanned sealskins. Then they shall insert its carrying poles in the rings.

12 They shall take all the sanctuary's service utensils and wrap them in blue wool cloths. Then they shall cover them with a box made of blue-tanned sealskins and place it on a carrying frame.

13 They shall remove all the ashes from the altar and cover the altar with a purple cloth.

14 They shall place on the altar all the utensils used for its service, such as the fire pans, hooks, shovels, and sacrificial basins. Then they shall put them in a box made of blue-tanned sealskins, and insert carrying poles in the rings.

15 Afterward Aaron and his sons shall finish covering the holy furniture and all the sanctuary utensils, and only then can the camp begin its journey. The Kehothites are permitted to carry these holy items only after the priests finish packing them, because they will die if they touch the sacred objects.

All these are the articles the Kehothites must carry from the Meeting Tent.

16 Eleazar son of Aaron the priest shall be in charge of the oil for the golden menorah, the perfume incense, the grain offerings for the daily sacrifice, and the anointing oil. He shall also be in charge of the entire Tabernacle and all its holy furniture and utensils.

Do Not Destroy the Kehothites   *Maftir*

17 Adonai instructed Moses and Aaron, saying:

18 Make sure that the Kehothites do not destroy themselves, **19** so that they live, and do not die, when they enter the Holy of Holies. Aaron and his sons must enter first and assign each load so that every Kehothite can do his job and carry his assigned load.

20 The Kehothites are not permitted to enter and see the holy furniture being packed. If they do, they will destroy themselves.

Naso נָשֹׂא

TAKE A CENSUS

21 Adonai instructed Moses, saying:

22 Take a census of Gershon's two Levite families, the Gershonites and the Meraris.

23 Count everyone from thirty to fifty years old who is able to work in the service of the Meeting Tent.

24 The Gershonites shall be responsible for maintaining and carrying the following:

25 They shall carry the tapestries for the Meeting Tent, the tanned ram skins for the roof and the blue-tanned sealskins for the over-roof, the drape at the entrance of the Meeting Tent, **26** the enclosure's hangings, the curtain at the entrance to the enclosure around the Tabernacle and altar, the ropes, and all the tools necessary for their maintenance.

27 Aaron and his sons shall supervise all the carrying and maintenance work of the Gershonites. The Gershonites shall be assigned to carry specific loads.

28 Ithamar son of Aaron the priest shall supervise the duties of the Gershonites at the Meeting Tent.

29 Take a census of the family of Merari.

30 Count the Meraris from thirty to fifty years old who are fit for service in the Meeting Tent.

31 The Meraris shall be responsible for carrying and maintaining these items in the Meeting Tent: the frames, crossbars, pillars, and bases of the Tabernacle, **32** the pillars of the surrounding enclosure, their bases, pegs, and ropes, all their tools, and all their maintenance equipment. The Meraris shall be specifically assigned by name to carry all the loads with which they are entrusted.

33 All the duties of the Meraris in the Meeting Tent shall be under the direction of Ithamar son of Aaron the priest.

34 Moses, Aaron, and the communal leaders counted the descendants of the Kehothites by families, **35** including everyone from thirty to fifty years old who was fit for service in the Meeting Tent **36** and the total number added up to 2,750.

37 This was the complete count of the Kehothite family who served in the Meeting Tent, as tabulated by Moses and Aaron. It was done as Adonai had directed Moses.

Gershon's Descendants   *2nd Aliyah*

38 This was the count of Gershon's descendants, **39** which included all males from thirty to fifty years old who were fit for service in the Meeting Tent. **40** The total added up to 2,630 Gershonites.

41 This was the complete count of the Gershonites who served in the Meeting Tent. The census was taken by Moses and Aaron as Adonai had directed.

42 The count of Merari's descendants **43** included everyone from thirty to fifty years old who was fit for service in the Meeting Tent. **44** The count of the Merari family added up to 3,200 males.

45 This was the complete count of the families of Merari's descendants. The census was taken by Moses and Aaron as Adonai had directed Moses.

46 The entire census that Moses, Aaron, and the communal leaders took of the Levites **47** included everyone from thirty to fifty years old who was fit for service in the Meeting Tent. **48** The total added up to 8,580 males.

49 At Adonai's request, each individual was given a special responsibility for what he would carry.

Do Not Contaminate the Camp   *3rd Aliyah*

5 Adonai spoke to Moses, and said:

2 Command the Israelites to send away anyone in the camp who has a skin disease or an infection, and anyone who is ritually unclean from touching a dead person.

3 You must remove all sick persons, male or female, from the camp so that they will not contaminate the camp where I live among you.

4 The Israelites did this, and removed all infected people from the camp. The Israelites did exactly as Adonai had instructed Moses.

5 Adonai instructed Moses, and told him to **6** speak to the Israelites:

If a man or a woman has committed a sin against his fellow man, thereby being unfaithful to Adonai and becoming guilty of a crime, **7** that person must confess the crime that he has committed and must repay what he has stolen. He must also pay one-fifth extra to the victim of his crime. **8** But if there is no relative to whom the money can be repaid, then the money belongs to Adonai and must be given to the priest. This payment is in addition to the ram of the atonement, and only then is the sin forgiven.

9 All the offerings that the Israelites present as elevated gifts shall belong to the priest.

10 The offerings are given to the priest and belong to him.

Adultery and Unfaithfulness   *4ᵗʰ Aliyah*

11 Adonai spoke to Moses and told him: **12** Speak to the Israelites and say to them: This is the law if any man's wife is suspected of committing adultery and being unfaithful to her husband.

13 If she willingly slept with a man and kept it hidden from her husband, and there was proof against the woman, **14** and the husband became suspicious of his wife, and even if she was innocent: **15** the law is that the husband must bring his wife to the priest and bring an offering of two quarts of barley flour without oil or frankincense on it, since it is a suspicion offering to determine the truth.

16 The priest shall confront the woman and have her stand before Adonai. **17** He shall pour holy water into a clay bowl and add some earth from the Tabernacle floor and mix it into the water. **18** Then the priest shall stand the woman before Adonai and loosen her hair. The priest shall put in her hands the suspicion offering to determine whether the husband's complaints are justified. The priest shall stand next to the woman and hold the curse-bearing bitter water in his hands. **19** Then the priest shall ask the woman to take an oath. He will say, "If a man has not slept with you, and you have not committed adultery, the curse-bearing bitter water will have no effect on you. **20** But if you have committed adultery against your husband and have slept with a man other than your husband—."

21 Then the priest shall continue and say to the woman, "Now Adonai will ruin your reputation and make it into a curse among your people, and you will become infertile and your belly will swell. **22** This curse-bearing water will enter your body and cause your belly to swell and make you infertile." The woman shall be required to respond, "Amen. Amen."

23 Then the priest will write curses on a piece of parchment, and wash the writing off into the bitter water.

24 Then he shall make the woman drink the curse-bearing bitter water, and it will make the woman sick with guilt feelings.

25 Next the priest shall take the suspicion offering from the woman, and wave the offering before Adonai, and carry it to the altar.

26 After he makes the woman drink the water, the priest shall take some of the grain offering and burn it on the altar.

27 If the woman has been untrue to her husband, the curse-bearing water will enter her body and make her sick and cause her belly to swell and she will become infertile, and she will lose her reputation and will become a curse among her people.

28 However, if the woman is innocent and has not been unfaithful to her husband, she will remain healthy and she will be able to give birth to children.

29 This is the law for dealing with jealousy if a woman commits adultery and becomes unfaithful, **30** or when a man becomes suspicious of his wife's actions. The priest shall stand the woman before Adonai and follow this entire ritual. **31** Then the husband will be clear of sin, but the woman will be held accountable for her behavior.

6 Adonai spoke to Moses and told him to **2** speak to the Israelites and say to them: This is the law when a man or

a woman wishes to take a Nazirite vow to Adonai. **3** He must not drink wine and liquor. He must not even use vinegar made from wine. He must not drink any grape juice or eat any grapes or raisins. **4** As long as he is a Nazirite, he must not eat anything made from grapes, including their seeds and skin.

5 As long as he is a Nazirite, he must never cut the hair on his head. During the entire Nazirite period he is holy to Adonai and he must let his hair on his head grow long.

6 As long as he is a Nazirite to Adonai, he must not have any contact with the dead.

7 As long as he is a Nazirite and the uncut hair is still on his head, he must not make himself unclean even when his father, mother, brother, or sister dies.

8 As long as he is a Nazirite, he is dedicated to Adonai.

9 If a person suddenly dies in the presence of a Nazirite, rendering the long hair of his Nazirite "crown" ritually unclean, then when he purifies himself on the seventh day, he must shave off the hair on his head. **10** On the eighth day, he must bring two doves or two pigeons to the priest at the entrance of the Meeting Tent. **11** The priest shall prepare one bird as a sin offering and one as a burnt offering to atone for his defilement by the dead. On that day, he shall resanctify his head **12** and again begin counting his Nazirite days to Adonai, and he shall bring a lamb as a guilt offering; since his Nazirite crown was made unclean, the days of his vow preceding this incident no longer count.

13 The following is the law of what the Nazirite must do when the term of his Nazirite vow is complete, and what he must bring to the entrance of the Meeting Tent:

14 The offering that he must present shall be one healthy male lamb for a burnt offering, one healthy female lamb for a sin offering, one healthy ram for a peace offering, **15** and a basket of unleavened bread mixed with olive oil and matzot spread with olive oil as well as a grain offering and a liquid offering.

16 The priest shall appear before Adonai and present the Nazirite's sin offering and burnt offering.

17 He shall then sacrifice the ram as a peace offering to Adonai, to go with the basket of unleavened bread. The priest shall also present the meal offering and libation.

18 After the service at the entrance of the Meeting Tent, the Nazirite shall shave off the hair on his head and place the hair from his head on the fire that is under the peace sacrifice.

19 After the Nazirite has been shaved, the priest shall take the cooked shoulder of the ram and one unleavened loaf and one flat matzah from the basket and place them on the Nazirite's hands.

20 The priest shall wave them before Adonai. These holy gifts belong to the priest, in addition to the animal's breast and right thigh. After all this, the Nazirite may drink wine.

21 This is the entire law concerning the Nazirite who takes a vow to bring his Nazirite sacrifice to Adonai. This is in addition to anything else that he may wish to present to fulfill his special vow, which must be brought above and beyond what the law requires for his Nazirite vow.

22 Adonai said to Moses, telling him to **23** instruct Aaron and his sons:
"You will bless the Israelites with this special blessing:

24 'May Adonai bless you and keep watch over you.
　　25 May Adonai bless you
　　and protect you.
　May Adonai smile on you
　and be kind to you.
　　26 May Adonai be good to you
　　and give you peace.'

27 With this special blessing I link My name with the people of Israel. And I Myself bless them."

Offerings of the Tribal Leaders

5ᵗʰ Aliyah

7 On the day that Moses finished erecting the Tabernacle, he anointed all its furniture and made each item holy. He also anointed the altar and all its utensils and made them holy.

2 The leaders of Israel, all of them the heads of their tribes, then came forward. They were the leaders of the tribes and the ones who had organized the census.

3 The offerings they presented to Adonai consisted of six covered wagons and twelve oxen. There was one wagon for each two leaders, and one ox for each one. They presented the gifts in front of the Tabernacle.

4 Adonai said to Moses, **5** "Take the offering from them, and let the wagons and oxen be used for service in the Meeting Tent. Give them to the Levites, to be used for carrying the sacred furniture." **6** So Moses took the wagons and oxen and presented them to the Levites. **7** He gave two wagons and four oxen to the descendants of Gershon, as gift for their work.

8 To the descendants of Merari, he gave four wagons and eight oxen. All their work was done under the direction of Ithamar son of Aaron the priest.

9 However he did not give any wagons to the descendants of Kehoth, because they had responsibility for the most sacred articles, which they were required to carry on their shoulders.

10 The leaders presented their dedication offerings for the altar. They placed their offerings before the altar on the day that it was anointed. **11** Adonai said to Moses, "Let each leader present his offerings on a different day." **12** Nachshon son of Aminadav, leader of the tribe of Judah, brought his offering on the first day. **13** His offering consisted of one silver bowl weighing 3.5 pounds, and one silver basin weighing 1.75 pounds, both filled with fine flour mixed with olive oil for a meal offering;

14 one gold bowl weighing 4 ounces filled with incense;

15 one young bull, one lamb for a burnt offering;

16 one goat for a sin offering; **17** and two oxen, five rams, five male goats, and five lambs for the peace offering. This was the offering of Nachshon son of Aminadav.

18 Nethanel son of Tzuar, leader of the tribe of Issachar, brought his offering on the second day.

19 His offering consisted of one silver bowl weighing 3.5 pounds, and one silver basin weighing 1.75 pounds, both filled with fine flour mixed with olive oil for a meal offering;

20 one gold bowl weighing 4 ounces filled with incense;

21 one young bull, one lamb for a burnt offering; **22** one goat for a sin offering; **23** and two oxen, five rams, five male goats, and five lambs for the peace offering. This was the offering of Nethanel son of Tzuar.

24 Eliav son of Helon, leader of the tribe of Zebulun, brought his offering on the third day.

25 His offering consisted of one silver bowl weighing 3.5 pounds, and one silver basin weighing 1.75 pounds, both filled with fine flour mixed with olive oil for a meal offering;

26 one gold bowl weighing 4 ounces filled with incense;

27 one young bull, one lamb for a burnt offering;

28 one goat for a sin offering; **29** and two oxen, five rams, five male goats, and five lambs for the peace offering. This was the offering of Eliav son of Helon.

30 Elitzur son of Shedeur, leader of the tribe of Reuben, brought his offering on the fourth day.

31 His offering consisted of one silver bowl weighing 3.5 pounds, and one silver basin weighing 1.75 pounds, both filled with fine flour mixed with olive oil for a meal offering;

32 one gold bowl weighing 4 ounces filled with incense;

33 one young bull, one lamb for a burnt offering;

34 one goat for a sin offering; **35** and two oxen, five rams, five male goats, and five lambs for the peace offering.

This was the offering of Elitzur son of Shedeur.

36 Shelumiel son of Zurishaddai, leader of the tribe of Simeon, brought his offerings on the fifth day.

37 His offering consisted of one silver bowl weighing 3.5 pounds, and one silver basin weighing 1.75 pounds, both filled with fine flour mixed with olive oil for a meal offering;

38 one gold bowl weighing 4 ounces filled with incense;

39 one young bull, one lamb for a burnt offering; **40** one goat for a sin offering; **41** and two oxen, five rams, five male goats, and five lambs for the peace offering. This was the offering of Shelumiel son of Zurishaddai.

The Leaders Continue
Their Offerings
6ᵗʰ Aliyah

42 Eliassaf son of Deuel, leader of the tribe of Gad, brought his offering on the sixth day.

43 His offering consisted of one silver bowl weighing 3.5 pounds, and one silver basin weighing 1.75 pounds, both filled with fine flour mixed with olive oil for a meal offering;

44 one gold bowl weighing 4 ounces filled with incense;

45 one young bull, one lamb for a burnt offering;

46 one goat for a sin offering; **47** and two oxen, five rams, five male goats, and five lambs for the peace offering.

This was the offering of Eliassaf son of Deuel.

48 Elishama son of Amihud, leader of the tribe of Ephraim, brought his offering on the seventh day.

49 His offering consisted of one silver bowl weighing 3.5 pounds, and one silver basin weighing 1.75 pounds, both filled with fine flour mixed with olive oil for a meal offering;

50 one gold bowl weighing 4 ounces filled with incense;

51 one young bull, one lamb for a burnt offering;

52 one goat for a sin offering; **53** and two oxen, five rams, five male goats, and five lambs for the peace offering.

That was the offering of Elishama son of Amihud.

54 Gamliel son of Pedahzur, leader of the tribe of Manasseh, brought his offering on the eighth day.

55 His offering consisted of one silver bowl weighing 3.5 pounds, and one silver basin weighing 1.75 pounds, both filled with fine flour mixed with olive oil for a meal offering; **56** one gold bowl weighing 4 ounces filled with incense; **57** one young bull, one lamb for a burnt offering; **58** one goat for a sin offering; **59** and two oxen, five rams, five male goats, and five lambs for the peace offering. This was the offering of Gamliel son of Pedahzur.

60 Avidan son of Gidoni, leader of the tribe of Benjamin, brought his offering on the ninth day.

61 His offering consisted of one silver bowl weighing 3.5 pounds, and one silver basin weighing 1.75 pounds, both filled with fine flour mixed with olive oil for a meal offering; **62** one gold bowl weighing 4 ounces filled with incense; **63** one young bull, one lamb for a burnt offering; **64** one goat for a sin offering; **65** and two oxen, five rams, five male goats, and five lambs for the peace offering. That was the offering of Avidan son of Gidoni.

66 Achiezer son of Amishaddai, leader of the tribe of Dan, brought his offering on the tenth day.

67 His offering consisted of one silver bowl weighing 3.5 pounds, and one silver basin weighing 1.75 pounds, both filled with fine flour mixed with olive oil for a meal offering; **68** one gold bowl weighing 4 ounces filled with incense; **69** one young bull, one lamb for a burnt offering; **70** one goat for a sin offering; **71** and two oxen, five rams, five male goats, and five lambs for the peace offering. That was the offering of Achiezer son of Amishaddai.

Asher and Naphtali Bring Offerings   *7ᵗʰ Aliyah*

72 Pagiel son of Okhran, leader of the tribe of Asher, brought his offering on the eleventh day.

73 His offering consisted of one silver bowl weighing 3.5 pounds, and one silver basin weighing 1.75 pounds, both filled with fine flour mixed with olive oil for a meal offering; **74** one gold bowl weighing 4 ounces filled with incense; **75** one young bull, one lamb for a burnt offering;

76 one goat for a sin offering; **77** and two oxen, five rams, five male goats, and five lambs for the peace offering. This was the offering of Pagien son of Okhran.

78 Achira son of Eynan, leader of tribe of Naphtali, brought his offering on the twelfth day.

79 His offering consisted of one silver bowl weighing 3.5 pounds, and one silver basin weighing 1.75 pounds, both filled with fine flour mixed with olive oil for a meal offering;

80 one gold bowl weighing 4 ounces filled with incense;

81 one young bull, one lamb for a burnt offering;

82 one goat for a sin offering; **83** and two oxen, five rams, five male goats, and five lambs for the peace offering. That was the offering of Achira son of Eynan.

84 These are the totals of the dedication offerings brought by the tribal leaders on the day that the altar was anointed. There were twelve silver bowls, twelve silver basins, and twelve gold incense bowls.

85 Each silver bowl weighed 3.5 pounds, and each silver basin weighed 1.75 pounds. All together the silver in the two bowls weighed 60 pounds. **86** There were twelve golden bowls filled with incense; each golden bowl weighed 4 ounces. All the gold in the incense bowls weighed 3 pounds.

Adonai Speaks to Moses   *Maftir*

87 For burnt offerings there were twelve oxen, twelve rams, and twelve lambs, along with their grain offerings. There were also twelve male goats for sin offerings.

88 For the peace offerings there were twenty-four bulls, sixty rams, sixty male goats, and sixty lambs. These were the dedication offerings after the altar was anointed.

89 Whenever Moses went into the Meeting Tent to speak with Adonai, he heard the Voice speaking to him from between the two cherubs on the cover of the ark with the Ten Commandments. That was how Adonai communicated with Moses.

Beha'alotecha בְּהַעֲלֹתְךָ
WHEN YOU LIGHT THE MENORAH

8 Adonai spoke to Moses and said to him: **2** Speak to Aaron and tell him: When you light the menorah, position the seven lamps and place them to illuminate the front of the menorah.

3 So Aaron did so, and positioned the lamps to illuminate the area in front of the menorah, just as Adonai had commanded Moses.

4 The menorah was hammered out of a single gold ingot. Everything extending from its base to its blossom consisted of a single piece of hammered gold. The menorah was made exactly to the design that Adonai showed Moses.

5 Adonai spoke to Moses, and said:

6 Remove the Levites from among the Israelites and make them ritually clean. **7** To make them acceptable to Me, you must sprinkle them with the water of purification, and have them shave their entire bodies with a razor, and wash their clothes and their bodies to make themselves ritually clean.

8 Then have them bring a young bull and a grain offering consisting of the finest flour mixed with olive oil. You shall also present a second bull as a sin offering.

9 Bring the Levites to the front of the Meeting Tent, and assemble the entire Israelite community. **10** Present the Levites before the Meeting Tent, and have the Israelites place their hands on the Levites. **11** Aaron is to present the Levites as a wave offering to Adonai from the Israelites, and thus the Levites will become the ones to perform Adonai's service. **12** Afterwards the Levites shall place their hands on the heads of the bulls, and you shall present one bull as a sin offering and one as a burnt offering to Adonai, to make an atonement for the Levites.

13 Next, assemble the Levites in front of Aaron and his sons, and present them as a wave offering dedicated to

Adonai. **14** With this ceremony you will separate the Levites from the other Israelites, and the Levites shall become exclusively Mine.

The Levites and Aaron   *2nd Aliyah*

15 After you have purified them and dedicated them with a wave offering, the Levites shall come to perform the service in the Meeting Tent.

16 From among the Israelites the Levites are given to serve Me in place of the first-borns of all the Israelites. I have chosen the Levites for Myself.

17 All first-borns of the Israelites are Mine, man and beast alike. I sanctified them for Myself on the day that I killed all the first-borns in Egypt. **18** Now I have chosen the Levites in place of all the first-born sons of the Israelites.

19 I have given the Levites as assistants to Aaron and his descendants. From now on they will perform the service for the Israelites in the Meeting Tent and make atonement for the Israelites, so that no plague will strike them when they approach the sanctuary.

20 Moses, Aaron, and the entire Israelite community dedicated the Levites and followed all the instructions that Adonai had given Moses. The Israelites followed all the instructions exactly.

21 The Levites purified themselves with a sin offering and washed their bodies and their clothing. Aaron presented them as a wave offering before Adonai and made atonement for them to purify them. **22** From then on, the Levites performed the service in the Meeting Tent under the direction of Aaron and his sons. The Levites did everything exactly as Adonai had commanded Moses.

23 Adonai spoke to Moses and said:

24 These are the rules for the Levites: They must begin serving in the Tabernacle at the age of twenty-five, and become a part of the workforce in the service of the Meeting Tent.

25 When they are fifty years old they must retire from the active workforce. **26** After retirement they can assist the priests in the Meeting Tent, but they must not officiate in the divine service. This is how you shall designate the responsibilities.

Passover in the Wilderness   *3rd Aliyah*

9 Adonai spoke to Moses in the Wilderness of Sinai, in the second year of the Exodus from Egypt, in the first month [Nisan], saying: **2** Tell the Israelites to prepare the Passover offering at the proper time.

3 The proper time to celebrate Passover shall be the fourteenth day of this month [Nisan] in the evening. They must prepare the Passover offering in accordance with all its regulations and laws.

4 So Moses spoke to the Israelites and told them to prepare the Passover offering. **5** They prepared the Passover offering in the Wilderness of Sinai, on the fourteenth of the first month in the evening. The Israelites did everything exactly as Adonai had instructed Moses.

6 But there were some men who had come in contact with the dead, and they could not prepare the Passover offering on that day because they were ritually unclean. During the day, they came to Moses and Aaron.

7 The men said to Moses, "We are ritually unclean because we came into contact with the dead. Why should we lose out and not be able to present Adonai's offering at the appointed time, along with the other Israelites?"

8 Moses answered, "Wait until I ask and receive instructions from Adonai about your problem."

9 Adonai answered Moses and said: **10** Speak to the Israelites, saying:

If any Israelite becomes ritually unclean because of contact with the dead, or is on a long trip, he may still celebrate Passover.

11 They too are to celebrate Passover on the evening of the fourteenth day of the second month, and they shall eat the Passover offering with matzot and bitter herbs.

12 They shall not leave over any of the offering until morning, and not break any bone in it. They shall prepare the offering according to all the Passover rules.

13 However, if a man is ritually clean, and not on a journey, and he refuses to prepare the Passover offering, then that person shall be cut off from the community. He shall suffer the consequences of his sin for not offering Adonai's sacrifice at the proper time.

14 Any foreigner who lives among you may also prepare Adonai's Passover offering and present it according to the regulations and laws of the Passover offering. The same law shall apply to you and the foreigner in your midst.

The Cloud and the Fiery Glow   *4ᵗʰ Aliyah*

15 On the day that the Tabernacle was erected, a cloud covered the Tabernacle and the Meeting Tent.

Then, in the evening, a glow like a fire covered the Tabernacle, and remained there until morning.

16 From then on it was a regular occurrence. A cloud covered the Tabernacle by day, and a fiery glow covered it by night.

17 Whenever the cloud rose up above the Meeting Tent, the Israelites would set out on the march, and they would camp wherever the cloud settled.

18 In this way the Israelites moved forward at Adonai's command. They remained in one place as long as the cloud remained over the Tabernacle.

19 If the cloud remained over the Tabernacle for a long time, the Israelites kept their trust in Adonai and did not resume their journey.

20 Sometimes the cloud would settle on the Tabernacle for just a few days, and so they remained camped for only a few days. They would move on only at Adonai's command.

21 Sometimes the cloud remained only overnight, and in the morning, when the cloud lifted, they would journey on. By day or by night, whenever the cloud lifted, they would break camp and move on.

22 Whether the cloud remained at rest over the Tabernacle for two days or a month or a full year, no matter how long, the Israelites would remain and not move on. But as soon as the cloud lifted they resumed their journey. **23** They placed their trust in Adonai and moved at Adonai's command. The Israelites obeyed Adonai's commands as delivered through Moses.

10

Adonai spoke to Moses, saying:

2 Make two silver bugles. Hammer them out of silver, and blow the bugles to assemble the community and to break camp.

3 When both of the bugles are blown with a long blast, the entire community shall assemble at the entrance of the Meeting Tent.

4 But if only one long blast is sounded on just one of the bugles, then the leaders of tribes shall assemble to meet with you.

5 When you blow a series of short blasts, the camps to the east of the Tabernacle shall begin the march.

6 And when you sound a second series of short notes, the camps to the south of the Tabernacle shall begin the march, following the other tribes. When the Israelites are to move on, you are to signal with a series of short bugle notes.

7 When the whole community is to be assembled, the bugles shall be blown with a long note.

8 Aaron's descendants, the priests, shall be the ones to blow the bugles. This shall be a permanent law to be followed in every generation.

9 When you go to war in your land against an enemy who attacks you, you shall blow a long blast on the bugles. Then Adonai will come to your aid, and you will defeat your enemies.

10 During your times of rejoicing, your festivals and your new moon celebrations, you shall sound the bugles for your burnt offerings and your peace offerings. The sounds will remind you of Adonai. I am Adonai. I will surely remember you.

From Sinai to Paran

5ᵗʰ Aliyah

11 In the second year of the Exodus, on the twentieth of the second month [Iyar], the cloud lifted from the Tabernacle.

12 So the Israelites resumed their journey, departing from the Wilderness of Sinai, until the cloud stopped in the Wilderness of Paran. **13** This was the first time that Adonai told Moses to order the Israelites to move forward. **14** The tribes under the marching banner of Judah set out first, led by Nachshon son of Aminadav.

15 Nethanel son of Zuar headed the tribe of Issachar, **16** Eliav son of Helon headed the tribe of Zebulun.

17 The Tabernacle was taken down, and the descendants of Gershon and Merari from the tribe of Levi, who carried the Tabernacle, began the march.

18 The tribes under the marching banner of Reuben then began to march, under the leadership of Elitzur son of Shedeur. **19** Shelumiel son of Zurishaddai headed the tribe of Simeon.

20 Eliassaf son of Deuel headed the tribe of Gad.

21 The Kehothites from the tribe of Levi, who carried the sacred furniture, then began their march. The Tabernacle would already be set up when they arrived at the new destination.

22 The tribes under the marching banner of Ephraim then began the march, under the leadership of Elishama son of Amihud.

23 Gamliel son of Pedahzur headed the tribe of Manasseh, **24** and Avidan son of Gidoni headed the tribe of Benjamin.

25 Then the tribes under the marching banner of Dan, the last of the camps, began their march, under the leadership of Achiezer son of Amishaddai. **26** Pagiel son of Okhran headed the tribe of Asher, **27** and Achira son of Eynan headed the tribe of Naphtali.

28 This was the marching order of the Israelites, in which the tribes marched group by group and banner by banner when they began to travel.

29 Moses said to his father-in-law, Hovev son of Reuel the Midianite, "We are now on our way to the land that Adonai promised to give us. Come with us and share the benefit of all the good things that Adonai has promised Israel."

30 Hovev replied, "No, I would rather not go. I wish to return to my land and my birthplace."

31 Moses said, "Please do not leave us. You can be our guide, because you know the good camping places in the desert. **32** If you come with us, we will share with you whatever good Adonai grants us."

33 The Israelites began their journey from Mount Sinai. They marched for three days, and the ark traveled three days ahead of them to scout out a suitable place to camp.

34 As they began the march, Adonai's cloud was continually with them.

Adonai, Stay with Us   *6th Aliyah*

35 When the ark traveled, Moses would say,

"Adonai, rise up,
and scatter your enemies!
Let your foes flee before You!"

36 When the ark came to rest, Moses would say,

"O Adonai, stay with us;
remain
with the people of Israel."

11 The Israelites began to complain. When Adonai heard them, He became angry, and a fire from Adonai blazed out and destroyed those at the edge of the camp.

2 The people begged Moses to save them, so Moses prayed to Adonai and the fire died down. **3** They named the place Taberah (Burning), because Adonai's fire had burned them.

4 Now the foreign rabble among the Israelites became homesick and had a strong yearning for the food of Egypt. The Israelites again began to complain, saying, "We are hungry for meat. **5** We remember the delicious fish and the cucumbers, melons, leeks, onions, and garlic that we ate in Egypt. **6** But now our appetites are gone, and day after day all we get is manna for breakfast, lunch, and supper."

7 The manna was shiny yellow in color and looked like coriander seed. **8** The people just gathered it up from the ground and ground it or crushed it into flour and cooked it in a pan or baked it into flat cakes. It tasted like a pancake fried in oil. **9** At night, manna would fall on the camp like dew.

10 Moses heard the people and their families complaining near the entrances of their tents. Adonai became very angry, and Moses was also upset.

11 Moses asked Adonai, "Why are You testing me so strongly, and why are You treating me like this? Why did You place so heavy a burden upon me? **12** The Israelites are not my children. I did not give birth to them. You made them a promise, and You told me that I would have to nurse them in my bosom, just as a nurse carries a new-born baby, until we conquer the land that You promised their ancestors.

13 Where in the middle of this forsaken wilderness can I find enough meat to feed all these people? They are always complaining and asking me to give them some meat to eat.

14 I cannot be responsible for this entire nation of whining cry-babies all by myself.

15 It would be much better if You did me a favor and just killed me! I just don't have the strength to carry this great responsibility."

16 Adonai said to Moses, "Gather seventy of Israel's elders and leaders. Bring them to the Meeting Tent, and I will meet you there.

17 I will come down and speak to you there. I will take some of the spirit that is in you and put it in them. Then you will not have to bear the responsibility all by yourself.

18 By the way, tell the people to be prepared, because tomorrow they will have meat to eat. Say to them, 'You have been whining in Adonai's ears, saying, "Who will give us some meat to eat? Life in Egypt was much better for us." Now Adonai is going to send you meat, and you will have to eat it. **19** You will eat it not just for one day, not just for two days, not just for five days, not just for ten days, and not just for twenty days.

20 You will eat meat until it is coming out of your nose and you are sick of it.'

I will do this because you have lost faith in Adonai, because even though He is right here among you, you continually ask, 'Why did we ever leave Egypt?'"

21 Moses said, "Here I am alone among 600,000 men, and You promise to give them enough meat to eat for a full month! **22** Even if we butchered all of our cattle and sheep, there could never be enough meat for all of them. Even if all the fish in the sea were caught, it still would not be enough for them."

23 Adonai said to Moses, "Is there any limit to My power? Now you will see whether My power is limited."

24 Moses went out of the Tabernacle and told the people what Adonai had said. He assembled seventy of the elders and stationed them around the Meeting Tent.

25 Adonai descended in a cloud and spoke to Moses. He took some of the spirit (responsibility) from Moses and placed it upon the seventy elders. When the spirit rested on them, they gained the gift of prophecy.

26 Two of the seventy elders, Eldad and Medad, remained in the camp, and the spirit also rested on them. Although they were among the seventy elders, they had not gone to the Meeting Tent, yet the spirit rested on them and they prophesied in the camp.

27 A young man ran to tell Moses, "Eldad and Medad are prophesying in the camp!"

28 Joshua son of Nun, the assistant of Moses, protested, "My lord Moses, make them stop!"

29 Moses replied, "Are you jealous for my sake? I wish that all of Adonai's people were holy enough to have the gift of prophecy! Let Adonai grant His spirit to everyone who deserves it."

The Hail of Quail   *7th Aliyah*

30 Then Moses along with the elders of Israel returned to the camp.

31 Adonai sent a strong wind, and it started to blow and swept the quail up from the sea. They ran out of strength over the camp, and the quail were scattered in piles three feet deep throughout the camp and for miles in every direction. **32** All that day, all night, and the entire next day the people gathered quail. Even the slowest person gathered ten chomer (60 bushels). The people spread them out to dry in the sun around the camp.

33 While still eating the meat, the people began to die because they ate too much. Adonai was angry at the Israelites, and He struck them with a plague.

34 Moses named the place Kivroth HaTaavah (Graves of Craving) because it was there that they buried the people who had greedy cravings for meat and died from overeating.

35 From Kivroth HaTaavah, the people traveled to Hatzeroth.

12 Miriam and Aaron began to criticize Moses because he had married a Cushite woman, a dark-skinned woman.

2 They complained, "Adonai speaks only to Moses. Why doesn't he speak to us?" But Adonai heard it.

3 However, Moses was very humble. He was more humble than any man on the face of the earth.

4 Suddenly Adonai ordered Moses, Aaron, and Miriam, "All three of you, come to the Meeting Tent!"

When the three of them got there, **5** Adonai descended in a pillar of cloud and stood at the entrance of the Meeting Tent. He called Aaron and Miriam, and they both stepped forward.

6 Adonai said, "Listen carefully to My words. With anyone else who experiences divine prophecy, I make Myself known to him in a vision, and speak to him in a dream. **7** But with My trusted servant Moses, **8** I speak to him face-to-face, and not in riddles. You have no reason to criticize My servant Moses."

9 Adonai was angry at them and left.

10 Suddenly the cloud over the Meeting Tent lifted. Miriam became leprous, and as white as snow. When Aaron saw what had happened to Miriam, **11** he said to Moses, "My lord, please do not punish us for acting foolishly and sinning. **12** Do not let your sister Miriam be like a stillborn child, born with its flesh rotting away."

13 Moses prayed to Adonai, "O Adonai, please heal her!"

Miriam Is Cured   *Maftir*

14 Adonai answered Moses, "Wouldn't Miriam be disgraced for seven days if her father had punished her by spitting in her face? So I will punish her by banishing her for seven days outside the camp, and then I will let her return home."

15 Miriam remained outside the camp for seven days, and the people did not move on until Miriam was cured and returned home. **16** Then the Israelites left Hatzeroth, and they made their camp in the Wilderness of Paran.

Shelach Lecha שְׁלַח לְךָ
SEND SCOUTS TO CANAAN

13 Adonai instructed Moses and said, **2** "Send out scouts as spies to explore the Canaanite territory that I am about to give the Israelites. Choose one scout from each tribe. Make sure that each scout is a leader of his tribe." **3** At Adonai's command, Moses sent them from the Wilderness of Paran. All the men were leaders of the tribes. **4** Their names were as follows:

From the tribe of Reuben, Shamua son of Zakur.

5 From the tribe of Simeon, Shaphat son of Chori.

6 From the tribe of Judah, Caleb son of Yefuneh.

7 From the tribe of Issachar, Yig'al son of Joseph.

8 From the tribe of Ephraim, Hoshea son of Nun.

9 From the tribe of Benjamin, Palti son of Raphu.

10 From the tribe of Zebulun, Gadiel son of Sodi.

11 From the tribe of Manasseh from Joseph, Gaddi son of Susi.

12 From the tribe of Dan, Amiel son of Gemalli.

13 From the tribe of Asher, Sethur son of Michael.

14 From the tribe of Naphtali, Nachbi son of Vafsi.

15 From the tribe of Gad, Geuel son of Makhi.

16 These are the names of the men Moses sent to explore the land. However, Moses gave Hoshea son of Nun a new name, Joshua.

17 When Moses sent the scouts to explore the Canaanite territory, he said to them, "Head north to the Negev, and then continue to the hill country.

18 See what kind of land it is.
Are the people who live there
strong or weak,
few or many?
19 Is the inhabited area good or bad?
Are the cities where they live
open or fortified?

20 Is the soil rich or weak?
Does the land have trees or not?
Make a special effort
to bring back
samples of the fruits."

It was the season when the first grapes were beginning to ripen.

The Cluster of Grapes   *2ⁿᵈ Aliyah*

21 The scouts headed north and explored the land, from the Wilderness of Zin all the way to Rechov on the road to Hamath. **22** On the way they passed through the Negev, until they came to Hebron. There they saw the Achiman, Sheshai, and Talmi, descendants of the Anakim (giants). Hebron was founded seven years before the Egyptian city of Zoan. **23** When they came to Nahal Eshkol (Cluster Valley), they cut a branch with a cluster of grapes. It was so large that it needed two men to carry it on a pole. They also took some pomegranates and figs. **24** Because of the grape-cluster that the Israelites cut there, the place was named Cluster Valley.

25 At the end of forty days they came back from exploring the land. **26** When they arrived, they went directly to Moses, Aaron, and the entire Israelite community, who were waiting for them in the Wilderness of the Paran near Kadesh. They brought their report to Moses, Aaron, and the entire community, and showed them fruit from the land.

27 They gave the following report: "We went to the land where you sent us, and as you can see from its fruit, it is really flowing with milk and honey.

28 However, the people living in the land are powerful, and the cities are large and well fortified. We also saw the descendants of the Anakim (giants). **29** Amalek lives in the Negev; the Hittites, Jebusites, and Amorites live in the hills; and the Canaanites live near the Mediterranean Sea and on the banks of the Jordan."

30 Caleb tried to encourage the people. Caleb said "We must advance and occupy the land. We can do it!"

31 The other scouts disagreed with Caleb. "We cannot conquer them! They are much too powerful for us!"

32 Then they began to spread discouraging reports about the land they had explored. They told the Israelites, "The land we scouted is a land that will defeat invaders. All the men we saw there were huge! **33** While we were there, we saw Anakim (giants). Compared with them we looked and felt like tiny grasshoppers!"

14 That night, after the report of the scouts, the entire community began to shout and cry. **2** The Israelites complained to Moses and Aaron. The entire community grumbled, "It would have been better if we had died in Egypt or in this desert! **3** Did Adonai bring us to this land so that we, our wives, and our children could die by the sword or spend our lives as slaves? It would be best for us to return to Egypt!"

4 The people began to plot among themselves. "Let's choose a new leader and return to Egypt."

5 Moses and Aaron bowed down and prayed before the assembled Israelite community.

6 Two of the scouts, Joshua son of Nun and Caleb son of Yefuneh, tore their clothes in shame. **7** They said to the whole Israelite community, "The land that we explored is a very good and fertile land!

The Israelites Rebel   *3rd Aliyah*

8 "If Adonai is pleased with us, He will bring us to this land flowing with milk and honey. **9** Only don't rebel against Adonai! Don't be afraid of the people in the land! Because they have lost their protection and Adonai is on our side."

10 The rebellious mob threatened to stone Moses and Aaron to death. Suddenly Adonai appeared in a cloud over the Meeting Tent.

11 Adonai said to Moses, "How long will this people continue to anger Me? How long will they refuse to believe in Me despite all the miracles that I have done for them? **12** I will kill them with a plague. Then I will make you and your descendants into a greater, more powerful nation."

13 Moses replied to Adonai, "Just imagine what the Egyptians would think when they hear about it. Remember that with Your great power You rescued this nation from out of Egypt. **14** Just imagine what they will tell the people who live in this land. They are aware that You, Adonai, have been with this nation Israel. They know that You, Adonai, have revealed Yourself to them face-to-face, and that Your cloud leads them. You lead them in a pillar of cloud by day, and a pillar of fire at night.

15 And now you want to slaughter this entire nation! The nations that have heard about You will say that **16** Adonai is weak and unable to lead this nation into the land that He swore to give them, and so He just killed them in the desert.

17 Now, O Adonai, prove to the world that Your power is great and exercise restraint. You once said,

18 'Adonai is slow to anger, rich in love, and forgiving of sin and rebellion. But He does not forgive those who do not repent. He does not leave the guilty unpunished, He punishes the children for the sins of their parents to the third and fourth generation.'

19 Please, with Your great love, forgive the sins of this nation, just as You have forgiven them from the time they left Egypt until now."

20 Adonai answered, "I will pardon them as you have requested. **21** But as surely as I live, and as surely as My glory fills all the world, **22** I will punish all the people who have witnessed My glory and the miracles I performed in Egypt and the wilderness but who still test Me and refuse to obey Me.

23 They will never see the land that I swore to give to their ancestors. None of those who doubted Me will ever enter the land.

24 Only my servant Caleb will enter the land, because he was loyal and showed a different spirit and followed Me wholeheartedly. I will bring him into the land that he explored, and his descendants will receive their share. **25** Beware the Amalekites and the Canaanites who are living in the valley. Tomorrow leave the place and march into the desert toward the Sea of Reeds."

You Will Wander for Forty Years   *4ᵗʰ Aliyah*

26 Adonai spoke to Moses and Aaron, saying, **27** "How long will you allow this evil mob to exist, and to complain against Me? I have heard the complaints of the Israelites about Me.

28 Tell them as follows: 'As surely as I live, I will do to them the things that they accuse Me of doing. **29** Because they complained about Me, they will all die in this desert.

Everyone over twenty years old who was counted will die **30** and will not enter the land which I swore to give to you. The only two exceptions will be Caleb son of Yefuneh and Joshua son of Nun.

31 The rebels predicted that their children would be taken captive; their children are the ones who will enjoy the land that they rejected.

32 Your bodies will rot in the desert. **33** Your children will wander from place to place in the desert for forty years, and suffer for your lack of faith until the last of your corpses drop here in the desert.

34 Your punishment of forty years will equal the number of days the scouts spent exploring the land. I will punish you for forty years, one year for each day, a total of forty years until your sin is forgiven. You will discover that I am very angry.

35 I, Adonai, have spoken! I will do this only to every member of the community that complained against Me. They will end their lives in this desert, and here is where they will die.'"

36 The scouts whom Moses had sent to explore the land, and who had circulated false rumors about the land, **37** who had brought discouraging reports about the land, died in a plague.

38 Among the twelve scouts who explored the land only Joshua son of Nun and Caleb son of Yefuneh remained alive.

39 When Moses reported Adonai's decision to the Israelites, there was great sorrow.

40 They got up early in the morning, and began to march toward Canaan, saying, "Now we are ready! We are ready to enter the land that Adonai has promised us. We know now that we were wrong."

41 Moses said, "Once again you are disobeying Adonai. **42** Do not go forward. Adonai is not with you. You will be defeated by your enemies!

43 The Amalekites and Canaanites will attack you, and you will fall by their swords. You have disregarded Adonai, and He will not be with you."

44 But the people refused to listen and climbed toward the hill country of Canaan. The ark of Adonai's covenant and Moses remained in the camp.

45 The Amalekites and Canaanites who lived in the hills ambushed the Israelites, and routed them, and chased them all the way back to Hormah.

15 Adonai spoke to Moses, and instructed him to **2** speak to the Israelites and say to them: When you finally come to your homeland that I am giving you, **3** you will wish to present fire offerings to please Adonai. They may be burnt offerings for a vow or a free-will offering for your festivals. The sacrifices must be taken from the cattle or sheep or goats as a thank you gift to Adonai.

4 The person presenting the sacrifice to Adonai must bring a grain offering of two quarts of the best grade of flour mixed with one quart of olive oil. **5** For each lamb presented as burnt or peace sacrifice you shall also present one quart of wine for the libation.

6 For a ram, you shall also present a grain offering of three quarts of flour mixed with 2.5 pints of olive oil. **7** You shall also present a libation of 2.5 pints of wine as a thank you gift to Adonai.

Grain Offerings   *5th Aliyah*

8 When you present an animal as a burnt offering to fulfill a special vow or a peace offering to Adonai, **9** you must bring with each animal five quarts of choice flour as a grain offering, mixed with two quarts of olive oil.

10 Also, as a libation, bring two quarts of wine as a thank you gift to Adonai.

11 You must do the same for each bull, ram, sheep, or goat.

12 You must present the same meal offering for each of your sacrifices.

13 Every Israelite who presents a fire offering as a thank you offering to Adonai must present his gift with the grain offering in the same way. **14** The foreigner who lives among you and presents a fire offering as a thank you gift to Adonai, he must follow the exact same procedure. **15** The same rule shall apply both to you and to the foreigner who lives among you. It is a law for all generations that the foreigner and you are the same before Adonai. **16** You and the foreigner who lives among you shall be judged by the exact same law.

The Dough Offering   *6ᵗʰ Aliyah*

17 Adonai spoke to Moses, and told him to **18** speak to the Israelites and say to them:

When you arrive in the land to which I am bringing you, **19** and you eat the crops of the land, you must remember **20** to set aside a gift from the first portion of your baking dough as an offering to Adonai; it must be separated just like the elevated gift that is taken from the threshing floor.

21 In future generations, you must set aside a gift to Adonai from your first batch of baking as a gift to Adonai.

22 This is the law if you mistakenly violate any of the commandments that Adonai has given to Moses:

23 If your descendants fail to obey a law that Adonai has commanded through Moses, **24** or if the community, because of its leader, has committed a sin by mistake, then the community must present a bull for a burnt offering as a thank you gift to Adonai, with a grain offering and a liquid offering as a libation. The community must also present one goat for a sin offering.

25 In this way the priest will make atonement for the entire Israelite community, and they will be forgiven. It was a mistake, and they presented a fire offering and a sin offering before Adonai to atone for their mistake.

26 The entire Israelite community as well as the foreigner who lives among you shall be forgiven for the mistake.

Individual Sin Offering   *7th Aliyah*

27 If a person unintentionally commits a sin, he must bring a young female goat for a sin offering.

28 In this way the priest will make atonement for the guilty person before Adonai, and the person will be forgiven for his sin. **29** The exact same law applies to Israelites and to the foreigners who live among you.

30 But if a person deliberately commits a sin, then it makes no difference whether he is an Israelite or a foreigner, he has willfully disobeyed Adonai and shall be cut off from the community.

31 He has violated Adonai's commandments, and therefore he shall be cut off from the community, and his sin will not be forgiven.

32 While the Israelites were in the desert, they found a man gathering firewood for the Sabbath. **33** He was brought before Moses, Aaron, and the entire community. **34** And they held him under guard because no one knew how to deal with the problem.

35 Adonai instructed Moses, "Tell the people to take him outside the camp and execute him."

36 So the entire community took him outside the camp, and they executed him, just as Adonai commanded.

Sew Fringes on Your Garments   *Maftir*

37 Adonai spoke to Moses, and told him: **38** Tell the Israelites to sew fringes (*tzitzit*) on the corners of their garments and insert a blue cord in each corner of the fringe.

39 When they see the fringes, they will be reminded to obey Adonai's commandments and not follow the evil in their heart and be blinded by the degraded sight of their eyes. **40** When they see the fringes, they will remember and observe all My commandments and be faithful to Adonai.

41 I am Adonai,
who brought you out of Egypt.
Remember: I am Adonai.

Korach קֹרַח
KORACH THE REBEL

16 Korach son of Yitzhar, a grandson of Kehoth and great-grandson of Levi, together with Dathan and Aviram, both of them sons of Eliav, and On son of Peleth, all three of whom were descendants of Reuben, began a rebellion. **2** They and 250 Israelite leaders challenged the authority of Moses.

3 They confronted Moses and Aaron with the accusation, "You have gone too far! Everyone in the community is holy, and Adonai is with us. So why do you two think that you are superior to everyone else?"

4 When Moses heard this, he began to pray. **5** Then he spoke to Korach and his followers and said, "Tomorrow morning, Adonai will show us the person He has designated as His holy spokesman. Adonai will choose those who shall be privileged to present offerings to Him.

6 Tomorrow this is what you must do: Korach, you and your associates must take your fire pans **7** and burn incense in them before Adonai. Then we will find out who Adonai has chosen to be the holy one. You Levites have overstepped and gone too far!"

8 Then Moses said to Korach, "Levites, listen to me. **9** Adonai has honored you and has separated you from the rest of the community of Israel and has brought you close to Him, allowing you to serve in the Tabernacle and help the community to worship with reverence.

10 He gave this honor to you and all your fellow Levites, and now you are also demanding the priesthood! **11** You and your followers are really rebelling against Adonai and not against Aaron. After all, who is Aaron that you should have grievances against him?"

12 Now Moses sent for Dathan and Aviram, the sons of Eliav, but they sent back this message: "We won't come!

13 It's bad enough that you brought us out of Egypt, a land flowing with milk and honey, just to kill us in the wilderness! You have no right to tell us what to do.

The Rebellion of Korach   *2nd Aliyah*

14 "Look around, you didn't bring us to a land flowing with milk and honey, or give us fertile fields and vineyards. Do you think that you can keep fooling us? We will definitely not come to meet with you!"

15 Moses became very angry, and he said to Adonai, "Do not listen to them or accept their offerings. I did not even take a single donkey from them! I did not harm any of them!"

16 Then Moses said to Korach, "Tomorrow you and your associates must come and present yourselves before Adonai. You and your associates and Aaron must appear tomorrow. **17** Make sure that each man brings his fire pan and fills it with incense, so that your 250 followers can present them before Adonai."

18 So the rebels all brought their burning fire pans filled with incense and stood at the entrance of the Meeting Tent with Moses and Aaron. **19** Meanwhile, Korach brought more of his followers to the entrance of the Meeting Tent. Suddenly Adonai's glory appeared to the entire community.

Moses Pleads with Adonai   *3rd Aliyah*

20 Adonai spoke to Moses and Aaron, and said, **21** "Separate yourselves from this band of rebels because I am going to destroy them."

22 But Moses and Aaron bowed and pleaded, "Adonai, Creator of all living souls. If one man sins, must you punish the entire community?"

23 Adonai spoke to Moses and directed him to **24** warn the entire community to move away from the tents of Korach, Dathan, and Aviram.

25 So Moses and the elders of Israel rushed to the tent of Dathan and Aviram.

26 Moses warned the community, "Hurry, run away from the tents of these wicked men. Do not touch anything that belongs to them or you too will be punished because of all their sins."

27 The people retreated from around the tents of Korach, Dathan, and Aviram. Dathan and Aviram, along with their sons, daughters, and infants, stood defiantly at the entrance of their tents.

28 Moses announced, "Now you will know that Adonai sent me to do all these deeds, and it was not my own doing. **29** If the rebels die like ordinary men, then you will know that Adonai did not send me. **30** But if Adonai performs a miracle and makes the earth open its mouth and swallow them and all their belongings, so that they descend to the depths alive, then you will know that these men were provoking Adonai."

31 As Moses finished speaking, the ground under Dathan and Aviram split open. **32** The earth opened its mouth and swallowed them and all the men who were with Korach and all their property. **33** They all fell alive into the earth, along with all their property. Then the earth closed over them, and they disappeared from the community.

34 The Israelites around them all heard their cries, and ran away as the earth swallowed them up.

35 Then streaks of fire came down from Adonai and burned up the 250 men who were offering incense.

17 Adonai spoke to Moses, saying, **2** "Tell Eleazar son of Aaron the priest to gather up all the fire pans because they have been sanctified, and scatter the burning coals.

3 The fire pans belonging to the rebels who sinned are holy. Save the copper pans and hammer the metal into sheets to cover the altar. The metal covering will be a warning to Israel that Adonai is in their midst."

4 So Eleazar gathered the copper fire pans of the rebels and hammered them into metal sheets as a covering for the altar.

5 The copper altar covering was intended to be a

visual reminder to the Israelites that only descendants of Aaron are authorized to burn incense before Adonai. Any others would be punished just like Korach and his followers.

6 The next day the entire Israelite community began to complain against Moses. Now they grumbled, "You have killed Adonai's people!"

7 The people, still complaining against Moses and Aaron, turned and faced the Meeting Tent. Suddenly the tent was covered with a cloud, and Adonai's glory appeared. **8** Moses and Aaron went to the front of the Meeting Tent.

Atonement for the Israelites   *4ᵗʰ Aliyah*

9 Adonai spoke to Moses, saying, **10** "Get away from this congregation because in one moment I will destroy all of them." Moses and Aaron threw themselves on their faces.

11 Moses said to Aaron, "Hurry! Take your fire pan and put some hot coals from the altar in it. Quickly, offer incense to make atonement for the community, because Adonai is angry and the plague has already begun!"

12 So Aaron took his fire pan, as Moses had ordered him, and bravely ran into the midst of the community. He offered the incense to atone for the people.

13 He stood among the dead and the living, until the plague stopped.

14 But 14,700 people died in the plague, in addition to those who died because of Korach's rebellion.

15 When the plague stopped, Aaron returned to Moses at the entrance of the Meeting Tent.

Aaron's Staff Blossoms   *5ᵗʰ Aliyah*

16 Adonai spoke to Moses, telling him to **17** speak to the Israelites and to take twelve staffs, one from each tribe, and let each leader write his name on his own staff.

18 "Write Aaron's name on Levi's staff because there must be only one staff for each tribe. **19** Place the staffs in the Meeting

Tent in front of the ark where I meet with you. **20** The staff of the man whom I choose will blossom. Then I will once and for all put an end to the Israelites' complaints against you."

21 Moses spoke to the Israelites, and each leader gave him a staff to represent his tribe. There were twelve staffs, with Aaron's staff among them. **22** Moses set the staffs before Adonai in the Meeting Tent.

23 The following day Moses entered the Meeting Tent, and Aaron's staff, representing the house of Levi, had blossomed and almonds were ripening on it.

24 Then Moses brought out all the staffs from before Adonai and let the Israelites see them. Each leader took his own staff.

The Symbol   *6ᵗʰ Aliyah*

25 Adonai said to Moses, "Put Aaron's staff in front of the ark as a symbol. Let it be a warning to anyone who wants to rebel and challenge Me. This should put an end to complaints against Me, and prevent any more deaths."

26 Moses did exactly as Adonai had instructed him.

27 The Israelites said to Moses, "We are as good as dead! We will all be destroyed! We are all lost! **28** Anyone who approaches the Tabernacle is as good as dead! We are all doomed to die!"

18 Adonai said to Aaron: You, your sons, and the members of your tribe will be responsible for the sanctuary. You and your descendants will also be responsible for any sins connected with the priesthood.

2 Enlist your relatives, the members of the tribe of Levi. Let them assist you and help you perform your sacred duties in the Meeting Tent.

3 The Levites shall perform their duties in the Meeting Tent under your supervision, but under no circumstances may they handle any of the sacred objects or the altar utensils or they will die.

4 The Levites shall be your assistants and they will be responsible for the care and maintenance of the

Meeting Tent, and no unauthorized person is permitted to join them.

5 Let them be entrusted with responsibility for the sanctuary and the altar, so that I will not become angry and punish the Israelites.

6 I have chosen your relatives the Levites from among the Israelites as a gift to you. They are dedicated to help and assist you to perform the service in the Meeting Tent.

7 Aaron, you and your sons shall perform all the priestly duties. These include conducting all the sacred services associated with the altar and all the services inside the cloth partition. The work of the priesthood is the gift of service that I have given you. Any unauthorized person who comes near the sanctuary shall die.

8 Adonai announced to Aaron: I have set you in charge of the sacred gifts and sacrifices brought by the Israelites. From now on you and your descendants will receive a regular share of the offerings.

9 This is what shall be yours: all the Israelites' sacrifices, and all their grain offerings, and all their sin and guilt offerings shall belong to you and your descendants.

10 All male priests may eat these offerings, but they must be eaten in a most holy area and must remain holy to you.

11 Remember, these sacred offerings are dedicated to you and can be eaten by your sons and daughters. Any person in your household who is ritually clean may eat them.

12 The best of the olive oil, wine, and grain that are presented to Adonai is given to you.

13 The first fruit of everything that grows in your land, which is presented to Adonai, shall be yours. Everyone in your household who is ritually clean may eat it.

14 Everything that the Israelites pledge to Adonai shall also be yours.

15 The first-born that is offered to Adonai, whether man or beast, shall belong to you. But you must redeem the first-born sons and the first-born unclean animals on the payment of five pieces of silver.

16 They must be redeemed when they are one month old by the payment of five silver coins.

17 However, the first-born of oxen, sheep, or goats cannot be redeemed, because they are sacred to Me. You must slaughter them and sprinkle their blood on the altar and burn their fat as a thank you gift to Adonai.

18 You are permitted to eat the meat of these animals just as you can eat the breast and right hind leg of a wave offering.

19 From now on, whatever is presented as a holy offering I give to you and your descendants as a regular share. This shall be a permanent covenant sealed with salt between Adonai and your descendants.

20 Then Adonai said to Aaron, You and your descendants will not own any property in the land of the Israelites.

I Myself shall be your share and your inheritance among the Israelites.

Tithes for Tithes   *7th Aliyah*

21 To the descendants of the Levites I am now giving all the tithes in Israel as their inheritance. This is in return for the services and work that they perform in the Meeting Tent.

22 From now on no other Israelites shall enter into the Meeting Tent or they will become guilty of sin and die.

23 Only the Levites shall conduct the necessary services in the Meeting Tent, and they will make an atonement for the Israelites.

It is a law for all future generations that the Levites do not have any inheritance of land. **24** The inheritance I am giving the Levites shall instead consist of all the tithes that the Israelites present as wave offerings. I have told the Levites that these gifts belong to them, and they have no need for an inheritance of land among the Israelites.

25 Adonai spoke to Moses and said to him: **26** Speak to the Levites and say to them:

When an Israelite presents his tithe that I have given you as your inheritance from them, you must separate a tithe from their tithes as a gift to Me, a tithe of the tithe. **27** The tithe given to you by the Israelites is your own gift from the threshing floor or wine from the winepress.

28 Now you must take a tithe from all the tithes that you have collected from the Israelites and must present it as Adonai's gift to Aaron the priest. **29** From the tithe of all the tithes you shall pick the choicest parts as Adonai's portion, to be given to Aaron the priest and his descendants.

A Tithe of the Tithes *Maftir*

30 Say to the Levites: After you have separated out the dedicated tithe for the priest, the remainder of the tithes shall be for all the Levites exactly as if it came from your own threshing floor and your own winepress. **31** You and your family can eat it anywhere because it is payment for your service in the Meeting Tent.

32 Once you have set aside the best of all your tithes, you will not be guilty of sinning, because you have not defiled the sacred offerings of the Israelites, and you will not die.

Chukkat חֻקַּת

THIS IS THE LAW OF THE TORAH

19 Adonai spoke to Moses and Aaron, and told them: **2** This is the law of the Torah that Adonai has commanded the Israelites. Speak to the Israelites and have them bring a completely healthy red cow, one that has never done any farm work.

3 Give it to Eleazar the priest, and he shall take it outside the camp, where it shall be slaughtered in his presence.

4 Then Eleazar the priest shall dip his finger in its blood and sprinkle it seven times toward the Meeting Tent.

5 The whole cow shall be burned; its skin, flesh, blood, and organs must be burned in the presence of Eleazar.

6 The priest shall then take a piece of cedar wood, some hyssop, and some red wool, and throw it into the fire.

7 After the ceremony the priest shall wash his garments and his body. He remains unclean until evening, and then he may return to the camp. **8** The person who burns the cow must also wash his clothing and body and will also remain unclean until evening.

9 A ritually clean person shall gather up the ashes of the cow and place them outside the camp in a clean place. The ashes of the cow are to be mixed in water by the Israelites for the ceremony of purification for the removal of sin.

10 The person who gathers up the ashes of the cow must wash his body and his clothing, and remains unclean until evening.

This shall be a permanent law for the Israelites and for any foreigner who lives among you.

11 Those who have any contact with a dead human being shall become ritually unclean for seven days.

12 They must purify themselves on the third and seventh days by sprinkling themselves with the purification water. Anyone who does not undergo purification on the third and seventh days will remain ritually unclean even after the seventh day.

13 Any person who touches a dead human being and does not have himself sprinkled shall be cut off from the community of Israel if he desecrates Adonai's Tabernacle by entering it. Since the purification water was not sprinkled on him, he remains unclean.

14 This is the law when a man dies in a tent: Anyone who enters the tent and everyone who lived in the tent shall remain unclean for seven days. **15** Every open container that was not sealed shall be declared unclean.

16 Anyone who touches the body of someone who was killed or of a person who died naturally, and so too a person who touches a human bone or an open grave—that person shall be unclean for seven days.

17 To remove defilement, mix some of the ashes from the burnt purification offering in a vessel that has been filled with water from a running spring.

The Purification Process   *2ⁿᵈ Aliyah*

18 A ritually clean person shall then dip a hyssop branch into the water and sprinkle the water on all the containers and people who were in the tent and on anyone who touched a bone, a murder victim, or any other dead body, or a grave.

19 On the third and seventh days, the ritually clean person shall sprinkle some of the purification water on the unclean person. The purification process is completed on the seventh day, when the person undergoing cleansing washes his clothing and body, and then becomes ritually clean in the evening.

20 If a person is unclean and refuses to purify himself, and desecrates Adonai's sanctuary by entering it, he shall no longer be a part of the Israelite community. As long as the purification water has not been sprinkled on him, he shall remain unclean.

21 This is a permanent law.

Anyone who sprinkles the purification water must bathe his body and wash his clothing. If he merely touches the purification water, however, he shall be unclean until evening.

22 Anything that an unclean person comes in contact with shall become unclean, and anyone who touches him shall be unclean until evening.

20 In the first month, the entire Israelite community reached the Wilderness of Zin, and the people camped in Kadesh. It was there that Miriam died and was buried.

2 There was no water to drink, and the Israelites blamed Moses and Aaron.

3 The people quarreled with Moses. They complained, "We wish that we had died together with our brothers! **4** Did you bring us into this desert so that we and our livestock should die here?

5 Why have you led us out of Egypt and brought us to this miserable place? There are no plants, no figs, no grapes, no pomegranates. And now there is not even a drop of water to drink!"

6 Moses and Aaron turned away from the angry crowd toward the entrance of the Meeting Tent and prayed.

Suddenly Adonai's presence appeared to them.

Water from the Rock   *3rd Aliyah*

7 Adonai spoke to Moses, **8** "Take your miracle staff, and you and Aaron assemble the community. Speak to the rock before their eyes, and it will gush out water. You will bring water from the rock, so that the Israelites and their cattle can drink."

9 So Moses took his staff from before Adonai. **10** Then Moses and Aaron assembled the Israelites in front of the rock.

Moses shouted, "You rebels, listen to me now! Now you will see water flow from this rock." **11** With that, Moses raised his hand, and struck the rock twice with his staff. A river of water gushed out, and the community and their cattle had plenty of water to drink.

12 But Adonai angrily said to Moses and Aaron, "I told you to speak to the rock. But neither of you trusted Me, and instead you struck the rock in the presence of the Israelites! Therefore, you shall not lead the Israelites into the land that I have given you."

13 That is why the place was called Mai Meribah (Waters of Dispute), because there the Israelites disputed with Adonai, and there He demonstrated His power and gave them water to drink.

Edom Refuses Israel   *4ᵗʰ Aliyah*

14 Moses sent ambassadors from Kadesh to the king of Edom with the following message:

"This is what your brother Israel says:

You are aware of all the troubles that we have encountered.

15 Our ancestors lived in Egypt for a long time. The Egyptians were cruel to our ancestors and to us.

16 So we cried out to Adonai. He heard our voice and sent a messenger to lead us out of Egypt. Now we are camped around the city of Kadesh, on the border of your land.

17 Please let us pass through your land. We will be careful not to trespass on any of your fields or vineyards, and we will not drink any water from your wells. We will only travel along the King's Highway, not turning right or left until we have passed through your lands."

18 The king of Edom answered, "No! you must not pass through my land. If you do, I will destroy you with my army!"

19 The Israelites answered, "We will stay on the main road. If we or our cattle drink any of your water, we will pay the full price. We only want to pass through your country on foot."

20 The king of Edom answered, "Keep out! Do not come into our country!" The king of Edom mobilized his army and opposed the Israelites with a large force of heavily armed soldiers.

21 Edom refused to allow Israel to pass through its territories, and Israel was forced to go around the area.

Aaron Dies   5*th* Aliyah

22 The Israelites proceeded from Kadesh to Mount Hor.

23 When they got there, Adonai said to Moses and Aaron,

24 "The time has come for Aaron to die and join his ancestors. He will not enter the land that I am giving the Israelites because you both disobeyed me at Mai Meribah.

25 Moses, take Aaron and his son Eleazar up to the top of Mount Hor. **26** Remove Aaron's priestly garments and put them on his son Eleazar. There Aaron will die and be gathered to his ancestors."

27 Moses did everything that Adonai had commanded him. The three of them climbed Mount Hor as the entire community watched.

28 Moses removed Aaron's priestly garments and put them on Aaron's son Eleazar. Aaron died on the top of the mountain. When Moses and Eleazar came down from the mountain, **29** the people knew that Aaron had died, and the entire community of Israel mourned for Aaron for thirty days.

21 When the Canaanite king of Arad, who lived in the Negev, heard that the Israelites were moving along the Atharim highway, he mobilized his army and attacked them and took some captives. **2** The Israelites prayed to Adonai and said, "If You help us to defeat the Canaanites, we will destroy their cities and everything in them." **3** Adonai answered their prayers and helped them to defeat the Canaanites. The Israelites completely destroyed the Canaanite cities. Therefore the place was called Harmah (Destroyed Place).

4 The Israelites marched from Kadesh toward the Sea of Reeds so as to go around the territory of Edom. The people became impatient and complained.

5 The people spoke out against Adonai and Moses: "Did you take us out of Egypt to die in the desert? We have no bread to eat and no water to drink! We hate our tasteless food."

6 So Adonai punished them and sent poisonous snakes that bit the people, and many of the Israelites died.

7 The people rushed to Moses and said, "We admit that we have sinned by insulting Adonai and you. Please pray to Adonai, and ask Him to remove the snakes from among us." So Moses prayed for the people.

8 Adonai answered Moses, "Make a metal image of a poisonous snake and mount it on a tall pole. Anyone who has been bitten can just look at it and live."

9 Moses made a copper snake and mounted it on top of a tall pole. Whenever a snake bit somebody, he or she would look at the copper snake and live.

Israel Defeats the Amorites   *6th Aliyah*

10 From there the Israelites moved on and camped in Oboth.

11 Then they proceeded from Oboth and camped at Iye-Abarim in the wilderness along the Moab border toward the east.

12 From there they continued their journey and camped along the Brook of Zered.

13 Then they went on and camped in the desert near the border of the Amorites, on the opposite side of the Arnon River. The Arnon was the border separating the Moabites from the Amorites.

14 This is a song in the Book of Adonai's Wars:

> "The town of Waheb near Suphah
> and the valleys
> of the Arnon River
> **15** with its valleys
> stretched as far as the city of Ar
> on the border of Moab."

16 From there the Israelites traveled to the well of Beer. This is the well where Adonai said to Moses, "Gather the people, and I will give them water."

17 It was here that Israel sang this song:
"O well, rise up, sing this song.
18 This well was dug by princes,
Sunk by the people's leaders,
Carved out with their scepters."

From the desert, the Israelites proceeded to Matanah, **19** from Matanah to Nachaliel, and from Nachaliel to Bamoth. **20** From Bamoth they went to the plain of Moab, situated near the top of Mount Pisgah, which overlooks the desolated area of Yeshimon.

Israel Defeats King Sichon   *7ᵗʰ Aliyah*

21 Israel sent ambassadors to Sichon, king of the Amorites, with the following message: **22** "Allow us to pass through your land. We promise to keep away from your fields and vineyards, and we will not drink any of your well water. We will stay on the King's Highway until we have passed through your territories."

23 But Sichon refused to allow Israel to pass through his territories. Instead, he mobilized his army and marched out to attack Israel in the desert.
Sichon's army attacked the Israelites near the town of Yahaz.
24 But Israel defeated the Amorites and occupied their land from the Arnon River to the Jabbok River, but only as far as the fortified borders of the Ammonites.
25 Israel captured all the Amorite cities. They settled in Heshbon and its surrounding towns.
26 Heshbon was the capital of Sichon, king of the Amorites. He had defeated the first king of Moab and taken over all of his land as far as the Arnon River.
27 That is why the minstrels used to sing:

"Come to Heshbon,
Sichon's capital city.
28 A fire has come out of Heshbon;
A flame from Sichon's capital
has consumed Ar of Moab,
the rulers of Arnon's heights.

29 Moab, woe to you;
Nation of Chemosh, you are destroyed,
Your sons have become refugees,
your daughters are captives
to Sichon, king of the Amorites.
30 Moab's kingdom was wiped out
from Heshbon as far as Dibon,
and was laid waste
as far as Nopheh and Medeba."

31 So Israel settled in the land of the Amorites.

32 Now Moses sent out scouts to explore the town of Yaazer, and later the Israelites captured the villages in its vicinity, driving out the Amorites who lived there.

33 From there the Israelites marched northward toward the land of Bashan. Og, king of Bashan, deployed his entire army at the town of Edrei to battle the Israelites.

Israel Defeats Og King of Bashan   *Maftir*

34 Adonai said to Moses, "Do not be afraid of King Og. I will help you defeat him and his army. I will give you his territory and all its inhabitants. I will do the same to him as I did to Sichon, king of the Amorites, who ruled in Heshbon."

35 The Israelites killed Og along with his sons and all his people, leaving no survivors, and they took possession of his territory.

22 From there the Israelites moved on, and they traveled to the western plains of Moab, and camped along the Jordan across from Jericho.

Balak בָּלָק

THE STORY OF KING BALAK

2 When Balak son of Tzippor heard how Israel had defeated the Amorites, **3** he was terrified because of the great victory won by the Israelite soldiers.

4 So Moab sent a message to the leaders of Midian: "The Israelite army will eat up everything around us, just as a bull eats up all the vegetables in the field."

Balak son of Tzippor, king of Moab, **5** sent messengers to Balaam son of Beor, who lived in Pethor near the Euphrates River. They brought him the following message:

"I desperately need your help.
This nation is too powerful
for us to defeat alone. **6** Please come
and curse this nation for me.
Then, perhaps, we will be able to defeat them
and drive them from the area.
I know that anyone you bless is successful,
and whoever you curse is doomed."

7 The leaders of Moab and Midian, who were expert magicians, went to Balaam and brought him Balak's message.

8 Balaam replied, "Spend the night here, and when Adonai speaks to me, I will be able to give you an answer."

So the Moabite leaders stayed with Balaam.

9 That night Adonai appeared to Balaam and asked, "Who are these men, and what do they want from you?"

10 Balaam replied to Adonai, "Balak son of Tzippor, king of Moab, has sent them to me with this message: **11** 'A mighty nation that covers the face of the earth has come here from Egypt. Come and curse them for me. If you do, I will be able to defeat them and drive them away.' "

12 Adonai warned Balaam, "Do not go with Balak's messengers. Do not curse the nation, because I have blessed them."

Balaam Refuses to Curse Israel   *2ⁿᵈ Aliyah*

13 In the morning, when Balaam got up he said to the leaders,

"Go back home! Adonai will not allow me to go with you."

14 The Moabite leaders returned to king Balak and said, "Balaam refused to come with us."

15 So Balak sent another delegation, this time with many more important leaders.

16 They came to Balaam and, in the name of Balak, gave him the following message: "Do not refuse to come to me. **17** I will honor you greatly and give you anything you want. Please come and curse this nation for me."

18 But Balaam replied to Balak's servants and said, "Even if Balak gave me his whole palace full of gold and silver, I am powerless to do anything against the wishes of Adonai. **19** But stay here overnight, and then I will know what Adonai wants me to do."

20 That night, Adonai appeared to Balaam and said to him, "Since the leaders have come for you, go with them. But be sure to do only what I tell you to do."

Adonai Sends an Angel   *3rd Aliyah*

21 In the morning Balaam got up, saddled his donkey, and went with the Moabite leaders.

22 Adonai was angry because Balaam was so eager to go with them. An angel of Adonai stood in the middle of the road to stop Balaam, who was riding his donkey. **23** When the donkey saw Adonai's angel standing in the road with a sword in his hand, it ran from the road into the field. Balaam beat the donkey to get it back on the road.

24 Then the angel of Adonai stood in the middle of a narrow path between two vineyards, where there was a fence on either side.

25 When the donkey saw the angel of Adonai, it moved against one of the fences, crushing Balaam's foot, and Balaam beat it even more.

26 The angel of Adonai moved again and stood in a narrow spot where there was no room to turn around. **27** When the donkey saw Adonai's angel, it lay down and refused to move. Once again Balaam lost his temper and beat the donkey with a stick.

28 When this happened Adonai gave the donkey the power of speech, and it asked Balaam, "What did I do to you, to make you beat me three times?"

29 Balaam shouted, "You made me look like a fool. If I had a sword, I would kill you!"

30 The donkey answered Balaam, "But I am the same donkey that you always ride. Have I ever done this to you before?" And Balaam answered, "No!"

31 Now Adonai gave Balaam the power to see, and he saw the angel with a sword in his hand standing in the road. Balaam kneeled and bowed down.

32 The angel of Adonai said to him, "Why did you beat your donkey three times? I have come out to stop you, because your mission is against my wishes. **33** When the donkey saw me, it turned aside three times. If it had not turned aside, I would have killed you and let the donkey live."

34 Balaam said to Adonai's angel, "I was wrong! I didn't know that you were standing on the road to stop me. If you are angry with me, I will return home."

35 Adonai's angel said to Balaam, "I want you to go with the leaders. But say only exactly what I tell you."
So Balaam went with Balak's messengers.

36 When Balak heard that Balaam had arrived, he went to meet him in the capital city of Moab, which is near the Arnon River.

37 Balak said to Balaam, " Why didn't you come to me the first time. Did you think I wouldn't pay you?"

38 Balaam replied to Balak, "Do you think I can prophesy any time I want to? I can only repeat the words that Adonai tells me to say."

Israel Is a Peaceful Nation   *4ᵗʰ Aliyah*

39 Balaam went with Balak to the town of Kiryat Huzoth.
40 There Balak sacrificed cattle and sheep, and sent the meat to Balaam and the leaders who were with him.
41 In the morning, Balak took Balaam to the town of Bamoth Baal (Altars of Baal), a place from which he could see the Israelite camp.

23

Balaam said to Balak, "Build seven altars here, and bring me seven bulls and seven rams."

2 Balak did as Balaam asked. Then Balak and Balaam sacrificed a bull and a ram as a burnt offering on each of the seven altars.

3 Balaam said to Balak, "Wait here with your burnt offerings, and I will see if Adonai wishes to meet me and tell me what to say." So Balaam went to a quiet place to meet with Adonai.

4 Balaam said to Adonai, "I have set up seven altars, and I have sacrificed a bull and a ram as a burnt offering on each of the altars."

5 Then Adonai gave Balaam a message and said, "Return to Balak, and say exactly what I tell you."

6 When Balaam returned, Balak and the Moabite dignitaries were still standing near the burnt offerings.

7 This was Balaam's prophecy:

"Balak, king of Moab, has brought me from Aram,
from the hills of the east,
And told me to come and curse Jacob
and bring divine anger against Israel.
8 But how can I curse
If Adonai will not allow me to curse?
How can I curse
If Adonai is not angry?
9 From mountaintops I see this nation,
and watch them from the heights.
It is a nation at peace,
Far away from other nations.
10 Jacob is numerous like the dust;
who can count his people?
Who can count the Children of Israel?
When I die a righteous death,
let my death be like theirs!"

11 Balak said to Balaam, "What have you done to me? I brought you to curse my enemies, but you have made every effort to bless them!"

12 Balaam interrupted and said, "Didn't I warn you that I must be very careful to say only what Adonai tells me?"

Balaam's Second Prophecy   *5ᵗʰ Aliyah*

13 Balak replied, "Please, come with me to a place where you will be able to see just a small part of the Israelite camp. Perhaps from there you will be able to curse just a few of them for me. **14** So Balak took Balaam to the field of Zophim at the top of Mount Pisgah. There Balak built another seven altars and offered a bull and a ram on each altar.

15 Balaam said to Balak, "Wait here with your burnt offerings, and I will go to meet Adonai."

16 Adonai appeared to Balaam and gave him a message. He said, "Go back to Balak, and prophesy exactly what I tell you."

17 So Balaam returned and found Balak and the Moabite leaders standing near the burnt offerings. Balak asked, "What has Adonai said to you?" **18** Balaam prophesied,

"Balak son of Tzippor, rise,
and pay attention to my words.
19 Adonai is not human, and He does not lie.
Adonai is not mortal
and does not change His mind.
He speaks and does it.
What He says, He fulfills.
20 I have been given a command to bless,
and I cannot reverse it.
21 Adonai does not see evil in Jacob,
and He sees no misery in Israel.
Adonai is with them,
they have His admiration.
22 Adonai brought them out of Egypt.
He supports them with his strength.
23 No curse can harm Jacob,
and no sorcery can overpower Israel.
Adonai has performed wonders for Israel.

24 It is a nation as powerful as the king of beasts,
majestic like a lion.
It does not rest until it defeats the enemy
and wins the victory."

25 Balak said to Balaam, "If you cannot curse them, at least don't bless them!"

26 Balaam replied, "I warned you before. I can only prophesy what Adonai puts in my mind and my mouth."

Balaam's Third Prophecy   *6ᵗʰ Aliyah*

27 Then Balak said to Balaam, "I will take you someplace else. Perhaps Adonai will allow you to curse them for me from there."

28 Balak took Balaam to the top of Mount Peor. **29** Then Balaam said to Balak, "Build seven altars here, and prepare seven bulls and seven rams." **30** Balak did as Balaam said, and he sacrificed a bull and a ram as a burnt offering on each of the seven altars.

24 By now Balaam realized that Adonai planned to bless Israel, so he no longer tried to use magic to find out what to do. Instead, he looked toward the desert. **2** Then Balaam clearly saw the tribes of Israel living in peace. Adonai's spirit enveloped him. **3** And he began to prophesy:

"These are the words of Balaam son of Beor,
the words of a man with a clear vision.
4 The words of a man who listens to Adonai,
who sees a vision of the Almighty
and falls into a trance with open eyes.
5 Jacob, how beautiful are your tents;
Israel, your tabernacles are very peaceful.
6 They stretch out like palm trees
in gardens by the river,
like aloe trees planted by Adonai,
like cedars near the water.
7 Israel's water shall overflow,
and their crops shall have abundant water.

When their kingdom is established,
their king will be mightier than King Agag.
8 With power Adonai brought them out of Egypt,
they are His strength.
They will defeat many enemy nations,
Crushing their fortresses and wounding them with arrows.
9 Israel crouches like a mighty lion,
Who will dare challenge him?
Those who bless you will be blessed,
and those who curse you will be cursed."

10 When Balak heard Balaam's prophecy, he became angry and shouted, "I brought you here to curse my enemies, but instead you blessed them three times! **11** Now run home as fast as you can! I promised to pay you, but now, thanks to Adonai, you will not be paid!"

12 Balaam answered Balak, "Right at the outset I told your messengers, when you sent for me, that **13** even if King Balak were to give me his whole palace full of gold and silver, I could not promise to do anything good or bad, because I must obey Adonai. I can only prophesy whatever Adonai tells me to say.

Balaam's Final Prophecy   *7th Aliyah*

14 "So now I am returning to my people, but first I must warn you about what the Israelites will eventually do to your people." **15** Balaam then prophesied:

"I am Balaam son of Beor,
The words of a man who sees clearly,
16 and hears Adonai's words.
I saw a vision of the Almighty,
and my mind and eyes were opened.
17 I see Israel's distant future.
A star will shoot out from Jacob,
and a ruler will arise in Israel
and crush the leaders of Moab,
and rule over the descendants of Seth.

18 Edom will be destroyed.
His enemy, Seir, will be decimated,
And Israel shall be triumphant.
19 A ruler shall rise out of Jacob
who will destroy the survivors."

20 When Balaam saw Amalek, he continued to prophesy,

"Amalek is a leader among nations
but in the end
he will forever be destroyed."

21 When he saw the Kenites, he again prophesied,

"Though you live in a fortress,
and have built your homes among the rocks,
22 In the end the Kenites will be destroyed,
When Assyria conquers them."

23 Balaam ended his prophecy:

"No one can survive Adonai's devastation.
24 Warships shall sail from the ports of the Kittim,
and they will destroy Assyria and Eber.
But in the end they too will be destroyed."

25 When Balaam finished, he returned home. Balak left and also went on his way.

25 While Israel was camped in Shittim, some of the young men became involved with Moabite girls.
2 The girls invited the boys to sacrifice and to worship the Moabite idols.
3 Some of the Israelites began to worship the idol Baal Peor, thereby angering Adonai.
4 Adonai said to Moses, "Take the leaders who are responsible for this behavior and have the idolaters publicly executed before Adonai. Then I will not be angry with Israel."
5 Moses said to Israel's tribal judges, "Each of you must put to death any of your tribesmen who have worshipped the idol Baal Peor."

6 The judges at the entrance of the Meeting Tent began to weep about this decision. At that very moment, an Israelite brought a Midianite woman into the Israelite community in front of Moses and all the people.

Pinchas Stops the Plague   *Maftir*

7 When Pinchas son of Eleazar, a grandson of Aaron the priest, saw this, he jumped up and took a spear in his hand. **8** He rushed into the tent of the Israelite man, and drove his spear through the Israelite man and the Midianite woman. Seeing this, Adonai stopped the plague against the Israelites. **9** In that plague, 24,000 Israelites died.

Pinchas פִּנְחָס
THE REWARD OF PINCHAS

10 Then Adonai spoke to Moses, and said, **11** "Pinchas son of Eleazar and grandson of Aaron the priest was faithful to Me and turned My anger away from the Israelites, so that I did not destroy them.

12 Therefore, tell him that I have made a covenant of peace with him.

13 In this covenant I promise that he and his descendants shall always be My priests. It is given to him because he was loyal to Me and made atonement for the Israelites."

14 The name of the man who was killed was Zimri son of Salul, a leader of the tribe of Simeon. **15** The name of the Midianite woman who was killed was Kazbi daughter of Tzur; her father was the leader of a Midianite family.

16 Adonai spoke to Moses, saying, **17** "Attack the Midianites and destroy them **18** because they tricked some Israelites into worshipping the idol Peor, and because of their sister, Kazbi, daughter of the Midianite leader, who was killed on the day of the plague at Peor. After the plague had ended,

26 Adonai spoke to Moses and Eleazar son of Aaron the priest, and said, **2** "Take a census of the men in the Israelite community, and count every male over twenty years old who is fit for military service."

3 Moses and Eleazar the priest spoke to the Israelites in their camp on the Plains of Moab near the Jordan River, just across from Jericho, saying, **4** "Count all the men over twenty years of age, just as Adonai commanded Moses when they left Egypt."

The Census of the Tribe
2nd Aliyah

5 Reuben was Israel's first-born.
The descendants of Reuben were
the Enochite family from Enoch,
the Paluite family from Palu,

6 The Hetzronite family from Hetzron,
and the Karmite family from Karmi.
7 There were 43,730 qualified men fit for military service in
the tribe of Reuben.
8 The sons of Pallu were Eliav. **9** The sons of Eliav were
Nemuel, Dathan, and Aviram. Dathan and Aviram were the
leaders who led Korach's rebellion against Moses and Aaron
and Adonai. **10** But the earth opened its mouth and swallowed them and Korach. At the same time a streak of fire from
Adonai destroyed the 250 followers of Korach. This was a
divine miracle. **11** The sons of Korach, however, were not
killed.
12 By families, the descendants of Simeon were
the Nemuelite family from Nemuel,
the Yaminite family from Yamin,
the Yakhinite family from Yakhin,
13 the Zarchite family from Zerach,
and the Saulite family from Saul.
14 There were 22,200 men fit for military service in the tribe
of Simeon.
15 By families, the descendants of Gad were
the Tzefonite family from Tzefon,
the Haggite family from Haggi,
the Shunite family from Shuni,
16 the Aznite family from Aznil,
the Erite family from Eri,
17 the Arodite family from Arod,
and the Arelite family from Areli.
18 There were 40,500 men fit for military service in the tribe
of Gad.
19 The sons of Judah were Er and Onan, but Er and Onan died
in the land of Canaan.
20 By families, the descendants of Judah were
the Shelanite family from Shelah,
the Partzite family from Peretz, and
the Zarchite family from Zerach.

21 The descendants of Peretz were
the Chetzronite family from Chetzron,
and the Chamulite family from Chamul.
22 There were 76,500 men fit for military service in the tribe of Judah.
23 By families, the descendants of Issachar were
the Tolaite family from Tola,
the Punite family from Puvah.
24 the Yashuvite family from Yashuv, and
the Shimronite family from Shimron.
25 There were 64,300 men fit for military service in the tribe of Issachar.
26 By families, the descendants of Zebulun were
the Sardite family from Sered,
the Elonite family from Elon,
and the Yachlielite family from Yachliel.
27 There were 60,500 men fit for military service in the tribe of Zebulun.
28 By families, the descendants of Joseph
were Manasseh and Ephraim.
29 The descendants of Manasseh were
the Makhirite family from Makhir.
Makhir's son was Gilead,
and from Gilead came the family of the Gileadites.
30 These were the descendants of Gilead:
The Iyezerite family from Iyezer,
the Helekite family from Helek,
31 the Azrielite family from Azriel,
the Shikhmite family from Shekhem,
32 the Shemidaite family from Shemida,
and the Hefrite family from Hefer.
33 Chefer's son, Tzelafechad, did not have any sons, only daughters. The names of Tzelafechad's daughters were Machla, Noah, Chaglah, Milkah, and Tirtzah.
34 There were 52,700 men fit for military service in the tribe of Manasseh.

35 By families, the descendants of Ephraim were
the Shuthalchite family from Shuthelach,
the Bakhrite family from Bekher,
and the Tachanite family from Tachan.
36 The descendants of Shuthelach were
the Eranite family from Eran.
37 There were 32,500 men fit for military service in the tribe of
Ephraim.
These are the descendants of Joseph by their families.
38 By families, the descendants of Benjamin were
the Bal'ite family from Bela,
the Ashbelite family from Ashbel,
the Achiramite family from Achiram,
39 the Shefufamite family from Shefufam,
and the Hufamite family from Hufam.
40 The sons of Bela were Ard and Naaman.
These gave rise to the Ardite family,
and the Naamite family from Naaman.
41 There were 45,600 men fit for military service in the tribe
of Benjamin.
42 By families, the descendants of Dan were
the Shuchamite family from Shucham.
This was the only family of Dan.
43 There were 64,400 men fit for military service in the tribe
of Dan.
44 By families, the descendants of Asher were
the Yimnah family from Yimnah,
the Yishvite family from Yishvi, and
the Berite family from Beriah.
45 The descendants of Beriah were
the Hevrite family from Hever
and the Malkielite family from Malkiel.
46 The name of Asher's daughter was Serach.
47 There were 53,400 men fit for military service in the tribe
of Asher.
48 By families, the descendants of Naphtali were

the Yachtzielite family from Yachtziel,
the Gunite family from Guni,
49 the Yitzrite family from Yetzer,
and the Shilemite family from Shilem.
50 There were 45,400 men fit for military service in the tribe
of Naphtali.
51 There was a total of 601,730 Israelite men fit for military
service.

Dividing the Land   *3ʳᵈ Aliyah*

52 Adonai spoke to Moses, saying: **53** "You shall divide the land
as an inheritance among the people, based on the number of
recorded names.
54 To a larger group you shall give a larger inheritance, whereas
to a smaller group you shall give a smaller inheritance. Each
group shall receive its inheritance according to the number of
people in it.
55 Make sure to allot the land to the tribes through a lottery
system. **56** The large tribal family will be assigned more land,
and the smaller tribal family will be assigned less land.
Whether a group is large or small, its hereditary property shall
be divided by a lottery system."
57 These are the families of the Levites:
the Gershonite family from Gershon,
the Kehothite family from Kehoth,
and the Merarite family from Merari.
58 These are the subfamilies of Levi:
the Libnite family,
the Hevonite family, the Machlite family,
the Mushite family, and the Korchite family.
Kehoth had a son named Amram. **59** While in Egypt, Amram
married Yoheved, a daughter of Levi. She gave birth to Aaron
and Moses, and their sister Miriam.
60 Aaron had four sons: Nadav, Avihu, Eleazar, and Ithamar.
61 But Nadav and Avihu died when they offered unauthorized
fire before Adonai.
62 There were 23,000 Levite males over one month of age.

They were not counted with the other Israelites because they were not allotted any land when it was divided among the Israelite tribes.

63 The above is the census that Moses and Eleazar the priest took of the Israelites on the Plains of Moab, across from Jericho, near the Jordan River. **64** Not a single person who was counted by Moses and Aaron forty years earlier in the Wilderness of Zin was still alive. **65** Adonai had told the Israelites that they would all die in the desert, and that not a single person would remain alive except for Caleb son of Yefuneh, and Joshua son of Nun.

27 One day a petition was presented by the daughters of Tzelafechad son of Hefer, son of Gilead, son of Makhir, son of Manasseh, of the family of Joseph's son Manasseh. The names of his daughters were Machlah, Noah, Haglah, Milkah, and Tirtzah. **2** They stood before Moses, Eleazar the priest, the tribal leaders, and the entire community at the entrance of the Meeting Tent with the following petition:

3 "Our father died in the wilderness. He was not one of the members of Korach's party who rebelled against Adonai, but he died because of his own sin without leaving any sons. **4** Why should our father's family be penalized because he did not have a son? Give us an inheritance of land just like our father's brothers."

5 Moses brought their petition before Adonai.

Inheritance for the Daughters   *4th Aliyah*

6 Adonai answered Moses, saying:

7 "The daughters of Tzelafechad are right. Give them a portion of land alongside their uncles. Give them their father's inheritance of land. **8** Now speak to the Israelites and tell them that if a man dies and has no sons, his hereditary property shall pass over to his daughters. **9** If he has no daughters, then his hereditary land shall be given to his brothers. **10** If he has no brothers, you shall give his land to his father's brothers.

11 However, if his father had no brothers, then you shall give his land to the nearest relative in his family. This shall be the law for the Israelites, as Adonai has commanded Moses."

12 Adonai said to Moses, "Climb up to the top of Mount Avarim, where you will be able to see the land that I am giving to the Israelites. **13** After you see it, you will die and be gathered to your people, just as your brother Aaron was. **14** When the community rebelled against My instructions in the Wilderness of Zin, you disobeyed My commandment and did not believe in my holy power." Adonai was speaking about Mai Meribah (Waters of Dispute) at Kadesh in the Wilderness of Zin.

15 Moses spoke to Adonai, saying, "Adonai, source of all living beings, appoint a new leader over the community.

16 Your people need a strong leader to lead them in battle.

17 Do not let Adonai's community wander like sheep without a shepherd."

18 Adonai said to Moses, "Choose Joshua son of Nun, for he is a man of spirit. Place your hands on him. **19** Present him to Eleazar the priest, and let the entire community watch as he appoints him.

20 Publicly hand him your authority so that the entire Israelite community will obey him. **21** Let him stand before Eleazar the priest, who will ask on his behalf the decision of the Urim before Adonai. At Joshua's command, the Israelite community shall go out, and at his command they will return."

22 Moses did as Adonai had ordered him. He took Joshua and had him stand before Eleazar the priest and before the entire community. **23** He placed his hands on him and publicly passed his authority to Joshua. It was all done exactly as Adonai had commanded Moses.

The Daily Sacrifices

5ᵗʰ Aliyah

28 Adonai spoke to Moses, telling him to **2** give the following instructions to the Israelites and tell them: Make sure to present My fire-offering food sacrifices, because they please Me.

3 The fire offering to be presented each day to Adonai shall consist of two healthy lambs without blemish each day as a regular daily burnt offering. **4** Present one lamb in the morning, and the second lamb in the late afternoon. **5** Also present two quarts of flour for the grain offering, mixed with three pints of pure hand-pressed olive oil.

6 This is the regular daily burnt offering, the same as was presented at Mount Sinai as a thank you fire offering to Adonai. **7** The accompanying libation shall consist of three pints of wine for each lamb, a drink offering to Adonai.

8 In the late afternoon you shall present the second lamb. Present it with the same meal offering and libation as the morning sacrifice; it is a thank you offering to Adonai.

9 On the Sabbath, you shall present two additional healthy lambs with six quarts of flour mixed with olive oil as a grain offering, and the usual libation. **10** This is the burnt offering for each Sabbath in addition to the regular daily burnt offering and its libation.

11 On the first of every month, on the new moon (Rosh Hodesh) festival, you shall present as a burnt offering to Adonai two young bulls, one ram, and seven lambs, all without defects.

12 There shall be a grain offering of six quarts of flour mixed with olive oil for each bull, a grain offering of six quarts of flour mixed with olive oil for the ram, **13** and a grain offering of three quarts of flour mixed with olive oil for each lamb. This shall be the burnt offering presented as a thank you gift to Adonai.

14 The wine libations shall consist of six quarts of wine with each bull, four quarts of wine for the ram, and three pints for each lamb. This is the new moon burnt offering, to be made every month of the year.

15 Besides these offerings you shall present one goat

as a sin offering to Adonai. This is in addition to the regular daily burnt offering and its libation.

The Passover Festival   *6ᵗʰ Aliyah*

16 You must celebrate Adonai's Passover on the fourteenth day of the first month [Nisan]. **17** Then, on the fifteenth day of the month, the Passover festival shall begin, and you shall eat matzot for seven days.

18 The first day shall be a sacred holiday when you do no regular work. **19** You shall offer two young bulls, one ram, and seven lambs, all without defects, as a burnt fire offering to Adonai. **20** These shall be accompanied by a grain offering of flour mixed with five quarts of olive oil for each bull **21** and three quarts for each of the seven lambs.

22 To make atonement for yourselves you shall also offer a male goat as a sin offering. **23** You shall present all of these in addition to the regular morning burnt offering.

24 On each of the seven days of the Passover festival, you shall prepare a similar sacrifice as a fire offering that is a thank you gift to Adonai. This shall be offered in addition to the regular daily burnt offering and its libation.

25 The seventh day of the festival shall be a sacred holiday to you, when you shall not do any regular work.

26 The day of first fruits is when you bring Adonai a new grain offering as part of your Shavuot festival. You shall observe it as a sacred holiday, and you must not do any regular work.

27 As a thank you gift to Adonai you shall present a burnt offering consisting of two young bulls, one ram, and seven lambs. **28** These shall be accompanied by a grain offering consisting of flour mixed with five quarts of olive oil for each bull, three quarts for the ram, **29** and two quarts for each of the seven lambs.

30 Also offer one male goat to atone for yourselves. **31** You must present all of these offerings in addition to the regular daily burnt offering and its meal offering. Be sure that the animals you present are without defects.

29

The day of sounding the ram's horn (*shofar*), on the first day of the seventh month [Tishri], shall be a sacred holiday [Rosh Hashanah] to you, and you must not do any regular work.

2 As a thank you gift to Adonai, you must present a burnt offering consisting of one young bull, one ram, and seven lambs, all without defects. **3** The grain offering of flour mixed with olive oil shall consist of five quarts for the bull and three quarts for the ram, **4** and two quarts for each of the seven lambs.

5 In addition you shall sacrifice one goat as a sin offering to make atonement for yourselves. **6** All these sacrifices shall be in addition to the new moon (Rosh Hodesh) offering and the regular required daily offerings which are a thank you gift to Adonai.

7 Ten days later, the tenth of the month [of Tishri] shall be a sacred holiday when you must fast and not do any work [Yom Kippur].

8 As a burnt offering and a thank you gift to Adonai, you shall present one young bull, one ram, and seven lambs, all without defects.

9 The grain offerings of flour shall be accompanied by olive oil: five quarts for the bull, three quarts for the ram, **10** and two quarts for each of the seven lambs.

11 You shall also sacrifice one goat as a sin offering, in addition to the atonement sin offering. All these sacrifices and their libations are in addition to the regular daily burnt and grain offerings.

The Holiday of Sukkot   *7th Aliyah*

12 On the fifteenth day of the seventh month you shall celebrate a sacred holiday when no regular work shall be done [Sukkot]. For seven days you shall celebrate this festival to Adonai.

13 As a thank you gift to Adonai, you shall present a burnt offering of healthy animals consisting of thirteen young bulls, two rams, and fourteen lambs, all without defects. **14** The grain offering of flour mixed with olive oil shall be six quarts for each of the thirteen bulls, three quarts for each of the two rams, **15** and two quarts for each of the fourteen lambs.

16 You shall also present one goat as a sin offering. This is in addition to the regular daily burnt offering, its grain offering, and its libation.

17 On the second day you shall present twelve young bulls, two rams, and fourteen lambs, all without defects, **18** in addition to the grain offerings and libations appropriate for the number of bulls, rams, and sheep. **19** You shall also present one goat as a sin offering. These offerings and their libations shall be in addition to the regular daily burnt offering and its grain offering.

20 On the third day you shall present eleven young bulls, two rams, and fourteen lambs, all without defects, **21** along with the grain offerings and libations appropriate for the number of bulls, rams, and lambs. **22** You shall also present one goat as a sin offering, in addition to the regular daily burnt offering, its grain offering, and its libation.

23 On the fourth day you shall present ten young bulls, two rams, and fourteen lambs, all without defects, **24** along with the grain offerings and libations according to the number of bulls, rams, and lambs. **25** You shall also present one goat as a sin offering, in addition to the regular daily burnt offering, its grain offering, and its libation.

26 On the fifth day, you shall present nine young bulls, two rams, and fourteen lambs, all without defects, **27** along with the grain offerings and libations according to the number of bulls, rams, and lambs. **28** You shall also present one goat as a sin offering. All this is in addition to the regular daily burnt offering, its grain offering, and its libation.

29 On the sixth day, you shall present eight young bulls, two rams, and fourteen lambs, all without defects, **30** along with the grain offerings and libations according to the number of bulls, rams, and lambs. **31** You shall also present one goat as a sin offering. All this is in addition to the regular daily burnt offering, its grain offering, and its libation.

32 On the seventh day, you shall present seven young bulls, two rams, and fourteen lambs, all without defects, **33** along with the grain offerings and libations for the number of bulls, rams, and lambs. **34** You shall also present one goat as a sin offering. All of this is in addition to the regular daily burnt offering, its grain offering, and its libation.

The Shemini Atzeret Offering   *Maftir*

35 The eighth day shall be a time of rest for you (Shemini Atzeret), and you shall do no regular work.

36 As a burnt fire offering and as a thank you gift to Adonai, you shall present one bull, one ram, and seven lambs, all without defects, **37** along with the prescribed number of meal offerings and libations. **38** You shall also present one goat as a sin offering, in addition to the regular daily burnt offering, its grain offering, and its libation.

39 On your festivals you must present all of these offerings to Adonai, in addition to your burnt offerings, grain offerings, libations, and peace offerings, together with the free-will offerings and pledges.

30 Moses spoke to the Israelites and told them everything that Adonai had commanded him.

Mattot מַטּוֹת
THE TRIBES OF ISRAEL

2 Moses spoke to the Israelite leaders, saying: This is what Adonai has commanded:

3 If a man makes a promise to Adonai, or promises to do something, he must not break his promise. He must do exactly what he promised.

4 If a woman makes a promise to Adonai while living with her parents, **5** and her father hears about her promise but says nothing, she must keep the promise.

6 However, if he learns about it and objects, then she is no longer obligated to keep her promise, because her father has forbidden her to fulfill the promise. Since her father has forbidden her, Adonai will forgive her.

7 If she marries and her promise is still in force, she is still obligated by her promise.

8 If her husband learns about it and remains silent and does not object, then her promise must be kept. **9** However, if her husband refuses to accept her promise, he can cancel all her promises and Adonai will forgive her.

10 Any promise made by a widow or a divorcee must be fulfilled, no matter what obligation she takes upon herself.

11 This is the law if a woman makes a promise while in her husband's house: **12** If her husband learns about the promise and remains silent without stopping her, then all her promises and obligations must be kept. **13** However, if her husband voids them when he hears about them, then all her promises and obligations need not be kept. Since her husband voided the promises, Adonai will forgive her.

14 Every promise of self-denial by a woman can be upheld or voided by her husband. **15** However, if the entire day goes by and her husband does not object, then he has automatically agreed to the promise she has assumed. He has agreed to the promised obligations by remaining silent on the day he heard them. **16** However, if he voids them after learning about them, he removes any guilt that she may have for violating them.

17 These are the laws that Adonai commanded Moses concerning the relationship between a man and his wife, and between a father and his daughter as long as she is living in her father's house.

Revenge Against the Midianites   *2ⁿᵈ Aliyah*

31 Adonai spoke to Moses, saying, **2** "Take revenge for the Israelites who were tempted by the Midianites, who tempted them into idol worship. After that, Moses, you will die and be gathered to your ancestors."

3 Moses spoke to the people, saying, "Choose men for armed conflict against Midian, so that Adonai's revenge can be taken against the Midianites. **4** Select one thousand soldiers from each of Israel's tribes for armed service."

5 One thousand men volunteered from each tribe, for a total of twelve thousand troops. **6** Moses sent an army of one thousand men from each tribe under the command of Pinchas son of Eleazar the priest, who was in charge of the sacred articles and the trumpets for sounding the battle signal.

7 Just as Adonai had instructed Moses, they mounted a surprise attack against Midian, and killed all the adult males. **8** And they also killed the five kings of Midian: Evi, Rekem, Tzur, Hur, and Reba. They also killed Balaam son of Beor.

9 The Israelites captured all of Midian and their women and children. They seized all their animals, and everything that belonged to them. **10** Then the Israelites burned down all the Midianite cities and forts **11** and assembled everything they had captured, both humans and beasts.

12 They brought the captives and everything they had captured to Moses, Eleazar the priest, and the entire Israelite community, who were camped in the hills of Moab, across from the city of Jericho.

Purification After the War   *3rd Aliyah*

13 Moses, Eleazar, and the communal leaders went outside the camp to greet the victorious troops.

14 However, Moses was angry at the army's commanders.

15 Moses angrily asked, "Why are the women still alive? **16** They are the ones who at Balaam's urging caused the Israelites to be unfaithful to Adonai at Mount Peor and brought a plague on Adonai's community. **17** Now kill every male child, as well as every woman who has had sexual relations with a man.

18 All the young girls who have not had sexual relations with a man, however, you may keep alive for yourselves.

19 You must all remain outside the camp for seven days. All those who killed anyone or touched a dead body must purify themselves on the third and seventh days.

20 You must also purify every garment, every leather article, anything made of goat hair, and every wooden article."

21 Then Eleazar the priest explained to the soldiers returning from the campaign: "This is the law that Adonai commanded Moses:

22 Anything that can withstand heat, such as gold, silver, copper, iron, tin, and lead, **23** must be put through fire and cleansed and then purified with the waters of purification. But everything that burns can be purified by immersion in water.

24 Remember, you must also cleanse your bodies and wash your clothing on the seventh day, and then you will be purified and entitled to return to the camp."

Dividing the Captured Property   *4th Aliyah*

25 Adonai spoke to Moses, saying, **26** "You and Eleazar the priest and the tribal leaders must count all the captives and animals. **27** Divide everything into two equal parts, giving half to the soldiers who went into battle and the other half to the community.

28 Levy a tax for Adonai on the soldiers who participated in the campaign, consisting of one of every five hundred of the captives, cattle, donkeys, and sheep. **29** Take this quota from

their half, and give it to Eleazar the priest as a gift to Adonai.
30 From the half-share that is going to the other Israelites, take
one of every fifty captives, cattle, donkeys, sheep, and other
animals, and give it to the Levites, who are in charge of
Adonai's Tabernacle."
31 Moses and Eleazar the priest did exactly as Adonai had
commanded Moses.
32 In addition to everything else the troops had captured,
there were 675,000 sheep, **33** 72,000 head of cattle, **34** 61,000
donkeys, **35** and 32,000 females who had never had sexual
relations with a man.
36 The half-share for the soldiers who fought the Midianites
was 337,500 sheep, **37** and Adonai's share came to 675 sheep.
38 There were 36,000 cattle, and Adonai's share was 72 animals.
39 There were 30,500 donkeys, and Adonai's share was 61
donkeys.
40 There were 16,000 captives, and Adonai's share was 32
individuals.
41 Just as Adonai had commanded, Moses gave the tax to
Eleazar the priest as a gift to Adonai.

A Gift to Adonai   *5th Aliyah*
42 The half-share that Moses took from the soldiers for the
other Israelites as **43** the community's portion consisted of
337,500 sheep, **44** 36,000 cattle, **45** 30,500 donkeys, **46** and
16,000 captives.
47 From the Israelite half, Moses selected one of every fifty and
gave them to the Levites, who were in charge of Adonai's
Tabernacle. It was all done exactly as Adonai had commanded
Moses.
48 Then the commanders, generals, and captains of the army
approached Moses.
49 They said to Moses, "We have counted the warriors under
our command, and not a single soldier has been lost.
50 Therefore we want to bring a gift to Adonai. Every soldier
who found a gold article, such as an anklet, a bracelet, a finger
ring, an earring, or a body ornament wishes to bring it to
atone for ourselves before Adonai."

51 Moses and Eleazar the priest took all the gold jewelry from them. **52** The entire gift of gold that was offered to Adonai by the officers of the army weighed 400 pounds. **53** But the ordinary soldiers kept their plunder for themselves.

54 So Moses and Eleazar the priest accepted the gold from the officers and brought it to the Meeting Tent to remind the Israelites of their battle against the Midianites.

Reuben and Gad Petition Moses   *6ᵗʰ Aliyah*

32 The descendants of Reuben and Gad had large herds and flocks, and they saw that the area of Jazer and Gilead had good grass for their livestock. **2** So the descendants of Gad and Reuben came and petitioned Moses, Eleazar the priest, and the tribal leaders, saying, **3** "The cities of Ataroth, Dibon, Jazer, Nimrah, Heshbon, Elaleh, Sebam, Nebo, and Beor **4** have a lot of grass, and the land is ideal for our livestock."

5 They continued, "Do us a favor, and give this land to us as our permanent possession, and do not make us cross the Jordan." **6** Moses answered the descendants of Gad and Reuben, "Why should your brothers go out and fight while you remain here? **7** Why are you discouraging the Israelites from crossing over to the land that Adonai has given them? **8** That is just what your fathers did when I sent them from Kadesh Barnea to explore the land. **9** They explored as far as the Valley of Eshkol, but then they discouraged the Israelites from entering the land that Adonai had given them.

10 That day Adonai became angry and said, **11** 'None of the men over twenty years old who left Egypt will ever see the land that I swore to give to their ancestors Abraham, Isaac, and Jacob, because they did not believe in My power. **12** The only exceptions shall be Caleb son of Yefuneh the Kenizite and Joshua son of Nun, because they totally believe in My power.' **13** Adonai was very angry at the Israelites, and He made them wander in the desert for forty years until the generation who did not believe in Adonai's power had died out.

14 Now you are following the model of your sinful fathers, and you are making Adonai even more angry.

15 If you again refuse to follow him, He will again leave you in the desert, and you sinners will be completely destroyed."

16 The Reubenites and Gaddites drew near to Moses and said, "First let us build sheepfolds for our flocks and fortified cities for our families. **17** Then we will arm ourselves and go ahead and fight side by side with the other Israelites until we have brought them to their homeland. Let our children stay in the fortified cities because of the danger from the inhabitants, **18** but we will not return home until every Israelite has taken possession of his inheritance. **19** Nonetheless, we will not take possession with them on the far side of the Jordan, since our inheritance shall come to us on the Jordan's eastern bank."

The Advance Force   *7ᵗʰ Aliyah*

20 Moses said to them, "If you do that and go forth as an advance force ahead of your brothers, your petition will be granted. **21** Your entire force must cross the Jordan before Adonai, and fight until He has driven away His enemies. **22** When the land is conquered for Adonai, you may return home, and you will be free of any obligation in the eyes of Adonai and Israel. This land will then be yours as your permanent property before Adonai.

23 But if you do not do so, you will have sinned before Adonai, and your sin will be your undoing. **24** Now go, build cities for your children and sheepfolds for your sheep."

25 The descendants of Gad and Reuben said to Moses, "We will do as you have ordered. **26** Our children, wives, property, and livestock will remain here in the cities of Gilead. **27** Meanwhile, our entire armed army will cross the Jordan, as you have said."

28 Then Moses instructed Eleazar the priest, Joshua son of Nun, and the tribal leaders. **29** Moses said to them, "If the entire Gaddite and Reubenite army crosses the Jordan to fight at your side, then when the land is conquered, you shall give them the land of Gilead as their permanent property. **30** But if they do not fight at your side, then they must accept property with you in the land of Canaan."

31 The descendants of Gad and Reuben responded, "We promise to do whatever Adonai has told us to do. **32** Our soldiers will cross into the land of Canaan, and then we will inherit our permanent hereditary property on this side of the Jordan."

33 Moses then gave the descendants of Gad and Reuben, and the half-tribe of Manasseh son of Joseph, the kingdom of Sichon, king of the Amorites, and the kingdom of Og, king of Bashan. He gave them the entire country, along with the cities and the territories around them.

34 The descendants of Gad built the cities of Dibon, Ataroth, Aroer, **35** Atroth Shofan, Jazer, Jagbehah, **36** Beth-nimrah, and Beth-haran. They built walls around the cities and sheepfolds for their flocks.

37 The Reubenites built Heshbon, Elaleh, Kiryathaim, **38** Nebo, Baal-meon, and Sibmah. They renamed the cities that they rebuilt.

Machir, Jair, and Novah   *Maftir*

39 The sons of Makhir son of Manasseh went to Gilead and conquered it, and drove out the Amorites who were living there.

40 Moses gave Gilead to Machir son of Manasseh, and he settled there.

41 Jair, a grandson of Manasseh, conquered the villages in this district, and he named them Havoth Jair (Villages of Jair).

42 Then Novah went and captured Kenath and its surrounding towns and renamed them Novah after himself.

Massay מַסְעֵי
THE JOURNEYS OF ISRAEL

33 These are the places where the Israelites who left Egypt camped under the leadership of Moses and Aaron. **2** At Adonai's command, Moses kept a written record of their stopping places along the way. These are the places where they camped:

3 The Israelites left the Egyptian city of Rameses on the fifteenth day of the first month [Nisan]. On the day after the Passover sacrifice the Israelites marched out in full view of the Egyptians, **4** who were still burying all their first-born, who had been killed by Adonai. Adonai had also defeated their idols.

5 The Israelites left Rameses and camped in Sukkoth.

6 Then they left Sukkoth and camped in Etham on the edge of the wilderness.

7 They left Etham and returned to Pi-haviroth (Freedom Valley) opposite Baal-zephon and camped near Migdal (Tower).

8 They left Freedom Valley and crossed the Sea of Reeds into the wilderness. Then they journeyed for three days into the wilderness of Etham and camped in Marah.

9 They left Marah and camped in Elim, where there were twelve water springs and seventy palms.

10 They left Elim and camped near the Sea of Reeds.

The Travels of the Israelites   *2nd Aliyah*

11 They left the Sea of Reeds and camped in the Wilderness of Sin.

12 They left the Wilderness of Sin and camped in Dofkah.

13 They left Dofkah and camped in Alush.

14 They left Alush and camped in Rephidim, where there was no water for the Israelites to drink. **15** They left Rephidim and camped in the Wilderness of Sinai.

16 They left the Wilderness of Sinai and camped in Kivroth HaTaavah (Graves of Craving).

17 They left Kivroth HaTaavah and camped in Hatzeroth.

18 They left Hatzeroth and camped in Rithmah.

19 They left Rithmah and camped in Rimmon-peretz.

20 They left Rimmon-peretz and camped in Livnah.

21 They left Livnah and camped in Rissah.

22 They left Rissah and camped in Kehelathah.

23 They left Kehelathah and camped at Mount Shefer.

24 They left Mount Shefer and camped in Haradah.

25 They left Haradah and camped in Macheloth.

26 They left Macheloth and camped in Tachath.

27 They left Tachath and camped in Terach.

28 They left Terach and camped in Mitkah.

29 They left Mitkah and camped in Hashmonah.

30 They left Hashmonah and camped in Moseroth.

31 They left Moseroth and camped in Bene-jaakan.

32 They left Bene-jaakan and camped in Hor-HaGidgad.

33 They left Hor-haGidgad and camped in Jatvatah.

34 They left Jatvatah and camped in Avronah.

35 They left Avronah and camped in Etzyon-gever.

36 They left Etzyon-gever and camped in Kadesh in the Wilderness of Zin, also called Kadesh.

37 They left Kadesh and camped at Mount Hor, on the border of the land of Edom.

38 At Adonai's command, Aaron the priest climbed to the top of Mount Hor, and he died there on the first day of the fifth month [Av] in the fortieth year of the Israelites' exodus from Egypt. **39** Aaron was 123 years old when he died on Mount Hor.

40 It was there that the Canaanite king of Arad, who lived in the Negev in the land of Canaan, heard that the Israelites were approaching his land.

41 The Israelites left Mount Hor and camped in Zalmonah.

42 They left Zalmonah and camped in Punon.

43 They left Punon and camped in Oboth.

44 They left Oboth and camped in Iye-avarim (Desolate Borders) in the land of Moab.

45 They left Iye-avarim and camped in Dibon-gad.

46 They left Dibon-gad and camped in Almon- diblathayim.
47 They left Almon-diblathayim and camped in the mountains of Avarim close to Mount Nebo.
48 They left the mountains of Avarim and camped on the plains of Moab beside the Jordan River, opposite the city of Jericho. **49** They camped along the Jordan River from Beth Hajeshimoth as far as Abel Shittim in the plains of Moab.

Drive Out the Inhabitants   *3rd Aliyah*

50 Adonai spoke to Moses while the Israelites were camped on the plains of Moab along the Jordan River opposite Jericho, and told him: **51** Speak to the Israelites and say to them:
"When you cross the Jordan into the land of Canaan, **52** you must drive out the land's inhabitants. You must destroy all their carved images and destroy all their metal idols and altars. **53** Settle the land and live in the land I have given you. **54** You shall divide the land among your families. Give a large portion of land to a large family, give a small portion of land to a small family. Distribute the land to the tribes, and give each tribe what the sacred lottery indicates. **55** If you do not drive out the land's inhabitants, those who remain shall be splinters in your eyes and thorns in your sides. They will cause you troubles in the land where you will live. **56** Then I will treat you cruelly, as I originally planned to treat them."

34 Adonai spoke to Moses, telling him to **2** give the Israelites these instructions:
I am giving you the land of Canaan as your inheritance, and these will be the boundaries of the land.
3 Your southern boundary shall begin in the Wilderness of Zin adjacent to Edom. Your southern border to the east shall be the edge of the Dead Sea. **4** Your border shall turn to the south of the Scorpion Pass (Akrabim) and then shall extend toward Zin. Its southernmost point will be at Kadesh Barnea, and then extend to Hatzar-adar and reach as far as Atzmon. **5** From Atzmon the border shall turn

north and follow the Wadi of Egypt and end at the Mediterranean Sea.

6 Your western boundary shall be the coast of the Mediterranean Sea. This shall be your western border.

7 Your northern boundary will begin at the Mediterranean Sea and run east to Mount Hor. **8** From Mount Hor your boundary will run to Lebo-hamath, and on, through Zedad **9** and Zephron, to Hatzar-eynan. This will be your northern border.

10 For your eastern boundary, you shall draw a line from Hatzar-eynan to Shefam. **11** The boundary shall then descend southward from Shefam to Rivlah to the east of Ain. From there the boundary shall continue to the south, along the eastern shore of the Sea of Galilee. **12** The boundary shall then continue southward along the Jordan River, until the Dead Sea. All these shall be the boundaries of your country.

13 Then Moses gave the Israelites the following instructions:

This is the land that Adonai has commanded you to divide by lottery and distribute to the nine and a half tribes.

14 The descendants of Reuben and Gad, and the half-tribe of Manasseh have already taken possession of their hereditary land. **15** These two and a half tribes have already been given their land east of the Jordan River opposite Jericho.

Divide the Land   *4th Aliyah*

16 Adonai spoke to Moses, saying:

17 These are the names of the men who shall divide the land. First, there shall be Eleazar the priest and Joshua son of Nun.

18 You shall also appoint one leader from each tribe to help them divide the land.

19 These are the names of the leaders:

Caleb son of Yefuneh for the tribe of Judah.

20 Shemuel son of Amihud for the tribe of Simeon.

21 Elidad son of Kislon for the tribe of Benjamin.

22 Bukki son of Yagli for the tribe of Dan.

23 Haniel son of Ephod for the tribe of Manasseh.

24 Kemuel son of Shiftan for the tribe of Ephraim.

25 Elitzafan son of Parnach for the tribe of Zebulun.

26 Paltiel son of Azzan for the tribe of Issachar.

27 Achihud son of Shelomi for the tribe of Asher.

28 Pedahel son of Amihud for the tribe of Naphtali.

29 These are the leaders whom Adonai has chosen to distribute the land to the Israelites in the land of Canaan.

Assign Cities for the Levites   *5ᵗʰ Aliyah*

35 Adonai spoke to Moses on the plains of Moab along the Jordan River across from Jericho. **2** Instruct the Israelites and have them assign cities for the Levites from their hereditary lands. Also, provide pasture lands for the Levites around their cities. **3** The cities shall be their residence, while the pasture lands shall be for their flocks and herds.

4 The pasture land that you shall assign to the Levites shall extend outward 1,500 feet from the city walls in every direction. **5** Measure 3,000 feet outside the city on the eastern side, 3,000 feet on the southern side, 3,000 feet on the western side, and 3,000 feet on the northern side. This shall be their pasture land, with the city in the exact center.

6 You shall also provide the Levites with six safe refuge cities, where a person who has accidentally killed someone can find refuge. In addition to these six cities you shall also provide them with forty-two additional cities. **7** In total you shall give the Levites forty-eight cities along with the surrounding pasture lands.

8 These cities shall be assigned from the lands of the Israelites, more from a larger tribe, and less from a smaller tribe. Each tribe shall give the Levites cities in proportion to the hereditary land that it has been given.

Cities of Safe Refuge   *6ᵗʰ Aliyah*

9 Adonai spoke to Moses and told him: **10** Speak to the Israelites and say to them:

Now that you are crossing the Jordan into the land of Canaan, **11** you must designate towns which shall serve as safe refuge cities where a murderer who has accidentally killed a person can find safe refuge. **12** These cities shall serve you as a safe refuge from an avenger. A murderer must not be judged until he has had a fair trial before a court. **13** You shall provide six safe refuge cities. **14** You shall provide three safe cities on this side of the Jordan River, and three safe cities in the land of Canaan. **15** These cities shall be safe havens for both foreigners and Israelites, so that anyone who accidentally kills a person will find safety there.

16 However, if someone deliberately strikes another person with an iron weapon and kills him, then he is a murderer, and he must be executed. **17** Or if he strikes someone with a large stone, and the person dies, then he is a murderer and must be executed. **18** Or if he strikes someone with a deadly wooden weapon, and the person dies, then he is a murderer and must be executed.

19 In such cases, after the trial, a relative of the victim is allowed to kill the murderer wherever he finds him.

20 It is murder if a person deliberately knocks his victim down or throws something dangerous at him and causes the victim to die. **21** It is murder if he deliberately strikes someone with his fist and causes the victim to die. The person striking the blow is a murderer and he must be executed. Once he has been judged guilty, a relative of the victim is allowed to kill the murderer wherever he finds him.

22 However, if a person accidentally pushes his victim or throws an object at him without planning to injure anyone, **23** even if it is a large stone that can kill, but he did not see the victim, and it killed him, then he is not a murderer, because he was not an enemy and did not even have a grudge against his victim.

24 In such cases, the community shall follow these laws and judge between the killer and the avenger. **25** The community must protect the accidental murderer from the blood avenger and send him to a safe city. The killer must remain there until the death of the High Priest.

26 If the killer leaves the boundaries of the safe refuge city to which he fled, **27** and the blood avenger meets him outside the borders of his safe refuge city, then the blood avenger may kill him, and it is not considered an act of murder. **28** The killer must continue to live in his safe refuge city until the High Priest dies. After the High Priest dies, the killer is free and can return to his hereditary land.

29 No matter where you live, these shall be the laws in all your cities for every generation.

30 If anyone kills a human being, the murderer shall be put to death only on the basis of eyewitness testimony.

A single eyewitness is not enough testimony against a person when the death penalty is involved.

31 Never accept ransom for the life of a murderer who is under the death penalty, because he must be executed.

32 You must not accept ransom from a murderer in a safe city and allow him to return to his home before the High Priest dies.

33 Do not desecrate the land in which you live, because blood pollutes the land. When blood is spilled on the land, it cannot be cleansed except by the blood of the person who shed it.

34 You must not desecrate the land upon which you live, for I live among you. I, Adonai, live among My people the Israelites.

Women Who Inherit Lands   *7ᵗʰ Aliyah*

36 The leaders of the family of Gilead son of Machir, son of Manasseh, son of Joseph, petitioned Moses and the elders who were the tribal leaders of the Israelites.

2 They said, "Adonai has commanded you to divide the land among the Israelites as hereditary land by a lottery system. Adonai has also commanded you to give the hereditary land of our relative Tzelafechad to his daughters.

3 But if they marry a member of another Israelite tribe, then the hereditary land belonging to us from our ancestors will became a part of the tribe into which they marry. In this way our hereditary land from the lottery system will became smaller. **4** Then, when the Jubilee Year comes, their hereditary land will be added to the land of the tribe into which they marry, and it will be subtracted from the land of our ancestors."

5 So Moses gave the Israelites instructions from Adonai. "The tribe of Joseph's descendants are right. **6** This is Adonai's decision concerning the daughters of Tzelafechad. You may marry anyone you wish as long as you marry within your ancestral tribe. **7** In this way the hereditary land of the Israelites will not be transferred from one tribe to another, and every Israelite will remain attached to the hereditary land of his father's tribe.

8 Every girl who inherits property must marry a member of her father's tribe. Then each Israelite will inherit his father's hereditary land, **9** and the hereditary land will not be transferred from one tribe to another. Each of the Israelite tribes will remain attached to its own hereditary land."

The Five Daughters Marry   *Maftir*

10 Tzelafechad's daughters did exactly as Adonai had commanded Moses.

11 Machlah, Tirtzah, Haglah, Milkah, and Noah, the five daughters of Tzelafechad, married their cousins. **12** They married into the families of Manasseh son of Joseph, and their hereditary land remained with their father's family.

13 These are the commandments and laws that Adonai gave the Israelites through Moses in the plains of Moab near Jericho on the Jordan River.

סֵפֶר דְּבָרִים
THE BOOK OF DEVARIM

Masoretic Torah Notes

Here is a list of some of the Masoretic notes for the Book of Devarim.

1. The Book of Devarim contains 955 verses.
2. The Book of Devarim contains 34 chapters.
3. The Book of Devarim contains 11 sidrot.

These are the sidrot in the Book of Devarim.

סֵפֶר דְּבָרִים

THE BOOK OF DEVARIM

Devarim, *meaning "words," is the Hebrew name for the fifth book of the Torah. The Greek-speaking Jews of ancient times called it Deuteronomy, meaning "second law." They gave it this name because it summarizes and reviews the laws given in the preceding books of the Torah.*

The old generation who had been slaves in Egypt have died in the desert, and the new generation of freedom-loving Israelites are eager to cross the Jordan River and claim the heritage that Adonai had promised them. Moses, however, will not enter the land of Canaan with them.

Moses led the Israelites from the brickyards of Egypt to a new life of freedom. They emerged from Egypt demoralized, undisciplined, and unorganized. During the forty hard years in the wilderness, Moses molded them into a cohesive nation. Now, at the ripe old age of 120, he hands the leadership over to Joshua.

However, before relinquishing his leadership, Moses delivers four sermons.

In his first sermon (1:6–4:40) Moses recalls the forty years of wandering and the battles against enemies such as Sichon and Og.

In the second sermon (4:44–28:69) Moses tells the Israelites how Adonai wants them to behave, summarizing the laws given earlier.

In the third sermon (29:1–30:20) Moses urges the Israelites to keep their agreement with Adonai, thereby choosing life and success.

The fourth sermon (32:1–33:29) contains the Song of Moses and the blessing of the tribes.

After the final sermon, Moses hands over the leadership to Joshua, and all alone he climbs to the top of Mount Pisgah. From a distance he views the Promised Land which he cannot enter. Then Moses disappears and no one has ever found his grave.

In all of Jewish history since, there has never been a prophet of the same stature and ability as Moses.

There has been much scholarly debate about the authorship of the Torah. Two statements in the Torah point to Moses as the author:

1. *"Moses wrote the last scroll of the Torah [Devarim] and gave it to the priests." (31:9)*

2. *"Take the (fifth) scroll of the Torah and place it in the ark." (31:24–26)*

Moses wrote all of the words of the Torah in a scroll to the very end, even including an account of his own death.

Devarim דְּבָרִים
THESE ARE THE WORDS

1 These are the words that Moses spoke to the Israelites when they were camped on the east bank of the Jordan River, in the wilderness, in the Jordan Valley, near Suf, close to the cities of Paran, Tolfel, Lavan, Hatzeroth, and Di-zahav. **2** It was an eleven-day journey from Horeb to Kadesh Barnea by way of Mount Seir. **3** Moses spoke to the Israelites in the fortieth year, on the first of the eleventh month [Shevat], and told them everything that Adonai had commanded him. **4** This was after he had defeated King Sichon of the Amorites, who lived in Heshbon, and Og, king of the Bashan, who lived in Ashtaroth, near Edrei. **5** It was on the east bank of the Jordan, in the land of Moab, that Moses reviewed the events of the past, saying:

Moses' First Address

6 Adonai spoke to us at Horeb, saying, "You have remained too long at this mountain. **7** Turn around and head toward the Amorite country and all the neighboring territories in the Jordan Valley, the lowlands, the Negev, the seashore, the Canaanite territory, and Lebanon, all the way to the Euphrates River.

8 Look! I am giving you this land. Go forth and conquer the land that Adonai promised to give to your ancestors, Abraham, Isaac, and Jacob, and to all of their descendants."

9 Then I said to you, "You are a burden, and I cannot lead you all by myself. **10** Adonai has multiplied your numbers, and now you are as many as the stars in the sky. **11** May Adonai increase your numbers a thousand times and bless you, as He has promised.

Appoint Tribal Leaders   *2nd Aliyah*

12 "But I cannot carry the burden and responsibility and settle your disputes all by myself. **13** Choose men from among your tribes who are wise and understanding, and I will appoint them as your leaders."

14 And you agreed with me and answered, "Your plan is wise."

15 So I chose wise and experienced men from every tribe and appointed them to lead you as captains of thousands, captains of hundreds, captains of fifties, captains of tens, as leaders for your tribes.

16 I then instructed your judges, saying, "Listen carefully and patiently to every problem that your brethren bring you, and judge fairly between each man and his brother, even when a foreigner is involved. **17** Do not favor any person when making a decision. Pay attention to great and small alike, and do not be influenced by anyone, since you are judging in place of Adonai. If a case is too complicated, bring it to me, and I will judge it."

18 And at that time I also gave you other instructions that you must do.

19 As Adonai instructed us, we then left Horeb and made our way all through that terrifying wilderness that you saw, and then we arrived in the hill country of the Amorites. And finally we arrived in Kadesh Barnea.

20 There I said to you, "You have come to the Amorite hills, which Adonai is giving us. **21** Look! Adonai has placed the land before you. March north and occupy it, as Adonai told you. Do not be afraid and do not be discouraged."

The Scouts Explore the Land   *3rd Aliyah*

22 At that time some of you approached me and said, "First let us send scouts ahead of us to explore the land.

Let them report the best way to invade and what kind of cities we will encounter."

23 I approved your idea and chose twelve men, one from each tribe. **24** They set out and headed up toward the hill country, going as far as Nahal Eshkol (Cluster Valley) and explored the area. **25** They brought back samples of the fruits. They reported to us and said, "The land that Adonai is giving us is very fertile."

26 However, you decided not to go ahead, and you rebelled against Adonai. **27** In your tents you complained, and said, "Adonai brought us out of Egypt because He hates us! He wants the Amorites to slaughter us!

28 Where are we going? Our scouts have brought back a terrifying report. They say that they saw people who were stronger and taller than we are. Their cities were fortified with high walls, and their children, too, were giants."

29 So I said to you, "Don't be afraid of them! **30** Adonai is going before you. He will fight for you, just as you saw him fight for you in Egypt. **31** You saw, as well, how Adonai took care of you in the desert as you journeyed to this place, just as a father cares for his son. **32** But now you have lost faith in Adonai!. **33** He guides you by fire at night and in a cloud by day to show us where to camp."

34 When Adonai heard your complaints, He became angry and said, **35** "Not one person of this generation will ever see the good land that I have sworn to give your ancestors.

36 The only exception will be Caleb son of Yefuneh, because he totally believes in Me. Not only will he see it, but I will give him and his descendants the land that he explored."

37 Adonai was also angry at me because of you, and He said, "You will not enter the Promised Land. **38** Joshua son of Nun, who stands at your side, will be the one to enter, and he will lead the Israelites into the Promised Land.

The Amorites Defeat Israel   *4th Aliyah*

39 "Your children, who you feared would be taken captive, and your little ones, who do not even know the difference between good and evil, will occupy the land that I will give you. **40** Now you must turn back and march into the desert toward the Sea of Reeds."

41 Then you confessed to me and said, "Yes, we have sinned against Adonai! Now we will march north and fight, just as Adonai has commanded us." Then each of you took his weapons, and marched north into the hill country.

42 Adonai said to me, "Warn them not to go and not to attack, because I will not go with them. If they attack, they will be killed by their enemies."

43 I warned you, but you refused to listen. You ignored Adonai's warnings and headed up to the hill country.

44 The Amorites, who lived in the hills, flew down to attack you, and chased you like bees. They pursued you from Seir as far as Hormah.

45 Then you returned and wept before Adonai, but He refused to listen to you.

46 You camped in Kadesh Barnea for a long time.

2 As Adonai had directed me, we then turned around and headed into the wilderness toward the Sea of Reeds. We wandered in the hills of Seir for a long time.

Israel Begins to Wander   *5ᵗʰ Aliyah*

2 Adonai said to me, **3** "You have wandered around these hills long enough. Turn around and march north.

4 Give the people the following instructions:

Soon you will be passing by the borders of your relatives, the descendants of Esau, who live in Seir. They are afraid of you. Be very careful **5** and do not start a fight with them. I will not give you even one thin slice of their land, for I have given Mount Seir to Esau as an inheritance.

6 You must pay for the food you eat and the water you drink."

7 Adonai has blessed every step of your forty-year journey through the wilderness. Adonai was with you, and you lacked for nothing.

8 We passed through the lands of our relatives, the descendants of Esau who live in Seir, and marched through the Jordan Valley from Elath and Etzion Gever. We turned back and passed through the Wilderness of Moab.

9 Adonai warned me, "Do not attack Moab, and do not start a war with them, because I will not give you their land as an inheritance, since I have already given Ar to Lot's descendants as their heritage.

10 The Emim who used to live there were a powerful and

numerous race, as tall as the Anakim (giants). **11** The Moabites called them Emim, and others called them Rephaim. **12** At one time the Horites lived in Seir, but they were driven out by Esau's descendants, who annihilated them and settled in their place, just as Israel must displace the Canaanites in the hereditary land that Adonai gave them.

13 Now get moving and cross the Brook of Zered!"

So you crossed the Brook of Zered. **14** From the time that we left Kadesh Barnea until we crossed the Brook of Zered, thirty-eight years had passed, in which time, as Adonai had decreed, this generation of warriors died.

15 Adonai's hand was directed against them, until all of them died.

16 When all the warriors had died, **17** Adonai said to me, **18** "Soon you will pass through Ar, which is Moabite territory. **19** And you will be coming close to the Ammonites. Do not attack or start a war with them. I will not allow you to occupy the land of the Ammonites, for I have given the land as a heritage to the descendants of Lot.

20 That area was once the territory of the Rephaim (giants), who originally lived there. The Ammonites called them Zamzumim. **21** The Rephaim were once a large and powerful race, as tall as the giants, but Adonai destroyed them so that the Ammonites could drive them out and settle in their place.

22 Adonai destroyed the Horites for Esau's descendants who lived in Seir, and He allowed Esau's descendants to drive them out and settle in their land.

23 This was also true of the Avim, who lived from Hatzerim to Gaza; the Kaftorim came from Crete and defeated them, and settled and occupied their lands.

24 Now get up and cross the Brook of Amon. Attack! I will help you defeat Sichon, the Amorite king of Heshbon, and I will give you his land. Begin the advance! Attack him!

25 Today I will begin to make all the nations in the area afraid of you. Whoever hears of you will tremble with fear and worry about your presence."

26 I sent ambassadors from the Wilderness of Kedemoth to

Sichon, king of Heshbon, with a message of peace, saying, **27** "Allow us to pass through your land. We will travel only along the main highway, and we will not turn to the right or to the left. **28** Sell us food to eat, and water to drink for a price in silver. We only want your permission to pass through, **29** just as we passed by the territory of Esau in Seir and Moab in Ar. We wish only to cross the Jordan River into the land that Adonai is giving us."

30 But Sichon, king of Heshbon, refused to allow us to pass through his land. Adonai had stiffened his will and made him stubborn, so that we could defeat him and occupy his land

The Defeat of Kings Sichon and Og   *6ᵗʰ Aliyah*

31 Adonai said to me, "Look! I am giving King Sichon's land to you. Attack and begin to occupy his land."

32 Sichon mobilized his troops and advanced to oppose us in battle at Yahatz. **33** Adonai helped us, and we killed him and his sons and defeated his army. **34** Then we captured all his cities, and destroyed every one, including the men, women, and children, and left no survivors. **35** All that we took as plunder were the animals and the goods in the cities we captured.

36 We conquered the territory from Aroer, the city in the valley on the edge of the Arnon River, as far as Gilead. There was no city that was strong enough to defend itself against us, because Adonai had weakened them.

37 But we did not trespass onto the Ammonite territory, along the Jabbok River, and the cities of the hill country, which Adonai had warned us not to enter.

3 Next we turned and marched toward the Bashan, where Og and his troops came to oppose us in battle at Edrei. **2** Then Adonai said to me, "Do not be afraid of him, because I will help you defeat him and his army, and you will take possession of his land. You will defeat him just as you defeated King Sichon of Heshbon."

3 Adonai helped us defeat Og, king of the Bashan, and his army, and we left no survivors. **4** Then we conquered all his cities. Og's kingdom in the Bashan included the entire Argov region with its sixty cities. **5** They were all fortified with high walls, gates, and bars, but there were also many open towns.

6 We destroyed the cities of Bashan just as we had done to those of Sichon, king of Heshbon, and killed every man, woman, and child. **7** But for ourselves, we kept all the animals and plundered the cities. **8** At that time we also conquered the lands of the two Amorite kings who lived to the east of the Jordan River, in the area between the Brook of Arnon and Mount Hermon. **9** The people of Sidon called Mount Hermon Siryon, while the Amorites call it Senir. **10** The conquered territory included all the cities on the plateau of Gilead, and the entire Bashan as far as the cities of Salhah and Edrei; these cities were part of Og's kingdom in the Bashan.

11 Of all the Rephaim (giants), only Og, king of Bashan, survived. His iron bed was thirteen feet long and six feet wide. It is now in the Ammonite city of Rabbah.

12 I gave the Reubenites and Gaddites all the captured territory between Aroer on the Arnon River and the southern half of the Mount Gilead area, including all the cities.

13 I gave to half of the tribe of Manasseh the rest of the Gilead and all of Bashan, which had been Og's kingdom. This included the entire Argov region and the entire Bashan, which was known as the land of the Rephaim.

14 Jair, a descendant of Manasseh, acquired the Argov region as far as the borders of the Geshurites and Machathites, and he renamed the area in the Bashan, Harvath Jair (Jair's Villages), a name that is still in use today.

Every Able-Bodied Man Must Fight   *7th Aliyah*

15 I gave the Gilead region to Machir.

16 To the Reubenites and Gaddites, I gave the territory between the Gilead and the Armon River, as far as the Jabbok

River, the border of the Ammonites. **17** It also included the Jordan Valley and the Jordan River, from the Kinnereth as far as the Dead Sea.

18 At that time I instructed you, saying, "Adonai has given you this land as your heritage. Every able-bodied man among you must join your fellow Israelites as a striking force. **19** I am aware that you have much cattle. Your wives, children, and cattle can remain in the cities I have given you.

Do Not Be Afraid   *Maftir*

20 "Only when your brothers finally occupy the land that Adonai is giving them across the Jordan River will each man be able to return to his inheritance that I have given you."

21 I instructed Joshua, saying, "With your own eyes you have seen all that Adonai has done to these two kings. Adonai will do the same to all the kingdoms in the land on the other side of the Jordan River. **22** Do not be afraid of them, because Adonai will be fighting for you."

Va'etchanan וָאֶתְחַנַּן

I PLEADED WITH ADONAI

23 At that time I pleaded with Adonai, saying, **24** "O Adonai, You have begun to show me Your greatness and power. Is there any power in heaven or on earth who can perform deeds and miracles as You do? **25** Please let me cross the Jordan River. Let me see the wonderful Promised Land, the beautiful hills, and the mountains of Lebanon across the Jordan."

26 But because of you Adonai was angry at me, and He would not listen. Adonai angrily told me, "That is enough! Do not speak to Me any more about my decision.

27 You can climb to the top of Mount Pisgah, and look to the west, north, south, and east. Take a good look, because you will not cross the Jordan River.

28 I want you to encourage Joshua and make him strong, because he will be the one to lead the Israelites across the river and he will distribute the land to them that you will see."

29 At that time we were camped in the valley facing Beth-peor.

4 And now, Israel, if you wish to be successful, listen carefully to the rules and laws that I am teaching you, so that you will remain alive and occupy the land that Adonai is giving you. **2** Do not add other laws or subtract from these commandments. You must carefully observe all the commandments of Adonai which I am giving you.

3 With your own eyes you have seen what Adonai did to the idol Baal Peor. Adonai destroyed every person among you who worshipped the idol Baal Peor.

4 Only you, the ones who have remained faithful to Adonai, are all alive today.

I Have Taught You Rules and Laws   *2nd Aliyah*

5 I have taught you the rules and laws that Adonai gave me, so that you will be able to observe them in the land where you will be living. **6** Obey and observe these rules, so nations will respect your wisdom and understanding. They will hear all these rules and say, "This great nation is certainly a wise and intelligent people."

7 No other nation is so fortunate as to have Adonai in its midst. Adonai is among us. **8** No other nation possesses such humane rules and laws as are in the Torah that I am giving you today.

9 Beware and be careful not to forget the miracles that you have seen with your own eyes. Do not let these memories escape your minds as long as you live. Teach them to your children and your grandchildren. **10** Recall the day you stood before Adonai at Mount Horeb (Sinai). It was there that Adonai said to me, "Gather the people and I will allow them to hear My words. I will teach them to respect Me as long as they live on earth, so that they can teach My commandments to their children."

11 You came and stood at the foot of the mountain. The mountain was ablaze with a fire reaching up to heaven, surrounded by darkness and clouds.

12 Then Adonai spoke to you out of the fire. You heard the sound of words but saw no image; there was only a voice.

13 He presented His covenant to you, and instructed you to observe the Ten Commandments, which He engraved on two stone tablets.

14 At that time, Adonai commanded me to teach you His rules and laws, so that you will be able to observe them in the land you are soon to occupy.

15 Be very careful! Just remember that you did not see an image in the fire on the day that Adonai spoke to you at Mount Horeb. **16** So do not commit a sin and make an idol to worship. Do not make any male or female idols, **17** or statues of animals or winged creatures that fly through the air, **18** or any form of animal that walks on land or any fish that swims in the ocean.

19 When you raise your eyes to the sky, and see the sun, moon, stars, and other heavenly bodies, do not bow down to them or worship them. Adonai created these heavenly bodies only to provide light for the nations of the world.

20 Remember, Adonai has chosen you, and He brought you out of the fiery furnace of Egypt, to be His special people as you are today.

21 Adonai was angry at me because of you. He punished me and decided that I would not cross the Jordan River, and that I would not enter the Promised Land that He is giving you as an inheritance. **22** I must die on this side of the Jordan River, but you will be the ones to cross over and occupy the Promised Land.

23 Beware, and do not break Adonai's covenant with you. Adonai has forbidden you to worship idols.

24 Remember! Adonai is like a devouring fire, and demands loyalty.

25 After you have fathered children and grandchildren, and have been settled in the land for a long time, perhaps you will anger Him by making a statue of some image and worshipping an idol and committing a sin in the eyes of Adonai. **26** Let heaven and earth be my witnesses that you will then quickly disappear from the land that you are crossing the Jordan to occupy. You will not remain there very long, for you will be totally destroyed.

27 Adonai will scatter you, and you will remain only a handful among the nations to which Adonai will exile you. **28** There you will worship gods of wood and stone, which cannot see, hear, eat, or smell. **29** Then you will once again begin to seek Adonai, and you will pursue Him with all your heart and soul, and you will, in the end, find Him.

30 When you are in distress because of these calamities that will have happened to you, then you will finally return to Adonai and obey Him. **31** Adonai is merciful, and He will not abandon you or destroy you; He will not forget the covenant that He made with your ancestors.

32 Search from the beginning of time, when Adonai created people on earth, and from one end of the heavens to the other end, and see whether anything as great as this has ever happened, or whether anyone else has ever known anything as great as this.

33 No nation except you has ever heard Adonai speak out of fire, and lived. **34** Has Adonai ever saved another nation with miracles, signs, wonders, and with a mighty hand and out-stretched arm, and such great acts of power as Adonai performed for you in Egypt before your very eyes?

35 He has shown this to you so that you will understand that Adonai is the Supreme Being, and there is none like Him.

36 You heard His voice from the heavens instructing you, and here on earth He showed you His pillar of fire, and you heard His words from the midst of the fire.

37 Adonai used His great power and brought you out of Egypt because He loved your ancestors and chose to bless their children. **38** He will help you to defeat nations that are greater and stronger than you, and will give you their lands as an inheritance, just as He is doing today.

39 Remember, treasure it in your heart. Adonai is the Supreme Being in heaven above and on the earth below; there is no other.

40 Observe His laws and commandments that I am giving you today; then He will be good to you and your descendants after you. And you will live to a ripe old age in the land that Adonai is giving you forever and ever.

The Cities of Safe Refuge   *3rd Aliyah*

41 Then Moses chose three safe refuge cities on the east of the Jordan River, **42** where a person who accidentally kills someone can find a safe refuge.

43 These cities were Betzer in the wilderness belonging to the Reubenites, Ramoth in the Gilead belonging to the Gaddites, and Golan in Bashan belonging to the Manassites.

Moses' Second Address

44 These are the words that Moses spoke to the Israelites.

45 These are the rituals, rules, and laws that Moses presented to the Israelites when they left Egypt.

46 They were camped at this time on the east bank of the Jordan River, in the valley near Beth Peor in the land of

Sichon, king of Heshbon, whom Moses and the Israelites had defeated when they left Egypt.

47 The Israelites occupied the land of King Sichon, as well as the land of King Og of Bashan. These were the two Amorite kings who ruled the land on the eastern side of the Jordan River. **48** Their territories extended from Aroer on the edge of the Arnon River to Mount Siyon, also known as Mount Hermon, **49** as well as the Jordan Valley on the eastern bank of the Jordan River, as far as the Dead Sea below the slopes of Pisgah.

The Second Ten Commandments *4ᵗʰ Aliyah*

5 Moses assembled all the Israelites, and said to them: Hear O, Israel, listen to the rules and laws that I am publicly giving to you today. Learn them and carefully follow them.

2 Adonai made a covenant with you at Mount Horeb.

3 It was not with your ancestors that Adonai made this covenant, but with those of us who are still alive here and now. **4** Adonai spoke to us face-to-face out of the pillar of fire on the mountain. **5** At that time I stood between you and Adonai and repeated Adonai's words to you, because you were afraid of the fire and did not dare to climb the mountain.

Then Adonai gave the Ten Commandments for the second time. This is what he said:

First Commandment

6 I am Adonai, who brought you out of Egypt, from the land of slavery.

Second Commandment

7 You must not worship any gods but Me.

8 You must not make any idol or statue or image of anything in the heaven above, on the earth below, or in the waters below.

9 You must not bow down to idols and must not worship them. I, Adonai, demand exclusive worship.

I will punish the children down to the third and fourth generations because of the sins of the father.

10 But I will show kindness to those who love Me and observe My commandments. To them I will show love for thousands of generations.

Third Commandment

11 You must not swear falsely by using the name of Adonai. I will not allow the person who uses My name falsely to go unpunished.

Fourth Commandment

12 You must observe the Sabbath to keep it holy, just as Adonai has commanded you.

13 You can work on the six weekdays and do all your tasks, **14** but Saturday must be devoted to Adonai, and you must not do any work.

This includes you, your son, your daughter, your male and female servants, your ox, your donkey, all your other animals, and the foreigner who lives in your lands. Your male and female servants must be able to rest just as you do. **15** Remember that you were once slaves in Egypt, and Adonai liberated you with a strong hand and a mighty arm. Therefore Adonai has commanded you to observe the Sabbath.

Fifth Commandment

16 You must honor your father and your mother as Adonai has commanded you. If you do, you will live long and prosper on the land that Adonai is giving you.

Sixth Commandment

17 You must not commit murder.

Seventh Commandment

You must not commit adultery.

Eighth Commandment

You must not steal.

Ninth Commandment

You must not be a false witness against your neighbor.

Tenth Commandment

18 You must not be envious of your neighbor's house, his field, his male or female servants, his ox, his donkey, or anything else that belongs to him.

When We Hear It, We Will Obey   *5ᵗʰ Aliyah*

19 From the mountain, out of the fire and mist, Adonai spoke these commandments in a loud voice to the entire assembly. He also wrote these words on two stone tablets and gave them to me.

20 When you heard the voice out of the darkness, the mountain was surrounded by flames. Then your leaders and elders approached me **21** and said, "Yes, Adonai has truly showed us His glory and greatness, and we have heard His voice in the midst of the fire. Today, with our own eyes and ears, we have seen and heard that a human need not die when Adonai speaks to him. **22** But we are still in danger. If we continue to hear the voice of Adonai much longer, this great fire will destroy us, and we will all die. **23** No human has ever heard the voice of the living Adonai speaking out of fire as we have and survived. **24** Moses, approach Adonai, and listen to all He says. And then you can tell us whatever Adonai tells you, and when we hear it, we will obey."

25 Adonai heard what you said, and He said to me, "I have heard what the people have said to you and they are right. **26** I wish that their hearts would always remain the same and be willing to obey Me. Then they would observe My commandments forever, so that they and their children would forever enjoy a life of success.

27 Now, go tell them to return to their tents. **28** You, however, must remain here with Me. And I will give you all the rules and commandments, and you will teach them the laws so that they can understand and obey them in the land I am giving them."

29 Be careful to do what Adonai has commanded you, and do not deviate to the right or to the left. **30** If you follow all of

Adonai's commandments, then you will live long and prosper in the land you are about to occupy.

6 These are the commandments and the laws that Adonai commanded me to teach you, so that you can observe them in the land you will soon occupy.

2 Respect Adonai and observe all of His commandments and laws that I am teaching you. In this way you and your children and your grandchildren will obey Adonai as long as they live.

3 Hear, O Israel, and be careful to observe them. If you do, then just as Adonai has promised you, your future will be successful and you will give birth to many children in the land flowing with milk and honey.

Teach Your Children   *6ᵗʰ Aliyah*

4 Hear, O Israel,
Adonai is supreme,
Adonai is one.
5 You shall love Adonai
with all your heart,
with all your soul,
and with all your might.
6 These words
which I am commanding you today
must remain on your heart.
7 Teach them to your children
and speak of them when you are at home,
when traveling on the road,
when you lie down
and when you rise up.
8 Tie these words
as a sign around your hand,
and wear them as a symbol
in the center of your forehead.
9 Write them on parchments
attached to the doorposts (*mezuzot*) of your houses
and your gates.

10 When Adonai brings you to the land that He swore to give to your ancestors, Abraham, Isaac, and Jacob, you will find large, busy cities that you did not build. **11** You will also discover houses filled with beautiful furnishings that you did not put there. You will find wells that you did not dig, and vineyards and olive trees that you did not plant.

After you have eaten and are filled, **12** be careful and do not forget that Adonai is the one who brought you as free people out of Egypt, the land of slavery.

13 Respect Adonai, worship Him, and be loyal to His name.

14 Do not worship the idols of the nations around you.
15 Adonai demands loyalty from you. Do not make Adonai angry, because He will destroy you from the face of the earth.
16 Do not anger Adonai as you angered Him in Massah.
17 Make sure to observe the commandments of Adonai, as well as the rituals and decrees that He has commanded you. **18** Do what is upright and good in the eyes of Adonai, so that He will be good to you. Then you will come and occupy the good land that Adonai promised your ancestors.

19 Adonai will defeat all your enemies that surround you, just as He promised.

20 In the future, when your child asks you, "What is the meaning of the rituals, rules, and laws that Adonai has commanded us?" **21** here is how you must answer him: "We were slaves to Pharaoh in Egypt, but Adonai brought us out of Egypt with a mighty hand.

22 Before our very eyes Adonai produced great miracles against Pharaoh and all his household. **23** He brought us out of Egypt to give us the land He promised our ancestors He would give to us.

24 Adonai has commanded us to observe all these commandments and remain faithful to Him for all time, so that we would survive, just as we are now. **25** If we faithfully observe Adonai's instructions, then all will be well with us."

You Are Adonai's Special People   *7ᵗʰ Aliyah*

7 When Adonai brings you to the land that you are soon to occupy, He will destroy seven nations who are more

numerous and powerful than you: the Hittites, the Girga-shites, the Amorites, the Canaanites, the Perizzites, the Hivites, and the Jebusites.

2 When Adonai weakens them and you defeat them, then you must completely destroy them, and refuse to sign any treaty with them or show them any mercy.

3 You must not intermarry with them. You must not marry your daughters to their sons, and you must not marry their daughters to your sons. **4** If you do, they will lead your children away from worshipping Me and lead them to worship idols. Then Adonai will be angry at you, and you will quickly be destroyed.

5 This is what you must do to them. Destroy their altars, smash their sacred pillars, cut down their holy Asherah trees, and burn their idols.

6 You are a nation dedicated to Adonai. From among all the nations on the face of the earth, Adonai has chosen you to be His special people.

7 He chose you not because you were more numerous than the other nations. In fact you were one of the smallest.

8 Adonai chose you because He loves you, and because He kept the promise that He made to your ancestors. That is why Adonai brought you out with a mighty hand and rescued you from slavery, and from the power of Pharaoh, king of Egypt.

Study the Rules and Laws   *Maftir*

9 I want you to know that Adonai is faithful to those who keep His covenant for thousands of generations, for He loves those who love Him and observe His commandments. **10** But He takes revenge against those who hate him. He does not delay their punishments and He punishes them publicly.

11 Therefore study the rules and laws that I am teaching you today, so you will know how to observe them.

Ekev עֵקֶב
IF YOU OBEY MY RULES

12 If you obey My rules and observe the commandments, then Adonai will remember His covenant which He made with your ancestors.

13 He will love you.
He will bless you,
He will make you numerous.
He will bless you with many children,
He will increase the crops of your land,
your grain, your wine, your oil,
the calves of your herds,
and the lambs of your flocks,
in the land that He promised your ancestors
to give to you.

14 Adonai will bless you more than any nation. Your families and your livestock will increase, and none of your animals will be barren.

15 Adonai will remove sickness from you. He will not allow you to become ill with any of the Egyptian sicknesses that you suffered from while you were there. He will give them to your enemies.

16 Show no mercy to the nations that Adonai delivers into your hands. Do not worship their idols, because that will be a deadly trap.

17 Perhaps you are thinking, "These nations are more numerous than we are. We will never be able to defeat them."

18 Do not be afraid of them. Just remember what Adonai did to Pharaoh and to all of Egypt. **19** Remember the great miracles that you saw with your own eyes—the signs, the wonders, the mighty hand and the outstretched arm with which Adonai liberated you out of Egypt.

Adonai will do the same to all the nations you fear. **20** Adonai will send deadly hornets to attack them, so that the survivors hiding from you will also be destroyed.

21 Do not be afraid of those nations, because Adonai is watching over you.

22 Little by little Adonai will drive out these nations. Do not drive them out too quickly; otherwise the wild animals will became too numerous.

23 Adonai will put these nations in your power and He will panic them until they are destroyed. **24** He will put their kings at your mercy, and you will destroy them.

25 You must burn their idols. You must not save the gold and silver that cover the idols. It will entrap you because it is hateful to Adonai. **26** Do not bring any idols into your house, because you must not worship them or you too will be destroyed. Totally reject them because they are absolutely forbidden.

8 You must obey all the laws that I am giving you today. Then you will survive, flourish, and come to occupy the land that Adonai swore to give to your ancestors.

2 Remember how Adonai led you these forty years in the wilderness. He sent hardships to test you, to determine what is in your heart: whether you would keep His commandments or not. **3** He made life difficult for you by letting you go hungry, and then He fed you the manna, which neither you nor your ancestors had ever eaten. This was to teach you that man does not live by bread alone, but by the words that come out of Adonai's mouth.

4 For forty years the clothing you wore did not wear out, and your feet did not become blistered.

5 Beware that just as a parent disciplines his child, so Adonai is disciplining you.

6 Observe Adonai's commandments, walk in His ways, and worship Him.

7 Adonai is bringing you to a fertile land with flowing streams and with springs gushing from valleys and mountains. **8** It is a land overflowing with wheat, barley, grapes, figs, and pomegranates—a land of olive and honey-date trees. **9** It is a land of plentiful food, where nothing is lacking, a land where iron stones are plentiful, and the mountains are filled with copper.

10 When you eat and are satisfied, you must thank Adonai for the good land He has given you.

Do Not Forget Adonai   *2ⁿᵈ Aliyah*

11 Be careful not to forget Adonai, and to observe His commandments, decrees, and laws, which I am giving you today. **12** When you have eaten well and built fine houses to live in, **13** and your herds and flocks have grown and you have earned much silver and gold, and everything you own has prospered, **14** then you may become forgetful, and you will no longer remember Adonai, who liberated you from slavery in Egypt.

15 He led you through the great, terrifying wilderness, overrun by snakes, vipers, and scorpions, and with no water to drink. When there was no water, it was He who brought you water from a solid rock. **16** In the wilderness He fed you manna, a food that was unknown to your ancestors. He sent you hardships to test your loyalty, so that He could later do more good things for you.

17 Later, when you are successful, take care not to say to yourself, "It was my own strength and my power that made me successful."

18 Always keep in mind that it is Adonai who gives you the ability to be successful. He does this to preserve the covenant that He made with your ancestors, just as He is keeping it today with you.

19 Here and now I warn you, do not forget Adonai and follow idols by worshipping and bowing to them, because then you will be totally destroyed. **20** If you do not obey Adonai, you will be destroyed just like the nations that Adonai is destroying right now for you.

9 Hear, O Israel, today you are about to cross the Jordan River. When you are on the other side, you will have to drive out nations greater and more powerful than you, with great cities whose walls reach to the skies. **2** You will encounter nations as tall as giants, and you have heard the expression, "Who is strong enough to stand up against a giant?"

3 Today be aware that Adonai is the One who will cross ahead of you. He is like a fierce fire, and as Adonai has promised you, He will weaken the nations before you and drive them out and destroy them.

You Made Adonai Angry   *3rd Aliyah*

4 After Adonai chases them out before you, do not say to yourselves, "It was because of my righteousness that Adonai brought me to occupy this land."

No! It was because of the wickedness of these nations that Adonai is driving them out before you. **5** It is not because of your righteousness and goodness that you are going to occupy their land, but because of the wickedness of these nations that Adonai is driving them out before you. Adonai is also keeping the promise that He made to your ancestors, Abraham, Isaac, and Jacob.

6 I want you to know that you are a very stubborn nation, and it is not because of your righteousness that Adonai is giving you this land to occupy.

7 Remember and never forget how you angered Adonai in the wilderness. From the day you left Egypt, you have been rebelling against Adonai.

8 Even at Horeb you angered Adonai. And He was ready to destroy you.

9 At that time I climbed the mountain to get the tablets of the Ten Commandments, the covenant that Adonai had made with you. For forty days and forty nights I remained on the mountain without food or water. **10** Then Adonai gave me two stone tablets engraved with His finger. On them were written all the words that Adonai had spoken to you out of the fire, on the day of assembly at Mount Horeb.

11 At the end of the forty days and forty nights, Adonai gave me the two stone tablets of the covenant. **12** Then Adonai said to me, "Quick! Get moving and hurry down! The Israelites that you brought out of Egypt are acting wickedly. They have strayed from the commands I gave them and have made themselves an idol."

13 Then Adonai said to me, "I realize that this is a very stubborn nation. **14** Just leave Me alone, so that I can destroy them and blot out their name from under the heavens. Afterwards I will make your descendants into a nation greater and more numerous than they are."

15 So I turned around and started down the mountain. The mountain was still blazing with fire, and the two tablets of the covenant were in my hands.

16 I saw at once that you had sinned against Adonai by making a golden calf and by so quickly abandoning the path that Adonai had made for you.

17 In anger I raised the two tablets, and threw them down and shattered them right before your eyes.

18 Then I bowed down before Adonai, and once again I did not eat or drink for forty days and forty nights. I did this on account of the sin you had committed, by doing evil in the eyes of Adonai.

19 I was afraid that Adonai was angry enough to destroy you. But Adonai listened to my prayer.

20 Adonai was angry at Aaron too, and threatened to destroy him. So I also prayed for Aaron.

21 I took the golden calf that you had made, and I burned it in fire. I ground it up until it was as fine as dust, and I threw the dust into the stream flowing down from the mountain.

22 You also angered Adonai at Taberah, and at Massah, and at Kivroth-HaTaavah (Graves of Craving). **23** Then, at Kadesh Barnea, when Adonai said, "March north and occupy the land that I have given you," you again rebelled against the word of Adonai and did not believe that He would help you.

24 From the very first day that I knew you, you have been rebelling against Adonai.

25 I was so sure that Adonai would destroy you that I threw myself down before Him and lay face-down for forty days and forty nights. **26** I begged Adonai, "Adonai! Please do not destroy your nation which You liberated with miracles and brought out of Egypt with a mighty hand. **27** Think about your servants, Abraham, Isaac, and Jacob. Overlook the stubbornness and wickedness of this nation.

28 Do not let the Egyptians in the land of slavery jeer and sneer, 'Adonai brought them out just to kill them in the wilderness, because He hated them and was powerless to bring them to the land He promised them.'

29 Remember, they are still Your people and Your heritage. You brought them out with Your great power and with Your mighty arm!"

The Second Ten Commandments   *4ᵗʰ Aliyah*

10 At that time, Adonai said to me, "Carve out two stone tablets like the first ones, and return to Me on the mountain and make a wooden ark. **2** I will engrave the tablets with the words that were on the first tablets that you broke, and you shall place them in the ark."

3 I made an ark out of acacia wood and carved two tablets like the first. Then I climbed the mountain with the two tablets in my arms. **4** Once again Adonai engraved the tablets with the original text of the Ten Commandments that He gave you out of the fire on the mountain on the day of assembly. Adonai gave them to me. **5** So I turned and went down from the mountain. I placed the tablets that I had made in the ark, and they remained there just as Adonai had commanded.

6 Later, the Israelites continued their journey, from Beeroth-bene-Jaaken (Wells of Jaakan) to Moserah, where Aaron died and was buried. His son Eleazar became the next High Priest. **7** From there, they proceeded to Gudgodah, and from Gudgodah to Yatvath, an area filled with flowing brooks.

8 After I came down from the mountain, Adonai appointed the tribe of Levi to carry the ark containing the Ten Commandments and to stand before Adonai and serve Him, and to offer blessings in His name.

9 That is why the tribe of Levi was not given any inherited land among the other tribes. As Adonai promised, He is their inheritance.

10 This time I remained on the mountain for forty days and forty nights, just like the first time, and Adonai listened to me and agreed not to destroy you.

11 Then Adonai said to me, "Get up and continue the march at the head of the people. Advance and occupy the land that I swore to their ancestors I would give them."

Observe Adonai's Commandments   *5ᵗʰ Aliyah*

12 And now, Israel, what does Adonai demand of you? Only that you revere Adonai and that you follow all His commands and love Him, and serve Adonai with all your heart and with all your soul. **13** You must, for your own good, observe Adonai's commandments and decrees that I am giving you today.

14 The heavens, the earth, and everything in it all belong to Adonai. **15** It was with your ancestors that Adonai entered into a loving relationship. He chose them and their descendants from among all the nations, and today you are still His people.

16 Now is the time to cleanse your heart and stop being so stubborn.

17 Adonai is the Supreme Being. Adonai is powerful, great, mighty, and awesome. Adonai's decisions are fair and He cannot be bribed. **18** He provides justice to orphans and widows, and takes care of foreigners, and gives them food and clothing. **19** You too must show respect toward foreigners, because you were once foreigners in the land of Egypt.

> **20** Respect Adonai, and worship Him,
>   cling to Him, and revere His name.
>   **21** Adonai is worthy of your praise.

He is the One who performed miracles
and great and awesome deeds
that you saw with your very own eyes.

22 Your ancestors went down to Egypt with only seventy individuals, but now Adonai has made you as numerous as the stars in the sky.

11

You must love Adonai, and obey His decrees, laws, and commandments.

2 Remember, I am not speaking of your children, who never knew and never experienced the lessons that Adonai taught by His greatness, His mighty hand, and the strength of His outstretched arm.

3 They never saw the signs and miracles that He performed in Egypt against Pharaoh, king of Egypt, and all his land. **4** They never saw how He drowned the army of Egypt—their horses and chariots, in the waters of the Sea of Reeds. Adonai destroyed them, and to this very day they have not recovered. **5** They did not see how He took care of you in the wilderness until you came to this place. **6** They did not see what He did to Dathan and Aviram, the sons of Reuben's son Eliav, when the earth opened its mouth and swallowed them, along with their houses, their tents, and all their families.

7 But you, with your own eyes, have seen all the miracles and great deeds that Adonai has done.

8 Observe all the commandments that I am giving you today so that you will have the strength to occupy the land you are soon to conquer. **9** Then you will enjoy long life on the land that Adonai swore to your ancestors and their descendants, a land flowing with milk and honey.

The Blessings of Obedience   *6th Aliyah*

10 The land you are soon to possess is not like Egypt, the place you escaped from.

There you could plant your seed and could easily water it by yourself, just like a vegetable garden.

11 But the land you are crossing to occupy is a land of mountains and valleys, watered mostly by the rain.

12 From the beginning of each year until the end of each year, it is a land constantly under Adonai's personal care.

13 If you observe My commandments, which I am giving you today, and if you love Adonai with all your heart and soul, then Adonai has promised **14** to send the fall and spring rains at the proper time so that you can harvest your grain, oil, and wine. **15** He will provide grass for your animals, and you will eat and be satisfied.

16 Take care, however, that your hearts do not turn away and worship other idols.

17 Then Adonai will be angry, and He will shut down the skies so that there will be no rain. The land will not grow crops, and you will soon disappear from the Promised Land that Adonai is giving you.

18 Keep these words of mine in your heart
and in your soul.
Wind them as a reminder (*tefillin*) on your arm,
and let them be a sign in the center of your forehead.
19 Teach them to your children,
and speak of them
when you are at home,
and when you travel on the road,
and when you lie down,
and when you rise up.
20 Write them on parchments
attached to the doorposts (*mezuzot*)
of your houses and gates.
21 If you do this,
you and your children will live long
on the land that Adonai
swore to give to your ancestors,
as long as the heavens are above the earth.

You Will Be Victorious   7th *Aliyah/Maftir*

22 If you carefully observe
and keep all the commandments
that I give you today,
to love Adonai,
and follow all His ways,
and stay close to Him,
23 Then Adonai will drive out all the nations
that stand in your way.

24 You will conquer every piece of land upon which you walk. Your borders will extend from the wilderness to the mountains of Lebanon, from the Euphrates River as far as the Mediterranean Sea. **25** No power will be able to stop you. Just as He promised, Adonai will make you feared and dreaded throughout the region.

Re'eh רְאֵה
YOU HAVE A CHOICE

26 You have a choice between a blessing and a curse. **27** You will be blessed if you obey the commandments of Adonai that I am giving you today.

28 You will be cursed if you do not obey the commandments of Adonai, and stray from the path that I have marked out for you, by worshipping the idols of other nations.

29 When Adonai brings you to the land that you will soon occupy, you must pronounce these blessings on Mount Gerizim, and these curses on Mount Ebal.

30 Both mountains are across the Jordan River, on the western road on the way to Gilgal, near the oak trees of Moreh, in the territory of the Canaanites who live in the Jordan Valley.

31 You soon will cross the Jordan River and conquer the land that Adonai is giving you.

When you have conquered it and settled down, **32** you must carefully observe all the commandments and laws that I am giving you today.

12 These are the commandments and laws that you must carefully observe in the land that Adonai is giving you, so that you will be able to occupy it as long as you live on earth:

2 Destroy all the places where the nations you are driving out worship their idols, whether they are on mountaintops, on the hills, or under flowering trees.

3 You must destroy their altars, flatten their sacred pillars, burn their Asherah trees, chop down the statues of their idols, and erase their names from their temples.

4 You must not worship Adonai in the same manner as they worship their idols.

5 You must worship Adonai only at a sanctuary that He will choose from among all your tribes. He will choose a sanctuary as a place to establish His name. It is there that you shall go to worship Him.

6 That will be the place to which you must bring your burnt offerings and sacrifices, your tithes, your elevated gifts, your pledges, and the first-born of your cattle and flocks. **7** It is in the sanctuary that you and your families shall eat in the presence of Adonai and rejoice after all your labors, because Adonai has blessed you.

8 You must not continue to act as you now do, whereby everyone does what is right in his own eyes. **9** You have not yet come to the Promised Land that Adonai is giving you. **10** Soon, however, you will cross the Jordan and live in the land Adonai is giving you. The moment you are safe and secure from the enemies around you, and you are living in peace,

Adonai Will Choose His Sanctuary   *2ⁿᵈ Aliyah*

11 then you must bring all your burnt offerings, sacrifices, tithes, elevated gifts, and pledges to the sanctuary Adonai shall choose for Himself.

12 There you will celebrate before Adonai, along with your sons, your daughters, your male and female servants, and the Levites from your settlements, who have no hereditary land.

13 Beware not to offer your offerings in any other sanctuary that you may see. **14** You must bring your sacrifices only to the sanctuary that Adonai will choose in the territory of one of your tribes. Only there is it permissible to bring sacrifices, and only there may you present offerings to Me.

15 In all your settlements, whenever you wish you may slaughter cattle and eat the meat that Adonai has given as His blessing. Any Israelite, whether ritually clean or unclean, may eat the meat, just like that of the deer and the gazelle.

16 However, you must not drink the blood; you must pour it on the ground like water.

17 You must not eat the tithes of your wheat, wine, and oil, or the first-born of your cattle and flocks, or any pledges that you make, or elevated gifts in your own settlements.

18 These must be eaten only in the sanctuary that Adonai chooses. You shall eat the tithes with your son, your daughter, your male and female servants, and the Levites who live in your settlements, and you shall thank Adonai for the blessings He has given you.

19 Make sure not to neglect the Levites when you are settled in the Promised Land.

20 When Adonai enlarges your lands, as He has promised you, and you say to yourself, "I am hungry for meat," you may eat as much meat as you desire. **21** If the sanctuary chosen by Adonai and dedicated to His name is far away, you may slaughter your animals that Adonai will have given you in the manner that I have commanded you. Then you may eat them in your settlements whenever you desire, **22** just as you do with a deer or gazelle. The ritually clean and the ritually unclean alike may eat them.

23 Be extremely careful not to drink the blood, because the blood is the life of the animal, and you must not eat anything that is filled with life. **24** You must not drink the blood; just spill it out on the ground like water.

25 You will be doing what is right in Adonai's eyes if you do not drink it. If you do this, then you and your descendants will have a good life.

26 Your sacred offerings and gifts must be brought to the sanctuary that Adonai will choose. **27** There you shall present your burnt offerings, both the flesh and the blood, on the altar of Adonai. The blood of the sacrifices must be poured on the sides of the altar of Adonai, but the flesh may be eaten.

28 Make sure to obey the commandments that I have given you, so that you and your descendants will always have a good life, because you will be doing that which is good and right in the eyes of Adonai.

You Must Not Worship Idols *3rd Aliyah*

29 Adonai will drive away the nations in the land where you will live. **30** When He has destroyed them, you must not follow their example and worship their idols.

Do not wonder about their idols and say, "How did these

nations worship their idols? I think that I will worship them and try their practices." **31** You must not worship Adonai in the same way. These nations, when they worshipped, committed all sorts of evils detested by Adonai. They even worshipped their idols by burning their sons and daughters.

13 You must carefully observe the commandments that I am giving you. Do not add rules and do not subtract rules. **2** Someday, a prophet or a dreamer may arise among you, promising to perform miracles and telling you about the future, **3** and he may say to you, "Come, let us worship the idols of other nations." **4** Do not listen to the appeals of that prophet or dreamer. Adonai is really testing you to know whether you love Him with all your heart and all your soul.

5 Follow Adonai and respect Him, and observe His commandments; obey Him and remain faithful to Him.

6 That prophet or dreamer must be put to death because he wanted you to reject Adonai, who brought you out of Egypt and freed you from the land of slavery. He was trying to lead you from the path that Adonai commanded you to follow. You must erase such evil from your midst. **7** This is what you must do if your brother, your son, your daughter, your wife, or your friend secretly tries to tempt you and says, "Come, let us go worship a new god whom we or our ancestors have never before worshipped."

8 That person is tempting you to worship the idols of some other nation from one end of the world or another.

9 Do not be tempted by him, and do not listen to him. Do not pity him, and do not be merciful to him, and do not find excuses for him, **10** because you must be the one to put him to death. You must be the first to kill him, and then the other people must follow.

11 Stone him to death, because he tried to make you abandon Adonai, who brought you out of the slavery of Egypt.

12 When all Israel hears about it, they will be afraid, and no one else will ever again do such an evil thing among you.

13 This is what you must do when you learn that in one of your cities Adonai is giving you to live in, **14** some worthless people among you have persuaded the inhabitants to stray by saying, "Let us worship an idol and enjoy a new experience."

15 You must carefully investigate, and ask many questions, and find out the facts. If such a hateful thing has really occurred in one of your cities, **16** you must execute all the inhabitants of the city. Destroy it and everything in it, and kill all the animals.

17 Then gather all the property of the city's inhabitants in the central square, and burn the city along with all its goods, as a burnt offering to Adonai. The city must remain a ruin forever and must never be rebuilt. **18** Keep none of the property for yourself.

Then Adonai will have mercy on you and no longer be angry, and He will make you successful, just as He promised your ancestors **19** if you do this and obey Adonai and observe all the commandments that I am giving you today, and do what is right in the eyes of Adonai.

You Are Children of Adonai   *4th Aliyah*

14 You are children of Adonai. Do not cut yourselves as a sign of mourning, and do not shave the hair in the middle of your head.

2 You are a nation dedicated to Adonai. He has set you apart from every other nation on the face of the earth to be His own special treasure.

3 You must not eat any forbidden foods.

4 These are the animals that you may eat: the ox, the

sheep, the goat, **5** the gazelle, the deer, the antelope, the chamois, the wild goat, and the wild sheep.

6 You may eat every animal that has a true hoof cloven in two parts and brings up its cud.

7 However, among the animals that bring up their cud or have a true cloven hoof, there are some that you may not eat. These include the camel, the hare, and the rabbit, which bring up their cud but do not have true hooves and are therefore unclean to eat.

8 Also included is the pig, which has a true hoof but does not bring up its cud and is therefore forbidden to eat.

You must not eat the flesh of these animals, and you must not touch their carcasses.

9 This is what you may eat among the fish in the water. You may eat anything that has fins and scales.

10 But you may not eat any fish that has no fins and scales, because it is forbidden to you.

11 You may eat every ritually clean bird.

12 You must not eat the following birds: the eagle, the vulture, the osprey, **13** the white vulture, the falcon, the buzzard, **14** the entire raven family, **15** the ostrich, the gull and the hawk, **16** the owl, the white and the great owls, the swan, **17** the pelican, the magpie, the cormorant, **18** the stork, the heron family, the hoopoe, and the bat.

19 You must not eat any unclean flying insect.

20 However, you may eat every kind of ritually clean insect.

21 Because you are a holy nation to Adonai, you must not eat any animal or bird that has not been ritually slaughtered. You may give it to the foreigners who live in your settlements, or you may sell it to a foreigner.

You must not boil a lamb in the milk of its mother.

The Second Tithe   *5ᵗʰ Aliyah*

22 Each year you must set aside some of the crops that grow in your fields. **23** You may eat this second tithe of Adonai in the place that He will choose as His sanctuary. There you shall eat the second tithe of your grain, wine, and olive oil, as well as the first-born of your cattle and flocks. In this way you will forever learn to respect Adonai.

24 But if the sanctuary that Adonai has chosen is too far away for you to transport the produce you have set aside, then you may sell the second-tithe part of your harvest and bring the money to the sanctuary that Adonai has chosen. **25** You may convert the tithe into silver money, which you can bring to the place that Adonai has chosen.

26 There you may spend the money on anything you desire, whether it be for cattle, small animals, wine, brandy, or anything else for which you have an urge or need. Eat it there before Adonai, so that you and your family will be able to rejoice.

27 This does not mean, though, that you can forget the Levites in your settlements. Every third year you must give them your first tithe, since they have no hereditary land among you.

28 At the end of each three-year period, you must bring out all the tithes of that year's crop and store them in your settlements. **29** In this way the Levites, who do not have a land share of their own, and the foreigners, orphans, and widows who live in your communities, will have enough food to eat and be satisfied. If you do this, Adonai will bless you in all your undertakings.

The Year of Shmittah   *6ᵗʰ Aliyah*

15 Every seven years, you shall practice the forgiveness of debts (*shmittah*). **2** During the *shmittah* year, every creditor shall cancel any debt owed to him by his fellow Israelites.

3 You may demand payment from the alien, but you must cancel all monetary claims against your brethren.

4 If you do this, there will no longer be any poor among you, because Adonai will make you prosper in the land that you will soon occupy.

5 However, you will be successful only if you obey Adonai and carefully observe all the commandments that I am giving you today. **6** Then Adonai will bless you, as He has promised. You will extend loans to many nations, but you will not need to borrow. Thus you will rule many nations, but none will rule over you.

7 When you settle the land that Adonai is giving you, you must not harden your heart against the needy.

8 Be generous, open your hands, and extend him any credit he needs to take care of his wants. **9** Be very careful not to act selfishly and say to yourself, "Soon the seventh year is coming, and it will be the year of debt forgiveness." Because then you will look unkindly at your needy brother and refuse to lend him any money. If he complains about you to Adonai, you will have committed a sin.

10 You must make every effort to freely give him what he needs and you must not complain about giving; then Adonai will bless you in everything you do.

11 Unfortunately, there will always be poor people in the land. That is why this commandment insists that you behave generously to your poor and to the unfortunate Israelites in your land.

12 If you purchase an Israelite man or woman, he or she may serve for six years, but you must free them in the seventh year.

13 When you free them, you must not send them away empty-handed. **14** You must give them generous gifts from your flocks, from your granary, and from your winepress, so that they will also have a share of all the good things with which Adonai has blessed you. **15** This is how you will remember that you were a slave in Egypt until Adonai freed you. That is why I am giving you this commandment.

16 But suppose the slave is happy to serve you and

your family and is pleased with you, and he says, "I do not want to leave you." **17** Then you must take an awl and push it through his earlobe and into the door. Then he will become your slave forever. Do the same with your female slaves.

18 Of course you may be reluctant to free your slave, because for six years he has done double the work of a hired worker. But if you free him, Adonai will bless you in all your undertakings.

Dedicate the First-born Animals   *7ᵗʰ Aliyah*

19 You must dedicate to Adonai every male first-born among your cattle and flocks. You must not work your fields with a first-born ox, and you must not shear your first-born sheep. **20** Every year you and your family must eat in the presence of Adonai in the sanctuary that Adonai will choose.

21 If the animal has a defect or is crippled or blind or has another type of blemish, you may not sacrifice it to Adonai. **22** Both the ritually clean and the ritually unclean may eat such animals in their homes, as you would eat the deer and the gazelle. **23** You must not drink the blood; just spill it on the ground like water.

16 Observe the month of Aviv [Nisan] and present a Passover sacrifice to Adonai, because it was during the month of standing grain that Adonai brought you out of Egypt at night.

2 You shall sacrifice the Passover offering with sheep and cattle in the sanctuary that Adonai will choose.

3 You must not eat any leaven with the sacrifice during the Passover holiday. During the Passover holiday you shall eat matzah for seven days. This is the bread of affliction, symbolizing how you left Egypt in a great hurry, and it will enable you to remember your escape from Egypt all the days of your life.

4 For seven days no leavening shall be found in all your territory. You must not eat the flesh that you sacrificed in the evening of the first day of Passover. **5** It is forbidden to slaughter the Passover offering in any of your settlements that Adonai is giving you.

6 The only place where you may sacrifice the Passover offering is in the sanctuary that Adonai will choose.

There, in the evening, you shall sacrifice the Passover offering just as the sun is going down, the same time of day that you left Egypt. **7** You shall roast it and eat it in the sanctuary chosen by Adonai, and then in the morning you may return to your homes.

8 For six days you shall eat matzah. On the seventh day you shall hold an assembly to Adonai, and you must not do any work.

9 Then count seven weeks from the time you first begin to harvest the standing grain.

10 Then you shall celebrate the Festival of Shavuot to Adonai by presenting an offering in proportion to the blessings Adonai has given you.

11 You shall celebrate in the sanctuary that Adonai has chosen. You shall celebrate together with your sons, your daughters, your male and female servants, the Levites in your cities, and the strangers, the orphans, and the widows living among you.

12 You must remember that you were a slave in Egypt, and carefully observe all these rules.

The Festival of Sukkot   *Maftir*

13 You shall celebrate the Festival of Sukkot for seven days after you bring in the grain from your threshing floor and the wine from your winepress. **14** During the Festival of Sukkot you shall rejoice with your son and daughter, your male and female servants, and the Levite, strangers, orphans, and widows in your cities.

15 You shall celebrate the Festival of Sukkot for seven days in the sanctuary that Adonai will choose. Then Adonai will bless all your harvests and all the work of your hands, and you will be happy.

16 Three times each year, all your males must appear before Adonai in the sanctuary that He will choose: on the Festival of Matzot, on the Festival of Shavuot, and on the Festival of Sukkot. During these three festivals you must not appear before Adonai with empty hands. **17** Everyone shall bring an offering in proportion to the blessings that Adonai has given him.

JUDGES AND JUSTICE

18 Appoint judges and officials for your tribes in the towns that Adonai has given you, and make sure that they judge the people fairly.

19 Do not distort justice and do not give special consideration to anyone. You must not take bribes, because bribery blinds the wise and ruins the words of the righteous. **20** Only pursue justice and honesty, so that you may live and occupy the land that Adonai is giving you.

21 Do not plant an Asherah tree or plant any other tree near the altar that you make for Adonai.

22 Do not build a sacred stone pillar, because this is something that Adonai detests.

17 You must not sacrifice to Adonai any ox, sheep, or goat that has a serious defect, because Adonai considers this an insult.

2 If you discover a man or a woman in one of your communities doing evil, dishonoring Adonai's covenant **3** by bowing down to the sun, the moon, or other heavenly bodies whose worship I have strictly prohibited, **4** when you learn about it, you must listen and carefully question the witnesses. If the accusation is true, and this revolting practice has taken place in Israel, **5** then you must take the man or the woman who did the wicked act out to the gates of the town, and you shall stone the man or the woman to death.

6 The accused must be put to death only by the testimony of two or three witnesses.

7 The witnesses shall be the ones to throw the first stones, and only then shall the other people continue the stoning. In this way you will eliminate evil from your midst.

8 If it is difficult to reach a decision in your tribal courts in a case involving capital punishment, legal disputes, or assaults, then you must send the case to the sanctuary that Adonai has chosen. **9** The Levitical priests and judges who are on duty will render a legal decision.

10 You must accept their judgment, because this decision comes from the place that Adonai has chosen.

11 You must follow the laws as they interpret them; you must not wander to the right or the left from the verdict they declare.

12 If anyone disobeys and refuses to accept the decision of the priest or the judge who represents Adonai as the head of the court, then that person must be put to death. In so doing you will rid Israel of an evil influence. **13** When the Israelites hear about it, they will be afraid to challenge the decisions of the court.

If You Appoint a King   *2ⁿᵈ Aliyah*

14 When you have conquered the land that Adonai is giving you, and you have occupied it and settled down, you will start to think, "We must appoint a king, just like the other nations around us." **15** Then you must appoint the king whom Adonai will choose. You must appoint an Israelite as your king. Do not appoint a foreigner who is not one of your brethren.

16 The king must not build up great herds of horses for himself and send buyers to Egypt to purchase more horses. Adonai has warned you that you must never again return to Egypt.

17 The king must not marry many wives, for they will divert his attention from his governmental duties. The king must not spend his time accumulating silver and gold. **18** When the king is chosen for the royal throne, he must have a copy of the Torah scroll written for him by the Levitical priests. **19** This scroll must always be in his possession, and he must read from it every day of his life. By doing so he will learn to respect Adonai and faithfully observe every commandment in the Torah. **20** He will not feel that he is better than everyone else, and it will prevent him from turning away to the right or to the left. In this way he and his descendants will have a long and successful reign on the throne.

The Levitical Priests   *3ʳᵈ Aliyah*

18 The Levitical priests and the entire tribe of Levi will not own any property in the land of Israel. Therefore they shall live only from Adonai's offerings and gifts. **2** Adonai promised them that He will be their heritage among the tribes, and therefore they will not own any land in Israel. **3** The Israelites must give the priests the foreleg, the jaw, and the cheeks when any ox, sheep, or goat is slaughtered as food. **4** You must also give the priests the first fruits of your grain, wine, and oil and the first wool from the shearing of your sheep. **5** This is to be done because Adonai has chosen Levi and his descendants from all your tribes to stand and serve in the name of Adonai for all time.

You Must Remain Faithful   *4ᵗʰ Aliyah*

6 The Levitical priests, no matter where they live, can move to any town they choose and go to the sanctuary that Adonai has chosen. **7** There he can officiate before Adonai just the same as any of his fellow Levitical priests who regularly officiate there. **8** During the festivals, he shall receive an equal share of the food and gifts from sacrifices, even though he may have an income from an inheritance. **9** When you settle in the Promised Land that Adonai is giving you, you must not imitate the revolting practices of its present inhabitants. **10** No Israelite shall sacrifice his son or his daughter by fire, or practice magic, or try to communicate with evil spirits, or tell fortunes or practice witchcraft, **11** or use mumbo-jumbo incantations, or consult wizards or hold séances or try to talk to the dead. **12** Anyone who does these things is detested by Adonai. It is because of these repugnant practices that Adonai is driving out these nations before you. **13** You must remain totally faithful to Adonai.

Beware of False Prophets   *5ᵗʰ Aliyah*

14 The nations that you are driving out believe in astrology and practice magic. Adonai forbids you to do such things and insists that you are to be different.

15 Instead Adonai will choose one of you from among your brethren to be a prophet like me, and you must listen to him.

16 This is what you asked from Adonai at Horeb on the day of assembly, when you said, "If we hear the voice of Adonai any longer, if we look at this great fire any longer, we will die!"

17 Then Adonai said to me, "The people are right.

18 I will choose a prophet from among them, just like you. I will teach him what to say, and He will speak in My name whatever I tell him.

19 I will punish anyone who does not listen to what he says.

20 Any prophet who speaks in My name when I have not told him to do so, or who speaks in the name of idols, shall die."

21 You have a right to ask, "How can we tell that a prophecy does not come from Adonai ?"

22 When a prophet speaks in Adonai's name, and what he says does not happen or come true, then the message was not spoken by Adonai. The prophet was a fake; do not believe his phony prophecies. You must not allow yourself to be impressed by a false prophet.

19 When Adonai removes the nations from the land that He is giving you, and you occupy it and live in their cities and houses, **2** then you must set aside three cities in the land that Adonai is giving you. **3** Build roads, and divide the land that Adonai is giving you into three districts. One city in each of these districts shall be a place where a murderer can find safe refuge.

4 The safe cities shall be places where a murderer who has accidentally killed someone can live.

5 Here is an example of why the safe cities are needed. A man and his neighbor are in a forest chopping wood, and the ax head slips off the handle and kills his friend. If an accident of this kind occurs, the man can escape to a safe refuge city and live.

6 If the safe refuge city is too far, the angry blood avenger would be able to catch the killer and kill him, but the slayer had no intent to harm his victim, and therefore cannot legally be put to death. **7** That is why I am commanding you to build three separate safe cities.

8 Adonai will enlarge your borders, as He promised your ancestors, and He will give you all the territory that He promised them. **9** He will do this if you carefully observe all the commandments that I have given you today, loving Adonai, and always walking in His path. When your borders are enlarged, then you will have to add three extra safe refuge cities.

10 This will ensure that innocent blood is not spilled in the land that Adonai is giving you as your heritage. If you do not do this, then you yourselves will be guilty of murder.

11 But if a person hates his neighbor, and ambushes him and deliberately attacks him, and the victim dies, and the killer finds refuge in one of the safe cities, **12** then the leaders of the killer's city must bring him back from the safe refuge city and hand him over to the blood avenger to be killed.

13 You must not have pity on the murderer. Your life will be safer if you rid Israel of those who have murdered innocent people.

False Witnesses   *6ᵗʰ Aliyah*

14 You must not move your neighbor's boundary marker, which was set in place by your ancestors to mark their property.

15 One witness is not enough to convict a person for a crime that he may have committed. Guilt must be established by the testimony of at least two or three witnesses.

16 If a false witness testifies against someone, **17** both the accused and the accuser must appear before the priests and judges who are involved in the case. **18** The judges shall carefully question both of them, and if the accuser is found to have lied, **19** he must receive the same punishment as was intended for the accused. This is how you must remove such evil from your midst. **20** In this way other people will learn and will be afraid and will never again commit such a crime. **21** You must have no pity for crimes of this kind. You must take a life for a life, a tooth for a tooth, a hand for a hand, and a foot for a foot.

20 Do not be afraid when you go to war against your enemies and you see horses, armored chariots, and an army larger than yours, because Adonai, who brought you safely out of Egypt, is on your side.

2 Before you approach the battlefield, the priest will speak to the soldiers.

3 He will say, "Soldiers of Israel, today you are about to do battle against your enemies. Do not be fearful, do not be afraid, do not panic, and do not run away from the enemy. **4** Adonai is the One who is going into battle with you. He will fight with you against your enemies, and He will make you victorious."

5 Then the tribal leaders shall speak to the troops and say, "Has any man among you just built a new house and not yet moved into it? You can return home, because you may die in battle and then another man will live in it.

6 Are there any soldiers among you who have just planted a vineyard and have not tasted the first grapes? You can go home, because you may die in battle and someone else will enjoy your grapes.

7 Is there any soldier among you who is engaged to be married? You may go home and get married, because it is not right for you to die in battle and for someone else to marry her."

8 The leaders shall then continue speaking to the soldiers and say, "Is there any man among you who is fearful and afraid? You must go home, because your cowardice will demoralize the other troops." **9** When the leaders have finished speaking to the soldiers, they will appoint experienced battle commanders to lead the troops.

War Regulations   *7ᵗʰ Aliyah*

10 When you attack a city, you must first propose a peaceful settlement. **11** If the city surrenders peacefully and opens its gates to you, then all the people inside shall become your subjects and serve you as laborers.

12 However, if they refuse your peace offer and decide to resist, you shall besiege the city. **13** When Adonai hands it over to you, kill all the males. **14** However, you may keep the women, children, animals, and all the goods in the city. You may use all the plunder from your enemies for yourself.

15 That is what you must do to the cities that are very far away from you and do not belong to the nations in the area.

16 You must not allow anyone to remain alive in the cities of the nations that Adonai is giving you as your possession. **17** Adonai has commanded that you must completely wipe out the Hittites, the Amorites, the Canaanites, the Perizzites, the Hivites, and the Jebusites. **18** Otherwise they will infect you with all the revolting practices with which they worship their idols, and tempt you to sin against Adonai.

19 Even if your siege of a city takes a long time, do not cut down any of its food-producing trees. Do not cut down any tree, unless it is being used against you by the enemy forces. **20** But if you know that a tree does not produce food, then you may cut it down to make wooden devices to help you capture the city.

21 When you are living in the Promised Land and you find a murder victim and the killer's identity is unknown, **2** the leaders and judges in the surrounding area must measure the distance to the cities around the corpse.

3 The leaders of the city nearest to the body must then bring a female calf that has never plowed a field or pulled a wagon.

4 The leaders of that city shall bring the calf to a swiftly flowing stream, in a place that has never been plowed or planted, and there at the stream they shall break the calf's neck.

5 Then the priests from the tribe of Levi, whom Adonai has chosen to serve Him and to pronounce blessings in His name, shall come forward. They are empowered to decide lawsuits and criminal cases.

6 The leaders of the city nearest to where the victim was found shall wash their hands over the dead calf beside the stream of running water.

Cleanse Yourself of Guilt *Maftir*

7 The leaders shall say, "Our hands have not spilled this blood, and our eyes have not witnessed it."

8 The priests shall then say, "Adonai, forgive your people, whom you have liberated. Do not accuse your people of Israel of murdering an innocent person." If you do this, you will be free of guilt. **9** This is how you will cleanse yourself of the guilt of spilling innocent blood, because you will have done what is right in the eyes of Adonai.

Ki Tetze כִּי תֵצֵא
WHEN YOU GO TO WAR

10 When you go to war against your enemies, Adonai will help you defeat them, and you will take many prisoners. **11** If you find a beautiful woman among the captives and are attracted to her, you may marry her. **12** When you bring her home, she must shave off the hair on her head and cut her fingernails. **13** Then she must change her foreign clothing and remain in your home, mourning for her father and mother for a full month. After that you may marry her and make her your wife.

14 However, if you do not marry her, you must send her away free, because you have slept with her as your wife. You may not sell her or keep her as a servant.

15 This is the law when a man has two wives, one whom he loves and one whom he dislikes, and both wives, the loved one and the unloved one, have given birth to sons, but the first-born is the son of the unloved wife. **16** When the man divides his property, he must not give the son of the beloved wife more then the first-born son of the unloved wife.

17 He must give the son of the hated wife a double portion of all his property because he is the first-born and it is his legal right.

18 When parents have a difficult son who does not obey his father and mother, they shall discipline him. If he continues to disobey them, **19** his parents must bring him to the elders of the community at the city gate.

20 The parents shall say to the elders of his city, "Our son is dangerous and out of control. He refuses to listen to us, and he eats like a pig and is a drunkard." **21** If the elders all agree that the youngster is dangerous and cannot be controlled, the men of the community shall stone him to death. In this way you will remove an evil influence from your midst.

When Israel's young people hear about the punishment, they will be afraid, and they will be respectful and obey their parents.

Regulations of Lost Property   *2nd Aliyah*

22 If a person is legally sentenced to death, you must hang him from a tree. **23** You must not allow his body to hang on the tree overnight, but you must bury him on the same day. A person who has been hanged is an insult to Adonai, and you must not let it desecrate the land Adonai is giving you as a heritage.

22

If you see an ox or a sheep wandering around lost, you must not ignore it. You must return it to the owner.

2 If the owner is not nearby, or if you do not know who the owner is, you must take the animal to your own farm. You must care for it until the owner claims it, and then you must return it to him.

3 You must do the same in the case of any animal, or an article of clothing, or anything else that someone loses and you find. You must hold it for the owner.

4 If you see that your neighbor's donkey or ox has fallen on the road, you must not ignore it. You must help it get up.

5 No woman shall dress in men's clothing, and no man shall dress in women's clothing. Adonai hates cross-dressing behavior. **6** If you find a bird's nest in a tree or on the ground, and it contains baby birds or eggs, and the mother is sitting on the chicks or eggs, you must not take the mother away from her chicks. **7** You must release the mother, and only then is it permissible to take the chicks. If you do this, you will be successful and live long.

Safety and Agriculture   *3rd Aliyah*

8 When you build a new house, you must build a railing around your roof. You must make your house safe so that no one can fall from the roof.

9 You must not plant two types of crops in your vineyard.

If you do, it is forbidden to eat the yield of the grapes you planted and the fruit from the second crop.

10 You must not plow with an ox and a donkey in the same team. **11** You must not wear clothing in which wool and linen are woven together in the same garment (*shatnez*).

12 You must sew tassels (*tzitzit*) on the four corners of the garments that you wear.

13 This is the law when a man marries a woman, and lives with her, and then decides that he hates her **14** and makes up lies against her by saying, "I married this woman and I found that she was not a virgin when I married her. I have evidence that she has not been faithful to me."

15 The parents of the girl shall bring evidence of their daughter's virginity from the marriage bed and present it to the judges in court. **16** Then the parents of the girl shall say to the judges, "I gave my daughter to this man in marriage, but he despises her. **17** He has invented lies against her and claims that she was not a virgin. But here is evidence of my daughter's virginity." With that, the parents of the girl shall present the bloody sheet from the marriage bed as evidence before the judges.

18 The judges shall then sentence the liar to be whipped.

19 As a penalty they shall fine him one hundred silver shekels for slandering an Israelite virgin. The payment must be given to the parents of the girl. The slanderer must then keep the girl as his wife and is forbidden to divorce her as long as he lives.

20 If the charge is true, however, and there is no evidence of the girl's virginity, **21** they shall take the girl out to the door of her father's house, and the people of her city shall stone her, because she has brought shame upon her parents' family and upon Israel by prostituting herself. You must cleanse immorality from your midst.

22 If a man is found sleeping with a someone else's wife, both the woman and the man lying with her shall be put to death. You must rid Israel of evil.

23 This is the law where a virgin girl is betrothed to one man, and another man meets her in the city and has intercourse with her. **24** Both of them shall be brought to the gates of the city, and both of them shall be put to death by stoning. The penalty shall be imposed on the girl because she did not cry out even though she was in the city, and on the man because he had sex with his neighbor's betrothed wife. You must rid yourselves of immorality in your communities.

25 However, if the man met the engaged girl in the fields and raped her, then only the rapist shall be put to death. **26** You must not punish the girl, because she has not committed a sin deserving the death penalty. The crime is like murder where a man sneaks up on his neighbor and kills him. **27** The man attacked her in the field, and even if the engaged girl had screamed, there would have been no one to help her.

28 If a man meets a virgin girl who is not engaged, and he is caught raping her, **29** the rapist must give the girl's father fifty silver shekels. He must marry the girl that he raped, and he cannot divorce her as long as he lives.

23

A son must not marry his father's wife. This would shame his father.

2 A man who has diseased testicles or an injured penis must not enter the sanctuary. **3** A man born illegitimately is forbidden to marry an Israelite woman. Even in the tenth generation his descendants may not enter the sanctuary.

4 An Ammonite or Moabite man may not marry an Israelite woman even after the tenth generation.

5 The reason for this law is that they did not welcome the Israelites with bread and water when they escaped from Egypt, and also because they hired Balaam son of Beor, from Pethor in Aram Naharaim, to curse you. **6** But Adonai refused to listen to Balaam, and Adonai changed his curse against you into a blessing, because He loves you.

7 Never, as long as you exist, seek peace or make a treaty with these nations.

Do Not Hate the Edomites
or the Egyptians

4th Aliyah

8 You must not hate the Edomite, because he is your relative. You must not hate the Egyptian, because you were once a stranger in his land. **9** Therefore, the grandchildren of the Egyptians who left Egypt with you may convert in the third generation and marry Israelites.

10 When you go to war against your enemies, you must stay away from anything evil. **11** A soldier who becomes unclean because of an emission while he is sleeping must leave the camp and remain outside **12** until evening; then he must cleanse himself and can return to camp at sunset.

13 You must set up a special place outside the camp to use as a latrine. **14** You must also keep a shovel to dig a hole to cover your feces when you go to the latrine.

15 Your camp must be clean and holy, so that Adonai can help you become victorious over your enemy. Your camp must be holy because Adonai is among you.

16 If a slave escapes from his master, you must not force him to return.

17 You must allow him to live alongside you in your cities wherever he chooses, and you must not discriminate against him. You must do nothing to hurt his feelings.

18 There must not be any male or female Israelite prostitutes among you.

19 You must not bring an offering to the temple of Adonai that is paid for by the earnings of a prostitute, because it would be shameful to Adonai.

20 You must not deduct advance interest from loans made to an Israelite, whether for money or for food or for anything else for which interest is normally taken.

21 You may take interest from a foreigner, but you must not do so from an Israelite. If you observe this rule, Adonai will bless you in all your undertakings in the Promised Land that you are going to occupy.

22 When you make a sacred pledge to Adonai, pay it on time, because Adonai demands that you honor all your promises. **23** It is not a sin to avoid making pledges. **24** But if you make a sacred pledge, be sure to keep your promise to Adonai.

Eating Someone Else's Produce   *5th Aliyah*

25 If you enter your neighbor's vineyard and you are hungry, you may eat as many grapes as you desire, but you are not permitted to take bunches of grapes home with you.
26 It is the same when you are in your neighbor's field of grain. You may pick and eat the grain with your hand, but you are not allowed to cut the stalks with a sickle and take them with you.

24 When a man marries a woman and she displeases him, or if he has evidence of disgraceful conduct on her part, he can hand her divorce papers and send her away from his house. **2** Then she can leave his house and marry another man.

3 However, if her second husband also rejects her and also divorces her, and sends her away from his house, or if her second husband dies, **4** her first husband, who divorced her, cannot remarry her, because she has slept with another man. To do so would be detestable to Adonai, and you must not bring immorality to the land Adonai is giving you as an inheritance.

Newlyweds and Loans   *6th Aliyah*

5 A newly married man must not be drafted for military service or forced into any other type of service. He must be allowed to remain with his bride for one year, so that he can be happy with his bride.
6 You must not take an upper or lower millstone as a pledge for a loan because the owner makes his living by grinding grain into flour.

7 If a man kidnaps a fellow Israelite, and forces him into slavery and then sells him, the kidnapper shall be put to death. You must rid yourself of such evildoers in your community.

8 You must take care about the signs of contagious leprosy and observe all My health rules. You must take care to do everything I have commanded the priest to do.

9 Keep in mind what Adonai did to Miriam after you left Egypt.

10 When you make a loan of any kind to your neighbor, you must not go into his house to take something as security.

11 You must stand outside, and the man who owes you the money will bring the security item outside to you.

12 If the man is poor and has only a coat to pledge, you must not keep the poor person's warm coat overnight as security.

13 You must return his coat to him at sundown, so that he will be able to sleep in his warm garment, and he will bless you for it. Then you will have performed a righteous deed (*mitzvah*).

A Poor Man's Wages   *7ᵗʰ Aliyah*

14 You must not withhold the wages that are due your poor laborer, whether he is an Israelite or a foreigner living in your land. **15** You must pay him on the same day, before the sun goes down. He is a poor man, and he needs his daily wages because his family depends on the money.

Do not give him a reason to complain to Adonai, because you will be guilty of a sin.

16 Parents shall not be convicted on the testimony of their children, and children shall not be convicted on the testimony of their parents. A person shall be convicted only for his own crime.

17 You must not deny justice to the foreigner or the orphan. You must not take a widow's clothing as a pledge for a loan.

18 Always remember that you were a poor slave in Egypt, and Adonai freed you. That is why I am commanding you to observe these rules.

19 When you harvest your grain and forget a sheaf of wheat in your field, you must not go back to pick it up. Leave it for the foreigners, orphans, and widows. If you do this, Adonai will bless you in everything you do.

20 When you harvest the olives from your trees, do not try to gather every last remaining olive. These olives must be left for the foreigners, orphans, and widows.

21 When you harvest the grapes in your vineyard, you must not harvest them a second time. You must leave the last remaining grapes for the foreigners, orphans, and widows.

22 I am ordering you to do this so that you will always remember that you were a poor slave in Egypt.

25

When there is a problem between people, the judges will decide who is guilty and who is innocent. **2** If the guilty person is to be punished by whipping, the judges will order the person to lie down and be whipped with the number of strokes the crime deserves. **3** Forty lashes is the most punishment you can inflict on him, because more strokes will injure and humiliate him in the eyes of the community.

4 You must not muzzle your ox while it is threshing grain.

5 When brothers live in the same area, and one of them dies childless, the widow must not be allowed to marry someone outside the family. It is the brother-in-law's responsibility to marry her.

6 The first-born son she bears will then assume the name of the dead brother, so that his name will not disappear from Israel.

7 If the brother does not wish to marry his dead brother's wife, the widow is to approach the judges in court and say, "My brother-in-law refuses to marry me so that I can bear a son who carries my late husband's name."

8 Then the judges in the city shall send for the brother and try to persuade him to marry the widow. If he continues to refuse to marry her, he must say, "I refuse to marry her." **9** Then his sister-in-law shall approach her brother-in-law and take a shoe off his foot and spit in his face. Then she must say, "This is what must be done to the brother who refuses to create a family for his dead brother."

10 From then on the house of the brother shall be known as "House of the man without a shoe."

11 If two men are fighting and the wife of one of them helps her husband by grabbing the attacker by his testicles, **12** you must cut off her hand and not have any pity on her.

13 You must not cheat by using two different weights, one heavy and one light. **14** You must not cheat by using two different measures, one long and one short.

15 You must have accurate weights and accurate measures. If you do this, you will enjoy a long life in the land that Adonai is giving you. **16** Using dishonest weights and measures is repugnant to Adonai.

Remember Amalek   *Maftir*

17 It is important to remember how Amalek treated you when you were leaving Egypt. **18** They watched you as you marched on your way out of Egypt, and when you were tired and exhausted, they killed those who were too weak to keep up with the march. They had no pity and no respect for Adonai.

19 Once Adonai has given you peace from all the enemies surrounding you in the land that He is giving you as a heritage, you must completely wipe out the memory of Amalek. Do not forget: you must avenge yourself against Amalek.

Ki Tavo כִּי תָבוֹא
WHEN YOU ENTER THE PROMISED LAND

26 When you enter the Promised Land that Adonai is giving you as an inheritance, and you are living there, **2** you must gather the first crops of your harvest in a basket, and you must bring the first and best of your crops (*bikkurim*) to the sanctuary where Adonai has chosen to be worshipped.

3 There you shall give the basket to the priest on duty, and say to him, "This is my gift to Adonai for bringing me to the land that He swore to our ancestors He would give us."

4 The priest will then take the *bikkurim* basket from you and place it in front of the altar of Adonai.

5 Then you shall make the following declaration before Adonai:

"My ancestor was a wandering Aramaean.
He went down to Egypt
with a small number of people
and lived there as a foreigner,
and it was there that my ancestors became a great,
powerful, and numerous nation.
6 The Egyptians were cruel to us,
making us suffer,
and they forced us into slavery.
7 So we cried out for help,
and Adonai heard our cries
and saw our suffering,
our hard labor, and our pain.
8 Then Adonai brought us out of Egypt
with a strong hand
and an outstretched arm,
with shattering events
and with signs and great miracles.

9 He brought us to this land,
and gave us this Promised Land
flowing with milk and honey.
10 In thanks I am now bringing
the first crops of the land
that Adonai has generously given me."

After that, you shall place the basket before Adonai, and bow down.

11 Then you and your family and the Levites and the foreigners shall enjoy a festive meal and thank Adonai for all the good things He has granted you and your family.

The Special Third-Year Tithe   *2nd Aliyah*

12 In the third year you must set aside a special tithe to be given to the Levites, the foreigners, and the orphans and widows in your cities, so that they will not go hungry.

13 Then you must make the following declaration before Adonai:

"I have taken the sacred tithe from my house. I have given it to the Levites and to the orphans and widows, and I have followed all the commandments You have given to us. I have not neglected or forgotten any of Your commandments.

14 I did not touch or eat any of the tithe while I was in mourning. Adonai, I have obeyed You, and I have done everything You commanded me.

15 Adonai, look down from Your heavenly dwelling and bless Your people Israel, and the land that You have given us—the land flowing with milk and honey that You promised to our ancestors."

Obey My Commandments   *3rd Aliyah*

16 Adonai commands you today to obey all the commandments and laws. You must carefully observe these laws with all your heart and with all your soul.

17 You have agreed today to obey Adonai and have declared allegiance to Adonai, and have pledged to walk in His ways and observe His decrees, commandments, and laws.

18 Today, as He promised you, Adonai has declared that you are His treasured nation. If you observe all His commandments, **19** He will make you greater than all the other nations, so that you will receive praise, fame, and glory. And just as He promised, you will remain a holy nation consecrated to Adonai.

Write the Laws on the Stones   *4ᵗʰ Aliyah*

27 Then Moses and the leaders of Israel gave the following instructions to the Israelites:

Observe all the commandments that I am giving you today.

2 As soon as you cross the Jordan to the land that Adonai is giving you, you must set up large stones and coat them with plaster. **3** Once you have crossed over, you shall write these laws on them. This is how you shall enter the land that Adonai is giving you, the land flowing with milk and honey that Adonai promised to give to your ancestors.

4 When you have crossed the Jordan River, you shall set up the stones that I am now describing to you on Mount Ebal, and you shall coat them with plaster.

5 Then you shall build an altar to Adonai from stones that have never been touched by iron tools. **6** Build the altar with whole uncut stones. On this altar you shall offer burnt offerings. **7** You shall also bring peace offerings and feast there, and rejoice before Adonai.

8 You shall write all the words of this law in a clear script on the stones. **9** Then Moses and the priests spoke to the Israelites, saying:

"People of Israel, pay attention and listen. Today you have become a treasured nation to Adonai. **10** Therefore you must obey Adonai and observe His commandments and decrees that I am giving you today."

Blessings and Curses   *5th Aliyah*

11 That very same day, Moses gave the Israelites the following instructions:

12 When you cross the Jordan, the tribal leaders of Simeon, Levi, Judah, Issachar, Joseph, and Benjamin shall stand on Mount Gerizim and bless the people.

13 The tribal leaders of Reuben, Gad, Asher, Zebulun, Dan, and Naphtali shall stand on Mount Ebal to curse the people.

14 Then the Levites shall speak in a loud voice and say the following to the assembled Israelites:

15 Cursed is anyone who makes an idol. It is repugnant to Adonai even if it is a beautiful piece of sculpture and is hidden in a secret place.

Let us all say Amen.

16 Cursed is anyone who disrespects his father and mother.

Let us all say Amen.

17 Cursed is anyone who moves his neighbor's boundary marker.

Let us all say Amen.

18 Cursed is anyone who leads a blind person astray.

Let us all say Amen.

19 Cursed is anyone who denies justice to the foreigner, the orphan, and the widow.

Let us all say Amen.

20 Cursed is anyone who sleeps with his father's wife, because he insults his father.

Let us all say Amen.

21 Cursed is anyone who has sex with an animal.

Let us all say Amen.

22 Cursed is anyone who has sex with his sister or with the daughter of his father or of his mother.

Let us all say Amen.

23 Cursed is anyone who has sex with his mother-in-law.

Let us all say Amen.

24 Cursed is anyone who kills his neighbor.

Let us all say Amen.

25 Cursed is anyone who takes a bribe to put an innocent person to death.
Let us all say Amen.
26 Cursed is anyone who does not obey the laws of the Torah.
Let us all say Amen.

28

If you obey Adonai, and carefully observe all His commandments that I am giving to you today, then Adonai will raise you above all the nations on earth.

2 As long as you obey Adonai, you will be blessed in many ways.

3 You will be blessed in your cities and blessed on your farm.

4 You will be blessed with many children and large crops.

You will be blessed with fertile herds and flocks.

5 You will be blessed with an overflowing food basket.

You will be blessed with kneading bowls filled with bread.

6 You will be blessed when you come in.

You will be blessed when you go out.

Blessing for Obedience   *6th Aliyah*

7 Adonai will make your enemies flee from you in panic. They will attack you from one direction, and they will flee from you in seven directions.

8 Adonai will bless your storehouses and give you success in all your business. Adonai will bless you in the land that He is giving you.

9 If you observe the commandments and walk in His ways, Adonai will make you His holy nation, just as He promised.

10 Then all the nations of the world will know that Adonai favors you, and they will respect you.

11 Adonai will give you many healthy children. Your livestock and the crops of your farms will increase on the fertile land that Adonai promised your ancestors to give you. **12** Adonai

will open up the rivers in the sky to water your land just at the right time, and will give you success in everything you do. You will help many nations, but you will not need their help.
13 Adonai will make you into a leader of nations and never a follower. You will be a winner and never a loser. You must observe the commandments of Adonai exactly as I am giving them to you today.
14 You must not wander to the right or the left from the laws that I am giving you today. I especially forbid you to worship and pray to idols.
15 However, if you do not obey Adonai and do not observe His commandments and laws as I am giving them to you today, then all these curses will afflict you.

16 You will be cursed in the city.
You will be cursed on your farm.
17 You will be cursed in your food basket.
You will be cursed in your kneading bowl.
18 You will be cursed with no children.
You will be cursed with no crops.
You will be cursed with no fertile herds.
You will be cursed with no lambs in your flocks.
19 You will be cursed when you enter.
You will be cursed when you leave.

20 Adonai will send misfortune and failure on everything you do until you are destroyed and have disappeared because you continued your evil ways and forgot My teachings.
21 Adonai will send diseases to infect you until you disappear from the land you are about to occupy. **22** Adonai will strike you with tuberculosis, fevers, rashes, war, heat, and cancer and fungus. These calamities will overpower and destroy you.
23 The skies above you will be as dry as brass, and the earth below will be as hard as iron.
24 Adonai will change your rain into powder, and it will gush down from the skies and bury you.
25 Adonai will make you flee before your enemies.
You will attack in one column, and flee from your enemies in

seven columns. You will become an example to be pitied by the whole world. **26** Your bodies will be food for the birds of the sky and the animals of the earth, and no one will drive them away.

27 Adonai will afflict you with Egyptian boils, and with incurable ulcers, open sores, and itching that can never be cured. **28** Adonai will strike you with insanity, blindness, and dementia. **29** In broad daylight you will wander aimlessly like a blind man in the darkness, and you will not succeed in any of your enterprises. Everyone will cheat and rob you, and no one will try to help you. **30** When you marry, another man will sleep with your wife. When you build a house, you will not live to enjoy it. When you plant a vineyard, you will not get to eat the grapes.

31 Your ox will be slaughtered before your eyes, and you will not eat any of it. Your donkey will be stolen from you, and you will never get it back. Your sheep will be given to your enemies, and no one will help you reclaim them.

32 Your sons and daughters will be sold as slaves to a foreign nation. You will see it happen before your own eyes, but you will be powerless to prevent it. **33** A foreigner will eat the crops of your land, and you will constantly be cheated and oppressed. **34** The sights you will see will drive you insane.

35 Then Adonai will strike you with a cancerous skin disease from head to toe, and there will be no cure for it.

36 Adonai will exile you and your king to a nation unknown to you and your ancestors. In exile you will be slaves to a nation that worships idols of wood and stone. **37** You will became a symbol of horror, a mockery, and a proverb among the nations to where Adonai will exile you.

38 You will plant much seed in your fields, but the locusts will devour your crops and you will gather a tiny harvest. **39** You will plant vineyards and tend them, but the worms will eat the grapes, so you will not even drink wine or have a harvest. **40** In all your territories you will have many olive trees, but the olives will drop off and you will not have enough oil for medicines.

41 Your sons and daughters will be taken into captivity.

42 The trees and crops of your farm will be destroyed by locusts.

43 The foreigners among you shall became richer and more powerful than you, while you will become poorer and weaker. **44** They will lend you money, but you will not have any money to lend them. They will become your master, and you will be their followers.

45 All these curses will pursue and catch you and destroy you, because you did not obey Adonai and did not observe the commandments and laws that He gave you.

46 These punishments will be a warning to you and your children forever.

47 When you had an abundance of everything, you refused to serve Adonai willingly and with a glad heart.

48 Therefore you will serve the enemies that Adonai sends against you, and you will suffer hunger, thirst, nakedness, and poverty. Your enemy will place the iron yoke of slavery on your neck until it destroys you.

49 Adonai will bring a far-off nation from the end of the earth, swooping down like an eagle, a nation whose language you do not understand, **50** a cruel, sadistic nation, that will have no mercy on old and on young.

51 That foreign nation will devour all your livestock and the crops of your land, and you will starve. All of your grain, wine, and oil, the calves in your herds and the lambs in your flocks will disappear. **52** They will surround all your cities, and break down the high fortified walls that you trust to protect you. That nation will attack every city in the land that Adonai has given you.

53 Then you will even eat your own children.

54 The hunger will degrade the most kind-hearted and gentle person among you, and he will refuse to share with his brother, his wife, and his other children **55** the flesh of the child he is eating, because he has nothing left for himself, and because of the desperate suffering your enemies will cause when they besiege your settlements.

56 The most gentle, delicate woman, who has been brought up in such luxury that she does not let her foot touch the ground, so great will be her lack of food and her desperation when your enemies besiege your cities that she will not share with her husband, her son, and her daughter **57** the flesh of her newborn baby.

58 If you do not observe all the laws that are written in this book, and respect the glorious name of Adonai, **59** then Adonai will punish you and your descendants with great plagues. The punishments will be terrible, and the diseases will be incurable.

60 Adonai will infect you with the diseases you feared in Egypt.

61 Adonai will also bring upon you diseases that are not mentioned in this book of laws until they have destroyed you.

62 Once upon a time you were as numerous as the stars in the sky, and now you will become just a handful of survivors because you refused to obey Adonai. **63** Once Adonai was happy to be good to you and to see you multiply and grow, but now He will be happy to exile and destroy you. You will be uprooted from the land that you are soon to occupy.

64 Adonai will scatter you among the nations, from one end of the earth to the other. There you will be slaves to idolaters who worship idols that your ancestors never knew. **65** You will be aliens among the nations and will find no peace there. Adonai will give you cowardly hearts, and your future will be hopeless.

66 Your life will hang in danger. Day and night, you will live in fear, and you will be so terrified that you will not believe you will ever again see the rising sun. **67** In the morning, you will say, "I wish it were night," and in the evening you will say, "I wish it were morning." You will say this because of the horrors you will experience and the sights your eyes will see.

68 Adonai will send you back to Egypt in ships, something I promised you would never happen. You will offer to sell yourselves as slaves to your enemies, but no one will want to buy you.

69 These are the terms of the covenant that Adonai commanded Moses to make with the Israelites in addition to the covenant that Adonai made with them on Mount Horeb (Sinai).

Moses' Third Address
Moses Spoke to the Israelites   *7th Aliyah*

29
Moses summoned all Israel and said to them:
With your own eyes you have witnessed everything that Adonai did to Pharaoh and to all his servants, and to all the people in the land of Egypt. **2** You saw the great miracles, the signs and the wonders. **3** But until now Adonai did not give you a mind to understand and eyes to see and ears to hear.

4 Now Adonai says to you: For forty years I led you through the desert, during which time your clothes did not wear out and the shoes on your feet did not tear. **5** I gave you no bread to eat and no wine to drink, so that you would realize that I, Adonai, was taking care of you.

Obey My Covenant   *Maftir*

6 When you first came to this area, Sichon, king of Heshbon, and Og, king of the Bashan, attacked you, but you defeated them. **7** Then you took their land and gave their territories to the Reubenites, the Gaddites, and half the tribe of the Manassites.

8 If you obey the terms of our covenant, then you will prosper in everything you do.

Nitzavim נִצָּבִים
YOU ARE STANDING BEFORE ADONAI

9 Today your leaders, your tribal chiefs, your elders, your judges, every Israelite man, **10** your children, your wives, and the foreigner in your camp, even your woodcutters and water drawers—you are all standing before Adonai.

11 Today you are about to be brought into the covenant with Adonai, sealed with the promise that He is making to you today.

Israel Is Adonai's Nation   *2nd Aliyah*

12 He is confirming that you are His nation, and that He will be your God, just as He promised you, and as He swore to your ancestors, Abraham, Isaac, and Jacob.

13 I am not making this covenant with you alone. **14** I am making this covenant with everyone who is standing here with us today before Adonai and with all the future generations of Israel.

Adonai Will Not Forgive   *3rd Aliyah*

15 You remember that we lived in Egypt, and that we journeyed through the territories of enemy nations. **16** You saw their stupid idols made of wood and stone, gold and silver. **17** Surely no man, woman, family, or tribe is unfaithful to Adonai by worshipping the idols of those other nations. Make certain that none of you are poisoned by their ideas.

18 When such a traitor hears the warning of this terrible oath, he may say to himself, "I am safe even if I do my own thing." This attitude will lead to his downfall and ruination.

19 Adonai demands exclusive worship and will not forgive such a person. Adonai's anger will be directed like angry flames against that person. All the terrible curses written in this book will bury him, and Adonai will erase his name from under the heavens. **20** Adonai will separate him from all the Israelites tribes, and he will suffer all the dread curses of the covenant that are recorded in this teaching scroll. **21** Then future generations of your descendants, and foreigners from far away, will see the punishment against the land, and the diseases with which Adonai has struck it, and they will say, **22** "Sulphur and salt have burned the soil. The soil is burned dry and has become a desert of salt, and not even grass can grow on it, just like the destruction of Sodom, Gomorrah, Adma, and Zevoyim, the cities that Adonai destroyed when He became angry." **23** Nations will ask, "Why did Adonai punish this land? Why was He so angry?"

24 They will be told, "It is because they abandoned the covenant that Adonai made with their ancestors when He freed them from slavery in Egypt. **25** They turned around and bowed down to idols and worshipped them—idols they did not know, that were forbidden to them.

26 Adonai was angry and devastated them with the curses written in this book. **27** With anger and great fury Adonai drove them from their land. He exiled them to another land, where they live today."

28 There are many secrets that Adonai has not told us. However, the rules and laws that have been revealed are meant for us and our children forever. They must be forever obeyed.

Adonai Will Rescue You   *4ᵗʰ Aliyah*

30
The time will come when you will experience the blessing and the curses that I have set before you. You will be scattered among many nations and then you will realize that He is punishing you. **2** Then you will return to Adonai, and you will obey Him, and do everything that I am commanding you today. Then you and your children will repent with all your heart and with all your soul.

3 Adonai will have mercy and rescue your remnants. Adonai will once again bring you back from among the nations where He scattered you. **4** Even though you are living at the ends of the earth, Adonai will gather you up from there and will bring you back.

5 Then Adonai will bring you to the land that

belonged to your ancestors, and now you will possess it once more. Adonai will do good for you, and He will make you even more successful than your ancestors. **6** Adonai will cleanse your minds and hearts, and the minds and hearts of your descendants, so that you will love Adonai with all your heart and soul, so that Israel will once again flourish.

You Must Return and Obey   *5ᵗʰ Aliyah*

7 Adonai will turn all these curses against your enemies and against those who pursue you.

8 But you must return and obey Adonai, and observe all His commandments which I am giving you today.

9 Then Adonai will prosper all the work of your hands, and give you many children, and increase your livestock and the crops of your land. Once again Adonai will be happy to do good for you just as He did good for your ancestors.

10 These good things will happen only when you obey Adonai, and observe all His commandments and laws, just as they are written in this book of laws, and if you return to Adonai with all your heart and soul.

The Commandments Are
Close to You   *6ᵗʰ Aliyah*

11 These commandments that I am giving you today are not impossible to obey. **12** These laws are not far away in heaven, so that you might say, "These rules are far away in heaven; bring them down to us so that we can hear them and obey them." **13** They are not far away across the ocean so that one can say, "Who can sail across the ocean and bring them to us so that we can hear them and obey them?" **14** No! The commandments are very close to you. They are on your lips and in your heart, so that you can easily obey them.

Choose Life or Death   *7ᵗʰ Aliyah*

15 Look! Today I have set before you a free choice: Choose between life and goodness on one side, and death and evil on the other side.

16 I have commanded you today to love Adonai, to walk in His footsteps and observe His commandments, decrees, and laws. If you do this you will live and be successful, and Adonai will bless you in the land that you are about to occupy.

17 But if your heart turns away and you refuse to listen, and if you decide to bow down and worship idols,

Heaven and Earth Are Witnesses   *Maftir*

18 then I warn you: If you do this you will be completely destroyed. You will not live a long and prosperous life in the land you are crossing the Jordan to occupy.

19 As witnesses I call heaven and earth. I have given you the choice of life or death, blessing or curse. Choose life, so that you and your descendants will live.

20 You must make the choice to love Adonai, and to obey Him, and to commit yourself to Him, for He is your life and the length of your days. Then you will be able to live peacefully in the land that Adonai swore to give to Abraham, Isaac, and Jacob.

Vayelech וַיֵּלֶךְ
MOSES WENT AND SPOKE
TO THE ISRAELITES

31 Once again Moses spoke to the Israelites and said to them:

2 Today I am 120 years old and I can no longer lead you. Adonai has told me that I shall not cross the Jordan River.

3 But Adonai Himself will go across before you. He will destroy the nations living there, and you will defeat them as Adonai has promised. Joshua is the one who will lead you across.

Be Strong and Courageous   *2nd Aliyah*

4 Adonai will destroy the nations just as He destroyed the Amorite kings Sichon and Og, and their lands. **5** When Adonai makes you victorious over them, you must do everything that I have commanded you.

6 Be strong and courageous. Do not be afraid of the other nations. Adonai is going with you, and He will never fail you.

Joshua Becomes the Leader of Israel   *3rd Aliyah*

7 Moses summoned Joshua and, in the presence of all Israel, said to him, "You must be strong and courageous, because you are the one who will bring this nation to the land that Adonai promised their ancestors He would give them. You are the one who will divide up the land among them. **8** But Adonai is the One who will go before you. He will never fail you or abandon you, so do not ever be afraid of your enemies."

9 Then Moses wrote the last scroll [Devarim] of the Torah and gave it to Levi's descendants, the priests who carried the ark of Adonai's covenant, and to the elders of Israel.

You Must Read the Torah   *4th Aliyah*

10 Then Moses gave them the following commandments:
At the end of every seven years, at the time of the forgiveness of debts (*shmittah*) during the Festival of Sukkot, **11** when all

Israel come to present themselves before Adonai in the sanctuary that He will choose, you must read the Torah before all Israel, so that everyone will be able to hear it.

12 You must assemble all the Israelites, the men, women, children, and all the foreigners who live in your cities, and let them hear it, so that they will learn to respect Adonai and to obey carefully all the commandments. **13** Do this so that your children, who have not yet learned the laws, will listen and learn to respect Adonai. If you do this, you will live a long time in the land you are crossing the Jordan to occupy.

Teach This Poem to the Israelites   *5th Aliyah*

14 Adonai said to Moses, "The time is approaching for you to die. Call Joshua to come to the Meeting Tent, where I shall give him instructions."

So Moses and Joshua went into the Meeting Tent. **15** Then Adonai appeared at the entrance of the Tent in a pillar of cloud.

16 Adonai said to Moses, "When you die and join your ancestors, this nation will begin to worship idols in the Promised Land which they are about to enter. They will forget Me and reject the covenant I have made with them. **17** Then I will be angry and abandon them. I will ignore them and they will be destroyed.

They will be surrounded by many troubles, and they will say, 'Adonai has abandoned us because we have sinned. That is why these evils have befallen us.' **18** When that time comes, I will completely abandon them because they have sinned and worshipped idols.

19 Now write down the words of this poem and teach it to the Israelites. Make them memorize this poem so that it will serve as a warning for the Israelites.

I Will Tolerate No Excuses   *6th Aliyah*

20 "I am bringing them to a land flowing with milk and honey—the land I promised to give to their ancestors— where they can eat and live in luxury. Then they will begin to worship idols and reject My covenant. **21** Then, when they are sur-rounded by disasters and troubles, this poem will be like a witness and will remind them that they have no excuse for their disobedience. Even before I brought them into the Promised Land I knew exactly what they were thinking and what they were going to do."

22 On that day, Moses wrote down the words of this poem, and he taught it to the Israelites.

23 Adonai also gave Joshua instructions and said, "Be strong and brave, and I will help you bring the Israelites into the land I have promised them."

24 Moses, at the very end of his life, finished writing the [fifth] scroll of the Torah [and he called it Devarim].

Place the Scroll in the Ark   *7th Aliyah*

25 Moses then instructed the Levites who carried the ark of Adonai's covenant, saying, **26** "Take this [fifth] Torah scroll and place it inside Adonai's holy ark so it will serve as a wit-ness against the Israelites. **27** I am well aware that you are rebellious and stubborn. Even now, while I am here with you, you are rebelling against Adonai. How much more rebellious will you be when I am dead.

Assemble the Israelites   *Maftir*

28 "Assemble all the leaders of your tribes and your judges, and I will teach them the words of this poem. I will call upon heaven and earth as witnesses against them. **29** I know that after I die you will become corrupt and turn away from the path that I have commanded you to follow. In days to come, disasters will surround you because you will do evil in the eyes of Adonai, and anger Him by making idols."

30 Then Moses recited all the words of this poem to the entire assembly of Israel from beginning to end.

Ha'azinu הַאֲזִינוּ

O HEAVENS, GIVE EAR

The Poem of Moses and His Blessings

32

O heavens, give ear
And I will speak;
O earth; hear the words
Of my mouth.

2 My truths shall fall like gentle rain,
My commandments like dew,
Like water on growing plants,
Like showers on tender grass.

3 I will shout the name of Adonai,
I will give glory to His name.

4 He is the Rock,
His decisions are just;
Adonai is faithful, never false;
He is true and upright.

5 Those who are unfaithful to Him,
That crooked and unworthy generation
Have not obeyed Him.

6 Is this how they repay Adonai?
You foolish, stupid people.
Is He not your Creator?
He formed you,
He gave you life.

Remember the Past   *2nd Aliyah*

7 Remember the generations gone by,
Think about times that have passed;
Ask your parents,
And they will tell you.
Ask your graybeards,
And they will explain.

8 When Adonai gave nations
Their territories
And created different races,

He set up boundaries for the people
According to the number of beings.
9 The people of Israel belong to Adonai,
The Children of Jacob are in His care.
10 He found Israel in the wilderness
Filled with howling wind;
He strengthened and protected them
Just like His own eyes.
11 Adonai was like an eagle
Teaching its newborn to fly;
So He spread His wings to protect them
And carried them aloft between His feathers.
12 Only Adonai guided them,
All alone with no foreign helpers.

They Turned Away from Adonai   *3ʳᵈ Aliyah*

13 He brought them to high mountaintops,
And they feasted on the crops of the land;
He fed them honey from the rocks
And olive oil from stony soil.
14 He fed them yogurt from the flocks
And milk from the herds.
He fed them fat lambs and male goats,
And rams pastured in Bashan
With the best of grain.
They drank fine wine
From blood-red grapes.
15 But soon Jeshurun [Israel] grew fat and rebelled,
They became bloated and crude;
They abandoned Adonai, who made them,
And rejected the help of the Rock.
16 They made Him jealous by worshipping idols,
They angered Him with revolting ceremonies.
17 They sacrificed to demons,
To useless foreign idols
Whom your ancestors never worshipped.

18 You turned away from the Rock
That gave birth to you,
You forgot the One who gave you life.

Adonai's Anger   *4ᵗʰ Aliyah*

19 Adonai saw this and was angry,
So He abandoned His children.
20 He said, "I will hide My face from them,
And then they shall see what will happen to them,
For they are a disloyal generation,
Unfaithful children.
21 They have made Me very bitter
And angered Me with their idol worship;
Now I will make them jealous with a nation of fools.
22 Now, My anger is blazing,
And it will flame down
Into the bowels of the underworld.
It will consume the earth and its crops,
And it will ignite the foundations of mountains.
23 I will bury them with calamities;
I will shoot arrows at them.
24 I will send famines and plagues;
Epidemics and wild beasts
And poisonous snakes will engulf them.
25 In the streets they will die by the sword,
And in their homes terror will reign.
Against young and old alike,
Against nursing children and against oldsters.
26 I said, 'I will reduce them to nothing';
I will erase the memory of their existence.
27 But I was afraid that their enemies might boast,
'We have achieved a victory,
And we won without the help of their Adonai.'"
28 People of Israel! You have no sense,
You cannot tell right from wrong.

The End Results   *5ᵗʰ Aliyah*

29 If you were smart,
You would stop and think;
You would see the end result.
30 Is it possible for one soldier to defeat thousands,
Or for two to rout ten thousand?
Yes! If the Rock stopped protecting them,
And Adonai allowed it to happen.
31 Remember! Their pebble is nothing
compared to our Rock.
Even our enemies know this.
32 Their wine is from evil Sodom,
From the vineyards of Gomorrah;
Their grapes are filled with bitterness,
Their clusters are poisoned.
33 Their wine is snake venom
And the poison of cobras.
34 I have secreted that poisonous wine,
Safely secured it in My vaults.
35 Vengeance is mine,
I will repay them
When their feet slip.
Then their time of doom nears,
And fate will finish them.
36 Adonai will save His people
And have pity on His servants
When He sees the weakness
Of their leaders and their people.
37 He will say: Where are their idols?
The rock that they depend on,
The idols who ate the best of their offerings,
38 And drank their wine offerings?
Can these idols now help you,
Can they now protect you?

39 Don't you realize
There is only one Elohim,
Who sends death and gives life,
Who sickens and heals?
None of your idols
Can save you from My decrees.

Vengence on Adonai's Enemies

6th Aliyah

40 I will raise My hands
and promise and swear:
As surely as I live forever,
41 When I sharpen My gleaming sword,
I will heap vengeance on My enemies,
On my enemies who hate Me.
42 I will drench My arrows in their blood,
And My sword will devour the flesh
Of corpses and prisoners
From the long-haired enemy chieftains.
43 Many nations will praise Israel.
He will heap vengeance
On His enemies,
And He will purify the land of Israel.

Teach Your Children

7th Aliyah

44 Moses came with Hoshea son of Nun and recited all the words of this poem to the people.

45 When Moses had finished reciting the poem to the Israelites, **46** he said to them, "Pay close attention to every word of my warning to you today, so that you will be able to instruct your children to observe carefully all the words of this Torah. **47** It is not an empty teaching. It is your life, and with it you will long endure on the land which you are crossing the Jordan to occupy."

Moses Views the Promised Land *Maftir*

48 On that very day, Adonai spoke to Moses, saying:

49 "Climb Mount Avarim to Mount Nebo, in the land of Moab facing Jericho, and see the land of Canaan that I am giving the Israelites as an inheritance. **50** You will die on the mountain that you are climbing, and be gathered up to your people, just as your brother Aaron died on Mount Hor and was gathered to his people.

51 This is because you broke faith with me in full view of the Israelites at Mai Meribah (Waters of Dispute) at Kadesh in the wilderness of Zin, and because you did not sanctify Me among the Israelites. **52** Therefore you will see the land from afar, but you will not enter the land I am giving the Israelites."

Vezot Ha'berachah וְזֹאת הַבְּרָכָה
THIS IS THE BLESSING

33 This is the blessing that Moses, man of Adonai, gave to the Israelites just before his death.
2 Moses said:

Adonai came down from Mount Sinai
And shone on us from Mount Seir;
He appeared from Mount Paran
And came with numerous angels.
He brought a fire with His right Hand.
3 You love all the nations,
but Your holy ones grasp You by the hand.
They step in Your footsteps,
and cherish Your words.
4 Moses brought us the Torah;
It is Israel's eternal heritage.
5 He was Israel's king
when the people's leaders gathered
and the tribes of Israel were united into one.
6 Let Reuben live
and not perish,
though the tribe is few in number.

7 Moses said to Judah:

May Adonai listen to Judah's voice
and return him to his people.
Although he is powerful,
Help him against his enemies.

The Blessings of Levi and Benjamin   *2ⁿᵈ Aliyah*

8 To Levi Moses said:

Your Urim and Thumim belong to you.
You tested Adonai at Massah,
and disputed him at the waters of Meribah.
9 He said of his parents,
"I do not consider them."

He disagreed with his family.
But he kept teaching
and guarded Your covenant.
10 They shall teach Your law to Jacob,
and Your Torah to Israel.
They shall place incense before You
and sacrifices on Your altar.
11 I pray that Adonai will bless his effort
and prosper the work of his hands.
May He smash the bodies
Of those who rebel against him,
so that his enemies will never rise.

12 To Benjamin he said:

You are Adonai's beloved.
You shall safely dwell beside Him.
Adonai constantly protects him
and dwells among their hills.

The Blessings of Joseph   *3ʳᵈ Aliyah*

13 To Joseph Moses said:

His land is blessed by Adonai,
with precious dew from heaven,
and running waters that lie below,
14 Your crops will ripen in the sun,
and sweeten in the light of the moon,
15 The best crops from the mountains
and abundance from the ancient hills.
16 The gifts of the land and its riches
and the blessing of the One
who dwells in the thornbush.
May blessings encircle Joseph's head,
Crowning the prince among his brothers.
17 Joseph has the strength of a bull,
and his horns are as powerful as a wild ox.
With his horns he shall wound nations
at the far ends of the earth.

They are the tens of thousands
of the tribe of Ephraim
and the thousands of the tribe of Manasseh.

The Blessings of Zebulun, Issachar, and Gad

4ᵗʰ Aliyah

18 To Zebulun Moses said:

Zebulun! Be happy when you travel.
Issachar! Rejoice in your homes.
19 They invite nations to the mountain,
To offer righteous sacrifices.
They will be fed by the bounty of the sea
and by the secret treasures of the sands.

20 To Gad Moses said:

Blessed is the One
who helps the territory of Gad expand.
He is like a fierce lion,
Waiting to bite the arm and the head.
21 Gad chose the best land for himself,
He received a special leader's share.
When the leaders came together,
they followed Adonai's decrees
and judgments about Israel.

Blessings of Dan, Naphtali, and Asher

5ᵗʰ Aliyah

22 To Dan Moses said:

Dan is a young lion,
Leaping out from the hills of Bashan.

23 To Naphtali Moses said:

Naphtali will be completely happy
And filled with Adonai's blessings.
He shall possess the land
to the south and west of Lake Kinneret.

24 To Asher Moses said:

Asher is the most blessed among the sons.
He shall be accepted as the favorite
by his brothers,
and may his land produce much olive oil.
25 Your defenses
are stronger than iron and copper,
and you will became more powerful each day.
26 Israel! Remember, there is none like Adonai,
He speeds through the heavens to save you,
He is majestic in the skies.

Sheltered by Adonai   6th *Aliyah*

27 Adonai is my refuge above,
and underneath are His everlasting arms.
He will shatter the enemy before you,
and shall shout, "Destroy!"
28 As prophesied by Jacob,
Israel will dwell in safety
in a land bursting with grain and wine,
Your heavens will also drip with dew.
29 Happy are you, Israel!
Who is like you?
You are a nation sheltered by Adonai,
He is the Shield who helps you,
He is your magnificent Sword.
Your enemies will bow down to you,
And you shall trample upon their backs.

Moses Dies   7th *Aliyah*

34 From the plains of Moab Moses climbed up to Mount Nebo, to the top of Mount Pisgah, facing Jericho. Adonai showed him all the land of the Gilead as far as Dan, **2** all of the land of Naphtali, all of the land of Ephraim and Manasseh, all of the land of Judah as far as the Mediterranean Sea, **3** as far as the Negev, the Jordan Valley and Jericho, the city of palm dates, as far as Zoar.

4 Then Adonai said to him, "This is the land that I swore to give to Abraham, Isaac, and Jacob, saying, 'I will give it to your descendants.' Now I have let you see it with your own eyes, but I will not allow you to cross the river and enter it."

5 So Moses, Adonai's servant, at His command, died in the land of Moab. **6** Adonai buried him in the valley in the land of Moab, near Beth Peor. No one, even to this day, knows the place where he was buried.

7 Moses was 120 years old when he died, but his eyes were sharp and he was still strong and healthy.

8 For thirty days the Israelites mourned Moses on the plains of Moab.

When the mourning period for Moses came to an end, **9** Joshua son of Nun acquired the spirit of wisdom, because Moses had laid his hands on him. The Israelites listened to him and obeyed him exactly as they had obeyed Moses.

10 There never was another prophet in Israel like Moses, whom Adonai knew face-to-face. **11** No one else could have performed all the wonders and miracles that Adonai allowed Moses to perform before Pharaoh in the land of Egypt, **12** or any of the powerful miracles and awesome deeds that Moses performed before the eyes of all the Israelites.

Each year the entire Torah is read aloud in the synagogue. When it is completed, the members of the congregation stand up and recite

חֲזַק חֲזַק וְנִתְחַזֵּק

"Be strong and have courage."

This means, "be strong and live according to the rules and teachings of the Torah."

Index